ACCEPT ONE ANOTHER

A Practical and Expository Commentary on the Book of Romans

JAMES E. ALLMAN

SEVEN
INTERACTIVE
Academic

First Edition

Published by Seven Interactive Academic
427 Rome Pike
Lebanon, TN 37087

For information regarding permissions or copies purchased for educational or promotional purposes, please email Admin@SevenInteractive.com or contact Seven Interactive Academic, 427 Rome Pike, Lebanon, TN 37087.

For general information about Seven Interactive, please visit SevenInteractive.com.

ISBN-13: 978-1976529900
ISBN-10: 1976529905

DEDICATION

To all of the students at Mid-South Bible College (Crichton College), the members of the adult Bible class at First Evangelical Church in Memphis, Tennessee, the Men of Memphis Class, and the Impact Adult Fellowship of Stonebriar Community Church, Frisco, Texas, I dedicate this book.

Thank you for your patience, tolerance, and questions that taught me so much.

ACKNOWLEDGMENTS

The writing and publication of this work would not have come about, humanly, without two influences. First to mention is the Men of Memphis class which I taught for about twelve years. During that time we studied Romans. Men in the class urged me to write the material contained in this book.

Additionally I wish to thank my friend, Dr. Stephen Carlson, who also edited the book, for his guidance.

CONTENTS

❖❖❖❖❖❖❖❖❖❖

EDITOR'S PREFACE

I have numerous commentaries on the Book of Romans on my shelves, and I'm sure many of you do as well. The list of authors of these commentaries is quite impressive—Calvin, Gill, Godet, Hodge, Sanday and Hedlam, Cranfield, Bruce, Stott, Dunn, to name a few. But for about a quarter of a century, ever since the author of this commentary graciously provided me with a copy of his original manuscript, I have turned first to his book for help with the interpretation and application of Paul's Epistle to the Romans. His approach to the book has a consistency in dealing with the book as a whole and with specific passages that makes his arguments about Paul's original intent quite convincing time and time again.

I first met Dr. James E. Allman over 30 years ago when we were teaching at the same Bible college in Memphis, Tennessee. Jim had been there four years and had received his doctorate from Dallas Theological Seminary two years earlier, and I had just become a doctoral candidate at a seminary in Memphis and was busy looking for a dissertation topic. Over the next few years that we taught at the same college, Jim and I had numerous discussions about everything from Genesis to Revelation and various aspects of theology. But one thing Jim kept coming back to in our discussions was the Book of Romans, and he eventually began writing his own commentary on that book.

For over two decades now, despite the fact that we have not lived in the same city, Jim and I have stayed in touch. When the opportunity arose to be involved in helping Jim get his commentary published, I was not only excited for him but wanted to be a part of the project. It has been my privilege to be the editor of this commentary, but any mistakes in the interpretation of Romans are solely his responsibility!

As Jim explains in the Introduction, this book is not an exegetical commentary on the Greek text or even a verse-by-verse commentary from the English. I have found that Jim's expertise in Greek is second to none, but he has chosen to refer to the original Greek on rare occasions and only when it's helpful to do so. Rather than using Greek and Hebrew fonts, we decided to stick with a transliteration of the Greek, and the handful of Hebrew words as well, for ease of reading and because Jim had the non-specialist in mind when he wrote the book. Since transliteration of Greek is not consistent from one book to another, a transliteration guide has been provided.

The Book of Romans is, for many, the flagship epistle of the New Testament, and its message needs to be studied and taught just as much in the churches today as it was to its original audience in first century Rome. I know of no commentary that does a better job of doing this than the one you are now reading, and that was my view long before I became involved in publishing it. I am confident that the reader will find this to be the case as well.

Dr. Stephen W. Carlson
Hendersonville, Tennessee
September 2017

TRANSLITERATION GUIDE FOR THE GREEK ALPHABET

Letter	Name	Transliteration
α	alpha	a
β	beta	b
γ	gamma	g
δ	delta	d
ε	epsilon	e
ζ	zeta	z
η	eta	e
θ	theta	th
ι	iota	i
κ	kappa	k
λ	lambda	l
μ	mu	m
ν	nu	n
ξ	xi	x
ο	omicron	o
π	pi	p
ρ	rho	r
σ, ς	sigma	s
τ	tau	t
υ	upsilon	u
φ	phi	ph
χ	chi	ch
ψ	psi	ps
ω	omega	o
‘	rough breathing mark	h

No distinction is made in transliteration between regular sigma (σ) and final sigma (ς), between epsilon (ε) and eta (η), or between omicron (ο) and omega (ω).

ABBREVIATIONS OF BIBLE BOOKS

Old Testament	New Testament
Gen.	Matt.
Ex.	Mark
Lev.	Luke
Num.	John
Deut.	Acts
Josh.	Rom.
Jdg.	1 Cor.
Ruth	2 Cor.
1 Sam.	Gal.
2 Sam.	Eph.
1 Kings	Phil.
2 Kings	Col.
1 Chr.	1 Th.
2 Chr.	2 Th.
Ezra	1 Tim.
Neh.	2 Tim.
Esth.	Titus
Job	Phlm.
Ps./Pss.	Heb.
Prov.	Jms.
Ecc.	1 Pet.
Song	2 Pet.
Isa.	1 John
Jer.	2 John
Lam.	3 John
Ezk.	Jude
Dan.	Rev.
Hos.	
Joel	
Amos	
Obad.	
Jonah	
Micah	
Nah.	
Hab.	
Zeph.	
Hag.	
Zech.	
Mal.	

INTRODUCTION TO
THE BOOK OF ROMANS

The Book of Romans has exercised an influence out of all proportion to its size. It was the Book of Romans that led to the conversion of Augustine of Hippo. As Martin Luther expounded Romans at the University of Wittenberg, he fell under the power of its message. That message ignited the Protestant Reformation that has brought the gospel of God's grace to virtually every nation on earth. The public reading of Romans brought a "strange warming" to John Wesley's heart and to the British Empire. This dynamic power of Romans is a hallmark of God's Word. It works not only at the grand level, in the lives of those who significantly shape history, but also in the lives of everyday people.

My goals for the present study of Romans are varied. First, I have wanted to expound the Book of Romans in a non-technical discussion for the broader Christian community. Second, in pursuit of this non-technical approach, I have explained the book in light of Romans 15:7, which I believe is a verse that summarizes the entire letter. Third, I've felt the need to clarify certain basic terms of the book, especially "righteousness," "faith," "works," and "grace." I have not provided an in-depth technical discussion of Romans, but while writing the commentary I discovered that some technical discussion would be necessary.

The Background of the Letter

The apostle Paul wrote the Book of Romans during his third missionary journey while he was in Corinth preparing to return to Jerusalem (Acts 20:2-3). His letter has at least three personal purposes. First, he told them about his planned trip to Jerusalem to meet the needs of the church there (Rom. 15:25-27), perhaps desiring their prayers and financial support. Second, he wanted to prepare them for his arrival in Rome since he hoped to raise support for his mission to Spain (15:22-25). Third, he asked them to provide aid for Phoebe, who was going to Rome on business (16:1-2).

However, Paul faced a much more significant problem in the church at Rome: the church was divided. Paul described the problem in chapters 14–15: on the one hand, the Jewish believers in Rome condemned the Gentile believers because they ate meat; on the other hand, the Gentile believers despised the Jewish believers who were "under law." He began dealing with this problem in chapter 1 (beginning especially with v. 16) and did not resolve the troubling issue until chapter 15.

To draw these groups together again, Paul had to call them back to the basics of the Christian faith. Both groups had forgotten the grace of God in their own lives. Thus, Paul climaxed his whole discussion at Romans 15:7: "Therefore accept one another, just as the Messiah also accepted you, to the glory of God." The main clause of this verse, "accept one another," summarizes chapters 12–15. The second clause, "just as the Messiah also accepted you," summarizes chapters 1–11.

In pursuit of his goal of drawing these two factions together, Paul first had to remind his readers of how Christ received them. To do this, he began at a critical place. Tragically, Christians often forget their own condition in sin without God's grace. So Paul began his discussion of grace with a discussion of sin. He had to prove that no one, neither Gentile nor Jew, can earn any favor with God. In chapters 1–3, Paul showed both groups their lost condition without Christ. The emphasis in these chapters is on the condemnation of the self-righteous. They make their boast in the law while blaspheming God's name by their transgression of it (2:1–3:20).

By the time Paul reached 3:20, he has shown that "no one will be justified in His sight by the works of the law." He went on to explain how God can accept sinful humans in a relationship with Himself. Job asked, "How can a mortal be righteous before God?" (9:1). Paul's discussion in 3:21–4:25 explains faith-righteousness (that is, justification by faith) and its basis in the sacrificial work of Christ. Furthermore, this passage explains faith's foundation in the Hebrew Scriptures, the implications of faith as the means of righteousness,

2

and, finally, the nature of the faith that is the means of righteousness before God.

In chapters 5–8 Paul explained the life of those who are righteous by faith. They are people who suffer as a means of character development, boasting in their suffering since through it they experience the love of God. They live their lives on the basis of the righteousness of Christ and His resurrection life. His righteousness and resurrection life are the foundation of hope for all of life. The believer lives all of this life in the freedom given by grace. That freedom is freedom for righteousness, to live out the life of Christ under grace and not under law. This means that neither Jew nor Gentile can lord it over the faith of others. All believers equally have the righteousness of Christ. All are equally free for obedience. All are equally free under grace. As a result, God accepts all equally through grace. His grace in accepting all of us calls each of us to accept others by the same grace.

In chapters 9–11, Paul explained Israel's response to the gospel. Israel as a group has rejected the gospel. Yet it is precisely this rejection of the gospel that provides the crowning evidence of God's grace. For in spite of their rejection God will surely bring Israel as a nation to faith in Christ. He will do it out of faithfulness to Himself and His promises. Thus, God in His immeasurable wisdom really does receive all by grace.

The model Paul provides in chapters 1–11 thus becomes the pattern of the exhortations in chaps. 12–15. Receiving one another is the reasonable service to which Paul called the Roman Christians in 12:1-2. Making one's body a living, holy, and acceptable sacrifice is as practical as serving others in our spiritual gifting (12:3-8). It means loving one another without pretense (12:9–13:10), and accepting one another by grace (14:1–15:13). We must serve, love, and accept others without demanding that they meet conditions we impose. Then we are acting as God does. Then we help prevent schism and disharmony in the body of Christ.

Paul called Christians to learn God's grace that we may learn to extend grace to each other. Learning the lessons of the Book of Romans can and will impact the life of the Christian church today. It will revitalize its gospel witness and build a community where people actually live the gospel.

The Importance of Studying Romans

Someone might think that the issues about which I write in this book on Romans are merely the ramblings of a teacher or preacher. But the truths of Romans are my life, in a most literal way. If Romans is not true, I have no reason to continue living.

When I was pastoring many years ago, I found myself in an almost impossible position. Engaged to minister the Word of God to God's people, I was struggling with my own salvation. Few who have not been through the experience know how desperate such a condition is. I had slipped into a persistent depression over a period of about three years. The pressure of the ministry and the responsibility to lead people spiritually led me into a profound spiritual despair. My growing understanding of God's grace and its efficacious work in our lives compounded the despair. I felt that I must show myself worthy of the pastorate, worthy to even claim to be a Christian. I learned later that depression is anger turned inward. For me this was true. The anger I felt against myself led me to self-destructive thoughts. The despair grew and deepened. For most of about four years I would awaken in the depths of the night planning ways to commit suicide. I wanted my family to receive the benefits of an insurance policy on my life. I actually thought that I was worth more to them dead than alive.

The beginning of the end of this despair came late one night when for the first time Romans 5:8 crashed into my consciousness. I finally became convinced that God saves man by His grace. I was equally convinced that God's grace does not work by halves. His grace is sufficient. Yet I could not see any evidence that His grace was effective in my life. For the first time, God made it clear to me that night that salvation is not for the righteous. This verse makes it plain that one key requirement for salvation is that God saves sinners. Though I could see no evidence of God's grace in my life, I could see that I was indeed a sinner. If God saves sinners, then perhaps I could be a saved man. I knew that I was trusting in nothing but Christ for salvation, since I could trust nothing in my life. For the first time it became clear to me that for salvation to occur, sin is absolutely necessary. That was the beginning of a six-year odyssey into God's grace.

The key problem I had to overcome was my own proud desire to be personally worthy and fit. I remember talking to a pastor friend at the time about the ministry. I said that I knew that we did not have to be capable of doing the work of the ministry (2 Cor. 3:5). Nevertheless, I felt that I had to. I wanted people to recognize me as personally worthy of their respect and honor. I didn't really want "our competence" to be "from God." Yet over the next years God patiently dealt with me, building me up for a few days, letting me see some success. Then He forced me to face my own imperfection. I could never rest in my own accomplishments. As surely as I ever accomplished anything, shortly thereafter something would arise to convince me that I was still unworthy.

Then about six years later, while talking with a student in my office, another of those spiritual quantum leaps occurred. As a result of teaching the truths of Romans five and sometimes six days a week for three years, God's Spirit made clear to me another fact from Romans. I suddenly realized that if God declares a man righteous (justification), then he really is righteous. This idea was revolutionary to me. I had always thought that when God declares us righteous, His action was some sort of theological "double-think." He says we are righteous, but He knows that we are really sinners. The function of sanctification, as I understood it, was daily to lift me out of my sin. The process, in time, would bring me to the legally true, God-declared condition of righteousness.

Suddenly, I realized that God's Word is always true, not simply as a legal fiction, but true with all the reality of space and time. When God said "Let there be light," light came into being. When God declares the believing sinner righteous, that sinner is righteous. But it is not infused righteousness. God has declared that we have a righteousness that is a right relationship with Himself. And that is true as literally and as historically as when light came into existence on that first creative day. God says that we who are in Christ Jesus are new creations in Him (2 Cor. 5:17). If, then, I am righteous, I need no longer punish myself. Christ has already born the punishment. I have now become "the righteousness of God in Him" (2 Cor. 5:21). My value, furthermore, was not dependent on me, but on the price paid for me. If I had been the only sinner in the history of humanity, the price of sin would have remained the same. Any sin requires the death of the infinite Son of God. Therefore, every human being is of infinite value, for sin imposes the same penalty for every sinner in history. His infinite sufferings have taken away all God's wrath against me. His obedience has satisfied God for all of my failure (Rom. 5:19). I am indeed "accepted in the beloved" (Eph. 1:6, KJV).

This commentary on Romans is not just what I believe the Word of God teaches. I am sharing the very foundation on which I now live. Only by God's grace can I face life. It is this grace that I want you to understand. If my writing this book means that some of God's people have come to a better understanding of the grace of God, I believe this undertaking to be worth any effort and cost. I invite you, therefore, to experience Christ's grace, so that you may glorify the great God of heaven.

Dr. James E. Allman
Dallas, Texas
September 2017

OUTLINE OF
THE BOOK OF ROMANS

Introduction (1:1-15)

I. Christ, through His self-sacrifice, receives us by grace (1:16–11:36).

   A. Christ, through His self-sacrifice, brings a life of right relationship with God to the believer (1:16–8:39).

      1. Introduction: Paul is profoundly proud of the gospel, which reveals that sinners, Jews preeminently but also Gentiles, can be right with God by faith alone (1:16-17).

      2. Faith in Christ, who gave Himself for lost and sinful man, is right relationship with God (1:18–4:25).

         a. All humanity, Gentiles and the self-righteous, whether Jewish or Gentile, is equally condemned before God (1:18–3:20).

            (1) God is universally and presently pouring out His wrath against all sinful men who refuse to honor Him, turning them over to greater sin (1:18-32).

            (2) The self-righteous all stand condemned by God for their sin (2:1–3:20).

               (a) Even self-righteous man must acknowledge God's condemnation since even he does not obey God's law (2:1-16).

               (b) The self-righteous Jew cannot boast his privileges before God since his sin brings blasphemy upon the name of God (2:17-29).

               (c) The profit the Jews derive is their preeminence, which by their unbelief only exposes them to God's justice without commending them in any way to God (3:1-8).

               (d) The Scriptures show that Jews are under sin (3:9-18).

(e) The Law proves the condemnation of those under Law, so that the whole world becomes liable to punishment before God, because no one can be righteous before God through law which only reveals sin (3:19-20).

b. But God has provided a way of relating to Himself without Law and through faith (3:21–4:25).

(1) God brings His grace-righteousness to believing sinners through the work of Christ (3:21-26).

(2) God excludes boasting for all, both Jews and Greeks, through the principle of faith since He is the God of all, thus showing the righteousness of the Law (3:27-31).

(3) All Scripture, and particularly the experience of Abraham, testifies that right relationship with God is by faith (4:1-25).

(a) The Law and the Prophets testify that justification is by faith not law (4:1-8).

(b) Circumcision does not achieve justification, but is a sign of the faith that inherits the promise to which law stands opposed (4:9-17a).

(c) Abraham risked everything on God who raised Jesus from the dead in proof of justification and proved that the promise comes to the seed marked by faith (4:17b-25).

3. Christ, through His self-sacrifice, brings life to those who are righteous by faith (Rom. 5–8).

a. Therefore, having peace with God, we receive all blessings through Christ and know God's love in saving and keeping us (5:1-11).

b. Christ, patterned on Adam's contrast, brought life through His obedient death in order to bring life to reign through righteousness (5:12-21).

c. Righteousness will mark the life of believers when they regard themselves as dead to sin and alive to God through Christ and therefore not under law but under grace (6:1-14).

d. Believers, since they are not under law, will not go on sinning under grace since grace has set them free from sin through Christ's death and has given them in marriage to Christ to bear offspring for God (6:15–7:6).

e. The law is not itself sin, but sin can only exercise its dominion in a world of law (7:7-12).

f. The good law did not become death for Paul, since indwelling sin uses the law to produce acts of sin that he hates (7:13-25).

g. Therefore, we who live by faith in Christ are not condemned, but we live the life of the Spirit of God who will raise us from the dead, giving us His fatherly love as we suffer with Christ, showing that we are joint heirs with Him (8:1-17).

   (1) There is no condemnation for those in Christ Jesus since He gives us His Spirit to fulfill the requirement of the Law through faith, not through works (8:1-4).

   (2) Life in the Spirit means that one is not in the flesh but lives by faith in God who will raise such people with Christ (8:5-11).

   (3) This all means that we are called and taught by the Spirit to live by faith and not law, and to know God's fatherly love that has given those who suffer with Christ the role of joint heirs with Him (8:12-17).

h. But suffering, while it causes us to groan as we await our redemption, is bringing great hope for us since we know that God has eternally planned everything to conform us to Christ (8:18-30).

   (1) The sufferings of our lives are not worth comparing with the glory that will be revealed in us (8:18).

   (2) The greatness of the glory is shown by the longing of creation for our revelation as children of God, and by the Spirit's own groanings in His intercession for us, all leading us to hope (8:19-27).

   (3) We know that whatever comes to us comes from God who has purposed for us to become con-

formed to the image of Jesus, as the purpose of
His age long plan (8:28-30).

    i. Therefore, we are indeed at peace (see 5:1) with God
who has freely given us everything, so that nothing at
all can separate us from the love of God that is in
Christ Jesus our Lord (8:31-39).

B. Israel, like the Gentiles, will receive life by faith alone
(9:1–11:36).

  1. God has hardened unbelieving Israel (9:1-29).

    a. Paul longs for the salvation of his Israelite kinsmen
who have incredibly great blessings from God (9:1-5).

    b. In every generation of Israel, God has made a dis-
tinction between the seed of promise, chosen by
grace, and the seed of the flesh (9:6-13).

    c. God is perfectly just in sovereignly dispensing His
own compassion as He wills (9:14-18).

    d. No one may legitimately call God's justice into ques-
tion in this, since he may do with His creatures as He
wills (9:19-21).

    e. God has sovereignly hardened unbelieving Israel, but
He has called out believers from both Jews and Gentiles, as the prophets said He would (9:22-29).

  2. Israel rejected God's righteousness (9:30–10:21).

    a. The Gentiles by faith received what Israel rejected,
who stumbled over Christ the rock in unbelief
(9:30-33).

    b. Paul desires that Israel's zeal for God would bring
them to faith, but they have rejected God's righteousness and have tried to establish their own (10:1-3).

    c. Christ is the true goal of all righteousness that is of-
fered to both Jew and Gentile who will call on Jesus
as Yahweh, mighty to save (10:4-13).

    d. But Israel has surely heard the message proclaimed
constantly by the prophets and has obstinately disobeyed in unbelief (10:14-21).

  3. But God preserved a remnant chosen by grace (11:1-10).

  4. God took the promises from Israel to give them to the
Gentiles who received them by faith (11:11-24).

    5. God will stir Israel to jealousy, bringing them to salvation through faith (11:25-32).

    6. Conclusion: God's Unfathomable Wisdom and Knowledge (11:33-36).

II. Believers, through their self-sacrifice, must receive each other by grace (12:1–15:13).

    A. The righteous by faith must practice living sacrifice as they are transformed in their minds (12:1-2).

    B. Those who are righteous by faith and called to living sacrifice must express God's grace in ministry through their spiritual gifting (12:3-8).

    C. Those who are righteous by faith must offer their living sacrifice through sincere love (12:9–13:14).

        1. Those who have received grace from God should love one another sincerely (12:9-16).

        2. Those who love one another with sincere love must avoid avenging themselves on their enemies, leaving vengeance to God and the ministers to whom He has given the execution of justice (12:17–13:7).

        3. Believers must have no unpaid debts except love, for love satisfies all the law could impose (13:8-10).

        4. Parenthesis: Since you know that the time of the Lord's coming and the culmination of your salvation is near, give no opportunity to the flesh but live like Jesus Christ in the world (13:11-14).

    D. Paul called those who are righteous by faith to living sacrifice through accepting one another (14:1–15:13).

        1. Those who are righteous by faith must avoid judging and despising each other in matters of personal preference and simply accept each other (14:1-3).

        2. The weak must receive their strong brothers whom the Lord has accepted, even if they do not follow their diet or worship restrictions, since both will give account of their actions to God (14:4-12).

        3. The strong who are righteous by faith must not flaunt their freedom, so that by their example they can lead the weak to violate their consciences, but they should limit their own freedom for the weak (14:13–15:4).

4. Closing Prayer (15:5-6)
5. Conclusion: Believers must accept each other as Christ accepted them since He is the minister for both Jews and Gentiles, as the Scripture says (15:7-13).

Conclusion (15:14-33)

A. Paul's confidence in the Roman believers (15:14).

B. Paul wrote boldly as a minister by God's gracious power so the Gentiles would be his offering sanctified by the Holy Spirit (15:15-21).

C. Paul planned to visit the believers in Rome on his way to Spain after completing the ministry of the Greek saints for the poor in Jerusalem (15:22-29).

D. Paul desired earnest prayer for his deliverance from unbelievers in Judea, for the reception of his ministry among the saints, and for a joyous trip to be with the believers in Rome (15:30-32).

E. Paul's Signature Closing (15:33).

Commendation and Greetings (16:1-27)

A. Paul's commendation of Phoebe (16:1-2).

B. Paul greets various brothers and sisters in the church in a way that befits the saints (16:3-16).

C. Believers must avoid false doctrine and must trust in God (16:17-20).

D. Paul and others send greetings to the church in Rome (16:21-24).

E. Benediction (16:25-27)

ROMANS 1

Introduction (1:1-15)

[1]Paul, a servant of Christ Jesus, called to be an apostle and set apart for the gospel of God—[2]the gospel he promised beforehand through his prophets in the Holy Scriptures [3]regarding his Son, who as to his earthly life was a descendant of David, [4]and who through the Spirit of holiness was appointed the Son of God in power by his resurrection from the dead: Jesus Christ our Lord. [5]Through him we received grace and apostleship to call all the Gentiles to the obedience that comes from faith for his name's sake. [6]And you also are among those Gentiles who are called to belong to Jesus Christ.

[7]To all in Rome who are loved by God and called to be his holy people:

Grace and peace to you from God our Father and from the Lord Jesus Christ.

[8]First, I thank my God through Jesus Christ for all of you, because your faith is being reported all over the world. [9]God, whom I serve in my spirit in preaching the gospel of his Son, is my witness how constantly I remember you [10]in my prayers at all times; and I pray that now at last by God's will the way may be opened for me to come to you.

[11]I long to see you so that I may impart to you some spiritual gift to make you strong— [12]that is, that you and I may be mutually encouraged by each other's faith. [13]I do not want you to be unaware, brothers and sisters, that I planned many times to come to you (but have been prevented from doing so until now) in order that I might have a harvest among you, just as I have had among the other Gentiles.

¹⁴I am obligated both to Greeks and non-Greeks, both to the wise and the foolish. ¹⁵That is why I am so eager to preach the gospel also to you who are in Rome.

Romans 1:1-15 follows the standard opening for a letter in the ancient world. Paul began by identifying himself (with a brief description, vv. 1-5) and his readers (with a brief description, vv. 6-7a), and then he gave a prayer (v. 7b) and finally a thanksgiving (vv. 8-13). Paul then added a short statement of his desire to come to Rome (vv. 14-15).

It is not the purpose of this commentary to deal in detail with everything in the Roman letter. Rather my purpose is to discuss the ideas Paul raised about Romans 15:7. I have dealt with the impact of the ideas of passages in general without detailed exegetical treatment of each verse. With this approach in mind, two basic subjects call for attention in 1:1-8. First, I want to connect Paul's thoughts in 1:1-8 with 15:7. Second, I want to discuss **the gospel** (Gk. *euaggelion* meaning "good news") as Paul defined it in verses 1-5.

In 1:1-5 Paul made some key statements by which he modeled for his readers the gracious attitude he wanted them to extend to each other. Among the titles he recorded for himself is **an apostle** (v. 1). His title is of no slight importance, for it enshrines his authority to speak. Indeed, in Galatians, he expressed the significance of his apostolic authority. He reminded the Galatian Christians he had the right to define truth (Gal. 1:8-9). This meant whoever disagreed with him would come under God's curse. Here in Romans, he approached a church with which he had no personal relationship since he was not the founder of the church in Rome. Consequently, from the beginning he stressed his apostolic authority, which he received by a direct call from Christ, so that they would be submissive to his instructions. However, his purpose was not at all self-serving. He did not seek their submission so he could lord it over their faith. Instead, he sought their submission to the authority of God who had made him an apostle. Romans has crucial points where Paul could have stressed his authority, such as at the beginning of his exhortation section (12:1-2), but in those passages he addressed his readers with loving exhortation.

Even though Paul stressed the exalted position he had as an apostle by God's call, he did not relegate the Roman Christians to a lesser position. For in addressing them, he twice hailed them as recipients of God's calling. They are people who **belong to Jesus Christ** and **called to be his holy people** (1:6-7a). Whatever privileges Paul gained by his calling, he gained them for the sake of those who, like him, were called by Jesus Christ. He had a calling to be an apostle. They had a calling to be saints. Thus, Paul extended to them the same grace he had received from God. His apostolic calling was a great privilege, but it was not a position of domination over God's people. God had called the Roman believers also.

The other subject I want to discuss in the opening verses of this chapter is the gospel as Paul defined it in 1:2-4. The gospel has two emphases according to these verses. First, Jesus was **as to his earthly life a descendant of David.** Second, He was **through the Spirit of holiness was appointed the Son of God in power by his resurrection from the dead.** This last statement draws together several passages of Scripture from both of the testaments. Two references are crucial to the understanding of the passage: Ps 2:7 and Acts 13:32-33 (which quotes Ps. 2:7). Some have interpreted the Psalm reference as referring to the doctrine of the eternal generation of the Son, that is, that the being of the Son in the Godhead is continually "generated" by the being of the Father.[1] But a careful examination of the context in Psalm 2 shows that the one who speaks these words—the one who says "I will proclaim the decree of the Lord"—is the one of whom the Lord said in verse 6, "I have installed my King on Zion, my holy hill." Whoever this person is in the context, he is already the established king on Zion. This means that the title "son" in Psalm 2 refers, not to the deity of Jesus, but to the king of Israel.[2]

Thus, the New Testament uses Psalm 2 to refer to the kingship of Christ, not His eternal generation, and ties its initiation to the resurrection. Paul linked the declaration of His sonship with the resurrection in Romans 1:4. This is not the only place where Paul made such a connection. During his first missionary journey, Paul addressed the Jews who were worshiping in the synagogue of Pisidian Antioch (Acts 13:32-33). There he affirmed that God had fulfilled in their generation the promises He made to the fathers, and He did this by raising Christ from the dead. Paul then quoted Psalm 2:7. It is in this setting that we may identify the "day." God appointed Jesus as the kingly Son on His resurrection day. Therefore, the resurrection day is the day of His proclamation as King. This means that Jesus is the King who has the right to rule the whole earth (see Ps. 2:8). The day of His resurrection was Jesus' coronation day.

Why did Paul consider this element of Christ's identity so crucial to the gospel? He included it in the introductory description of the gospel in Romans and in his preaching in Pisidia. Yet there may be at least one reason for its prominent placement in Romans. Later in chapter 1, Paul stated that mankind is hostile to God, even though hostility to God is not the conscious condition of people outside of Christ. Most people do not feel hostile to God; they simply have no particular sentiment about Him at all. Hence, when a Christian witness approaches them with their need of Christ through the gospel and confronts them with their hostility toward God, they cannot understand. They may even argue that they are not God's enemies at all. However, kings are notoriously undemocratic. They are not so concerned with what their enemies think hostility is. They are much more concerned with what they think hostility is. As a result, it is incumbent on mankind to discover how King Jesus defines hostility to Himself, how He identifies His friends, and to show themselves to be His friends. Otherwise, He will surely come to destroy His enemies when they show themselves irremediably opposed to His reign.

Paul had been praying for several years that God would permit him to go to Rome. He earnestly desired to share with them his **spiritual gift** to bring them strength (1:11). When he made this statement as he dictated the letter to Tertius (see 16:22), he must have realized how arrogant it sounded spiritually. He remembered God's grace and the grace he wants his readers to practice. This he shows in verse 12 by the expression **that is.** Paul knew that he stood as much in need of strengthening from these divisive Romans as they were from him. Their faith would benefit him and his faith would benefit them, so they all would be **mutually encouraged.** Once again he expressed the grace of God, the same grace that he had received, to the Romans, indicating that he received them just as God had received him. Paul modeled for the Romans what he wanted them to do. The grace of God made Paul a debtor **both to Greeks and non-Greeks, both to the wise and the foolish.** Receiving grace from God places on the recipient a debt to extend that grace to others. Thus Paul, by grace an apostle of Jesus Christ (1:5), stood ready to serve the people at Rome also (vv. 14-15).

I. Christ, through His self-sacrifice, receives us by grace (1:16–11:36).
A. Christ, through His self-sacrifice, brings a life of right relationship with God to the believer (1:16–8:39).

Paul moved to the body of his letter in 1:16. I have already briefly sketched the structure of the body, but some amplification is necessary here. The body of the letter consists of two main parts or sections: 1:18–11:36 and 12:1–15:13. The first major section shows that God has always dealt with man by grace. We can further divide this section into two subsections: 1:16–8:39 and 9:1–11:36. I believe the first subsection can be summarized by the quotation in 1:17, "The righteous by faith shall live" (using the word order of the original). C. E. B. Cranfield suggested this rearrangement of the translation. He pointed out that the first part of the quotation, "The righteous by faith," summarizes 1:16–4:25. In this sub-subsection, Paul proved that righteousness is by faith. The rest of the quotation, "will live," summarizes chapters 5–8. In this sub-subsection, Paul explained how those who are right with God by faith should live.

1. Introduction: Paul is profoundly proud of the gospel, which reveals that sinners, Jews preeminently but also Gentiles, can be right with God by faith alone (1:16–17).

¹⁶For I am not ashamed of the gospel, because it is the power of God that brings salvation to everyone who believes: first to the Jew, then to the Gentile. ¹⁷For in the gospel the righteousness of God is revealed—a righteousness that is by faith from first to last, just as it is written: "The righteous will live by faith."

Paul began his whole discussion of grace and righteousness by faith with a general statement of his attitudes toward the gospel. He was **not ashamed of the gospel** because he took pride in it since he knew its **power.** Although he did not immediately explain that power, we may draw some conclusions from what follows. This divine power has two major effects in Romans. First, God's power in the gospel frees man from the wrath of God (compare 1:18 with 5:10). Second, it restores man to the glory of God (compare 3:23 with 5:1–3 and 8:29–30). Therefore, salvation from sin delivers from us from God's wrath and culminates in our glorification.

But this power in the gospel is not indiscriminately available since it is specifically **to everyone who believes.** God has not limited the gospel to Jews, or to Gentiles for that matter. It is available for all equally on the sole condition of faith.

In fact, Christian life is faith. It is **by faith from first to last** (literally, "from faith to faith"). The Christian life is faith from start to finish. To emphasize the validity of this statement, Paul quoted Habakkuk 2:4: **"The righteous will live by faith."** Since **faith** is so important in the particular context, we must define the term. Theologians have analyzed faith into three elements: knowledge, assent, and trust. (For lack of a better term I have used trust. Theologians have often used the Latin term *fiducia* which includes trust and commitment.) For reasons that I hope will become clear later, I have redefined *fiducia* ("faith" or "trust") as "love commitment." Finally, Paul made it clear in Romans 4:18 that an additional element to be included in faith is hope.

The objection could be made that in various places, (such as Rom. 5:1-5) that faith and hope are distinguished from one another. The contention here is that they are not to be distinguished from one another, but are so interdependent that one includes the other. The full discussion of this will come in Romans 4. However, a short justification of hope as an element of faith is in order. In Romans 4:17-21, Paul develops his explanation of what the faith that he is interested in is like. He gives as his example the faith of Abraham, particularly in the birth of Isaac. Abraham's knowledge of the person and plan of God led him to look past his awareness of his own age and his wife's barrenness. Both would normally mean that they had *no hope* of having a child. But God's promise and power gave him confidence to approach Sarah, and that confidence[3] led to the conception of a son.

Additionally, Romans 5:1-5 specifies that the life of faith is a life of hope, whether in relation to the promise of sharing in God's glory, or in the face of suffering. In suffering the child of God may know that God's purpose is to use pain to produce approved character. That approved character then generates more confidence in God as we experience the love of God given to us in the midst of hardship. How could one embrace hardship, except in the knowledge (faith, confidence) that God will use it to produce Christlikeness in us. When speaking of faith, hope, and love, we are not enumerating three distinct ideas. We identify different aspects of the same idea.[4]

But perhaps of most significance is Hebrews 11. The whole of the chapter aims to demonstrate the importance of hope for faith, virtually equating the concepts. There is no faith without hope. And where there is no hope, no confidence about the future, faith cannot operate. So faith has four elements: knowledge, assent, love commitment (trust), and hope.

Paul did not merely quote suitable language when he cited Habakkuk 2:4. Habakkuk is especially a book about faith in God. The book is largely about the development of faith in the prophet himself. Martin Lloyd-Jones wrote a brief commentary on the book that he entitled *From Fear to Faith*, showing that Habakkuk is peculiarly well adapted to help understand what faith is.

Habakkuk's ministry occurred in the last years of the Southern Kingdom, during the final moral degeneration of Judah. He saw his people breaking covenant on every hand. Yet God, who had promised to punish those who violate the covenant, was strangely ignoring Habakkuk's prayers for justice. He could not understand why the just and holy God did not keep His own covenant. He had a basic problem of faith. God's silence on this matter was not consistent with what he knew of God. His problem of faith is initially a problem of knowledge. The reason Habakkuk had to start with knowledge is that you cannot trust someone you do not know, and you come to trust others as you know more about them.

Habakkuk 1:1-4 expresses the prophet's problem of knowledge. God's response comes in verses 5-11. God informed His prophet that He will indeed bring justice to Judah, for He will punish the Israelite covenant breakers at the hands of the Babylonians. With this answer God solved Habakkuk's problem of understanding but created a new problem, a problem of acceptance. Habakkuk could not agree that the Lord's plan is appropriate. For him, knowledge was not yet faith.

Now Habakkuk has a problem of assent. Habakkuk's problem of assent appears especially in 1:13: "Why are you silent while one who is wicked swallows up one who is more righteous than himself." He found it difficult to accept God's plan as appropriate for the sins of Judah. Habakkuk was now in position to hear God's answer that comes in chapter 2.

God reminded the prophet that the one who is righteous will live by his faith, but He recounted the sins of the wicked. The sins listed in the chapter are peculiarly the sins of Babylonia, as is clear from verse 5. Yet as the list of sins lengthens, the reader becomes increasingly aware that the sins are not only Babylon's. Judah is also guilty of the same sins. From this Yahweh made it clear that Judah was as wicked as Babylon, not more righteous. In fact, from God's perspective, Judah was more wicked since they had sinned against centuries of God's grace and blessings.

Chapter 2 solved Habakkuk's problem of assent. He expressed his acceptance of God's plan in the opening of chapter 3. In 3:2 Habakkuk acknowledged that God's plan was right. Yet all of this was almost too much for the beleaguered prophet. He was unable to give himself confidently to God's plan. Starting at this point, he had a problem of commitment.

In response to Habakkuk's prayer that God in wrath would remember mercy, Yahweh sent His servant a vision (3:3-15). The vision drew on motifs of God's past deeds of salvation, such as the exodus and the conquest. Since the Old Testament consistently used God's past deeds of salvation as promises of His future saving work, this vision came to Habakkuk as comfort and encouragement. The God of the exodus had not forgotten how to redeem from foreign oppressors. The God of the conquest would ultimately lead His people to victory. He would come in His earth-shattering glory to bring redemption to His people. Now, seeing a God who is greater than the events of life, Habakkuk could move beyond merely assenting to the justice of God's plan. He moved on to give himself wholeheartedly to God in all that He was doing. Habakkuk acknowledged that God might bring all the covenant curses upon Judah in his lifetime (3:17). Yet he also said, "I will rejoice in the God of my salvation" (3:18). Now his faith was squarely in His God, not solely on God's deeds. He rested in faith without demanding that God live up to his expectations. Rather, his faith depended on the God of all history who molds history to suit His purposes. The prophet trusted a God who sustains those who rely on Him with supernatural strength and hope.

Indeed, from verse 16, Habakkuk's faith has blossomed into full flower, for he moved beyond mere acceptance to hope. He confidently believed that in spite of present circumstances, Yahweh would bring salvation in the future. His hope was a confidence born of faith in God. He was no longer dependent on surrounding circumstance for his confidence. He trusted in his God alone. From that time on he would take God so seriously that he could have hope in the midst of despair.

It becomes clear that Habakkuk has entered a love relationship. He has entered it as truly as one enters a marriage. It is not merely love that constitutes a marriage, for people love each other without marrying. What constitutes a marriage is the commitment that we make to the loved one. That love commitment is what holds us to the relationship in the midst of difficulties. It was Habakkuk's love relationship that would sustain him in his relationship with God, even in the face of the coming covenant curses (compare Deut. 28 and Lev. 26 with Hab. 3:17). Indeed, because of his love and hope he can even rejoice in his God (3:18)! For though he cannot trust his circumstances, he can trust his God. His faith is a confidence in the future because of his confidence in his God. It is an eschatological faith, a faith looking with confidence to the future.

Habakkuk modeled faith for us. When the creature contemplates God and His ways, no other relationship could possibly be right in God's eyes. The only right relationship is to take God more seriously than the reality sensed by the eyes and ears. Habakkuk refused to allow his attitude toward God and the world to depend on the experiences of the world. He refused to depend on the appearances of events. He judged the word of God to be so powerful and significant that for him it had more reality than the reality of the eyes. He refused to look at the world from the inside out. By faith he laid hold of the divine perspective on the world. This faith not only governed his thought. It mastered his desires and emotions. Perhaps the most significant evidence of his faith in chapter three is his rejoicing amid disaster. The Babylonians were to come to destroy all that gave his life meaning. But Habakkuk rested in, indeed delighted in, his God. This is righteousness by faith.

Once we have considered Habakkuk's teaching on faith, we can readily see the problem of the lost man. The problem is not what he knows (as will be clear from vv. 18–20). The problem of the lost man is what he loves. John 3:19 states, "This, then, is the judgment: The light has come into the world, and people loved darkness rather than the light because their deeds were evil." Faith is not primarily intellectual. The first two elements of faith, knowledge and assent, are indeed intellectual. But faith becomes saving faith only when the third element, the love commitment, is included, and this kind of faith is then peculiarly not intellectual but affective.[5] Men love darkness; therefore, they do not love God. Their sin consists just in this fact.

Indeed, Paul defined sin in these terms. Romans 14:23 says that "everything that does not come from faith is sin" (NIV). This is a more complete definition of sin than John's statement, "sin is lawlessness" (1 John 3:4), since Paul showed that there was a time when no law existed, but this does not mean sin did not exist (Rom. 5:12–14). If there was a time when God had given no law, then no one could sin if sin is simply lawlessness. But Paul affirmed that men sinned during that time. The only conclusion we can draw is that sin is not exclusively lawlessness. Even though no law exists, sin still exists. Therefore, sin must be something else, such as living with no faith in God. If faith is the only right relationship for the creature with the Creator, then unbelief must be the greatest affront to the living God.

The conclusion of all this is that a right relationship with God is, and always has been, by faith. It is by faith from first to last. The whole of the Christian life is simply faith in God.[6] To say this is to say that the Christian life is not just a way of living. It is only and completely a love relationship with God through Jesus Christ.[7] We can find support for this idea in John 17:3, where Jesus said, "This is eternal life: that they may know you, the only true God, and the One You have sent—Jesus Christ." Consider also Philippians 3:1-10 and Jesus' comments in John 14–15.

One more observation is necessary concerning Romans 1:16-17. If faith is as we have described it, and if righteousness is by faith, what is righteousness? The Christian community answers this question in different ways. Some say that righteousness in verse 17 is God's attribute. While this is certainly possible, the usage of the term elsewhere in Romans, and particularly in verse 17, does not support it, since God's attribute of righteousness is not by faith.

Another alternative for defining the term is "obedience." The point is that the gospel reveals the obedient lifestyle God requires of those related to Himself. Students of Romans have suggested at least three ways of interpreting this phrase. Some have called it the obedience God requires of those He saves. Others call it the obedience God imparts to those He saves. Finally, a third form of this view is that righteousness is the obedience God imputes to those whom He saves. Again, while these are all possible interpretations in general terms, they do not fit well in verse 17 or in the rest of the epistle. Righteousness, Paul explained, is not by works but by faith.

A final option for interpreting righteousness is "right relationship."[8] This means those who have right relationship with God are those who have faith in God. To understand this view it will be helpful to review two passages: Romans 3:19-22a and 4:5. In the third chapter Paul concluded his treatment of the sinful condition of all humanity. There he says, "Now we know that whatever the law says it says to those who are under law so that every mouth may be silenced and the whole world held accountable before God Therefore, no one will be declared righteous in his sight by observing the law; for by the law is the knowledge of sin" (my own translation). "But now a righteousness of God, apart from law, has been made known, to which the law and the prophets testify. This righteousness from God comes through faith in Jesus Christ to all who believe." In this passage Paul showed that righteousness in Romans is altogether apart from works. The righteousness of which he speaks is a "by faith" righteousness, a "without-law-through-faith righteousness."

The other reference that is basic for Paul's view of righteousness in Romans is 4:5. Paul affirmed that faith is counted as righteousness to him who "does not work but trusts God who justifies the ungodly." Two expressions in this verse are critical. God justifies those *who do not work*! They have no obedience! Indeed, they are "ungodly." The ungodly have no obedience. They have nothing to commend them to God. Yet even this does not solve all the problems of interpreting the statement of verse 5. The climaxing argument comes at the end of the verse, where Paul explained that, for the one who believes, his "faith is credited for righteousness." This should bring all discussion to an end. Faith is righteousness. Righteousness cannot be obedience. Righteousness must be right relationship.

An illustration from the Old Testament may help us understand the concept. Genesis 38 is a remarkable passage where an unusual person is declared righteous. As the story unfolds, we read that Judah had found a (Canaanite?) woman, Tamar, as a wife for his son Er. Because Er was evil, God took his life. According to the customs of the time, Judah gave Tamar to her brother-in-law Onan. He also died for his sin. But this time Judah refused to give her to his youngest son Shelah. When she was confident of his refusal, she hatched a plan that would protect herself, the family of Judah, and her husband's inheritance in the family. Driven to drastic measures by Judah's disloyalty, she dressed as a cult prostitute. Along the road she set an ambush for Judah, captured him in her plan, and by him conceived twins.

When Judah learned that she had committed adultery, he went into a rage at her breach of loyalty to the family and demanded she be put to death. At that critical moment, Tamar proved to Judah that he had fathered her children. Properly chastened by her loyalty to himself and her dead childless husband, Judah proclaimed, "She is more righteous than I, since I wouldn't give her to my son Shelah" (Gen. 38:26).

Surprising righteousness! How can a woman who has committed the sins of idolatry, prostitution, and incest be righteous under any circumstance? Obviously, we cannot define righteousness in Genesis 38 as obedience. Rather, Tamar's righteousness consisted of going beyond the duty of a widowed childless woman to provide offspring for her dead husband. She did what was necessary to protect and maintain the family relationship. This is righteousness! So when Paul says that the gospel reveals the righteousness of God "from faith to faith," he means that people have a right relationship with God by faith from start to finish.

2. Faith in Christ, who gave Himself for lost and sinful man, is right relationship with God (1:18–4:25).

In this section Paul explained that righteousness is by faith alone. He will do this by proving that no one can ever be obedient and by his obedience gain God's favor (1:18–3:20). Then he will show what God has done in making righteousness available (3:21-31). Finally, he will demonstrate that faith alone gives one access to such righteousness and explain what that faith looks like (ch. 4).

The problem Paul faced in the Roman church is that both the weak (mainly Jewish believers) and the strong (mainly Gentile believers, but including people like Paul) considered themselves superior because of their personal distinctions. The weak believed themselves superior to the Gentiles because they abstained from eating certain meats (14:1–12) and thus they condemned the Gentile Christians in the church. On the other hand, the Gentiles, who knew their freedom in Christ, despised the Jewish Christians in the church because of their weak faith. Each group urgently needed to learn that their personal distinctions in no way commend them to God. Indeed, their personal distinctions stood in the way of their relationship with God. Only those believers who understood that they had nothing to commend them to God would ever understand grace and live freely in it. Only in the freedom of God's grace can the church ever be free to be the church. This is the first step Paul took to teach the Roman Christians to "accept one another just as Christ accepted you, for the glory of God" (15:7).

a. All humanity, Gentiles and the self-righteous, whether Jewish or Gentile, is equally condemned before God (1:18–3:20).

In the history of theological discussion, Christians have defined sin in different ways. Three definitions have enjoyed special favor in the church. First, on the basis of 1 John 3:4, some have defined sin as any lack of conformity to God's law, or a transgression of God's law.[9] While this is a useful description of sin, it is inadequate as a full definition of sin. Human history has known times when no law existed (see Rom. 5:13–14). Yet even when law exists, some actions, while not specifically contrary to law, are nevertheless wrong. However, we have suggested above that humanity's sin problem is deeper than his actions. It is not so much what a man does as what he loves that is sinful. Yet this failure of love is not precisely a violation of a commandment. All the more is this true when God has given no commandment.

Second, some define sin as selfishness. Three objections make this view less likely. (1) Not every sin is ultimately selfish (e.g., the sin of Uzzah in 2 Sam. 6:7), although many and perhaps most are. (2) Chafer correctly stated, "No self-interest need be present in malice, enmity toward God, or in unbelief."[10] (3) Under this view the solution to sin would be selflessness, but that would be a work. That is, the sinner who would change from his selfishness to selflessness would by that change earn God's favor.

Third, still others define sin as anything that proves unlike the character of God.[11] This definition is much nearer to the truth. In fact, the only real objection to this view is that the creature must always be unlike God. Thus, this definition reduces sin to finiteness or creatureliness. Yet creatureliness is proper, as the creation of Adam and Eve proves. The heart of this definition, of course, deals not with creatureliness but with the creature failing to reflect the character of God. The creature can reflect God's character, but the definition leaves us with hopelessness since we must always be creatures— whether redeemed or lost.

All of this leaves room for another definition, this one taken from Paul. Even if this definition fails to satisfy the rigor of a carefully constructed theological definition, it certainly represents Paul's idea of sin. It is the one that he used in Romans. He defined sin as "everything that does not come from faith" (14:23). This explains how sin can exist when no law exists (see 5:12-14). It avoids the problem of defining sin as selfishness and as creatureliness. Furthermore, it is consistent with other passages. For example, John 3:36 says that condemnation is for those who do not believe, and there are a great number of passages that require faith as a condition for salvation.

Certain key implications of this definition of sin capture our attention. First, the beginning of sin is then contemporaneous with the beginning of unbelief. In this sense unbelief is not a positive act or a conscious decision. Rather, unbelief is a disposition of the soul to leave God out of life. This is the condemnation Scripture levels at the wicked: "In his pride the wicked does not seek him; in all his thoughts there is no room for God" (Ps. 10:4). It is painful to say, but the Scriptures teach that this disposition of hostility to God begins with the beginning of human life. David lamented and confessed in Psalm 51:5 that his mother conceived him in iniquity. We might interpret this statement, so far as I know, in one of two ways. It could mean that the act of conceiving a child is itself sinful. Yet God endowed humanity with the blessing of bearing children before the fall into sin (Gen. 1:26–28). This leaves only one other interpretation: that the child at conception already has an innate disposition to leave God out of his life. He is "by nature an object of wrath" (Eph. 2:3). Thus, the sin problem begins with the beginning of life, in the womb, at conception.

A second implication of saying that sin is unbelief is that sin is not inherently "doing bad things." This is not to say that lying is not sinful. Lying is sinful, not because we lie, but because unbelief motivates lying. Paul explained later in Romans that faith leads us to do the righteousness the law requires (8:4). If faith, then, leads to righteous living, unbelief leads to sin. Paul made a similar point in 2 Thessalonians 2:10… Those who follow the man of sin will come under God's judgment, not because they break commandments, not because they are selfish, not because they are unlike God, but because "they refused to love the truth and so be saved." It is their unbelief that seals them in their doom.

Finally, to define sin as unbelief is to affirm that one who does what is externally a good act, but in unbelief, is sinning. If unbelief is the essence of sin, then what makes an act sinful is the motive for which it is done. In the Scriptures we read that Judas betrayed Jesus. The Greek word for "betray" is the *paradidomi* (e.g., Matt. 10:4). But we also read that God the Father did this to Jesus (see "gave up" translating *paradidomi* in Rom. 8:32), and that Jesus did it to Himself (see "gave" translating *paradidomi* in Gal. 2:20). By what standard do we conclude that it was a terrible sin for Judas to do it when both the Father and Jesus themselves do the very same action? Is it not just this? Judas acted out of unbelief, that is, in rebellion against God and His will, and the Father and Jesus acted out of most holy and righteous motives. Many sins are inherently sinful, but not because of the inherent nature of the acts. Motive determines the moral quality of actions. Sins that are inherently sinful are so because we cannot do them by faith in God. On the other hand, some actions that are morally neutral in themselves become sinful because they are motivate by unbelief.

To illustrate the point, suppose the president of a Christian college were to approach two millionaires for his college. Suppose that one of the two millionaires is a committed follower of Jesus Christ, and the other is not. Suppose further that the president approaches the committed Christian and says, "You know that our college is providing a unique service in our community. No other institution is challenging young people to develop as Christians, not only spiritually, but also in their professional and academic lives. The service this will bring to our community is incalculable. That's why I'm here asking you to contribute one million dollars to the work of this institution." The Christian millionaire says to himself, "What he is saying is true. I can multiply my impact for the kingdom of God, see Christ's name glorified here, and bring integrity and Christian witness into the marketplace of this community by contributing to this college. Therefore, I'll give one million dollars to them." Would God consider his gift acceptable in His sight? Especially consider what Paul said to the Philippians: "I am amply supplied, now that I have received from Epaphroditus the gifts you sent. They are a fragrant offering, an acceptable sacrifice, pleasing to God" (4:18). You would certainly conclude that such gifts would bring great pleasure to God.

On the other hand, suppose that the president of the college went to the unbelieving millionaire.[12] As the president approaches the second man, he offers him the same opportunity to contribute to the college on the same basis as he offered the Christian. But the unbeliever thinks to himself, "This is a good idea. I need a good tax break

28

this year anyway, so I'll give to this college. Besides, maybe God will go a little easier on my sins when I come before Him." Will that gift please God? Does He not say that even the sacrifice of the wicked is an abomination to Him (Prov. 21:27)? We must conclude that it is primarily the motive for which actions are done that determines the moral quality of the actions.

The implications of this statement are frightening. If it is true, as I believe it is, then it means that lost men never do anything but sin. Even the externally good acts that they do are spiritually sinful. It is the nature of the lost man to be unbelieving. Isn't it true that if a lost man acted out of faith in God, God would save him? Then everything he does is sin. I drew the conclusion from Psalm 51:4 that hostility to God starts with the beginning of human life. This means that no lost person has ever done anything but sin—not beginning with the first conscious decision of life but from the very inception of life itself. Thus, unbelieving hostility to God dominates all of life—that is, until the Spirit of God moves to redeem and justify believers in Christ.

(1) God is universally and presently pouring out His wrath against all sinful men who refuse to honor Him, turning them over to greater sin (1:18-32).

[18]**The wrath of God is being revealed from heaven against all the godlessness and wickedness of people, who suppress the truth by their wickedness,** [19]**since what may be known about God is plain to them, because God has made it plain to them.** [20]**For since the creation of the world God's invisible qualities— his eternal power and divine nature—have been clearly seen, being understood from what has been made, so that people are without excuse.**

[21]**For although they knew God, they neither glorified him as God nor gave thanks to him, but their thinking became futile and their foolish hearts were darkened.** [22]**Although they claimed to be wise, they became fools** [23]**and exchanged the glory of the immortal God for images made to look like a mortal human being and birds and animals and reptiles.**

²⁴Therefore God gave them over in the sinful desires of their hearts to sexual impurity for the degrading of their bodies with one another. ²⁵They exchanged the truth about God for a lie, and worshiped and served created things rather than the Creator—who is forever praised. Amen.

²⁶Because of this, God gave them over to shameful lusts. Even their women exchanged natural sexual relations for unnatural ones. ²⁷In the same way the men also abandoned natural relations with women and were inflamed with lust for one another. Men committed shameful acts with other men, and received in themselves the due penalty for their error.

²⁸Furthermore, just as they did not think it worthwhile to retain the knowledge of God, so God gave them over to a depraved mind, so that they do what ought not to be done. ²⁹They have become filled with every kind of wickedness, evil, greed and depravity. They are full of envy, murder, strife, deceit and malice. They are gossips, ³⁰slanderers, God-haters, insolent, arrogant and boastful; they invent ways of doing evil; they disobey their parents; ³¹they have no understanding, no fidelity, no love, no mercy. ³²Although they know God's righteous decree that those who do such things deserve death, they not only continue to do these very things but also approve of those who practice them.

With the above definition of sin in mind, it is now appropriate for us to turn to the study of the sinfulness of humanity as explained in Romans 1:18–3:20. As Paul began his discussion, he elaborated on the sin of all humanity (1:18-32). This point of departure is excellent tactically. The self-righteous of humanity will accept all that Paul said about "all those other folks." Beginning at Romans 2:1, Paul turned to address the self-righteous themselves, with the Jewish Christians as the special addressees of the passage. In 2:1–3:32 Paul showed them that for all their pretensions to righteousness, they are equally as guilty as the rest of humanity. Although they condemn others for their sins, these self-righteous people are guilty of the very sins they condemn.

The verses now under consideration divide into two parts: verses 18-23 and verses 24-32. In the first part, Paul stated that God is presently at work punishing men who reject Him by substituting the worship of creatures for the worship of the Creator.

Paul affirmed here that God is presently pouring out His **wrath** on the world of wicked men **who suppress the truth by their wickedness.** But it would be wrong to say that the world is awaiting the outpouring of God's wrath. For over a century, it is common to find biblical scholars who deny the reality of God's wrath. Their view is that since He is a God of love (which He is; see 1 John 4:7–8), He cannot show wrath because love and wrath are incompatible. It certainly may be true that human love and wrath are incompatible. Yet is the nature of humanity the model on which we must understand God? Is it necessary to understand God in this way? I fear that the old saying would become true, "God created man in His own image, and man has returned the favor."

The biblical evidence for the wrath of God is unmistakable. The word occurs with two emphases: human anger (see Rom. 12:19; Eph. 4:31; Col. 3:8; 1 Tim. 2:8; Rom. 13:4–5 of governmental officials in particular) and divine anger. In the latter case the New Testament uses the term with two subcategories: present wrath (John 3:36; Rom. 1:18; 4:15; Heb. 3:11; 4:3) and future wrath (Matt. 3:7; 21:23; Rom. 2:5,8; 9:22; 1 Th. 1:10; 2:16; Rev. 6:16,17; 11:18; 14:10; 16:19; 19:15).

The pattern of the Old Testament is of crucial importance in a discussion of this kind. E. Johnson's comment on this issue is appropriate: "Words for anger are connected with God three times as often as they are connected with man in the Old Testament."[13] Clearly, the Bible does not hesitate to associate wrath with God.

In Romans 1:18 God's wrath is not a distant peril facing man. The careful reader may have already noticed that Paul described this wrath as something that is presently looming immediately over the lives of all humanity, and he referred to this wrath again later (see especially 1:24–32). God directs this wrath at a particular class of humanity: those **who suppress the truth by their wickedness.**

We should carefully observe that the problem with men is not that they do not know the truth. They do know the truth; otherwise they could not suppress it. The reason they know the truth is that God has revealed the truth to them. It is not normally necessary to teach children that God exists. The existence of God is a normal assumption of a normal mind. When the human mind meets it, it makes perfectly good sense. But it takes enormous effort to convince the mind, even one's own mind, that God does not exist.

The reason for humanity's ready assumption that God exists is twofold. God has created the human mind to prepare for an encounter with the concept of God. The concept of God may even be what theologians call an intuitive idea. Intuitive ideas are initially unknown to the mind. However, when the mind meets them, it is not surprised. In fact, intuitive ideas are not always completely provable, but all of reality is based on them. They include such ideas as the appropriateness of human reason for understanding reality, the principle of cause and effect, and the existence of the self. God constructed a world in which these principles function, and then He constructed the human mind to recognize them when it should meet them. This, then, is the first reason for humanity's ready assumption of the existence of God.

The second reason that all mankind universally presupposes the existence of deity appears in our passage. God has revealed His existence within man (Rom. 1:19). Furthermore, He has given sufficient revelation of Himself in the created order so that every man stands stripped of every legal defense before God (v. 20). The creation reveals that deity exists and that deity possesses **eternal power.** Every human being is, therefore, obligated to seek God out. Yet it is a universal reality that no one seeks God (3:11). The tragedy of this is that the revelation of God in nature is enough only to condemn; it is not enough to redeem. Therefore, those who stifle what they might know of God leave themselves no escape from the wrath of God.

We may rightly conclude from what Paul says in verses 18–20 that a true atheistic stand is not possible. People may conclude that God does not exist, but biblically it is not because the evidence has forced them to this conclusion. Atheists struggle wildly against those who believe in God because they are terrified that the theist may be right, that God may exist after all. Our text teaches us that God has revealed Himself to all humanity. So we may say that, in the innermost part of his mind, an atheist is in fact certain that God does exist.

For all his reasonings, he cannot escape the nagging terror in his heart that God is there. It is this unsettling dread that fuels his violent opposition to theism.

Paul explained the defenseless posture of the unrighteous, especially the sin that **suppresses the truth.** Even though the unrighteous know about God, they refuse Him due honor and exchanged His **glory** for the likeness of [NIV, **made to look like**] the **images** of creatures. Such people became witless **fools,** while confidently asserting their wisdom by exchanging the glory of God who is **incorruptible.** These fools exerted great effort in their craving to be rid of God. They did not seek the creature nor even the image of the creature. They sought only the likeness of the image of the creature! Instead of bowing humbly before God's radiant glory, they worshiped **mortal human being and birds and animals and reptiles.**

At this point in His dealings with man, God begins the work of His wrath. The great Judge of mankind determined to give man just what he wanted: more skill in sin. He handed such men over to dishonor their bodies as they exchanged the glory of God for a lie (vv. 24–25). Interpreters of Scripture have taken different positions about the meaning of Paul's threefold expression **God gave them over** (vv. 24,26,28) One cannot help but wonder just what this statement means. It would be more congenial to our concept of God to think of Him abandoning us to our sins. One commentator explained Paul's statement this way: "When we refuse to 'let God be God' and do not acknowledge Him, He abandons us to our vicious impulses."[14] But is this the point Paul was making? I have already discussed the Greek verb that Paul used here (*paradidomi*). This is the same word used for Judas's betrayal of Jesus (Matt. 10:4 and several other places that the name Judas appears in the Gospels). Did Judas's sin specifically consist in abandoning Christ? Or did he deliberately set out to find an opportunity to deliver Jesus into His enemies' hands? Mark's Gospel says: "Then Judas Iscariot, one of the Twelve, went to the chief priests to betray Jesus to them. They were delighted to hear this and promised to give him money. So he watched for an opportunity to hand him over" (14:10–11). So Judas's act was not a passive abandoning of Christ to His fate; no, he actively set out to turn Jesus over to the priests.

The impact of these observations on Romans 1:24 is profound. What God does as He turns men over to sin is not a passive abandoning. He actively turns man over. In saying this, however, we must be careful not to imply that we make Him the author of sin in some way. What preserves us from heresy here is the recognition of the truth that God in His marvelous grace is now restraining sin in the world. Man is not as evil as he can be. But as man goes on in his sin, as a judgment of the present wrath of God, He actively makes it possible for mankind to develop more and more competence in sinning. He enables mankind to go deeper and deeper into sin. Therefore, we do not conclude that God has forced men to sin. He simply grants them more opportunities to express the sin that dwells them. He does this, as we shall see, "that they might at last learn from their consequent wretchedness to hate the futility of a life turned away from the truth of God."[15]

The peculiar form that this judgment against sin takes is the dishonoring of **their** bodies, that is, the abuse of their bodies. They had dishonored God. Now God dishonors them. They abused God's glory, desiring in exchange the likeness of corruptible creatures. Now God hands them over to abuse their own bodies. Here God acts in poetic justice to prove that the judgment is indeed from heaven and to remind mankind of the cause of their judgment

In response to this judgment, these people—who had exchanged the glory of God for a lie—fell under the wrath of God again: **God gave them over to shameful lusts.** They exchanged God's truth for a lie. In response, God removes His restraints on sin so that mankind also exchanges God's purpose for the sexes, exchanging the natural sexual function for what is contrary to nature: homosexuality. In this passage, homosexuality is not so much a judgment on individual sinners as it is a judgment on humanity. The growth of homosexuality shows the bankruptcy of humanity and is a verdict on a whole culture. It is not just the homosexual that this passage condemns. It is all of humanity and all of human culture without God. Even the AIDS epidemic is not so much a judgment on the homosexual community as it is a judgment on a culture that has exchanged the glory of God for the worship of the creature. We may legitimately show mercy to the sufferer under the scourge of

AIDS. But we must realize that the judgment is on the world of men who suppress the truth in ungodliness.

Now that man had embraced this depth of sin, **God gave them over to a depraved mind.** The Greek word for **depraved** (*adokimos*) can also mean "disapproved." The wicked disapproved of God, and now God has given them, in His poetic justice, a disapproved mind. "Because they have rejected God as not worth reckoning with, God has delivered them into a condition in which their minds are fit only to be rejected as worthless, useless for their proper purpose, disreputable."[16] The fruit of this disapproved mind is all kinds of evil behaviors, several of which Paul listed in verses 29–31. Those who read this list carefully may notice that the list has no conjunctions. This is a figure of speech called *asyndeton*, too few conjunctions. The purpose of asyndeton is to alert the reader that the author's main point is at the end of the list. The author encourages the reader to read the list without dwelling on it.

Indeed, the point of the list is at the end in verse 32. Mankind knew that God has already declared that those who commit such sins to be worthy of death. Nevertheless, they not only do them but also take pleasure in those who do them. We might expect that as man sinks lower and lower into sin, he would become more and more appalled at his own debased condition. Here is the spectacle of sin. In his perversion, man has lost moral insight and perception. He delights in sin, enjoying in himself and others what he ought to despise in himself. Worse, he does this in the face of the full knowledge of God's just decree that those guilty of such sins **deserve death.** Is this not depravity?

Some Christians hesitate to affirm the doctrine of total depravity. One prominent Christian is supposed to have said that he did not believe in man's total depravity because no man is as bad as he can be. While the statement is true, the conclusion reached on the basis of it is not. Total depravity does not refer to how bad mankind is or can be. Rather it refers to how bad off mankind is. Technically the term means "(1) that corruption extends to every part of man's nature, including the faculties of his being; and (2) that there is nothing in man that can commend him to a righteous God."[17] Paul has taught that man under sin has become foolish in his imaginings. On a later occasion, Paul affirmed that we are dead in our trespasses and sins (Eph. 2:1). Man's mind is darkened (Rom. 1:21). He is sick and helpless (Rom. 5:6). His eyes are blind (John 9:41), and Satan works to keep him that way (2 Cor. 4:3–4). Thus, total depravity affirms that, in every part of his existence, man is incapable of being what God requires His creatures to be. Romans 1 proves the truth of that statement, for the chapter tells not simply the truth about the worst of men, but the truth about all men.

Notes for Romans 1

[1]So Louis Berkhof, *Systematic Theology*, p. 93; John F. Walvoord, *Jesus Christ Our Lord*, pp. 40-42.

[2]E.g., Geoffrey W. Grogan, *What the Bible Teaches About Jesus*, p. 43, who says, "As the term *son of God* has been used with reference to the nation as a whole we are not surprised to find it applied to them in its plural form (Deut. 14:1; Isa. 1:2). Once again, however, we find no use of it in the singular to designate an individual, with the important exception of the king. He is called 'son of God' in three passages. 2 Samuel 7:14 is the basic one, because both Psalm 2:7 and Psalm 89:27 assume the certainty of the promises in 2 Samuel 7 and so are founded on them.... It is a term applicable to the king because he sums up the chosen nation and because he foreshadows the great King of the future.... It is a term of relationship rather than one of office, and this relationship was seen in all its fullness, indeed in a unique form, when Jesus of Nazareth came into our world as *the* Son of God. It was this relationship that fitted him for the kingly office *par excellence*."

[3]*Merriam-Webster's Collegiate Thesaurus*, 373, gives confidence as the first synonym for hope!

[4]1 Corinthians 13:13 requires us to think of different kinds of faith. Verse 2 of the chapter mentions something like the gift of faith (inferred from chapter 12) which is not the same as the faith of James 2, for example. One would need, thus, to differentiate it, also, from what one would call saving faith in other places in Paul.

[5]In the field of education, the affective domain "includes all behavior connected with feelings and emotions. Thus, as we earlier stated, emotions, tastes and preferences, appreciations, attitudes and

values, morals and character, and aspects of personality adjustment or mental health are included" (Thomas A. Ringness, *The Affective Domain in Education*, p. 5).

[6]J. H. Merle D'Aubigné said, "Faith, according to St. Paul, is the means by which the whole being of the believer—his understanding, heart, and will—enter into possession of the salvation purchased for him by the incarnation and death of the Son of God. Jesus Christ is apprehended by faith, and from that hour becomes all things to man and in man. He communicates a divine life to our human nature; and man thus renewed, and freed from the chains of sin and self, feels new affections and performs new works.... If faith be not an appropriation of salvation, it is nothing; all the Christian economy is thrown into confusion, the fountains of the new life are sealed, and Christianity is overturned from its foundations" (*History of the Reformation of the Sixteenth Century*, 1:51-52).

[7]It is surprising that the Old Testament commandment to love God with all our heart, soul, and strength is not repeated in the New Testament outside the discussions Jesus had with the Jews. This omission, however, is only apparent, for in my opinion, faith *is* loving God with all our heart, soul, and strength.

[8]Koch defined righteousness in the Old Testament as "reciprocal fidelity and loyalty" that goes beyond the fulfillment of duty. Ernst Jenni and Claus Westermann, *Theological Dictionary of the Old Testament* (Peabody, MA: Hendrickson Publishers, 1997), s.v., "[*tsadaq*] to be communally faithful, beneficial," by K. Koch, 1049.

[9]Westminster Shorter Catechism, Question 14.

[10]Louis Sperry Chafer, *Systematic Theology*, 2:258.

[11]Chafer, 7:287.

[12]In defense of this part of the illustration, I would remind my reader that an "unsanctified" dollar buys the same amount of gasoline that a "sanctified" dollar does! Furthermore, once we Christians have received it with thanksgiving to God as the real Giver, the money is sanctified to His use.

[13]Jan Bergman and Elsie Johnson, "אָנַף," ed. G. Johannes Botterweck and Helmer Ringgren, trans. John T. Willis, *Theological Dictionary of the Old Testament* (Grand Rapids, MI; Cambridge, U.K.: William B. Eerdmans Publishing Company, 1977), 356.

[14]William M. Greathouse, *Romans,* p. 33.

[15]C. E. B. Cranfield, *A Critical and Exegetical Commentary on the Epistle to the Romans,* International Critical Commentary (London; New York: T&T Clark International, 2004), 121.

[16]Cranfield, 1:128.

[17]*Baker's Dictionary of Theology,* s.v. "Depravity, Total," by Charles C. Ryrie, p. 164.

ROMANS 2

In Romans 1:18-32 Paul demonstrated the sinful condition of all humanity, and in 2:1–3:20 he applied to the self-righteous among humanity what he has already said about humanity in general. They include the Gentiles, to be sure, but especially the Jews. This is the point of the "therefore" with which the chapter begins. Paul shows the sinfulness of the self-righteous while he proves the sinfulness of the human race.

> (2) The self-righteous all stand condemned by God for their sin (2:1–3:20).
> > (a) Even self-righteous man must acknowledge God's condemnation since even he does not obey God's law (2:1-16).

¹You, therefore, have no excuse, you who pass judgment on someone else, for at whatever point you judge another, you are condemning yourself, because you who pass judgment do the same things. ²Now we know that God's judgment against those who do such things is based on truth. ³So when you, a mere human being, pass judgment on them and yet do the same things, do you think you will escape God's judgment? ⁴Or do you show contempt for the riches of his kindness, forbearance and patience, not realizing that God's kindness is intended to lead you to repentance?

⁵But because of your stubbornness and your unrepentant heart, you are storing up wrath against yourself for the day of God's wrath, when his righteous judgment will be revealed. ⁶God "will repay each person according to what they have done." ⁷To those who by persistence in doing good seek glory, honor and immortality, he will give eternal life. ⁸But for those who are self-seeking and who reject the truth and follow evil,

there will be wrath and anger. [9]There will be trouble and distress for every human being who does evil: first for the Jew, then for the Gentile; [10]but glory, honor and peace for everyone who does good: first for the Jew, then for the Gentile. [11]For God does not show favoritism.

[12]All who sin apart from the law will also perish apart from the law, and all who sin under the law will be judged by the law. [13]For it is not those who hear the law who are righteous in God's sight, but it is those who obey the law who will be declared righteous. [14](Indeed, when Gentiles, who do not have the law, do by nature things required by the law, they are a law for themselves, even though they do not have the law. [15]They show that the requirements of the law are written on their hearts, their consciences also bearing witness, and their thoughts sometimes accusing them and at other times even defending them.) [16]This will take place on the day when God judges people's secrets through Jesus Christ, as my gospel declares.

Self-righteousness is among the most serious sins in Scripture. The four Gospels contain no account of Jesus ever preaching an entire sermon against adultery. He preached none against drunkenness or any of the other sins that our culture condemns so regularly. Yet He addressed the Pharisees' self-righteousness in two lengthy sermons: the Sermon on the Mount (Matt. 5–7) and the Woes to the Pharisees (Matt. 23). In the Sermon on the Mount, Jesus said, "For I tell you that unless your righteousness surpasses that of the Pharisees and the teachers of the law, you will certainly not enter the kingdom of heaven" (Matt. 5:20). He also announced divine condemnation on their whole system of righteousness: "Woe to you, teachers of the law and Pharisees, you hypocrites! You travel over land and sea to win a single convert, and when he becomes one, you make him twice as much a son of hell as you are.... Woe to you, teachers of the law and Pharisees, you hypocrites! You give a tenth of your spices—mint dill, and cumin. But you have neglected the more important matters of the law—justice, mercy, and faithfulness" (Matt. 23:15,23). The Jewish leaders' failure to recognize their own sin left them hypocritical and judgmental fools (v. 17).

In fact, self-righteousness may be the most serious sin mankind can commit from God's point of view. On the one hand, we don't need to tell an adulterer that he is a sinner. Drunks know that they have a problem. Thieves and murderers expect, in their guilty consciences, judgment from God. On the other hand, the self-righteous never recognize their condition before God. They disregard their need of Christ's atonement, while hypocritically acknowledging His work. It may even be that the hardest of lost men to win to Christ are the morally upright. They are self-sufficient and thus feel no need of God or His grace. But both the morally upright pagan and the morally acceptable Christian expect only justice from God. They do not know that justice must mean condemnation. Grace is not for the righteous. It is for the ungodly—those who are sinful, helpless, enemies of God (Rom. 5:6-10).

Scripture has already condemned the sinfulness of the human race. Therefore, the self-righteous of humanity, **those who pass judgment on someone else** but insist on their own goodness, must surely fall under the same condemnation. They condemn others for what they do **yet do the same things.** Such people think that they are free from condemnation even though they practice the same sins (Rom. 2:1–3). They would not condemn others so freely if they thought differently. In Romans 2, Paul developed and proved the sinfulness of the self-righteous.

In verses 4-5 Paul reminded his readers that everyone who practices sin will fall under God's judgment. Nevertheless, the sanctimonious, though they know this, despise God's **kindness.** For in His kindness God sends events into their lives that should lead them to repentance. We should note how sinful the heart of these pious frauds is. For while God sends them experiences to lead them to repentance, they reject His kindness. Paul attributed their rejection of God's kindness to their **stubbornness** and **unrepentant heart.** Because of their pious sin, they are storing up wrath from God when He judges humanity's sin.

In chapter 1, Paul explained the judgment that God sends against sin. But even God's present wrath mingles with mercy. When God drove our first parents from Eden in His wrath, He mercifully barred the way to the tree of life. If they had eaten from the tree in their fallen state, they would have remained fallen forever (see Gen. 3:21-24). By barring their way, He preserved them for the redemption He was preparing. The same principle is present here in Romans. In turning man over to more sin, God is dealing in great mercy with man's sin.

Paul's statement in verse 5 seems to indicate that it is God's intention for His present wrath to lead man to repentance. That man scorns His kindness proves how sinful even the self-righteous are. If man were in the least responsive to God spiritually, he would repent as he sees himself slipping deeper into sin. He would cry out to God, begging for the mercy He has already begun to show in His judgment. How sinful, then, is the heart of man! How hard and unrepentant he is! Such observations make it all the more clear that these impostors will come under God's judgment. They condemn others, and with their own mouths they condemn themselves. They commit the very sins they condemn.

These pretenders by their own testimony acknowledge that God will reward every person according to his works (Rom. 2:6–16). They simply believe that God is wrong about them. He pronounces all humanity sinful, but they believe that they have overcome in their own lives the judgment of God. Still God does certainly reward each according to his works. He will reward those who actually practice righteousness with life, but the wicked He will surely punish with death. In fact God always rewards the obedient, even the Gentile who does not have the written law but has the law in his conscience.

One may wonder which law these statements refer to. While we do not yet have enough data in Romans to define law fully, we must point out that when Paul talks about the law, he means the Mosaic Law. The following reasons make this a necessary conclusion. First, as Paul developed his discussion, he posed law as a possible means of right relationship with God, though he rejected it. No Christian or Jew would ever think of any law other than God's as offering life before God. Indeed, no one would think that keeping the law of Rome or of America would offer life with God. If any law existed that could offer eternal life, it would surely be God's.

Second the usage of the term "law" in Romans argues for the meaning "the law of God." This can be seen in verse 14 where Paul said that some people do not have the law. Then the Jew takes his rest in the law (see v. 17). Again, the law speaks to the Jew who is under law (3:19). The law and the prophets testify to God's way of righteousness without law (3:21). It is the law itself that faith-righteousness establishes (3:31). The promise comes both to the seed of faith and to the seed that was under law (4:16). Perhaps the most significant passage in this discussion is Romans 5:13–14: "For before the law was given, sin was in the world. But sin is not taken into account when there is no law. Nevertheless, death reigned from the time of Adam to the time of Moses." The point is that for centuries before Moses, no law existed. When Moses came, the law came. We should also note 7:1–3 where Paul discussed the Mosaic legislation about marriage and adultery. In 7:7 Paul quoted from the Ten Commandments. In 8:7 Paul stated that those who are of the flesh are not subject to the law of God. Finally, in 10:5 Paul said that Moses wrote about the righteousness that is in the law. From these references we must conclude that Paul was talking about the Mosaic law that God gave the Israelites on Mount Sinai.

Paul made an astonishing statement in 2:13 when he said that **it is those who obey the law who will be declared righteous.** This statement would appear to contradict 3:20: "No one will be declared righteous in God's sight by observing the law." The commentaries struggle with the affirmation of verse 13. One fine writer said, "Rather is Paul thinking of that beginning of grateful obedience to be found in those who believe in Christ, that though very weak and faltering and in no way deserving God's favour, is, as the expression of humble trust in God, well-pleasing in His sight."[1] His explanation, however, does not fit the context, which is the way of obedience as a means of acceptance with God. He explained that those who claim to have acceptable obedience, the self-righteous, fall short of God's righteousness. Yes, God will reward the obedient with life. The self-righteous will not inherit life since they are not obedient.

These observations lead to an alternative interpretation. From one point of view, we grant that if anyone perfectly obeyed the law, he would inherit life. But no human being has ever kept the law perfectly, that is, except Jesus Himself. God properly calls Jesus righteous through His obedience. Nonetheless, He is the only person born of woman who has perfectly obeyed. No other has or can! Thus, Paul was correct. Those who perfectly obey God will inherit life. That the self-righteous do not inherit life by their lifestyle proves that they have not kept the law.

No Gentile has ever been under the Mosaic law of God; only Israel has been subject to it. Yet even the pagan Gentiles, who have never had the law, demonstrate that the work of the law has been **written on their hearts.** This means that the conscience is a sufficient testimony that all people know they ought to be obedient to some outside power. When those without the law obey the leading of conscience, they show themselves nearer to pleasing God than those who have the law while breaking it. For those who have no law, Paul explained, God will pronounce judgment without the law. For those who have the law, God will pronounce judgment by the law. But He will condemn all. All people stand under their condemning consciences, even the self-righteous. The defiled conscience of each person (with or without the law) is clear evidence that the whole race stands under condemnation.

(b) The self-righteous Jew cannot boast his privileges before God since his sin brings blasphemy upon the name of God (2:17-29).

[17]Now you, if you call yourself a Jew; if you rely on the law and boast in God; [18]if you know his will and approve of what is superior because you are instructed by the law; [19]if you are convinced that you are a guide for the blind, a light for those who are in the dark, [20]an instructor of the foolish, a teacher of little children, because you have in the law the embodiment of knowledge and truth—[21]you, then, who teach others, do you not teach yourself? You who preach against stealing, do you steal? [22]You who say that people should not commit adultery, do you commit adultery? You who abhor idols, do you rob temples? [23]You who boast in the law, do you dishonor God by breaking the law? [24]As it is written: "God's name is blasphemed among the Gentiles because of you."

²⁵Circumcision has value if you observe the law, but if you break the law, you have become as though you had not been circumcised. ²⁶So then, if those who are not circumcised keep the law's requirements, will they not be regarded as though they were circumcised? ²⁷The one who is not circumcised physically and yet obeys the law will condemn you who, even though you have the written code and circumcision, are a lawbreaker.

²⁸A person is not a Jew who is one only outwardly, nor is circumcision merely outward and physical. ²⁹No, a person is a Jew who is one inwardly; and circumcision is circumcision of the heart, by the Spirit, not by the written code. Such a person's praise is not from other people, but from God.

In verse 17 Paul turned directly to the Jew to face him with his disobedience to God's law in which he boasts. It is the law that forms the basis of his confidence (vv. 17–29). In this section Paul listed the privileges that the Jew boasts of before God (vv. 17–20); he called the Jews to account for their sin that blasphemes God's name (vv. 21–24); and finally, he explained that the privileges the Jew boasts in bring him into condemnation since privilege always brings responsibility before God (vv. 25–29). It is the tragedy of religion that those who preach so vehemently against sin and boast so readily in their righteousness are so liable to the very sins they condemn. Whether it is universally true or not, it is certainly true that Paul directed this precise charge against his self-righteous Jewish readers.

I must emphasize that Paul was not merely singling out Jewish sins. His accusation against the Jews in this passage is nothing more than what their own rabbis have said. Bird commented that "the sharp barb of truth at the end of this rhetorical whip is that his opponent has not lived up to the vocation that the mandate in the Torah has placed on him. It would only take a little introspection, wrestling with his own 'evil impulse'... and meditating on the penitential psalms, for this imaginary opponent to realize that he might not be much better than his pagan neighbor."² The self-righteous wish to exempt themselves from the charge of hypocrisy. Nevertheless, they must bear it. The self-righteous Jew who sets himself up as judge of righteousness stands condemned by the Scripture itself as one who dishonors God (2:23). Any Jew in Rome would feel the force of the quotation, **God's name is blasphemed among the Gentiles because of you** (Isa. 52:5), where the prophet lamented the fact that the pagan nations mock God's name because of Israel, which was dispersed in their midst. Therefore, the quotation powerfully drives home the groundlessness of the Jews' pretensions to righteousness. This same charge stands against all the self-righteous. The best the world has produced, the Jewish people, stand under the condemnation of dishonoring God. Thus, all other hypocritically righteous people stand condemned as well.

Now since Jews have great privileges, they also have great responsibilities before God through those privileges. Paul addressed the special responsibility implied by **circumcision** in 2:25–29. The privileges of the self-righteous Jew bring him into condemnation since circumcision brings responsibility, not privilege. According to Paul circumcision can only be profitable to one who does the law. Indeed, Gentiles who do not have the law, yet practice some parts of it, are more acceptable to God than the circumcised law-breaker. Paul goes so far as to define the obedient Gentile as circumcised (2:26), obviously not in the flesh, but in the heart. Furthermore, this circumcised Gentile will judge the circumcised law breaker, and, as Nygren pointed out, "the positions are reversed."[3] At the beginning of this chapter, Paul explained that the Jews felt obliged to judge the Gentiles. Now the Gentiles, by their lifestyle, judges the Jews. For the only true Jew is not one only **outwardly, in the physical,** but one whose circumcision occurs **inwardly,** from **the heart** and **by the Spirit.** He is this one who receives God's praise, even if he does not receive man's (vv. 28–29).

It is often important to discuss for the Christian reader the meaning of circumcision for the Jew. God first gave circumcision to His people at the same time God changed Abram's name to Abraham (see Gen. 17:9-27). God gives circumcision to Abraham as the sign of the covenant He had made with him. Ever since then, those who desired to participate in the blessings promised to Abraham had to have the sign of circumcision. Abraham is preeminent in the Old Testament as a man of faith. Indeed, Paul made a connection between circumcision and Abraham's faith (Rom. 4:11) and described circumcision as the sign of the faith-righteousness he had while being uncircumcised.

The second important passage in this connection is Deuteronomy 10:16, which occurs in the midst of a passage expounding the Great Commandment (see 6:5). Moses instructed the people, "Circumcise your hearts, therefore, and do not be stiff-necked any longer." Carefully note the association of ideas in this verse. One who is circumcised in heart, that is, who indeed has the circumcision of Abraham, is not stiff-necked. The imagery of the stiff neck is important here. It draws on the background of plowing. It is impossible to guide an animal that bows its neck and refuses to respond to the plowman. The plowman would be unable to guide the animal and would become incapable of doing the plowing. The converse of being stiff-necked, then, would be sensitivity, teachability, responsiveness to the plowman, that is, to God. So circumcision is a sign of faith and the faith response to God. Indeed, the person with circumcised heart will "love the LORD his God" with all his heart, soul, and strength (6:5). This, then, is the key to the covenant relationship God gave to Israel.

The final key passage in discussing the meaning of circumcision is Deuteronomy 30:6, which is central to this discussion since it explains how one's heart becomes circumcised. God told Israel: "With your own eyes you saw those great trials, those miraculous signs and great wonders. But to this day the Lord has not given you a mind that understands or eyes that see or ears that hear" (29:3-4). They were utterly devoid of understanding the spiritual significance of God's works in Egypt on their behalf. Indeed, Israel's lack of spiritual understanding would lead, as Moses pointed out, to worldwide dispersion. But after their worldwide dispersion, they would return to the Lord. Moses explained to the Israelites what would be behind their return: "The LORD your God will circumcise your hearts and the hearts of your descendants, so that you may love him with all your heart and with all your soul, and live" (Deut. 30:6). Heart circumcision means that God brings to pass in the life of the circumcised the whole-hearted love that He seeks in His people. Therefore, physical circumcision is nothing more than the external sign of an internal spiritual condition. Without the accompanying spiritual condition, the sign is hypocrisy and vanity.

Notes for Romans 2

[1]C. E. B. Cranfield, *A Critical and Exegetical Commentary on the Epistle to the Romans*, 1:155.

[2]Michael Bird, *Romans*, The Story of God Bible Commentary, ed. Tremper Longman III and Scott McKnight (Grand Rapids: Zondervan, 2016), 81; cp. also Douglas J. Moo, *The Epistle to the Romans*, The New International Commentary on the New Testament (Grand Rapids, MI: Wm. B. Eerdmans Publishing Co., 1996), 159.

[3]Anders Nygren, *Commentary on Romans*, p. 132.

(c) The profit the Jews derive is their preeminence, which by their unbelief only exposes them to God's justice without commending them in any way to God (3:1-8).

[1]What advantage, then, is there in being a Jew, or what value is there in circumcision? [2]Much in every way! First of all, the Jews have been entrusted with the very words of God.

[3]What if some were unfaithful? Will their unfaithfulness nullify God's faithfulness? [4]Not at all! Let God be true, and every human being a liar. As it is written:

"So that you may be proved right when you speak
and prevail when you judge."

[5]But if our unrighteousness brings out God's righteousness more clearly, what shall we say? That God is unjust in bringing his wrath on us? (I am using a human argument.) [6]Certainly not! If that were so, how could God judge the world? [7]Someone might argue, "If my falsehood enhances God's truthfulness and so increases his glory, why am I still condemned as a sinner?" [8]Why not say—as some slanderously claim that we say—"Let us do evil that good may result"? Their condemnation is just!

Paul has left himself open to a serious objection. At the end of chapter 2, he implied that physical circumcision is of no value whatever, thus raising the question he posed in 3:1: **What advantage, then, is there in being a Jew, or what value is there in circumcision?** Yet, as C. E. B. Cranfield pointed out, such a conclusion "would have called in question the truthfulness of the Old Testament or the faithfulness of God. . . The question raised is nothing less than the question of the credibility of God."[1] Paul wanted all his readers, Jews as well as Gentile, to understand that the Jews have great privileges, not the least of which is that God entrusted them with the Scriptures, **the very words of God.** Other privileges he discussed in chapters 9–11. "But this tremendous preeminence never involved exemption from God's judgment—in fact, it meant that the Jews were always in a particularly exposed position in relationship to it (see Amos 3:2)."[2] Now then, if they were entrusted with God's oracles, and were themselves found untrustworthy, doesn't this prove that God is unfaithful (3:3)?

The interpretation of verse 3 depends on the interpretation of the expression **God's faithfulness,** or "the faithfulness of God." In Greek it is possible to interpret the word we have translated **faithfulness** as "faith." That interpretation of the word would mean that Israel's **unfaithfulness** or unbelief annuls faith in God. While this is a rather popular interpretation, it does not satisfy the demands of the context here. For the response Paul gave in verse 4 does not depend on man's attitude to God (faith in God). It depends on God's character (the faithfulness of God). Therefore, Paul's meaning is that Israel's unbelief cannot prove that God is unfaithful. The connection between these ideas is not immediately plain. Yet if we remember the importance of the question posed in verse 1, perhaps the connection becomes clearer. If Israel has received none of the promised privileges in their covenant relationship with God, then we must question God's faithfulness and the truthfulness of Scripture.

Of course, it cannot be that God is unfaithful and His word untrue since whatever God says is by definition true (v. 3). God is a God of truth. He must always speak the truth even if that makes **every human being a liar.** God is what truth is. Even David acknowledged that God must be right no matter the implications for his own life. In Psalm 51 David confessed his sin of murdering Uriah. He confessed it, as he said, "that You may be proved right when you speak and justified when you judge."[3] His confession condemned him as a murderer. Nevertheless David understood that God must be right and true in whatever He says and does.

Verses 5-8 present significant problems for interpreters. The specific course of Paul's thought is not altogether clear. It may be, as Nygren suggested,[4] that Paul connected this section with the quotation from Psalm 51:4. Man's confession of sin, and indeed man's sin itself, shows the righteousness of God. Therefore, if we by our sin bring praise to God, why does God still find fault (3:5,7)? How can God justly bring His wrath on those who reveal so well and fully His character? But Paul rejected this question as completely false, since God is the judge of the world. As such He must be and must do what is righteous. In fact, Paul did not even dignify the questions of verses 5 and 7 with answers. Rather, he fully rejected them. We should recall that Paul had faced the charge that he was making God out to be unjust by his teaching on an earlier occasion (v. 8). He informed his readers that all who think such thoughts receive a just reward.

(d) The Scriptures show that Jews are under sin (3:9-18).

[9]**What shall we conclude then? Do we have any advantage? Not at all! For we have already made the charge that Jews and Gentiles alike are all under the power of sin.** [10]**As it is written:**
   "There is no one righteous, not even one;
   [11]**there is no one who understands;**
   there is no one who seeks God.
   [12]**All have turned away,**
   they have together become worthless;
   there is no one who does good,
   not even one."
   [13]**"Their throats are open graves;**
   their tongues practice deceit."
   "The poison of vipers is on their lips."
   [14]**"Their mouths are full of cursing and bitterness."**
   [15]**"Their feet are swift to shed blood;**
   [16]**ruin and misery mark their ways,**
   [17]**and the way of peace they do not know."**
   [18]**"There is no fear of God before their eyes."**

Verse 9 begins the conclusion of Paul's discussion of sin. Starting at 1:18 Paul has been showing that no human being can in any way by his own obedience achieve righteousness before God. His method has been to examine the life of mankind at large, and then of self righteous (Jewish) humanity in particular. In this section, he summarized his findings. In verses 9-18 Paul used the Scriptures to show that all Jews are under sin.

What Paul has been saying shows that neither Jews nor Gentiles have any way to protect themselves against the charges made in chapter 1. All are under sin. With this conclusion, the prophets from the Old Testament agree. Beginning in verse 10, Paul cited a chain of passages from the Old Testament proving that all Jews are guilty before God. The order of citations is important. In verses 10-12 (quoting Ps. 14:1-3) he described the character of Jews as foolishly sinful. In verses 13-17 he described the Jews' works: first their speech (vv. 13-14, quoting Ps. 5:9; 140:3; 10:7), then their actions (vv. 15-17, quoting Is. 59:7-8). Their actions are sinfully destructive since they do not know the way of peace. Finally, in verse 18 he gave the reason for their sinfulness: they have **no fear of God before their eyes** (quoting Ps. 36:1).

Writing about Psalm 14, Weiser said that the psalm directs its threat against Israel's leaders.[5] They lack any sense of duty, either to God or man. They steal from the poor to satisfy their own greed. Thus "they devour my people as though eating bread; they never call on the LORD" (Ps. 14:4). The same conclusions will come from the study of the other passages quoted. Thus, Paul used these quotations to prove the Jews' sinfulness. The best that the world has produced stand condemned under their own law, the law in which they put their hope. We must conclude that all humanity stands condemned under sin (3:20).

From Psalm 14 Paul proved that the character of the Jews is foolishly sinful. None may stand before God and claim any righteousness or goodness in His sight. Indeed, not even one righteous person lives on earth. No one understands; no one seeks God. The understanding that man lacks is the kind that discerns God's hand in the affairs of the world (Isa. 41:20). If there were such a person, he would submit to God's warnings and reverently worships Him (Ps. 2:10-11). He would seek after God (Ps. 14:2; 53:3) and do good (Ps. 36:4). He would be diligent (Prov. 10:5), sparing in speech (Prov. 10:19), and obedient to God (Josh. 1:8). He would remember God's abundant kindnesses without rebellion (Ps. 106:7). Perhaps the most significant characteristic of a person with this understanding would be that he knows the Lord (Jer. 9:24), and prays to Him and turns from wickedness (see Dan. 9:13). But a person with such an understanding is lacking in the world of humanity.

The next line of the quotation explains and specifies this lack of understanding: "There is no one who seeks God." From God's divine perspective the "hungry heathen" simply do not exist. Missionary stories about the heathen who have been waiting for years for the coming of the gospel may be true, but such stories are evidence that God has been at work through His Holy Spirit to prepare a people for His name. But left to himself, no man ever seeks God. We must remember this is God's verdict on all humanity. Out of all of them in the entire human race, no one—not Jew, not Gentile—seeks God.

Indeed, the psalm says that all humanity has turned away and become useless. If we were to take a census of all the earth seeking those who do what is really good, the total of all such would not even reach the sum of one!

Verses 13-17 describe the deeds of human beings, first their use of language (vv. 13-14) and then their actions (vv. 15-17). Paul's quotation of Psalm 5 describes man's throat as an **open grave.** This description must have been exceptionally repugnant to an Israelite. If a Jewish man left the land of Israel on a trip, he would knock the dust of Gentile territory off his feet before reentering the land. This action testified to the laxity he perceived among Gentiles in the disposal of their dead. A good Jew could never be sure in Gentile territory that he had not come into contact with a dead body. The very dust of Gentile territory would make him unfit for worshiping God and would defile the holy land. The imagery of the verse draws on similar ideas. The open grave makes those who contact it unfit for God's worship and service.

But Paul stated that every man carries death's contagion around with him. It is not some danger we face in the external world. The awful noisome pestilence of death pours from the throat of every human being. Every man is thus defiled and unfit for worshiping and serving God.

The rest of this quotation describes the contagion pouring from man's mouth. In their deceitfulness, people hide their motives and purposes. Behind the facade of compassion and concern, under a man's flattering tongue is the asp's poison. Their words bring death and destruction wherever their words go. Their words, indeed, are words of cursing and bitterness.

Their words match their deeds. For if their mouths pour out the venom of death, their feet are swift to shed blood. Everywhere they go they leave destruction and misery in their wake. Anyone who meets them risks his life. All of this testifies to their utter ignorance of the way of peace (v. 17). They do not know what peace is. They do not know the way to it. They do not know the way peace works.

To cap it all off, Paul gave the reason for the horrors he has described: **There is no fear of God before their eyes** (v. 18; quoting Ps. 35:2). Some Christians reject the fear of God as appropriate for life with God. Yet we must see that fearing God would solve all the problems detailed in verses 10-17. It is the failure to fear God that has led man into the depths of sin.

God even encourages His people to fear Him in both testaments. After God gave Israel the Ten Commandments (Ex. 19:16), the people trembled in terror at the base of the mountain (the Hebrew verb indicates dread of disaster; for this nuance of the term, see Gen. 27:33; 42:28; Judg. 8:12; 1 Sam. 14:15). They begged Moses to be their go-between with God, since they were confident that they would, otherwise, God would destroy them. God's response appears in Deuteronomy 5:29. It is a matter of profound surprise that God commended the people for their fear: "Oh, that their hearts would be inclined to fear me and keep all my commands always, so that it might go well with them and their children forever!" God values His people's fear. This pattern is not unique to the Old Testament. Peter commanded his Christian readers to "fear God" (1 Pet. 2:17). We must conclude, then, that the fear of God is not out of harmony with Christian living.

But doesn't the apostle John teach us that Christians should not fear God? "There is no fear in love. But perfect love casts out fear" (1 John 4:18). Those who use this verse often intend to suggest that in the Old Testament fear of God was appropriate, but not in the New Testament. This verse teaches that in Christ we come to perfect love and should never fear God. On the other hand, can it be possible for any creature to stand before God without trembling, and especially God's redeemed? Peter stated that believers are "scarcely saved" (1 Pet. 4:17-18, KJV).

Nevertheless, my intent is not to set Peter against John but rather to suggest a way to harmonize Peter and John. Fear of God occurs in Scripture with two different aspects, one positive and one negative. John never used fear in a positive sense. For him it is always negative. Another statement in 1 John 4:18 is, "Fear has to do with punishment [Gk. *kolasis*]." One of the standard dictionaries for the study of New Testament Greek gives significant aid in understanding the word *kolasis*. The authors stated: "Fear checks development and is the antithesis of [the maturing] which love works."[6] So for the apostle John, fear paralyzes. It prohibits activity. It prevents development. One who fears is unable to reach maturity, or what John calls perfection.

By contrast the fear that God values is not negative but positive. God values fear in His people precisely because it is what drives them to godliness, as in Deuteronomy 5:29. One sort of fear paralyzes God's people; another fear drives them to action. In fact, this positive fear is inherent in love. It is a fear that prohibits a lover from doing anything to hurt the one loved. It drives the lover to search for ways to please the one loved. This is the fear God seeks. This fear is absent in the heart of all mankind! This is the explanation of sin's horrors listed in Romans 3:9-17.

Paul has drawn together this chain of quotations as the summary of his discussion begun in 1:18. In 3:19-20 he explained the implications of all he has been saying. His Jewish Christian readers might have thought that all that he has said leaves them untouched. Therefore, he told them, "Whatever the law says, it says to those who are under the law" (3:19). The verdict of Romans 1:18–3:18, and especially of 3:9-18, rests squarely on every Jew.

Remember that Paul was seeking to restore the unity of the church at Rome. The Jewish believers condemned their Gentile brothers for eating meat (chap. 14). The only way a Christian can condemn a brother in Christ is if he believes himself somehow superior to his brother. In this passage Paul proved that no Jew (or Gentile) has any ground for merit before God. He is saved by grace and grace alone, without works of law. No believer in Christ is superior to any other. No recipient of grace is inferior to any other. The judgmental spirit is an absolute contradiction of our standing in grace.

The law can only address those who are under it. Therefore, what Paul has said from the Old Testament, he has said about Jews. It is the Jew whom the law condemns. When God looked for one who is righteous, it was specially the Jew of whom he said, "There is no one righteous, not even one" (3:10). It is the Jew, the best the world has produced, who is unrighteous and does not seek God. The best of humanity have **open graves** for throats and **the poison of vipers on their lips.** It is they who have not known **the way of peace.** They, of all humanity, have **no fear of God before their eyes.** By these judgments from the law every Jew must understand that by his works, his obedience, his righteousness, he has no hope before God. Therefore, no Jew can judge a Gentile for failure to keep the law, since no Jew has kept it either.

> **(e) The Law proves the condemnation of those under Law, so that the whole world becomes liable to punishment before God, because no one can be righteous before God through law which only reveals sin (3:19-20).**

[19]Now we know that whatever the law says, it says to those who are under the law, so that every mouth may be silenced and the whole world held accountable to God. [20]Therefore no one will be declared righteous in God's sight by the works of the law; rather, through the law we become conscious of our sin.

On the other hand, no Gentile can exalt himself over Jews. The reason is that Israel's condemnation implies that God condemns the whole world (3:19). If the best the world has produced stand condemned before God, then all nations stand under His wrath. All Gentiles bear the same condemnation and punishment as the Jews.

All of this means that no human distinctives can ever earn the love and favor of God. Thus, in Christ, no one can ever judge another. The judge assumes a position of legal superiority over the one he condemns. Yet when the judge himself bears the law's condemnation, he must be disqualified from passing judgment. Additionally, as James pointed out (4:11-12), the one who judges his brother also judges the law itself! Therefore, in Christ, judging is wrong. Indeed, all the world stands condemned precisely because God never intended the law to do anything else. The law can never bring justification. Instead, it had a different purpose: to bring the knowledge of sin (3:20).

Chapter 7 returns to this idea. For our purposes it is enough to summarize what this knowledge of sin is. Paul said that the knowledge of sin came to him through the ministry of the law (Rom. 7:7). But in that passage the knowledge of sin is not specifically intellectual. In fact it is not particularly intellectual. In 7:8 Paul explained his knowledge of sin: "But sin, seizing the opportunity afforded by the commandment, produced in me every kind of coveting." For Paul the knowledge of sin was the experience of sin in his life. Law stirred up sin in Paul. The purpose of the law, as a result, was not to bring righteousness, but to expose the latent sinfulness in all people. It is no wonder, then, that "no one will be declared righteous in God's sight by the works of the law."

Ending at verse 20, Paul's argument has shown that no one can achieve righteousness by human merit. It may be important then, to recall where we are and what Paul has accomplished. Beginning in 1:16-17 Paul introduced the idea that "the righteous by faith shall live." This he developed through chapter eight. In the present section, 1:18–4:25, Paul explained the first part of his idea—righteousness by faith. Yet it is very difficult even for Christians to accept that we are righteous by faith and not by works. Thus, he had to take up the possibility of righteousness by law, that is, by works. By 3:20 he has shown that no one can be righteous by works of law. Having completed this theological demolition work, Paul was ready to begin reconstruction. In 1:18–3:20 Paul proved that righteousness is not by works; in 3:21–4:25 he proved that righteousness is by faith alone.

b. But God has provided a way of relating to Himself without Law and through faith (3:21–4:25).
(1) God brings His grace-righteousness to believing sinners through the work of Christ (3:21-26).

[21]**But now apart from the law the righteousness of God has been made known, to which the Law and the Prophets testify.** [22]**This righteousness is given through faith in Jesus Christ to all who believe. There is no difference between Jew and Gentile,** [23]**for all have sinned and fall short of the glory of God,** [24]**and all are justified freely by his grace through the redemption that came by Christ Jesus.** [25]**God presented Christ as a sacrifice of atonement, through the shedding of his blood—to be received by faith. He did this to demonstrate his righteousness, because in his forbearance he had left the sins committed beforehand unpunished—** [26]**he did it to demonstrate his righteousness at the present time, so as to be just and the one who justifies those who have faith in Jesus.**

But now. If we may infer anything about Paul's writing procedure, we might see Paul in the atrium of the house in Corinth. He paces the floor dictating to Tertius. Since he has completed the "hall of horrors" (3:10-18), we might see him give Tertius a coffee break. He leaves the house to walk in the garden. He breathes deeply of the freshness, of the scent of flowers that pour into his body, reaching even his soul, bringing a renewed mental freshness. Then rejuvenated, he calls Tertius back to the task and resumes. Though this is all fiction (and not very good at that) we might see something of this behind Paul's words in verse 21: **But now.**

With these words Paul turned from the conversation of sin, condemnation, and death, and turned to what is true, noble, righteous, pure, lovely, reputable, full of virtue, and full of praise (see Phil. 4:8). He turned to the grace of God at work for us in bringing us righteousness in Jesus Christ.

In the first two verses of this section (3:21-22) Paul identified a new kind of righteousness. As in 1:16-17 **the righteousness of God** could be a reference to God's attribute. But this context discusses man's relationship to God, not God's character. So this expression describes the relationship that the sinful man receives with God.

It may be helpful to review what Paul meant when he talked about righteousness. Two expressions in verses 21-22 aid in our definition. Verse 21 says faith is "apart from the law."[7] Now if it is a without-law-righteousness it is not a righteousness gained by obedience or determined by obedience. Rules, laws, and condemnation are all excluded. Righteousness is on an entirely different basis. When we have made these observations, it becomes necessary to define what this righteousness is. In my commentary on 1:16-17, I concluded that righteousness is relational, that is, righteousness is right relationship with God. Paul's point there, as in the preceding section, is that righteousness is not by law. Thus he ruled out obedience, rules, and condemnation as part of our relationship with God.

Then what is the basis of our relationship with God? Paul explained this in verse 22 where he described the relationship as "through faith." Righteousness before God is a "without-law-through-faith" righteousness. It is a relationship set up by and maintained through faith (see 1:17, where Paul says that this relationship is "by faith from first to last").

The course of Paul's argument in 3:21–4:25 develops these ideas. We said earlier that faith, the basis of our relationship with God, begins with knowledge. In 3:22-26 Paul explained the facts—that is, the knowledge—with which our faith begins. In 3:27-31 he applied what he has said to the situation at the church in Rome. In 4:1-12 he showed from the law and the prophets (as he said in 3:21) that right relationship with God is by faith. In 4:13–17a Paul discussed the ramifications of faith-righteousness on our relationship with God. Finally, in 4:17b-25 he modeled the faith that is right relationship with God.

The right relationship God has granted to us by faith is **to all who believe.** Neither Jew nor Gentile has any advantage before God, for each one receives right relationship by faith equally. They are equally sinful: **there is no difference: all have sinned and fall short of the glory of God.** Furthermore, God justifies all believers **freely by his grace.**

Paul's explanation of how sinners can have a right relationship with God is amazing. People of faith are right with God. But people of faith have a special character: they have sinned and **come short of God's glory.** This connection of ideas becomes necessary because of what Paul says in verses 22-23. Yet these ideas are not usually welcome in the Christian community. Christians usually do not want to connect sinfulness and righteousness in any way. We want to keep sin out of Christianity. We believe God requires of us that we walk above sin. Sin, we believe, separates us from God. Therefore, we do not and cannot tolerate sin in ourselves or in others. The result of these commitments is a persistent sense of guilt preying on the Christian conscience. No one lives above sin. No one lives obediently so consistently as to fulfill the requirements laid on us by these teachings. The collective guilty conscience of the church has sapped it of its strength and drained it of its service. Guilt has emptied prayer of power and made the gospel message unbelievable. We offer forgiveness of sins to the world, but we carry the load of sins on our own consciences. It is no wonder that the world does not believe our gospel. A statement attributed to J. I. Packer expresses the problem well:

> Our minds have been conditioned to think of the Cross as a redemption which does less than redeem, and of Christ as a Savior who does less than save, and of God's love as a weak affection which cannot keep anyone from hell without help, and of faith as the human help which God needs for this purpose.[8]

Amazingly, Christians fear to believe their own gospel! Yet it is not the good whom God saves; it is sinners! Someone will almost certainly respond, "That's true; but He does not save us in our sin. He saves us from our sin." True; no one who reads the Bible can long maintain any different position. On the other hand, those who make such statements often, though not always, have some other thought in the background. Often what is on their minds is the idea that saved people are obedient people. Where there is no obedience there is no salvation. Such people major on words such as "ought" and "should" and "must" and "duty." For the class of people I am speaking of, the Christian life comes down to one thing—obedience.

The problems with such an approach are serious. First, such people easily become self-righteous. As Paul has shown, they do not themselves obey God so they redefine God's standards to make themselves appear righteous. They believe that they are giving God great service by their obedience, but their only service is to their own egos. Second, such people become judgmental. Since they have attained a lifestyle that they believe pleases God, those who do not follow their teaching are not pleasing to God. They recognize that sin is always an affront to God. The problem is that they do not believe that their own sin is an affront to God, since they have obedience. Third, such people become exclusive. They do not want to sully their garments with the sins of those around them. They build a fortress mentality to keep the world out of their circle. If Jesus had lived this way, none of us would know salvation! By their rules they can tell who is right with God and who is not. What is more, anyone who is not right with God is not welcome in their circle. Fourth, such an emphasis on obedience can achieve outward conformity to the group's standards, but it can never grip the heart. Anything that man can measure, such as conformity to the standards of the group, man can counterfeit. They have forgotten the heart. No particular or merely external characteristic distinguishes those who are pleasing to God from those who are not. People who press primarily for obedience as the sign of salvation ignore righteousness, peace, and joy in the Holy Spirit, which Paul stated are essential characteristics of the kingdom (Rom. 14:17). Jesus was incarnate righteous, peace, and joy. But He was crucified as a law breaker. For the legalist, as long as people conform to the standards of the group, they are happy. Finally, and most distressingly for the legalist, conformity to the group standard gives no decisive sense of the grace and love of God. They are unceasingly laboring to gain God's favor. They can never rest in what Christ has accomplished. They always believe that God is out to get them. He is still a God of mercy. But they live in sorrow and guilt and defeat, having never experienced the Christ's victory in the cross. In their pride they exalt what they can do, what man can do, over what God has done in Christ in receiving us.

These observations ought to force us to seek another way of life with God. That way is the righteousness that God gives—a right relationship with Himself. If righteousness is right relationship by faith, by what means does God bring it to man? Job posed this very question. He knew that he was right with God, but he did not know how. He said, "Indeed, I know that this is true. But how can a mortal be righteous before God?" (Job 9:1.) Romans 3:24-25 explains how God brings sinful people into right relationship with Himself. They are **justified freely by His grace through the redemption that came by Christ Jesus. God presented Christ as a sacrifice of atonement, through the shedding of his blood—to be received by faith.** God has declared sinful believers righteous! Christians have discussed for centuries the meaning of **justified** (Gk. *dikaioo*). Does it mean "to make righteous" or "to declare righteous"? Two Old Testament passages help define this term. In Deuteronomy 25:1 there is a situation in which two Israelites have a dispute that they cannot settle. They are to bring it to the judges. The judges will hear the case and "justify the righteous" and "condemn the wicked" (NASB). In the circumstance envisioned, justify certainly cannot mean to make righteous. No human judge can ever make anyone righteous. The function of a judge is not to change the character of those brought to trial. The judge's function is to recognize and declare the facts of the case. Only if one of the parties to the case is actually righteous can the judge declare him to be righteous. So "justify" here means "to declare righteous."

The other verse is Psalm 51:4, where David prayed and confessed his sin of murdering Uriah. As he contemplated his sin and its enormity, he exclaimed, "Against you, you only, have I sinned and done what is evil in your sight." Then he explained why he said that. He openly confessed his sin: "so you are right in your verdict and justified when you judge." Clearly, no one can make God righteous. So in this context "justify" must mean "to show to be righteous" or "to declare righteous." Our use of Psalm 51 is all the more important in that Paul has quoted it in Romans 3:4, showing that in this third chapter Paul had already used "justify" in the sense of "declare righteous." The point, then, is that God has declared sinful believers righteous.

Yet Job's question still stands: "Indeed, I know that this is true. But how can a mortal be righteous before God?" Paul gave an answer in two parts, one very brief, the other much longer. Job asked "How?" Paul answered that sinners are justified **freely.** The same Greek word appears in John 15:25, where Jesus said, "They hated me without reason." One man hates another because he has some quality to cause the hatred. But Jesus had no character quality to cause men to hate Him. Thus **freely** can mean "without reason." One other passage uses the word in a similar way. Paul stated that when he was in

Thessalonica, he had worked with his own hands so that he could provide for his and his companions' needs. He did not eat anyone's bread "without paying for it" (2 Th. 3:8).

With these two references in mind, we may return to Romans 3:24. Paul says that God justifies sinful believers freely. Borrowing from Jesus' words in John 15:25 and Paul's in 2 Thessalonians 3:8, we may better explain his expression. He justifies them "with no cause in themselves," "without paying for it," or simply, for free. God receives no benefit as payment for declaring believers righteous.

These people have absolutely no cause in themselves why God should declare them righteous. Of course, this is a terrible blow to the self-righteous of the world. God delights to declare that sinners who have faith in Christ are righteous. Chapter 4 shows that faith cannot be the cause of justification. Justification is by grace, and faith is part of that grace. Otherwise, Paul could not add what he does next in our verse. No, God declares them righteous with no reference to their moral character. They are righteous **freely by His grace.** No reason exists for God to justify anyone. Yet I believe that I can show why God has chosen to justify, to save, those He does.

In 1 Corinthians 1:26-29 Paul explained why God chose whom He did. God chose the foolish, the weak, and the despised of the world "so that no one may boast before him." If we were a small nation conquering a new land, we would seek the best of the land to include in the government. That would be the only wise plan, since we would be too small a people to provide all of the civil servants needed for the government. This is man's way, but it is not how God works. He is in the process of conquering the earth and setting up His kingdom here. Yet He does not look for the wise, the powerful, or the noble to staff His government. He seeks those whom no one else would choose. Therefore, when they accomplish great things, the praise, the excellence, and the glory belong to God, as Paul said in verses 30-31: "It is because of Him that you are in Christ Jesus, who has become for us wisdom from God—that is, our righteousness, holiness, and redemption. Therefore, as it is written: 'Let the one who boasts boast in the Lord.'"

What we have read in 1 Corinthians 1 addresses the second part of Paul's answer to Job's question, How can a man be right with

God? In Romans 3:24, after saying that we are justified freely, he added, **by His grace.** The idea presented in 1 Corinthians 1:26-31 is His grace! Grace means that God extends His favor to those who have no hope for His favor. We often define grace as unmerited favor. But it means more. God has declared that all humanity is condemned because of sin. By our unbelief that has issued in our sinful life patterns, we have forfeited all expectation of anything but wrath from God. We might give undeserved favor to people who have done no wrong. They may have done nothing to merit the favor we show, but they may otherwise be relatively nice people. What God has done in justifying us by His grace is to extend His favor, not to those who do not merit it, but to those who deserve nothing but wrath—nothing but His righteous burning anger against sin.

A third observation about God's grace clarifies the reason for His grace: it comes for the sake of another, that is, for Jesus' sake. An illustration from the Old Testament may help to understand this point.

In 2 Samuel 9, David brought Mephibosheth to his court. In the ancient political setting, Mephibosheth could only expect death. He was one of the few surviving members of King Saul's house, David's mortal enemy. Therefore, he would be a rival claimant to the throne of Israel. Furthermore, Mephibosheth was lame in both feet. It was possible to conceive of lameness in those days as a curse from God. Thus no one would ever want to bring him to court since that would mean bringing the curse into the royal court. Israel's royal court needed God's blessing, not His curse.

Yet David brought Mephibosheth to his court anyway and bestowed on him the honors and dignity that would have been his if Saul's dynasty still ruled. David restored Saul's lands to him. He gave him a place at the royal table to eat, like one of the princes of Israel. He returned Saul's servants to Mephibosheth so they would work his land and give him a regular income the rest of his life. Mephibosheth was astounded that David should honor him so. As he approached the king for the first time, he expressed his amazement and said, "What is your servant, that you should notice a dead dog like me?"

To anyone who has read the story, the question is obviously the wrong one. Three times in the passage David gave the reason for his actions. David wanted to show God's kindness (2 Sam. 9:3) to anyone from Saul's house for Jonathan's sake (vv. 1, 7). David showed Mephibosheth God's favor, not for Mephibosheth's sake, but for the sake of another, the beloved Jonathan. Similarly, God shows His favor to lost condemned sinners, and if they ask why God does this, He replies, "It is not for your sake, O sinner, that I am about to do this. It is for the sake of My dear Son" (see Ezk. 36:22). The very faith that God has given each of us is for Christ's sake (see Phil. 1:29). God has forgiven our sins for His name's sake (1 John 2:12; see 1 Cor. 6:11). It is for Christ's sake that God shows us His favor, not for our sake. Of course, this is painfully humbling to the pride of the saints. Yet all that we have from God we have for Christ's sake. No distinction exists among mankind in sin, and no distinction exists among mankind in grace. Paul said it this way: "He has saved us and called us to a holy life—not because of anything we have done but because of his own purpose and grace. This grace was given us in Christ Jesus before the beginning of time" (2 Tim. 1:9).

A final observation about grace is necessary. We have thought that God might conceivably have saved no one. He *may* be merciful, but He *must* be rightous. Therefore, as we have thought, it would be perfectly possible for God to save no one, for Him to destroy all humanity equally in His justice. This would be true if God were only a God of justice, but He is equally a God of grace. But He is a person in whom grace and justice are in perfect harmony. Thus, God's own nature makes it necessary for Him to save. He is, after all, the God of all grace (1 Pet. 5:10).

Though we have thought at some length about God's grace, we have not exhausted it. Paul gave a two-part answer to Job's question, How can a man be right with God? One part of the answer is short, and the other is longer. The short part of the answer is that God has justified us freely and with no cause in ourselves. The longer part of the answer begins with Paul's statement that God has justified us by His grace. The latter part of verse 24 and verses 25-26 explain God's magnificent grace.

God's grace operates by means. The first of its means mentioned by Paul is redemption. Redemption in its broadest sense is the payment of a price to regain ownership of something lost. It also bestows benefit on the redeemed object. For instance, if a man consecrates his house to God (Lev. 27:14-15), he may buy it back by paying the full price of the house plus 20 percent. The benefit bestowed, in this case, is that the family may continue living in the house. The concept of adding a penalty of 20 percent is important to the idea of human redemption. When one wishes to redeem, one must not merely pay the total worth of the thing. The redeemer must pay more than is due based on strict values. Redemption, then, is more costly than mere purchase. It requires a payment of more than the object is worth.

When applied more narrowly to spiritual redemption, we are building on the foundation laid in the Old Testament law. God intended those old practices of redemption to illuminate our understanding of how He redeems us now. Indeed, it is from Old Testament teaching on redemption that we begin to understand what Christ has done. "No man can redeem the life of another or give to God a ransom for them—the ransom for a life is costly, no payment is ever enough—so that he should live on forever and not see decay" (Ps. 49:7-9). The Old Testament law has a way of valuing a human being (Lev. 27:1-13). Yet this verse in Psalm 49 has taught us the enormous value of a soul. Unless we can make full payment, no redemption can occur. Then how will a soul's redemption occur? We have further learned that redemption involves paying more than the value of the redeemed object. How can a payment exceeding the value of a soul occur?

The answer begins in Romans 3:24. Grace is at work **through the redemption that came by Christ Jesus.** God redeems in Christ, the payment price for the soul. Sin that has subjected us to God's curse (Gal. 3:13) has required redemption. But in Christ's redeeming work, God sets us free from paying the penalty of sin because He has forgiven our transgressions (Eph. 1:7; Col. 1:14). Jesus accomplished this great work by shedding His blood (1 Pet. 1:18; Eph. 1:7; Rev. 5:9), having become a curse for us (Gal. 3:13).

As in the Old Testament if one would redeem an unclean animal whose death God required, one must substitute a sacrificial animal to die in its place. A man, however, is not redeemable, genuinely, by the death of a sacrificial animal. Only a sacrifice that is clean and pure, that is more valuable than any human being, can redeem anyone.

The condemned animal, when redeemed by sacrificial death, lives. Similarly, when sinners are redeemed, they gain the life bought by the redeeming sacrifice. That life includes justification (Rom. 3:24); forgiveness of sins (Eph. 1:7; Col. 1:14), that is, release from bearing sin's penalty (see Luke 7:36-50); cleansing of the conscience (Heb. 9:12-15); and the experience of God's mercy and covenant (Luke 1:68-75). This redemption is eternal (Heb. 9:12) and reaches into our daily experience (Rom. 3:24; Eph. 1:7; Col. 1:14). But it reaches its consummation only at the second coming and kingdom of the Savior (Luke 21:28; Rom. 8:23; Eph. 1:14; 4:30), when God will redeem even our bodies.

Considering all this, we might ask how much Jesus actually paid to redeem us. He was on the cross only a few hours. Some Christians have even held that He paid only a token amount of what was due for our sins. Sinners who bear their own sins suffer forever in the terrors of hell. How can a few hours on the cross be even an equivalent payment?

The response to these questions comes in three parts. First, God prepared the way for Jesus' work as He gave the Old Testament teaching about redemption. The biblical teaching on redemption requires the payment, not of a token, but of the full price plus penalty. God in the Old Testament has prepared us to understand that when He redeems, He pays the complete price to redeem us from our sins.

Second the price paid to redeem us is nothing less than Jesus Christ, the Son of God. Our redemption does not rest on payment made in gold or silver (1 Pet. 1:18). Our God has not redeemed us with the blood of goats or calves (Heb. 9:12). God has bought us at the price of His own Son (Acts 20:28). It is the King, who is Himself true God, who gave Himself to redeem us. In addition, His was no involuntary offering. His was the most amazing sacrifice of all. His was fully voluntary! The infinite, holy Son of God gave Himself to redeem sinful man. How can we limit the value or efficacy of such a sacrifice? Can we measure the value of His sacrifice by time? Must we not rather measure it by the excellence of the Person? Indeed, the excellence of the Person is the measure of the value of His sacrifice.

Third, the sacrifice of Christ must be measureless (certainly not by time) because it accomplished eternal redemption (Heb. 9:12).

Eternality is a characteristic of God. When we call God eternal, we mean that He possesses the whole of His existence in one indivisible present.[9] This means that He exists without time at all. Thus, when God poured out on Jesus His wrath against sin, the man Jesus suffered in time on the cross. But as the eternal Son of God, Jesus bore in eternity all of sin's penalty without reference to time. Indeed, the effect of His eternal redemption is eternal salvation (Heb. 5:9). Therefore, time does not enter into His work of redeeming.

Redemption has great meaning for us. It means, first, that we have nothing at all to pay for our sins! The Lord Jesus has released us from our sins (Rev. 1:5). This leaves no room for any grief, sorrow, pain, or sacrifice that we must undergo in order to deal with our sin. "We have peace with God through our Lord Jesus Christ" (Rom. 5:1).

But more importantly, we ought to learn that the one we have wronged is the one who paid the penalty. It is the role of the sinner to receive redemption. It is also the role of the spiritual to do what is necessary to receive every believer who is in the body of Christ. Remember Paul's words: "Accept one another, then, just as Christ accepted you, in order to bring praise to God" (Rom. 15:7). What Christ has done in bringing us to God must be the pattern for our treatment of each other. Therefore, since Christ paid the redemption price for our sins, we must pay whatever price is necessary for our fellowship with other believers. Thus grace uses redemption in bringing us to faith righteousness.

Job said, "Indeed, I know that this is true. But how can a mortal be righteous before God?" (Job 9:1). Redemption is one of the ways by which man can be right with God, but there is more. Another means that grace uses is propitiation (Gk. *hilasterion*). The word translated this way is a difficult word. In fact, many in this century have even denied that the word should have this meaning and prefer the meaning "expiation" instead. Expiation is the sacrifice that brings cleansing from sin (e.g. Heb. 9–10). The reason for this opposition is that in non-biblical Greek, propitiation is a sacrifice offered to turn away a god's wrath. The verb form of *hilasterion* (*hilaskomai*) appears in this sense in Homer's Iliad (1.100, 147). The objection is that such an idea is unworthy of the God of the Bible. It is unworthy, they claim, because the God of love could not also be a God of wrath. Therefore, He would not require a sacrifice for sin to win His favor and appease His wrath.

We may give two responses to this approach. First, Paul has already confronted us with the wrath of God (1:18). Indeed, God is love, but He is also equally a God of wrath. The wrath of God is an important part of His self-revelation in the Old Testament as well as in the New Testament. In fact, one scholar has pointed out that the Old Testament associates wrath with God twice as often as it does with man.[10] Second, it is of equal importance to note the difference between propitiation in pagan Greek religion and propitiation in the New Testament. Among the ancient Greeks, a man offered a sacrificial bribe in the hope of turning away the deity's wrath. In the New Testament God Himself gave the sacrifice to turn away His own wrath. This is no pagan idea unworthy of the God revealed in Jesus Christ. His love is thoroughly consistent. It is love indeed! The wrathful God, in His love for sinners, turned away His own wrath by the gift of His Son. Note how Paul explained this: **God presented him as a propitiation.** God's grace was propitiation's cause, and appeasing God's wrath was propitiation's goal.

Therefore, propitiation is the sacrifice (it is in Christ's blood) that turns God's wrath away from the sinner. But, one may ask, if God turns away His own wrath, what remains? If He is no longer wrathful against the believer, how does He act toward us? What is His attitude? Obviously, God has no neutral attribute halfway between wrath and love. Having propitiated Himself, God does not look at the believer in indifference.

Rather since Jesus' sacrifice turned away God's wrath, all that remains is the love of God. More directly, the verb form of "propitiation" appears in Luke 18:13, where the tax collector prays, "God, **have mercy** [*hilaskomai*] on me, a sinner." Jesus' own comment alerts us to God's attitude to this man, and to all for whom He has propitiated Himself. The publican, He said, went home justified (v. 14). God declared that those for whom He has propitiated Himself are in right relationship with Him. They are righteous; they have His favor.

To apply this, we must say God Himself provides what is necessary to turn away His own wrath and to bring sinners into His favor.

He poured out His wrath on Jesus so no wrath now remains for the believing sinner. Paul later summarized this truth when he said, "Therefore, there is now no condemnation for those who are in Christ Jesus" (Rom. 8:1). In Christ we are free from God's wrath. He has released us to live in the love and gracious favor of God. Grace works by propitiation.

However, we not only receive personal benefit from propitiation. We receive a new relationship—a new relationship with God and with mankind. Paul will command his readers, This demands that we who have received God's grace to accept Christ's propitiation for our brothers, which is Paul's point in Romans 15:7. How can we bear anger toward brothers and sisters in Christ when God does not? When we do, we act as if we are more righteous than God! Our role is not to be ministers of God's wrath, which is the government's role (Rom. 13:1-7). Our role is to be ministers of God's redemption and propitiation. We must find ways to communicate God's saving work to others. We must show it to those outside the fellowship of the church. Even more, we must show it to those who are in Christ with us.

It is no wonder that the world does not believe our gospel—it would seem that we don't! We bear grudges. We long to see punishment fall on our enemies. We do not love one another, and we do not love the lost. Jesus always astonishes me in this respect. The people who followed Him were not the leaders of His day. They were the outcast and despised, the tax collectors and sinners. The self-righteous despised Him. Those who knew they were sinners flocked to Him. But we cultivate the self-righteous while the sinners of our day despise us and our gospel.

After Tony Campolo gave a birthday party for a Honolulu prostitute, a man asked him, "Hey! You never told me you were a preacher, What kind of church do you belong to?" He answered, "To a church that throws parties for prostitutes at 3:30 in the morning." A bystander responded, "No you don't. There's no church like that. If there was, I'd join it. I'd join a church like that!"[11] This is God's grace reaching out to a world dying for grace. How much better our churches would be if we expressed God's grace to one another. How much better if we Christians were content with Christ's sacrifice. He paid the price to redeem us from our sins and turned God's wrath away from us. How wonderful if we could accept our own lost condition and God's grace that comes to us in Christ.

The method God used to bring His grace to the believer is found in the phrase **in His blood.** Leon Morris provided a study of blood and concluded rightly that blood is a symbol of sacrifice. The shedding of blood proves that the sacrificial animal has died.[12] So also with Christ, the blood is the evidence that a gruesome and violent death has occurred. It is this gruesome and violent death that is the method by which God accomplished redemption and propitiation. Christ alone provided it. Like Yahweh in Isaiah, Jesus could have said, "I looked, and there was no one to help, I was appalled that no one gave support; so my own arm achieved salvation for me" (Isa. 63:5). He alone suffered the horror of God-forsakenness. He alone knew the terror of the silence of God. When Jesus cried out, "My God, my God, why have you forsaken me" (Matt. 27:46), He was suffered for the sins of humanity. He suffered under the abandoning wrath of God. Because Jesus suffered for us, the author of Hebrews could say to his readers, "God has said, 'Never will I leave you; never will I forsake you.' So we say with confidence, 'The Lord is my helper; I will not be afraid. What can mere mortals do to me?'" (Heb. 13:5-6).

God has in His free grace made justification possible through redemption and propitiation. All of this He has done through Christ's sacrifice (Rom. 3:24-25). It is all available to sinners on one condition—the condition of faith.[13] As we have shown before, faith is a love commitment to God through Jesus Christ. Those who commit themselves in such love look to God alone for righteousness. They have no thought of standing before God by their works. They accept, even risk their lives on, the redeeming and propitiating blood of Christ. Having risked themselves, they can extend grace to others in the body of Christ. They have come to rest in all that Christ is. They can extend that rest to others who are suffering with sin.

Paul then explained further why God has done all this. It is surprising to see in verses 25-26 that God's purpose in the work of Christ was not primarily the salvation of the lost. From what we have seen in Romans 1–4, God's work imposes a great measure of humility upon its prime beneficiaries. The sins of mankind mean that we have no righteousness to offer God by which He may declare us right with Himself. The work of Christ expounded in Romans 3:24-25 means that all of our hope rests outside ourselves. So in verses 25-26 Paul showed the reason for it all, again humbling mankind. In Christ God showed His own righteousness in His past treatment of sin. That is not all. In Christ, God showed His righteousness in His present act of justifying believers.

Paul gave two reasons for the work of Christ in this passage. First, it was **to demonstrate his righteousness** that God **left sins committed beforehand unpunished.** Two events from the Old Testament help us understand Paul's point: the sin of Achan at Jericho and David's sin with Bathsheba. God commanded the Israelites to destroy what they found during the conquest of Jericho and to bring whatever was indestructible to the tabernacle. During the battle Achan stole some gold and silver and a Babylonian garment from the city and hid them in his tent. When God led Joshua to the sinner, He commanded Israel to stone Achan and all his family to death and to burn all of Achan's belongings (Josh. 7:16-26).

Turning to the sin of David (2 Sam. 11–12), we are told that at the time kings normally led their armies to war David decided to stay in Jerusalem (11:1). David was where he should not have been. Israel's armies were pursuing their divinely ordered task of subduing the Gentile nations to the rule of the Lord (see Deut. 20). As king, David held responsibility to lead the nation in covenant obedience. Of course, Israel had asked for a king for the very purpose of leading them in battle. Yet the king was at ease in Jerusalem while the army pursued the covenant without him. Thus, David was unfaithful to Israel, and he was unfaithful to God.

On the other hand, Bathsheba was where she had a right to be. The roof of a house was the coolest part of the house. While she was in the right place (or at least, not in a wrong place), she was there at the wrong time. David sought the cool of his roof at night as the beautiful Bathsheba was bathing. Captivated by her beauty, the king sent for her and had sexual relations with her. The adultery David committed was bad enough, but verse 3 states that she was Uriah's wife. Two facts make this important. First, Uriah was one of David's mighty men (see 2 Sam. 23:39) who was with the army at Rabbah. He was with Israel's armies fighting in loyalty to God's covenant. Thus, Bathsheba was alone in Jerusalem with no protector. Therefore, not only was David unfaithful to God and to Israel, but he was also unfaithful to his responsibilities to Bathsheba and his loyal servant Uriah. Since her husband was not there to protect her, it fell to the king to protect her within the nation.

The other significant fact about Uriah is that he was a Hittite. This means that he was a convert to the worship of Israel's God. He had sought refuge under the wings of the Lord (see Ruth 2:12). As a resident alien, he had no natural civil rights since the normal and proper agency to protect civil rights was the family. Now that he had left his father's house and his native land, no one would protect his rights. No one would protect him, that is, except the king. As the chief representative of God before the people, it was his responsibility to protect the rights of the helpless, the widow, the orphan, and the alien (see Deut. 10:18; 17:19-20). Instead of protecting Uriah and his wife, he forced himself on Bathsheba. He had Uriah, the Canaanite who was faithful to God and his king, killed to cover up his adultery. Nevertheless, when God led Nathan to the sinner, He forgave David's sin. The proper penalty for David's sins of adultery, murder, and blasphemy (for he misrepresented the just character of God to Israel and the nations) was death. Yet David did not die. The child he and Bathsheba conceived died, but the sinner did not. That God forgave David is clear from 2 Samuel 12:13. The consequences that followed David's sin were directly related to his sin, but they were in no way the just penalty for his sin. Rather they were chastening for sin (see Ps. 89:30-35).

What conclusions can we draw from these events? Looking at them without the New Testament, we might conclude that God is unjust—that He shows favoritism. He favors adulterous, murdering kings, but He hates pilfering commoners. Without the cross we might draw no other conclusion. But at the cross God proved His righteousness in passing over David's sin. God proved that He is righteous, in fact, by executing His just wrath at David's sin against the Great King, King Jesus. Now the greatest of all kings, the King of kings and Lord of lords, died paying the penalty for David's sin. Yet it was not only for the sins of kings but also for the sins of commoners that King Jesus died. He paid the price in full. God showed Himself righteous in dealing with all sins in Old Testament times.

The second reason for the work of Christ that Paul provided in this passage is that God must not only show His righteousness in His dealings with sin in Old Testament times, He must also show it as He **justifies those who have faith in Jesus.** God plans to justify multitudes of those who have faith in Christ. Paul has shown already that not one of these can be righteous by works: we are all under God's righteous condemnation of our sins. Therefore, all those whom God justifies are condemned sinners. Later in chapter 4, Paul marked out two qualities in all those whom God justifies: God justifies wicked believers (v. 5). But how can a just God declare wicked believers righteous? How can He justify them and remain righteous? Only by the cross can God remain righteous while declaring believers in Christ to be righteous. One of God's key problems (if we may even speak of God having a problem!) in dealing with sin was His own character. He is both gracious and just. If He is just, He must punish sin. If He is gracious, He must forgive sin. But He must forgive justly. Only in the cross does God finally demonstrate both His justice and His grace. The greatest cause for which God can act, and of course the greatest cause for which we can act, is for the vindication and revelation of the excellence of God's person. The justification for God's actions is His own character. The rationale for our actions is the character of God. The rationale for our very existence is the character of God. He is the supreme motivation and validation of all our life, our service, and our sufferings. Indeed, He is the reason we are saved. No other reason could be right.

> **(2) God excludes boasting for all, both Jews and Greeks, through the principle of faith since He is the God of all, thus showing the righteousness of the Law (3:27-31).**

[27]Where, then, is boasting? It is excluded. Because of what law? The law that requires works? No, because of the law that requires faith. [28]For we maintain that a person is justified by

faith apart from the works of the law. [29]Or is God the God of Jews only? Is he not the God of Gentiles too? Yes, of Gentiles too, [30]since there is only one God, who will justify the circumcised by faith and the uncircumcised through that same faith. [31]Do we, then, nullify the law by this faith? Not at all! Rather, we uphold the law.

Paul asked, **Where, then, is boasting?** And he concluded, as was certainly necessary, that **it is excluded.** No boasting is possible. Man brings no merit, no works, and no obedience to God. God has done all that is necessary to save man. We are helpless and hopeless before His wrath. We are idle and silent before His grace. We have no recourse but God Himself. Our only hope is to receive humbly the grace God has offered through faith. Boasting is only possible under law, under works. However, when we stand before God by faith, none of us will boast, either before God or before man. He has banished all condemning and despising in the family of God (Rom. 14:3). Paul said, **We maintain that a person is justified by faith apart from the works of the law.** Law has no part in our right standing with God. Obedience has no part in our right standing with God. Works have no part in our right standing with God. Only faith commends us to God.

If this is not true, then God is God of the Jews only, and not God of the Gentiles. But He is also **the God of the Gentiles,** and He will justify all alike, Jew and Gentile, **through that same faith.** It would seem from these thoughts that Paul here sounded the death knell of the law. Chapter 5 discusses faith more fully, while chapters 6–8 teach that grace establishes the law.

Notes for Romans 3

[1]C. E. B. Cranfield, *The Epistle to the Romans* in The International Critical Commentary (Edinburgh: T&T Clark), 1:176-77.

[2]Cranfield, 1:177.

[3]As a matter of interest, Cranfield (1:183) explained how some Rabbis interpreted Psalm 51:4: "The Rabbinic explanations of Ps 51:4 [MT: 6] in Yalkut Reub. on Gen 8:21 and Sanh. 107a, quoted in SB 3,

p. 135, are startling: according to them, David's motive in sinning with Bathsheba was to prevent God's word in Gen 8:21 ('the imagination of man's heart is evil from his youth') from being falsified."

[4]Nygren said, "It is by man's falseness, not in spite of it, that the truthfulness of God is glorified" (p. 139).

[5]Artur Weiser, *The Psalms: A Commentary* Old Testament Library, ed. G. E. Wright (Philadelphia: Westminster, 1962), 164.

[6]James H. Moulton and George Milligan, *The Vocabulary of the Greek Testament Illustrated from the Papyri and Other Non-literary Sources,* s.v., "kolasis," p. 352.

[7]In many English versions the words "apart from the law" or "without the law" appear to be adverbial, that is, they appear to explain *the way* God's righteousness is revealed (e.g., KJV, NASB). In the Greek text the words immediately precede the expression "the righteousness of God." Normally, Greek places a modifying element immediately around what it modifies. This observation would suggest that "without law" is adjectival, explaining *the kind* of righteousness that is in view. In fact, the adverbial interpretation runs afoul of the rest of the verse and of chapter 4, where we learn that the law itself testifies to the righteousness of God. Indeed, 3:21 states that the law bears testimony to God's righteousness. Therefore, I have explained the passage as discussing "without-law-righteousness of God."

[8]J. I. Packer, "Introductory Essay to John Owen's *Death of Death in the Death of Christ,*" accessed at http://www.all-of-grace.org/pub/others/deathofdeath.html on May 17, 2017.

[9]Louis Berkhof, *Systematic Theology,* p. 60. The full definition as he gives it is, "that perfection of God whereby He is elevated above all temporal limits and all succession of moments and possesses the whole of His existence in one indivisible present."

[10]*Theological Dictionary of the Old Testament,* s.v. "πna, 'anaph," by E. Johnson, 1(1974): 356.

[11]Tony Campolo, *The Kingdom of God is a Party* (Nashville: Thomas Nelson, 1992), p. 8.

[12]Leon Morris, *The Apostolic Preaching of the Cross* (Grand Rapids: Eerdmans, 1965), Kindle Locations 1898-1915.

[13]Chapter 4 shows that faith is the sole condition of righteousness and explains the nature of this faith.

(3) All Scripture, and particularly the experience of Abraham, testifies that right relationship with God is by faith (4:1-25).

Chapter 4 deals with faith-righteousness. Paul summarized Romans 1–8 in 1:17 where he quoted Habakkuk 2:4: "The righteous by faith shall live." The first part of that statement ("the righteous by faith") summarizes chapters 1–4. In pursuit of that idea, Paul has shown that obedience brings no righteousness (1:18–3:20). Then he began explaining righteousness without works based on Jesus' atonement (3:21-30). Here in chapter 4, Paul explained faith's role in right relationship with God. Paul's purpose in this chapter is to show that his teaching is also the teaching of the Old Testament.

Chapter 4 divides into three sections (vv. 1-8, vv. 9-17a, and vv. 17b-25). Verses 1-8 show that the Law and the Prophets testify to faith-righteousness (see 3:21). Verses 9-17a show that circumcision is a sign of the faith that inherits the promise. Verses 17b-25 use the life of Abraham as a model for faith.

(a) The Law and the Prophets testify that justification is by faith not law (4:1-8).

¹What then shall we say that Abraham, our forefather according to the flesh, discovered in this matter? ²If, in fact, Abraham was justified by works, he had something to boast about—but not before God. ³What does Scripture say? "Abraham believed God, and it was credited to him as righteousness."

⁴Now to the one who works, wages are not credited as a gift but as an obligation. ⁵However, to the one who does not work but trusts God who justifies the ungodly, their faith is credited

as righteousness. ⁶David says the same thing when he speaks of
the blessedness of the one to whom God credits righteousness
apart from works:
⁷"Blessed are those
whose transgressions are forgiven,
whose sins are covered.
⁸Blessed is the one
whose sin the Lord will never count against them."

Paul returned to the Old Testament to prove that his doctrine is the
teaching of the Old Testament. If Paul contradicted previous revelation, he would prove himself to be a false prophet. This is why he
appealed to the testimony of **the Law and the Prophets.** The testimony of the Law comes first, specifically Genesis 15:6.

Paul used Abraham's experience since he is the honored father
of Israel. Therefore, what is true for him must also be true for Israel.
Even Abraham had nothing to **boast about...before God.** He was
indeed a wonderful man, but Scripture makes it clear that his obedience was not the basis of his right relationship with God. The Scripture testifies that **Abram believed God, and it was credited to
him as righteousness.** Abraham had faith-righteousness, not
works-righteousness.

We can understand Abraham's faith better if we return in
thought to the Old Testament and see it in its historical setting. Some
have taken the position that Abraham's faith began in Genesis 15, for
some of the English translations of the Bible imply that. However,
the grammar of Genesis 15:6 makes it necessary to identify the verse
as background information in the chapter. The verse gives the reader
enough information to be able to understand the discussion going on
between Abraham and the Lord. When we look for the beginning of
Abraham's faith, we must go back to Genesis 12:1-3, where God appeared to him and commanded him to leave his family. Abraham had
to leave his father's house and his native land to go to a land that
God would show him. As Hebrews 11:8 says, he left his home even
though he did not know where he was going. This may be the greatest act of faith in human history. The two reasons for this statement
are of vital importance to our discussion.

First, faith begins with knowledge of a person, but Abraham knew almost nothing about God. From the testimony of Genesis, all we can say for sure that Abraham knew at the time he set out for Canaan appears in Genesis 12:1–3. This is remarkable. Normally, it would require enormous trust for a man to uproot his whole life to set out on what must have appeared to people in his day as a wild goose chase. He cut himself off from his whole past.[1]

Second, Abraham set out to become a sojourner. The social status of a sojourner in the ancient Near East is not quite like anything in our experience. The sojourner "has come among a people distinct from him and thus lacks the protection and benefits ordinarily provided by kin and birthplace."[2] They were "travelling foreigners who could count on the customs of hospitality but were not protected by law (Deut. 15:3; 23:21)."[3] This status as a sojourner is what made Abraham's act such a powerful expression of faith. He abandoned everything that could provide for his needs in life, casting all his hope on God for protection while he sojourned in Canaan. Few modern missionaries have set out on their ministries in such a condition. American missionaries still have the protection of the constitution and of the American embassy wherever they go. But Abraham went out trusting in God. In abandoning everything that guaranteed life, Abraham revealed his deep love commitment to God. It was in this love commitment that he found his hope and his life. He risked everything on God. Abraham was truly a man of great faith and he proved it by becoming a sojourner.

In verses 4-5, Paul explained the significance of the grand fact that God justified Abraham by faith. When blessing comes to the obedient, the reward is the payment of a debt or **obligation.** But "grace" (Gk. *charis*; NIV **gift**) plays no part in it. In fact, verse 4 is a basic verse for defining "work" as Paul used it in this book. Paul did not always use the word in a negative way. In Ephesians 2:8–10 he used it both positively (v. 10) and negatively (v. 9) in the same context. Romans 4:4-5 reveals two basic facts about "works" used negatively. First, works originate with man, as Paul says, "to him who works." Works are what man does, not what God does. Second, works bring reward. The converse is also true: disobedience brings punishment. Works earn rewards or penalties from God. This is why works and

79

grace never go together. Grace is God's favor shown for Jesus' sake to those who have forfeited all claims on God's favor. If works are the basis of our relationship with God, we can receive no grace from God. We can only receive what we deserve, only what is just. Law and works absolutely exclude grace. Paul made this same point again in Romans 11:6, "And if by grace, then it is no longer by works; if it were, grace would no longer be grace." Grace and works exclude each other because of the nature of works. A work, then, is anything that man originates that either obligates or allows God to bless him.

On the other hand, Paul explained in verse 5 that Abraham's righteousness is **by faith.** For those who have faith-righteousness, faith is exactly opposite works-righteousness. The one who works receives a just reward. The one who receives grace is the one who **does not work!** Receiving grace requires no obedience. Man brings no works to God, for he has none. In fact Paul is so urgent to drive home this lack of works that he describes the object of God's justifying grace as "wicked."

The truth about the grand man Abraham is that he was wicked. Abraham could not be righteous by his works, because the Bible tells us the truth about Abraham. Genesis 20 records that King Abimelech caught 99 year-old Abraham in a lie. This was not the first time he had told this lie about Sarah, his sister-wife. In verse 13 he admitted that they had been saying she was his sister everywhere they went since they left his father's house 24 years earlier! He was a practiced, habitual liar. Abraham was a wicked man and it is clear that good works did not save him.

In our passage, Paul described faith-righteousness. A man like Abraham could never be righteous by works. He has no righteousness to offer. The good news of verse 5, however, is that God justifies people who have two characteristics. They are qualities that all the justified have. All the justified are believers, and they are wicked. To be right with God, we must be wicked. Then we can receive grace. Only sinners are qualified for salvation.

This means that faith is not a work. We must conclude this from our verse. As Paul stated it, the believer is the one **who does not work.** What is it about faith that keeps it from being a work? Let's review our definition of work. A work is anything that man originates that either obligates or allows God to bless him. What is different about faith?

Faith differs from work because faith does not originate with man. When faith is present, man truly believes. But faith is a gift of God. Paul says in Philippians 1:29, "For it has been granted to you on behalf of Christ … to believe on him." Romans 3:11 says, "There is no one who seeks God," and verse 18 says, "There is no fear of God before their eyes." Then how does anyone ever come to faith in God? God gives it (Phil. 1:29). This should be clear from the Old Testament's teaching on circumcision that Paul addressed in v. 11. Circumcision was the sign of faith-righteousness. We can infer the same idea Paul used from Deuteronomy 30:6, where Moses said to rebellious Israel, "The Lord your God will circumcise your hearts and the hearts of your descendants, so that you may love him with all your heart and all your soul, and live." But one must understand this verse in light of 10:16, which is part of the exposition of the great commandment that covers chapters 6–11. Moses explained loving God with all one's heart by means of a figure, the circumcised heart. What God requires, God provides. God requires faith. He has since the days of Abraham. Therefore, God provides faith.

We have defined faith as consisting of four elements: knowledge, assent, love commitment, and hope. The third element, love commitment, is the crucial element in faith. It is there that we can see that faith does not focus on itself any more than love focuses on itself. One who loves does not treasure love, but the object of his love. Similarly, faith does not treasure itself or see itself as valuable. It treasures its object, the God it trusts.

Works must be the center of focus for the obedient. The life of obedience depends on it. But the life of faith depends, not on faith, but on God. For the believer, God is the focus of faith. Faith earns no rewards. Faith cannot obligate God. When faith receives blessing from God, it does not, indeed it cannot, congratulate itself. It hardly even recognizes itself. Faith focuses all its affection, all its attention, all its devotion, all its energies on God. Faith means that the God who reveals Himself through the Lord Jesus Christ is all in all. Therefore, faith is not a work; faith always stands opposed to works. Therefore, faith is right relationship with God.

Some have claimed that faith is a token obedience that man can give in place of the full obedience that God would otherwise require. Paul rejected this idea in these verses. Faith stands in contrast with work. Faith opposes work. Righteousness is "through faith" (Rom. 3:21). "For we maintain," Paul stated, "that a man is justified by faith apart from observing the law" (Rom. 3:28). Faith is a way of life entirely unrelated to law.

In verse 6 Paul appealed to the Prophets to give their testimony to faith-righteousness,[4] specifically from the prophet David in Psalm 32. Paul summarized David's testimony in verse 6 as **the blessedness of the one to whom God credits righteousness apart from works.** David went even further in Psalm 32, where he said that there are some whom the Lord has **forgiven** and thus He does not **count** their sins **against them.** If God does not take into account their sins, then works do not enter into their righteousness at all. Rather, their faith is the ground of their righteousness.

The believer is right with God! God takes no account of his sin. In fact, God has forgiven his sin. God gives the believer righteousness! Therefore, if faith is right relationship with God, works do not increase our righteousness. If faith is right relationship with God, disobedience cannot decrease it. Paul describes this wonderful truth another way in 2 Corinthians 5:21: "God made him who had no sin to be sin for us, so that in him we might become the righteousness of God." Hear what the apostle Paul said. We are not righteous; we are God's righteousness in Christ. The former statement describes us; the latter identifies us. Righteousness is not what we have, for that would be the righteousness of works. Righteousness in Christ is what we are. We are, according to the Bible, the righteousness of God.

(b) Circumcision does not achieve justification, but is a sign of the faith that inherits the promise to which law stands opposed (4:9-17a).

[9]**Is this blessedness only for the circumcised, or also for the uncircumcised? We have been saying that Abraham's faith was credited to him as righteousness.** [10]**Under what circumstances was it credited? Was it after he was circumcised, or before? It**

was not after, but before! [11]And he received circumcision as a sign, a seal of the righteousness that he had by faith while he was still uncircumcised. So then, he is the father of all who believe but have not been circumcised, in order that righteousness might be credited to them. [12]And he is then also the father of the circumcised who not only are circumcised but who also follow in the footsteps of the faith that our father Abraham had before he was circumcised.

[13]It was not through the law that Abraham and his offspring received the promise that he would be heir of the world, but through the righteousness that comes by faith. [14]For if those who depend on the law are heirs, faith means nothing and the promise is worthless, [15]because the law brings wrath. And where there is no law there is no transgression.

[16]Therefore, the promise comes by faith, so that it may be by grace and may be guaranteed to all Abraham's offspring— not only to those who are of the law but also to those who have the faith of Abraham. He is the father of us all. [17a]As it is written: "I have made you a father of many nations."

Verses 9–12 show that God credited faith-righteousness to Abraham before he received circumcision. The timing of this justification proves that justification is available for all believers, not only the circumcised. Indeed, circumcision is a sign, the seal of faith (v. 11, see Deut. 10:16). Therefore, Abraham has become the father of two sorts of children. The one sort of children is uncircumcised and the other is circumcised, but all are believers. Therefore, faith is the common characteristic among Abraham's children.

This discussion of circumcision showed the first century Jew clearly that Abraham's righteousness was altogether apart from law. He did not receive righteousness when he had kept any law. Therefore, his righteousness is by faith, not by works. So the Jewish believer in Christ must also accept his Gentile brother, both in Christ and in Abraham. Then Gentiles are righteous. They have right relationship with God, as Jews do, by faith in Christ. Regarding right relationship with God, circumcision profits nothing, but only "faith expressing itself through love" (Gal. 5:6).

This must be the case. For if God gave Abraham the promise to be heir of the world by law, then faith is irrelevant and the promise is null (Rom. 4:13-14). It was not even the purpose of the law to produce righteousness. Paul's letters have several statements about the law's purpose. Romans 4:15 says that **the law brings wrath. And where there is no law there is no transgression.** The law makes punishment possible. Romans 5:20 says, "The law was brought in so that the trespass might increase," and 7:13 he says that the law's purpose was that "sin might become utterly sinful." Galatians 3:19–22 says that God gave the law so that everything would be "locked up…under the control of sin" so that the promise "might be given to those who believe." Ladd made this comment about Paul's view of the law: "The heart of Old Testament religion cannot be characterized as legalism, nor was the Law given as the means of achieving a right relationship with God by obedience."[5] God never intended the law to give eternal life. He gave the law so that the Israelites "may live long in the land the LORD your God is giving you" (Ex. 20:12).

The law, however, brought condemnation (Rom. 4:15). The law is only for sinners, not for the righteous (1 Tim. 1:9). Righteous people do not need law. If every businessman in America were thoroughly ethical and moral our government would not need to regulate business by law. The existence and number of laws regulating our business community prove the extent to which businesses have failed to play fair. It proves that the business community is not trustworthy. Law, then, is not for the righteous; it is for the sinner. This is why Paul stated that the law brings wrath, meaning that its function is to inflict the penalty of justice on transgressors. Verse 15 adds one more basic observation about law. This observation furthers Paul's conclusion that the promise does not come to fulfillment by law (vv. 13-14). The observation is this: **where there is no law there is no transgression.** This statement has two implications.

The first implication relates directly to the conclusion reached in verses 13-14. Law would nullify the promise because of its relationship to transgression. If I am under law and I violate it, as I surely will (see Rom. 1:18–3:20), then I have transgressed. I must receive punishment (**the law brings wrath**). The punishment rules out the fulfillment of any promise. Law nullifies faith and promise.

The statement requires us to draw another implication. If I am not under law but still sin, as I surely will, I have not transgressed. Indeed, I cannot transgress. Sin takes on a whole new character and role in life when there is no law.

I have explained that the best definition of sin is unbelief. In the life of faith one major obstacle hinders our faith: lack of knowledge. Faith grows by means of knowledge of God revealed in Scripture. Sometimes, however, God leads us out beyond our knowledge of Himself. He does this because, in our struggles, we learn to know Him. Yet in our struggles we must make decisions uninformed by revelation, uninformed by the knowledge of God. We are not unbelievers at such times; we simply do not know how to trust God. At such times we often make sinful choices, choices inconsistent with the nature and revelation of God. To the degree that we are unaware of God's revealed character, to that degree we are immature in our faith, and to that extent we make sinful choices. At those times we are not rebellious; we are only immature.

Two passages may help us to understand this better. The first is 1 Corinthians 3:1–3 where Paul contrasted the Corinthians' condition when he first came to them with their current condition. At first they were not spiritual, but babies. From this we should learn that Paul used the term "spiritual" primarily to mean "mature." The Corinthians' current carnal condition, then, is a condition of arrested growth. People in every day life reach a plateau of growth emotionally and do not continue. We may also stop growing spiritually. Both conditions are pathological. Loving parents search for help for children who are not growing, sometimes radical help. So also God, our heavenly Father, sets out to aid His children to grow spiritually, sometimes with radical aid.

Paul then described two symptoms of babyhood: the need for milk instead of solid food, and strife and division. The baby's need for milk appears again in Hebrews 5:11-14, another key passage in understanding the nature of a Christian's sin. It is helpful because it allows us to define milk and therefore the specific quality of immaturity. The author of Hebrews described a baby with two characteristics. First, "Anyone who lives on milk, being still an infant, is not acquainted with the teaching about righteousness" (v. 13). I suggest that "the word about righteousness" is a reference to Scripture since it teaches about right living. The baby has no skill, when he reads the Bible, in applying it to life (which is the point of the context). Baby Christians need the Bible's application made as clear as possible. Therefore, milk refers to Scripture that makes application very clear, books like 1 Corinthians. Solid meat would refer to books or passages where the application is not absolutely clear, such as Genesis 14 and its fascinating teaching about Melchizedek. Thus, the first characteristic of babies is their lack of skill in understanding and applying Scripture to life.

The baby's second characteristic appears by inference from Hebrews 5:14: "But solid food is for the mature, who by constant use have trained themselves to distinguish between good and evil." Mature Christians do a better job of applying Scripture than do baby Christians. They can also go one step further. When Scripture does not speak to a particular life situation, mature Christians can discern what is appropriate and inappropriate, what is right and wrong. Since baby Christians cannot even apply Scripture to life, how will they fare in areas of life where Scripture is not clear?

The mature can make fine distinctions because they are trained. But how did they gain this skill? Anyone would know that in learning a skill we always do everything correctly in the training process. No piano student who ever learned to play has ever played a wrong note either in practice or in performance. Right? No successful athlete has ever blown a play, either in practice or in competition. Right? Then surely we should expect to gain skill in distinguishing good and evil without ever failing. No! Of course not. The only way to grow in any skill is by failure. Failure is the necessary condition of growth in any skill. But when we fail, we must learn to know the grace of our loving Father-God for failure, for our immaturity, for our sin. When God leads us out beyond our knowledge of Himself, He leads us out into the immaturity of our faith. In that way He can expose and deal with it. He leads us to places where we cannot understand Him, to teach us about Himself. If we are listening, even when we fail, we will grow from our failures. In such a circumstance we have not transgressed. Therefore, no punishment is possible. On the other hand, God has exposed our immaturity; so he does discipline us.

We have been pursuing the implications of Paul's statement **where there is no law there is no transgression** (Rom. 4:15). One key difference between sin as transgression and sin as immaturity is God's response to it. When God views sin as transgression, He executes His wrath against it in order to vindicate justice. When, however, He views sin as immaturity, He cannot bring wrath. Rather, He deals in love. His love seeks the restoration and growth of His beloved, but immature, children.

This is the point of Hebrews 12:5-12. Notice verse 6: "For whom the Lord loves He disciplines and punishes everyone whom he accepts as a son" (NIV with slight modification). Note that every son receives discipline, not just the disobedient, but the obedient as well. They receive discipline because of God's Fatherly love. God does not discipline sinners. He disciplines sons whom He loves. Even Jesus received discipline! Hebrews 5:7-8 teaches that as "Son," Jesus learned obedience through what He suffered. Thus, whether we sin or not, we receive discipline from the Lord so that we may grow up to share His great holiness. Paul stated, **The law brings wrath. And where there is no law there is no transgression** (Rom. 4:15). This means that sin now, for the Christian, has the character of immaturity rather than transgression. We come under, not the wrath of God, but His disciplining, restoring love. I would suggest, then, that sin does not cause us to lose fellowship with God. We gain intimate fellowship in the disciplining love of God, and because of that discipline we live.

In this way God has offered the promise by faith so that it might be by grace. The result is that the promise comes **to all Abraham's offspring** (Rom. 4:16-17a), not only to those who have been under law. For Abraham received God's promise that he would become the father of many nations and inherit the earth. But what is this faith like? What is the faith that receives the promise? Paul described this kind of faith in 4:17b-25.

> **(c) Abraham risked everything on God who raised Jesus from the dead in proof of justification and proved that the promise comes to the seed marked by faith (4:17b-25).**

[17b]He is our father in the sight of God, in whom he believed—the God who gives life to the dead and calls into being things that were not.

[18]Against all hope, Abraham in hope believed and so became the father of many nations, just as it had been said to him, "So shall your offspring be." [19]Without weakening in his faith, he faced the fact that his body was as good as dead—since he was about a hundred years old—and that Sarah's womb was also dead. [20]Yet he did not waver through unbelief regarding the promise of God, but was strengthened in his faith and gave glory to God, [21]being fully persuaded that God had power to do what he had promised. [22]This is why "it was credited to him as righteousness." [23]The words "it was credited to him" were written not for him alone, [24]but also for us, to whom God will credit righteousness—for us who believe in him who raised Jesus our Lord from the dead. [25]He was delivered over to death for our sins and was raised to life for our justification.

Faith, as we have defined it, begins with knowledge. In this last half of verse 17 we learn what Abraham knew, what the basis of his faith was. In the passage before us, Paul modeled this faith that God gives, that is, justifying faith. He drew from Genesis 21, the birth of Isaac. God had promised Abraham a son in Genesis 15, but He waited until Abraham was 100 years old to fulfill the promise. We recognize that by that time in his life, Abraham's body was dead concerning having children. We can say the same about Sarah: "Sarah was past the age of childbearing" (Gen. 18:11). She was not only barren, but she was well past the time of childbearing, being 89 years old at the time God promised Isaac to her. Indeed, concerning childbearing, Paul said that **Sarah's womb was also dead** (Rom. 4:19).

The God whom Abraham knew, however, was sufficient for such problems. He is **the God who gives life to the dead and calls into being things that were not** (Rom. 4:17b). Abraham knew his own deadness, but he knew a God who is more powerful than death. Abraham knew his wife's barrenness and age, but he also knew a God who calls the nonexistent into existence. Abraham's faith did not ignore or deny the reality of his world or common sense. Faith takes full account of the world and the senses. It is not a world-denying thing; it is a God-affirming thing. Faith does not deny the world; it only looks at the world through God's Word. It assesses the future through the reality-changing Word of God.

This is Paul's description of believing Abraham: **Against all hope, Abraham in hope believed and so became the father of many nations. . . Without weakening in his faith, he faced the fact that his body was as good as dead. . . and that Sarah's womb was also dead. Yet he did not waver through unbelief regarding the promise of God, but was strengthened in his faith and gave glory to God, being fully persuaded that God had power to do what he had promised** (Rom. 4:18-21).

Here is faith! Abraham's knowledge of God gave him confidence about the future (that is, hope) in spite of the impossibilities of the world. When we know God, we can take risks; we can put ourselves in places where we are vulnerable. Abraham at age 99 knew his God. He grew confident about his future, not only nine months hence, but especially for the days that immediately followed God's promise. Remember that Isaac's conception was not a virgin conception. Only one virgin in history has conceived. Abraham believed God. He had such strong confidence in God that he and his wife conceived a son born of the promise of God. He saw the impossibilities through the lenses of God's promise and watched reality change. His faith did not change reality; God did. In fact, by His Word, He created a new reality: Abraham's body and Sarah's womb were **as good as dead.** God changed them that they could bear Isaac. So by his faith he became the recipient and participant in God's promised blessing.

All of this stands written in Scripture for our sake. We need to know what faith is. We need to know a God who makes alive the dead and calls the nonexistent into existence. This is the God **who raised Jesus our Lord from the dead.** Faith knows such a God. Faith knows that this God handed Jesus **over to death for our sins.** Faith sees the death of one unknown Jew in a remote corner of the Roman Empire as the only payment for sin. Faith knows that this God raised that crucified Man **to life.** Faith recognizes that Jesus' resurrection is God's testimony that believing people receive **justification**—right standing in His eyes!

Abraham's faith is the critical model for our relationship with God, not only in its beginning, but throughout our lives. Abraham's faith is crucial in accepting God's verdict on our lives. Without faith no one could accept the verdict that "There is no one righteous, not even one" (Rom. 3:10). For without faith we will believe what our eyes tell us, not what God says. Our eyes tell us that multitudes of humanity are righteous, especially those we love.

Without faith no one could accept that those who are right with God by faith have peace with God (Rom. 5:1). For without faith we will believe that people who have good works, the obedient, have peace with God. Unbelief acknowledges no other route to God's favor than the route of works. Without faith no one could believe that those who are in Christ Jesus have no condemnation (Rom. 8:1). Unbelief wrestles with the discomfort of God's pure grace. To unbelief, grace looks like lawlessness. Without faith no one could ever believe that all suffering is worthwhile (Rom. 8:18). For unbelief knows for certain that suffering proves God's condemning wrath against us. Only faith can see things from God's point of view. Only faith can understand that God makes all things work together for good, which is to bring us into Christ's image (Rom. 8:28-29). Faith knows that God brings suffering into our lives to test our love for Him. As in Job's life and sufferings, God confronts us in our pains with a probing question. He asks, "Do you love me, or do you love my blessings?" Unbelief loves only God's blessings. Only faith based on grace can love God when He does not give prosperity.

Without faith no one could accept God's verdict on faith: "For we maintain that a person is justified by faith apart from the works of the law" (Rom. 3:28). So without faith no one can accept the message about life that God gives in Romans 5–8. Faith takes God so seriously that in confidence about the future (hope) it risks everything on Him and watches reality change.

Notes for Romans 4

[1]Gerhard von Rad, *Genesis: A Commentary*, p. 239.
[2]*IDB*, see "Sojourner," by T. M. Mauch, 4 (1962): 397.
[3]Roland De Vaux, *Ancient Israel: Social Institutions*, 1:74.

[4]As we will see later, faith produces obedience; but righteousness is not obedience. Righteousness in Romans is right relationship with God, and the only right relationship with God is faith. Righteousness is faith.

[5]George Eldon Ladd, *A Theology of the New Testament*, ed. Donald A. Hagner, Rev. ed. (Grand Rapids, MI: William B. Eerdmans Publishing Company, 1993), 540. Ladd later suggested that Paul's problem was "that Judaism had in reality substituted the law for the covenant, or identified the covenant with the law" (p. 499). He has himself fallen afoul of an important point. The Old Testament identifies the law as the Mosaic Covenant. Ladd's discussion appears to distinguish the Mosaic Covenant as law and the Abrahamic Covenant as covenant. This is an unfair and unbiblical distinction. The law is a covenant, but it is not the only covenant. In Romans 7:7-12 Paul did not distinguish between Pharisaic misinterpretation and the commandment of God. It is God's commandment that condemned him.

ROMANS 5

3. Christ, through His self-sacrifice, brings life to those who are righteous by faith (Rom. 5–8).

In verse 1, the word **Therefore** looks all the way back to the beginning of the book and draws a conclusion from chapters 1–4: **since we have been justified by faith, we have peace with God.** Paul has now turned to a new dimension of his discussion. In 1:17 Paul quoted Habakkuk 2:4, "The righteous by faith will live" (using the word order from the Hebrew and Greek). The first part of that quotation ("The righteous by faith") summarizes chapters 1–4. The second part of that quotation ("will live") summarizes chapters 5–8, which describes the life of those justified by faith.

These four chapters are best divided into six parts (5:1-11; 5:12-21; 6:1-14; 6:15–7:25, which is parenthetical; 8:1-17; 8:18-39). Paul began by describing the life of the justified as a life of peace boasting in suffering since they have come to know God's love (5:1-11). That life is further a life of alien righteousness that we receive from Christ's one obedient act (5:12-21). That righteousness, however, comes to be our experience as we learn to live out our participation in the death and resurrection of Christ (6:1-14). The passage 6:15–7:25 is parenthetical and explains the significance of Paul's statement in 6:14, which says, "For sin shall not be your master, because you are not under law, but under grace." That life is only possible for those whom the Spirit of God leads to live by faith and by grace. Though they suffer greatly (8:1-17), their suffering produces a life of Christ-likeness and a victorious life through God's love in Christ (8:18-39).

a. Therefore, having peace with God, we receive all blessings through Christ and know God's love in saving and keeping us (5:1-11).

¹Therefore, since we have been justified through faith, we have peace with God through our Lord Jesus Christ, ²through whom we have gained access by faith into this grace in which we now stand. And we boast in the hope of the glory of God. ³Not only so, but we also glory in our sufferings, because we know that suffering produces perseverance; ⁴perseverance, character; and character, hope. ⁵And hope does not put us to shame, because God's love has been poured out into our hearts through the Holy Spirit, who has been given to us.

⁶You see, at just the right time, when we were still power-less, Christ died for the ungodly. ⁷Very rarely will anyone die for a righteous person, though for a good person someone might possibly dare to die. ⁸But God demonstrates his own love for us in this: While we were still sinners, Christ died for us.

⁹Since we have now been justified by his blood, how much more shall we be saved from God's wrath through him! ¹⁰For if, while we were God's enemies, we were reconciled to him through the death of his Son, how much more, having been reconciled, shall we be saved through his life! ¹¹Not only is this so, but we also boast in God through our Lord Jesus Christ, through whom we have now received reconciliation.

Some scribe in copying the Book of Romans may have been afraid of saying so openly that the **justified by faith** actually have peace with God. We always want to make sure that people maintain an atti-tude of anxiety in God's presence. So he changed the text from "we have" to "let us have" peace with God. But Paul had no such pur-pose. Paul wanted the justified to know their position before God: **we have peace with God.**

It will take all of this section (chaps. 5–8) to explain what this peace is. Yet Paul begins immediately in the opening verses of chap-ter 5: **we have peace with God through our Lord Jesus Christ.** Everything we have before God, we have in Christ. In fact, "he him-self is our peace" (Eph. 2:14). Peace is not so much what God gives. It is the One God gives, Jesus Himself.

In Him we also have **access by faith into this grace in which we now stand.** Many people think that somehow we humans have a right to God's grace. Some of us think that somehow God owes grace to us. Paul explained that we stand in grace only in Christ. In Christ we have **peace** and we stand in **grace.** Peace is, then, the result of our standing in grace in Christ.

Indeed, because of Christ our life of peace and grace leads us to experience great boasting. We make two boasts, first, our **hope** to share in God's **glory,** and then **in our sufferings.** In 1:16 Paul described the gospel as "the power of God." We learned in chapter 3 that God's power in the gospel breaks the cycle of sin. What power this is! Now we learn that the power of God in the gospel gives us hope of God's glory. Lest we misunderstand, Paul was not talking here about glorifying God but that we will share in God's glory (see "we shall be glorified with Him" in 8:17). He said that all creation yearns for the revelation of God's children in all their glory (8:18–21). Indeed, Peter said that those who have fled the corruption of the world will be participants in the divine nature (2 Pet. 1:4). God's power in the gospel restores us to the glory of God. In this we make our boast!

Yet Paul wanted his readers to understand that we have more to rejoice in than simply a future that we cannot now see. God intends His justified people to know peace as they live a life of joy throughout their days. Joy should mark our whole lives. This is not normal human joy, however, for this joy, this boasting, is peculiar: we boast **in our sufferings.**

Suffering can only bring boasting when we understand the plan of God. Our boastful rejoicing and suffering relate directly to one another. Paul explained that relationship in verses 3-5. First, **suffering produces perseverance.** Second, **perseverance** produces **character.** Finally, **character** produces **hope** that brings no **shame.** It is the purpose of suffering to bring confidence to us, confidence in the future that God promised us. Indeed, we can rejoice amid sufferings. In suffering, we come to experience **God's love** that **has been poured out into our hearts through the Holy Spirit, who has been given to us.** Therefore, the life of the justified is a life of suffering; but it is especially in suffering that we come to know God's love for us. Then the life of the justified is a life experiencing God's love.

Do not short-circuit the work of suffering in your life. All God really wants from us in suffering is our endurance. In addition to verse 3, consider James 1:12: "Blessed is the one who perseveres under trial because, having stood the test, that person will receive the crown of life that the Lord has promised to those who love him." Endurance is the crown of Christian living and suffering is the means to attain it. We come to know God's love when we endure suffering. Do not short-circuit the work of suffering in your life. This is the path to intimacy with God.

God's love is no weak emotionalism. Weak emotional love depends on the beauty or attraction of its object. Such is not God's love. Verses 6-11 describe His love. These verses give two great measures for God's love. First, the objects of His love measure its greatness; and second is the gift He gave for them. For God expresses His inalienable love as He gives His Son to hostile, ungodly sinners. His Son's death saves us and His life keeps us.

In verses 6-10 Paul described the recipients of God's love in four ways. He says they are **powerless** and **ungodly** (v. 6), **sinners** (v. 8), and **enemies** (v. 10). A righteous man or a benefactor[1] might attract benevolent, even sacrificial, action from other men. But God's love proves its character by sacrificing for ungodly, sinful enemies. This is an incomparable love. Paul explained the significance of such a love in verses 9-10. When we were His enemies, God gave the reconciling sacrifice. Now that He has reconciled us, He will save us from His own wrath (v. 9) by the life of Christ (v. 10). His saving work is as sure as the life of Christ. As Christ, having died to sin once, no longer dies (6:8–9), so those He saves live by the certainty of His life.

How significant these truths are! Christ died for the ungodly! God loves sinners! He offers no love to the "righteous." The "godly" have no hope before Him. The "obedient" cannot be saved. But all who know themselves condemned, all who know their guilt, all who know they are drowning in sin, all who hold in their hearts hostility against God, have hope. For Christ offers no hope to the righteous. Christ died for the ungodly. No one who thinks he has something to offer God can have God's salvation. Self-righteousness stands excluded. Someone has said that the church is the only institution in the world whose members must meet the qualification of having no qualifications. Here is hope for the weak, ungodly, sinful enemy of God. This is just the kind of person He saves!

God proves His love by the nature of those who receive His love. But He also proves it by the gift He gives. While some men might die for a righteous man or a benefactor, God proves His love by giving His Son, the Messiah, His anointed king, to die to save His own enemies.

We do not fully comprehend the measure of this gift just by considering His identity. We come to know its measure, the dignity of His person, as well, by contemplating what He accomplishes. Paul went beyond what we have already seen in chapter 3 and in the early part of this chapter. In verses 9-10, he mentioned two more effects of Christ's work. First, **since we have now been justified by His blood,** we shall be saved from **wrath** (v. 9). The wrath mentioned here might refer to one of two ideas. In 1:18 Paul referred to God's present wrath. But then he referred to future wrath on sinners that God will inflict in the day of judgment (2:5-11). It may be that both of these ideas are present in 5:9. The death of Christ frees us from all God's wrath. It breaks the cycle of sin (1:24–32) and frees us from the dread of God's future wrath. This is what Christ did for sinners. He did not do it for the righteous. He did not do it for benefactors. He died for weak, ungodly, sinful enemies of His rule. Here is amazing and divine love!

Verse 10-11 carries us another step further. God has seized the initiative with His **enemies.** He has not required His enemies to sue for His favor. He has Himself done what was necessary to reconcile His enemies to Himself. **Reconciliation** might be hard to understand, but it may be helpful to compare it to something common to our experience. Anyone who has balanced a checkbook will understand what reconciliation means. I am so poor at math that when I must balance my personal checkbook, I always assume that the bank is right. They have computers, after all. So as long as my records show that I have less money in my account than the bank says I have, I am satisfied. But if the bank shows less than I do, without hesitation I change my records to agree with theirs—I reconcile my account to the bank's.[2] While this may not be good finance, it is good theology.

We are by nature enemies of God (Rom. 5:10), alienated from Him. By the death of Christ and because of it, God has changed the whole equation. He has solved the issues that made us enemies (our sin and debt to Him) and fitting us to have fellowship with Himself (Paul will spell out a key part of what reconciliation is in 5:12-25, namely, His identification of us, in Christ, as righteous by His obedience). So we live through the life of Christ, and we live His life. Here is the change God is making in us so that we now become His children. Such is God's love. Such is the life of those justified by faith. It is a life reveling in the love of God.

b. Christ, patterned on Adam's contrast, brought life through His obedient death in order to bring life to reign through righteousness (5:12-21).

[12]Therefore, just as sin entered the world through one man, and death through sin, and in this way death came to all people, because all sinned—

[13]To be sure, sin was in the world before the law was given, but sin is not charged against anyone's account where there is no law. [14]Nevertheless, death reigned from the time of Adam to the time of Moses, even over those who did not sin by breaking a command, as did Adam, who is a pattern of the one to come.

[15]But the gift is not like the trespass. For if the many died by the trespass of the one man, how much more did God's grace and the gift that came by the grace of the one man, Jesus Christ, overflow to the many! [16]Nor can the gift of God be compared with the result of one man's sin: The judgment followed one sin and brought condemnation, but the gift followed many trespasses and brought justification. [17]For if, by the trespass of the one man, death reigned through that one man, how much more will those who receive God's abundant provision of grace and of the gift of righteousness reign in life through the one man, Jesus Christ!

[18]Consequently, just as one trespass resulted in condemnation for all people, so also one righteous act resulted in justification and life for all people. [19]For just as through the disobedience of the one man the many were made sinners, so also through the obedience of the one man the many will be made righteous.

²⁰**The law was brought in so that the trespass might increase. But where sin increased, grace increased all the more, ²¹so that, just as sin reigned in death, so also grace might reign through righteousness to bring eternal life through Jesus Christ our Lord.**

The life of the justified, this peace we know in Christ, is also a life of alien righteousness. To help us understand what alien righteousness means, Paul contrasted our righteousness in Christ with our condemned condition in Adam. Just as we humans stand condemned for nothing we have done, so also we stand justified for nothing we have done.

Paul introduced this section with the term **therefore.** What he said earlier (vv.1-11) is that what we have before God, we have in Christ. This will be his point in verses 12–21 also. All we have, we have in Christ. Yet this idea is hard to grasp, since we are so accustomed to think that we earn everything we get. Paul clearly explained the basis of our standing before God, so he contrasted the effects of Christ's work and the effects of Adam's work, since Adam is a model of Christ (v. 14). However, to understand Adam as a type of Christ, we must turn him inside out. For what Adam's one deed has accomplished is the precise opposite of Jesus' one deed.

The word **therefore** requires a closer relation between verses 12-21 and verses 1-11. Specifically, it forces us to see how we became God's enemies and how, in Christ, God has reconciled us. The connection of ideas, then, is something like this. In verses 10–11 Paul reminds us that God has reconciled us to Himself by the death of His Son. **Therefore, just as sin entered the world through one man** (Adam), so righteousness entered the world **through the one man, Jesus Christ** (vv. 12-17). To be specific, it is by imputed sin that we became enemies of God, and it is by imputed righteousness that God has reconciled us to become His sons (vv. 18-19).

Verses 12-14 give evidence of how excited Paul was about his subject. Notice that verse 12 begins with **just as.** Normally such an expression correlates with a "so also." But Paul in his excitement never expressed the "so also." He found it necessary to develop some other ideas before coming back to his contrast between Adam and Jesus. This sort of construction often marks the writer's excitement over what he is saying.

Verses 12-14 explain our relationship to sin and death in Adam. Sin and death entered the world through Adam. All die because **all sinned.** Death is surely the punishment of sin. God warned Adam not to sin, "for when you eat of it you will certainly die" (Gen. 2:17) We die, not because of our own sin, but because of Adam's. Paul made this clear in verses 13-14. From Adam to Moses sin existed in the world, even though no law existed. Since God had given no law, He kept no record of sins as a basis for judging sinners. Yet sinners died. Indeed, he says that **death reigned from the time of Adam to the time of Moses.** Even people who did not sin as Adam did suffered death. People who had none of God's commandments, and thus did not break any commandments, died. Therefore, they died because of Adam's sin.

Paul introduced here ideas based on a concept foreign to the western world. This approach to life views the individual as a member of a corporate group. From the group, and from its head, an individual receives his meaning, his identity, and his destiny. Scholars call this concept "corporate solidarity." This idea was dominant in the ancient Near East and is common throughout the Bible. Jacob's family is Israel because they all share in the meaning, identity, and destiny that God established for Jacob. Similarly, all humanity stands in one of two corporate solidarities: all are either "in Adam" or "in Christ." To be in Adam is to share his meaning, identity, and destiny. To be in Christ is to share His. This is the foundation for verses 15-19.

On the one hand, one man's transgression brought **death** to multitudes. On the other hand, the gracious **gift** of One Man brings grace to multitudes. On the one hand, one man's sin brought condemning **judgment** to multitudes. On the other hand, the gracious gift brings **justification** in face of the transgression of multitudes. On the one hand, death reigned by one man's transgression. On the other hand, those who receive grace reign in life through the One Man, Jesus Christ.

Consider the significance of just one sin! Paul traced every human being's death to Adam's one sin. If that one sin had not occurred, there never would have been a World War I or World War II.

The Bubonic Plague, in which a third of Europe died, would never have swept the world. No Nazi Party would have slaughtered six million Jews along with six million Gentiles. None of us would wear glasses. Humanity would have known no disease, no discomfort, no war, no sorrow, no pain, no death. Ultimately, the horror of that one sin appears most clearly in that Jesus, the spotless Son of God, would never have needed to die. Such is the significance and the horror of one man's sin.

Paul's main point, however, is summarized in verses 18-19. Unfortunately, we normally only turn to verses 12-21 to struggle with what it teaches about Adam's sin. Yet this is not Paul's point at all. The apostle only introduced Adam as an aid to understand the work of Christ. This emphasis on Jesus' work is clear in these two verses. The one act of Adam brought condemnation to all identified with him. God has declared every human being a sinner because of Adam's sin. The point of the verb **made** in verse 19 is just this. The same verb appears in Luke 12:42 and Hebrews 5:1 where it refers to appointing someone to an office. Paul uses the verb in the same sense here. God appointed all humanity to the official position **sinner** because of Adam's one sin. Additionally, in the two passages just mentioned where this verb occurs, the person once appointed begins to act in his position: he acts as high priest or steward. So it is with every human being: all of us whom God has appointed to the office of sinner have carried out our office by sinning.

This is great good news! If I am a sinner by appointment because of Adam's sin, then I can be righteous by appointment because of Jesus' obedience. It is by the obedience of this one man that many shall be **made** (i.e., appointed) righteous. So our righteousness is not our own. It is an alien righteousness. I have become **sinner** without sinning. Then I become **righteous** without acting righteously, without works of law! My sin does not make me a sinner. I am a sinner, and therefore I sin. My obedience, then, does not make me righteous. I am righteous in Christ, with the righteousness of Christ.

I mentioned in the commentary on chapter 3 that God faced two great problems in justifying us, both caused by His own nature. First, He is just. Then, He is gracious. The solution of the first problem (His justice) appears in chapter 3, where Paul showed how God solved our need for someone to pay the just penalty of our sins. Jesus died to redeem us from sin. I owe no more to God's justice. The other problem we have as sinners is the need to give perfect obedience to God. God has commanded us to love Him with all our heart, with all our soul, and with all our strength. No matter how long we live, no matter how obedient we may become or attempt to become, we have not perfectly loved God and perfectly obeyed Him all the days of our lives.

Paul solved the second problem God faced as a result of His nature (His grace) by what He revealed in vv. 18-19. God has appointed us righteous because of the one obedience of Jesus Christ.[3] The one disobedience of Adam, eating the fruit of the tree of the knowledge of good and evil, brought sin and death upon all mankind. The one act of obedience by Jesus, dying on the cross to bear the punishment for mankind's sins, now graciously brings God's righteousness to all who believe. But His obedience is no mere law keeping. His obedience summed up the law and transcended it. No law could ever demand that anyone die for another. Yet in dying, Jesus fulfilled all righteousness, completely satisfying God's righteous demand against the sinner and His demand for obedient submission to His will.

Paul expressed the same truth in 2 Corinthians 5:21: "God made him who had no sin to be sin for us, so that in him we might become the righteousness of God." Do you hear what Paul said? We are not merely righteous. We are *God's* righteousness. We have no righteousness by what we have done, but we become the righteousness of God. So we have not merely 10 percent or 50 percent righteousness. We have the complete righteousness of God in Christ. God's righteousness is infinite, and this is what we are. God has declared it so. This implies that in Christ we have—as Jesus said of Himself— fulfilled all righteousness. We, in Christ, have satisfied all the demands of the law already. Consequently, we do not need the law. Law is for sinners (1 Tim. 1:9). Since God has appointed us to be as righteous as Christ, we have fulfilled all demands of the law. No wrath can come to us. No penalty can be appropriate for us since we are in Christ, God's righteousness. Here is alien righteousness. Here is peace with God.

Why then the law? Paul answers this question in verses 20-21. The law came in alongside the promise to Abraham **so that the trespass might increase.** Galatians 3:15-22 explains that God intended the law to lead Israel to Messiah. Israel could only come to Messiah Jesus as they came to understand their own incapacity for obedience. The law accomplished its function very well. Paul's verdict on Israel from the law makes that plain (see Rom. 3:10-18). Israel stood fully condemned by the very law in which they boasted. Peter bore testimony to this fact in Acts 15:10, where he said, "Now then, why do you try to test God by putting on the necks of Gentiles a yoke that neither we nor our ancestors have been able to bear?" The law makes nothing perfect (Heb. 7:19). Rather, God intended the law to stir up sin so people would long for His grace. So Paul says, **where sin increased, grace increased all the more.** This happened **so that, just as sin reigned in death, so also grace might reign through righteousness to bring eternal life through Jesus Christ our Lord.**

The message of grace means the end of the law. It means the end of works, the end of obedience, the end of demand, the end of obligation and duty. It means the end of condemnation, wrath, and penalty. "For Christ is the end of the law for righteousness to everyone who believes" (Rom. 10:4, NASB).

The problem with the message of grace is that it seems to leave us free to do anything we want. Particularly, it seems to leave man free to sin, and in a sense this is true. Some time ago a colleague came to my office. "Jim," he said, "I need to talk to you. Some of the students in your Romans class are telling others that since we are under grace we can sin all we want." I thanked my friend who honored me by confronting me with a problem I had caused. I responded, "Great, I'm glad they're saying that. It means I've been teaching Romans, because I'm getting the same response Paul did. Now all I need to do is teach them Romans 6." Teaching the doctrine of grace nearly always raises the charge of lawlessness.

Paul's statement in 5:21 helps us understand this. He said that grace reigns through righteousness. That one statement should solve all the questions that people pose, but he expanded on that idea in chapters 6–7.

Notes for Romans 5

[1]Cranfield suggested this as the proper reference of the word "good" in this verse.

[2]Louw and Nida (*Greek-English Lexicon,* 40.1) defines the word *reconcile* as meaning, "to re-establish proper friendly interpersonal relations after these have been disrupted or broken." They give four components of the word's meaning: "(1) disruption of friendly relations because of (2) presumed or real provocation, (3) overt behavior designed to remove hostility, and (4) restoration of original friendly relations" (see 2 Cor. 5:18).

[3]The Greek verb used here appears in Luke 12:42 and Hebrews 5:1; 7:28, for appointing someone to office.

ROMANS 6

Paul had just said, "The law was brought in so that the trespass might increase. But where sin increased, grace increased all the more" (5:20). This statement seems to imply that Christians can do anything they want, even sin, since grace abounds over our sin. It is curious that Christian people in general believe that if we do not have law, we will abandon ourselves to an orgy of sin. Do we believe that grace makes obedience irrelevant? Thus the ideas at the end of chapter 5 raised the question that begins chapter 6, making the discussion in this chapter necessary.

The question in verse 1 ("Shall we go on sinning so that grace may increase?") controls Paul's thought through verse 14. But the implied "no" in that question is so radical that it raises two more questions. The first one is in 6:15 and is answered in 6:16–7:6; the second is in 7:7 and is answered in 7:8–12. Paul's discussion in 7:8–12 raised a third question in verse 13, which he answered in 7:14-25.

> **c. Righteousness will mark the life of believers when they regard themselves as dead to sin and alive to God through Christ and therefore not under law but under grace (6:1-14).**

¹**What shall we say, then? Shall we go on sinning so that grace may increase? ²By no means! We are those who have died to sin; how can we live in it any longer? ³Or don't you know that all of us who were baptized into Christ Jesus were baptized into his death? ⁴We were therefore buried with him through baptism into death in order that, just as Christ was raised from the dead through the glory of the Father, we too may live a new life.**

⁵**For if we have been united with him in a death like his, we will certainly also be united with him in a resurrection like his. ⁶For we know that our old self was crucified with him so that**

the body ruled by sin might be done away with, that we should no longer be slaves to sin— [7]because anyone who has died has been set free from sin.

[8]Now if we died with Christ, we believe that we will also live with him. [9]For we know that since Christ was raised from the dead, he cannot die again; death no longer has mastery over him. [10]The death he died, he died to sin once for all; but the life he lives, he lives to God.

[11]In the same way, count yourselves dead to sin but alive to God in Christ Jesus. [12]Therefore do not let sin reign in your mortal body so that you obey its evil desires. [13]Do not offer any part of yourself to sin as an instrument of wickedness, but rather offer yourselves to God as those who have been brought from death to life; and offer every part of yourself to him as an instrument of righteousness. [14]For sin shall no longer be your master, because you are not under the law, but under grace.

Paul asked, **Shall we go on sinning so that grace may increase?** His answer appears differently in various English translations, but my favorite is, "Good heavens, no!" One of my students described the impact of this exclamation this way: "You've got all the facts straight, but your conclusion is all wrong." The apostle gave his answer to the question particularly in verses 1-10, summarized it in verse 11, and spelled out some of its detail in verses 12-13.

The answer Paul gave has two parts: the first part in 6:2-4a; the second in 6:4b-10. We **who have died to sin** will not live in it any longer since our baptism with Christ means that we **were baptized into His death**—baptism being our burial into His death. The problem I have with this statement is that I do not feel dead to sin. Sin seems to control me so easily. But Paul clearly said that we are indeed dead to sin, so our task is to discover in what sense this is true.

It is certainly not true to say that our death to sin means we no longer sin since this death has not eradicated sin in our lives. Paul did not deny the presence of sin in the lives of believers, but he did affirm that believers still relate to sin. This is clear in the rest of chapter 6 and in chapter 7. Paul cannot mean that the Christian no longer sins.

So what did Paul mean? First, our death to sin relates directly to our baptism with Christ. Baptism into Christ means baptism, indeed burial, into His death. Since we only bury the dead, we must be dead if we have been buried.

Many have assumed that baptism into Christ Jesus must refer to baptism into Christ's body, the church: "For we were all baptized by one Spirit into one body" (1 Cor. 12:13). The problem with this view is that this verse does not describe our union with Christ's death, as Romans 6:3-4 does. It describes our union with Christ's life. That life shows itself when the spiritual gifts operate through the body. But in Romans 6:3-4 Paul associated our baptism with death (**baptized into his death; baptism into death**), not with life. In fact he called it a burial (**we were buried**). Baptism into Christ's body is fullness of life. Baptism into His death is a sharing in His cross (see v. 6). For these reasons it is better to define baptism into Christ's death as water baptism.[1] As we immerse the believer, we are in figure burying him. Why do we do that? The only reason for burial is that a death has occurred. In verse 6 Paul pointed out that we have been **crucified with him.** So when we immerse, we are burying one who has shared in Christ's crucifixion.

Does baptism cause our death with Christ? One might think I have come dangerously close to baptismal salvation, but I have not. Instead, we are dealing with an idea that the New Testament shares with the Old Testament, which scholars have called *reactualization*, or ritual reenactment. It is "the process by which a past event is contemporized for a generation removed in time and space from the original event."[2] Another definition may also help in understanding the idea: "That which happened once with basic significance for the religious community is still present in its consequences, and the commemoration of the event renews these consequences in the faith of the worshipper."[3]

When reactualization occurs, the participants experience what it was like to go through some unrepeatable historical event. They experience that event through a ceremony or ritual. According to Noth,[4] reactualization involves six elements. First, the ceremony includes an interpretive narration. Second, it heavily emphasizes the Word of God. Third, the ritual will include certain elements of dramatic action. Fourth, all of this will take place in a recognized gathering of God's people. Fifth the whole ceremony deals with God's saving actions in history. Sixth, the ceremony *confronts the participants* with the promising and demanding Word of God. Dentan stated: "The ancient worshipper did not approach the cultus primarily to feed his intellect or stimulate an act of mental recollection; his purpose was to achieve actual participation in the events portrayed and existential involvement in the blessings proclaimed." He continued: "What such a ceremony would have meant, therefore, was that Yahweh himself appeared in the assembly, performing once again the mighty acts that brought the community into existence and continually sustained it, proclaiming anew his Torah—the way of life that he had ordained for it—dispensing the blessings and curses connected with its observance or non-observance, and personally accepting from his priests the sacrifices that were offered in his honor and for his pleasure."[5] Childs said: "[Re]Actualization occurs when the worshipper himself sees himself as a partaker in those non-repeatable historical events."[6] This rather technical discussion can be summarized in this statement: reactualization is "a means of showing the relevance of unique, unrepeatable historical events to contemporary man."[7]

The ancient Israelite, at Passover and similar times, confronted his past in such a way that the events became experiences of his own life. Those celebrations called him to decision as they did for his fathers. Moses declared: "It was not with our ancestors that the LORD made this covenant, but with us, with all of us who are alive here today" (Deut. 5:3). Later Moses confronted Israel with the significance of the exodus events: "Your eyes have seen all that the Lord did in Egypt to Pharaoh, to all his officials and to all his land. With your own eyes you saw those great trials, those signs and great wonders" (29:2-3). Now the fact is that most of those gathered in the plains of Moab had not seen what happened in Egypt. Only those who were between about 45 and 60 years old were old enough to remember what had occurred. Joshua, Caleb, and Moses were the only men of Israel over sixty since all the rest of their generation had died in the wilderness. Then how could Moses say, "With your own eyes saw. . ."?

Those who are familiar with the ritual of the Passover may already know the answer. In the Seder the host of the meal says,

In every generation each individual is bound to regard himself as if he had gone personally forth from Egypt, as it is said, 'And thou shalt relate to thy son on that day saying, this is on account of what the Eternal did for me, when I went forth from Egypt.' Thus it was not our ancestors alone, whom the Most Holy, blessed be he, then redeemed but us also did He redeem with them, as it is said, and He brought us forth from thence, in order to bring us in, that He might give us the land which He swore unto our ancestors.[8]

Every observant Jewish household treats the Passover celebration as though it were their own experience of deliverance from Egyptian bondage. The event itself is a long past, unrepeatable event. Yet through the means of the Passover Seder, all obedient Jews can know what it is like in their own experiences to go through the first Passover. This is reactualization.

The relevance of this discussion to baptism in Romans 6:3-4 should be clear. When we baptize, we are burying a crucified believer. As the believer enters the water, he experiences in his own life, what it was like for Christ to undergo death and burial. By faith the believer shares in Christ's crucifixion; in the waters of baptism, by faith he shares in Christ's burial.

Baptism is an apt symbol for our death and burial with Christ. It is appropriate not only because of its mode, immersion, but also because of its meaning elsewhere in the New Testament. A statement Paul made elsewhere helps us understand the significance of baptism: "They were all baptized into Moses in the cloud and in the sea" (1 Cor. 10:2). Many interpreters explain the preposition translated "into" in this verse as expressing the reason for baptism or its result. However, because of its use in other baptism contexts, it is better to understand it as expressing the sphere the baptized person enters. Those baptized into Moses came under his leadership, so baptism symbolizes Israel's identification with Moses. The Israelites became identified with him through the cloud and the sea. Baptism in John's ministry identified Israelites with those who have repented (Matt. 3:11). Baptism in the Great Commission identifies believers with each person of the Trinity (Matt. 28:19). Peter said that baptism identifies believers with those whose sins God has forgiven (Acts 2:38). Similarly, in Romans 6:3-4 baptism identifies believers with the death and burial of Christ.

It should be clear to anyone who has ever gone through immersion that the most important part of immersion is not going under the water. The most important part of immersion is coming out of the water! It is at this point in peculiar that we symbolize entry into the body of Christ. But it is at this point that we leave the place of death. In Israel's experience of baptism, Israel entered through the place of death to the place of life. When Egypt's soldiers tried to cross the Red Sea, they died. Baptism in water is a peculiarly appropriate symbol for death. The idea is not new. Similar ideas arose at times in Jewish thought. Edersheim described proselyte baptism as practiced by the Jews of Jesus' day. He said that baptism represented a complete change in legal status. The baptized convert should consider all connections of country, home, habits, and relations as changed—the old was buried in the waters of baptism. "This was carried out with such pitiless logic as not only to determine such questions as those of inheritance, but that it was declared that, except for the sake of not bringing proselytism into contempt, a proselyte might have wedded his own mother or sister. . ."[9]

When someone undergoes baptism, that person peculiarly enters the place of death. Now as one enters that place of death in Jesus' name, he identifies himself with His death. He has undergone burial with Him through baptism. There he has his own experience of what it was like for Jesus to die and enter the grave, and rising out of the water identifies him with Jesus' resurrection.

Our death does not mean that we cannot sin; it means that we no longer relate to anything as we once did. In fact in verse 6 Paul explained the significance of death with Christ. It means that we are no longer **slaves to sin.** Our death to sin means our slavery to righteousness. Death to sin means ability to live righteously.

We said before that the most significant part of immersion is not our *entry into* the water but our *leaving* the water. Similarly, our death with Christ is not the most significant part of our experience with Christ. If in immersion I remain long enough under the water, I will not only be in the place of death; I will certainly die. It is critical that I come out of the water. So also it is critical in the spiritual sense that I come out of the grave with Christ. So, having died and been buried with Christ and thus identified with Christ, I also arose with Him to "walk in newness of life" (6:4 KJV). *My death and resurrection with Christ make it impossible for me to continue in sin.*

Paul's answer to the question he posed in verse 1 is in two parts. He has said that we cannot continue in sin that grace might abound. The first reason he has given is that we have died with Christ to sin. In verses 4-6 he gave the second part of the answer: we live the res- urrected life in Christ. As we have shared in His death, we also share in His resurrection. In verse 4 the result of our death with Christ is that we "walk in newness of life" (**live a new life** in the NIV). We cannot continue in sin because in Christ's resurrection we have new resurrected life. Paul emphasized this again in verse 5, and then ex- plains its significance in verses 6-10. Since we have shared in His death, we will also share in His resurrection. Not only do we not con- tinue in sin, we have an entirely new relationship to sin. All that we were in Adam (our **old self**) **was crucifixion with him** to take away the power of sin. The result of nullifying our relationship with Adam is that we would **no longer be slaves to sin**. The dead have no more relationship to the world in which they died. And we have died to sin! This means that we no longer have the same relationship to it and thus we are free from it.

That statement includes at least two ideas. Those who have died cannot suffer punishment for breaking the law. On November 25, 1963 many people watched the television in horror as Jack Ruby murdered Lee Harvey Oswald, the accused assassin of President Kennedy. It would have solved so many problems and so much money if the government had only put Oswald on trial. Over five decades after his death, debate still rages about whether Oswald really assassinated the President. On the other hand, if they had tried and convicted Oswald, what could they have done to him? They could not execute him. He was already dead. They might have put him in jail, but what good would that do? Oswald was dead. The law and his crime held no more power over him.

Similarly, believers in Jesus Christ have died and risen with Him. Unlike Oswald, they have already paid, in their substitute, the penalty for sin. Christ has died once to sin, and He has risen from the dead; so death has no more power over Him. We, in Him, have also died to sin. We have risen in Him. Death, therefore, has no more power over us. He died to sin and lives to God, and so do we.

Our death and resurrection mean that sin's penalty, all of sin's penalty, is now irrelevant to us. In spiritual terms we are all Lee Harvey Oswalds. It would be as foolish for one who believes in Christ ever to come under sin's penalty again, just as it would be foolish for the government to put Oswald on trial. Also, since we are resurrected beings, sin has no more authority over us. We are no longer **slaves to sin**! Consequently, we have no more obligation to sin to obey it.

A few years ago I was teaching this passage in a home Bible study. When I got to this point, one of the women stopped me and said, "Then this makes a Christian's sin all the worse, because we don't have to sin." I had to agree with her. Unbelievers sin because they cannot help themselves. Paul defined sin as "unbelief" (Rom. 14:23). The lost are preeminently unbelievers, and their unbelief is the cause of their lost condition. Since sin is unbelief, they can do nothing but sin. Even the good things they do are sin, since they act in unbelief. But the justified are not unbelievers. We are people of faith. Faith now ought to mark and motivate every act of our lives. Now we do not have to sin. Now we have an entirely new relationship to everything in our experience. Now we are as dead to sin as we are dead to water. I can get into water. I can even stay in water for a time. But I cannot live in water. I am dead to it. Such is my relationship to sin. I can get into sin. I can even stay in sin for a time. But I cannot live in it any more. The justified can no more live in the atmosphere of sin than they can live in the atmosphere of water. Paul said, "Therefore, if anyone is in Christ, he is a new creature: the old things passed away; behold, new things have come" (2 Cor. 5:17, NASB). Even the world has changed for us, or rather it has a new relationship to us. All things are new, a truth Paul developed further in Romans 8:17-39.

When I was a new believer, I learned this passage from a different point of view. I learned an approach to the passage that someone called "positional truth." This interpretation said that we are dead with Christ, but not really. We have risen with Christ, but not really.

We are righteous in Christ, but not really. Our relationship to the Lord Jesus in His righteousness, death, and resurrection is our position before God. But the reality of our life on earth is that we are sinners. We are very much alive to sin, very much un-resurrected. In this view the purpose of sanctification is to bring my present sinful life on earth into harmony with my position before God. Thus sanctification meant obedience, and every act of disobedience proved that sanctification was idle in my life.

What we are seeing in this passage leads in an entirely new direction. We have already learned that at justification God declares us righteous. This is not just our position before God; it is our identity. We are not now sinners. We are righteous. The process of sanctification brings us not to righteousness but to maturity. The author of Hebrews exhorted his readers continue on to maturity (6:1). We do not grow to be more righteous, for in Christ we are the righteousness of God (2 Cor. 5:21). Rather we start from righteousness, and through sanctification we express more and more of the righteousness that we already are. Our lifestyle grows in obedience, but we are not therefore more righteous. We grow in righteousness, not in degree, but in expression. We grow from our righteous identity, not toward a righteous lifestyle. We need to know our righteousness to live before God.

In just the same way, we need to know our death and resurrection with Christ. We not only need to know this, we need to consider it to be true. This is why Paul said, "In the same way, count yourselves dead to sin but alive to God in Christ Jesus" (Rom. 6:11). This verse gives the first of three reasons why Christians struggle with sin. We do not recognize that we are actually **dead to sin.** Or we do not believe that we are indeed living by the power of Christ's resurrection life. We must become like Abraham (see comments on Rom. 4:16-21). He believed in a God who gives life to the dead. He believed in a God who calls things that do not exist into existence. He risked himself on God's promise that his dead body would produce a son from Sarah's dead womb. He watched the reality of his physical weakness change into a new reality determined by God's will and described by God's word. We Christians must learn that God's Word is more real and more potent than the reality of weakness we know so well. We believe ourselves incapable of righteousness.

Someone may object, "But I don't feel dead to sin! I don't feel free from sin's power. So how can such a thing be true?" Our death and resurrection with Christ are as true as our justification. Death and resurrection are not simply our position; they are our identity. "God's honor," Bridges said, "is to take precedence over our feelings."[10] The problem is that we have not learned faith. This is why I have made such a point of Abraham's faith. He knew a God who makes alive the dead and calls things into existence that do not exist. He simply believed that what God had promised He was able to do. Now we meet this teaching about our death to sin and our resurrection with Christ. Does God mean what He says? Is God able to break the power of sin in our lives? Can He enable me to live a life expressing the full righteousness He has given me? In chapter 4 we saw that Abraham's faith was a risk taking faith. Abraham made himself vulnerable because of God's self-revelation and watched his reality change.

We too must make ourselves vulnerable because of God's self-revelation so we can see our reality change. This is why we elaborated on Abraham's faith in chapter 4. Believers must understand Abraham's faith before they can understand their relationship to God. So the issue for us is clear. Will we take God so seriously that we put ourselves at risk for what we know of God? When temptation comes, even one of our pet temptations, will we take God seriously? When we see all the power of temptation and when we sense our own yearnings for sin, will we take God seriously? If we do, we will watch reality change. We will risk ourselves on a God who crucified and raised us together with Christ. We will watch as the power of pet temptations and our yearnings for sin fade as obedience grows. This is the meaning of Paul's command: **In the same way, count yourselves dead to sin but alive to God in Christ Jesus.**

In verses 12-13 Paul gave a second dynamic that will guarantee that Christians remain under sin's dominion, which is when we remain ignorant of our resurrection with Christ. We may not entrust ourselves to it—that is, we do not believe it. But then we will be likely to put ourselves at sin's disposal. How sad that we continue to offer ourselves to sin to fulfill its desires. Paul's two commands in these verses are about this problem, the first negative and the second positive.

The negative one is in verses 12-13a: **Therefore do not let sin reign in your mortal body so that you obey its evil desires. Do not offer any part of yourself to sin as an instrument of wickedness.** Christians can allow sin to be king in their bodies. This statement has two implications. First, sin relates especially to our bodies. I have developed and written about this more fully in chapter 7 where I have defined "flesh." Sin and flesh have a peculiar relationship to one another. Paul said in 8:23 that our bodies are not yet redeemed, so sin remains in the flesh.

The second implication of the statement is that we control or permit sin's reign in our lives. We do not have to sin. Yet we allow sin to become king by presenting ourselves to sin to accomplish its desires. Each of us has favored temptations, or perhaps not so favored ones. But we know, whatever we do, that eventually we will have to face some old habit, some old temptation that has beset us for years. We also know that we will face those temptations in special places or settings. Paul's instruction in verse 12 is simple. Avoid anyone, anything, any time, any place, where you are peculiarly susceptible to temptation. After all, you are dead to sin. How can you live anymore in it?! Why feed it any longer?

Yet it is not enough simply to avoid temptation.[11] We have, every one of us, known temptation when we least expected it. Thus Paul gave his positive instruction in verse 13b: **but rather offer yourselves to God as those who have been brought from death to life, and offer every part of yourself to him as an instrument of righteousness.** We should not present our bodies to sin; but we should present ourselves to God to become instruments of righteousness in His hands. The point is quite simple and down to earth. Because of our death to sin, we should look for opportunities to live out the righteousness that we are in Christ. As we fill our time living out our identity in Christ, we will have no time for sin. Thus Paul gave us a second means of avoiding sin, and a second means of remaining under sin's power.

Paul explains how this can be true in verse 14 while also giving the third means of remaining under sin's power. We have control over sin's reign in our lives, and the reason is in verse 14: **For sin shall no longer be your master,[12] because you are not under the**

law, but under grace. The reason we can control sin's reign in our lives is that we are **under grace.** Therefore, not only do we control sin's reign, but sin will not be lord over us. We have no obligation to sin at all. We are under grace.

This verse is extremely important for the context, for it controls the thought to the end of chapter 7. The reason for its importance is clearest if we consider its implications. Sin is not our master because we are not under law, but under grace. So if we are under law, what then? If under grace we are not under sin's dominion, then under law sin will be our master. Thus, trying to live by law will keep us enslaved to sin. Paul expanded on the implications of this verse from 6:15–7:25. He considered the positive implications of verse 14 in 6:15–7:6, and then the negative implications in 7:7-25.

EXCURSUS: ROMANS 6:15–7:25 AS PARENTHETIC
Life before God can never be lived
under law, only under grace.

Romans 6:15–7:25 is parenthetic to Paul's thought in chapters 5–8. The reason for the parenthesis is Paul's statement in verse 14 of chapter 6: **For sin shall no longer be your master, because you are not under the law, but under grace.** The implication of this statement is clear: sin can only rule those who are not under grace. Specifically, it can rule only over those who are under law. On this point, Lloyd-Jones writes:

> He seems to be striking another blow at the Law. He has already knocked it down, as it were, in chapter 5, verse 20; he is now trampling on it. At once his opponents take up the cudgels and say, 'Surely these are very wrong and very dangerous statements to make; surely if you are going to abrogate the Law and do away with it altogether, you are doing away with every guarantee of righteous and holy conduct and behaviour [sic]. Sanctification is impossible without the Law. If you treat the Law in that way and dismiss it, and rejoice in doing so, are you not encouraging lawlessness, and are you not almost inciting people to live

a sinful life?' Law, they believed, was the great guarantee of holy living and sanctification.[13]

The idea that the law is not the great guarantee of holy living and sanctification seems inconsistent with all human expectation and even contrary to reason. Most people believe that if we can give good men good laws, they will be better men. However, Paul's point is just the opposite. The power of the law actually stirs up sin in men (see Rom. 5:20).

Therefore, Paul's statement raises two questions that appear in the following context. First, one might think that the proclamation of the lordship of grace would lead to license to sin. Thus Paul posed the question of 6:15: **What then? Shall we sin because we are not under the law but under grace?** Paul's answer is in 6:16–7:6. Grace brings true freedom. The ability to sin is no freedom at all, but the most abject form of slavery. So grace, which is true freedom, cannot lead to more sinfulness. Second, if sin is not lord over those who are under grace, but will be lord over those under law, one might think that the law itself is sin. This is the background of the question posed in 7:7: **What shall we say, then? Is the law sinful?** Paul's answer is in 7:7b-12, and his conclusion is that law stirred up sin that brought death. But the law itself is **holy, righteous and good** (v. 12). The problem is not with the law, but with man's indwelling sin. The ideas in 7:11-12 raise a third question, **Did that which is good, then, become death to me?** (v. 13), and 7:13b–25 gives the answer. The law is not at fault, but indwelling sin fed by law. It is not the fault of the good that evil people pervert its use.

Therefore, the foremost issue raised in chapter 7 is whether anyone can live before God by law. The answer is that law only stirs up sin. Thus we can only live life before God by grace. Otherwise sin will dominate a person, even against his or her will.

These three questions with their answers are parenthetical to Paul's thought in Romans. In support of this idea, consider the connection implied in 8:1 where Paul introduced the chapter with the word **therefore: Therefore, there is now no condemnation for those who are in Christ Jesus.** The word **therefore** implies a connection with the preceding context. But attaching the word **there-**

fore to 7:25, achieves little sense. Consider carefully what Romans says: **So then, I myself in my mind am a slave to God's law, but in my sinful nature [lit. "my flesh"] a slave to the law of sin.** (I have explained the change from the NIV in my comments on chapter 7). Now go directly to, **Therefore, there is now no condemnation** in 8:1. How could Paul argue that anyone who is a slave to the law of sin possibly be free from condemnation? Further, 8:2 requires us not to relate the **therefore** of 8:1 to 7:25. In 8:2 Paul stated that **the law of the Spirit who gives life has set you free from the law of sin and death.** He specifically denied what he seems to have affirmed in 7:25.

In consequence of these observations it seems best, most natural, and most logical to connect **therefore** in 8:1, not to 7:25—in fact, not to anything in chapter 7— but rather, considering the previous discussion, we should connect **therefore** to 6:14. Note the easy connection and ready sense of connecting 6:14 with 8:1-2: **For sin shall no longer be your master, because you are not under the law, but under grace. . . Therefore, there is now no condemnation for those who are in Christ Jesus, because through Christ Jesus the law of the Spirit who gives life set you free from the law of sin and death.**

In sum, Paul is exploring the Christian life and the possible ways to live it. In the section 6:1-14 he shows that sin will not be characteristic of the life of those who are under grace. In 6:15–7:25 he shows that sin as a life characteristic is only possible when one is under law. But since the Christian is under grace (6:1-14), he is free to fulfill the law's decreed righteousness (8:4; cp. 3:31) and to live the life of the Spirit (8:5-16).

> d. **Believers, since they are not under law, will not go on sinning under grace since grace has set them free from sin through Christ's death and has given them in marriage to Christ to bear offspring for God (6:15–7:6).**

¹⁵What then? Shall we sin because we are not under the law but under grace? By no means! ¹⁶Don't you know that when you offer yourselves to someone as obedient slaves, you are slaves of

the one you obey—whether you are slaves to sin, which leads to death, or to obedience, which leads to righteousness? [17]But thanks be to God that, though you used to be slaves to sin, you have come to obey from your heart the pattern of teaching that has now claimed your allegiance. [18]You have been set free from sin and have become slaves to righteousness.

[19]I am using an example from everyday life because of your human limitations. Just as you used to offer yourselves as slaves to impurity and to ever-increasing wickedness, so now offer yourselves as slaves to righteousness leading to holiness. [20]When you were slaves to sin, you were free from the control of righteousness. [21]What benefit did you reap at that time from the things you are now ashamed of? Those things result in death! [22]But now that you have been set free from sin and have become slaves of God, the benefit you reap leads to holiness, and the result is eternal life. [23]For the wages of sin is death, but the gift of God is eternal life in Christ Jesus our Lord.

Shall we sin because we are not under the law but under grace?
Paul's answer is that people under grace do not continue in sin. (The verb **sin** is in the present tense, indicating continuous action.) Christ's death has freed them from sin and enslaved or married them to Christ to bear offspring to God (see 6:16–7:6). If we obey sin, then we prove ourselves to be under its lordship, and thus **under the law.** But God's grace has freed us from sin and has made us **slaves to righteousness.** The Roman Christians had proved this in their own experience. For they had known themselves **slaves to sin,** but they had come to freedom from sin and enslavement to righteousness. Now Paul encouraged them to treat themselves as **slaves to righteousness** to accomplish sanctification in their lives. They know that the fruit of sin is shame and death. So they also know, in mind and in life, the fruit of righteousness, and its result, **eternal life.**

Verses 15-23 raise the issue of our freedom. It is one of the Bible's key passages on freedom, so we must consider its contribution to our understanding. Theologically, we usually discuss human freedom as it contrasts with divine sovereignty. It is interesting that the Bible regularly associates statements about human freedom and

God's sovereignty without sensing or trying to solve any tension between the two (see Mark 14:21; Isa. 10:5-15; 45:1-4; Gen. 20:4-6). This is probably because our western interest in freedom is not of primary importance for the Bible.

The passage before us does not take up those issues. Freedom here relates only to sin or to righteousness. In fact, our passage teaches that all humanity is free. One group is free with respect to righteousness, and thus enslaved to sin. The other group is free with respect to sin, and thus enslaved to righteousness. We might almost conclude from this passage that for Paul, freedom involves slavery. One definition of freedom reads this way: freedom is "exemption from external control, interference, regulation, etc."[14] Such a definition may be helpful in this context. Slaves to sin are exempt from the control, interference, and regulation of righteousness. Slaves to righteousness are exempt from the control, interference, and regulation of sin.

Thus the only true freedom, so far as Romans 6 is concerned, is slavery. Slavery to sin (freedom from righteousness) is the most abject slavery. Sin binds its slave in the cycle of sin (Rom. 1:18-32). Under sin's slavery, sin begets more sin. Slavery to righteousness, on the other hand, is the fullest kind of liberty. Righteousness enables its slave to develop to his fullest potential, for it releases him from the control of sin. Indeed, slavery to sin, in the end, produces shame (Rom. 6:21) and death (v. 23). Slavery to righteousness, on the other hand, brings sanctification and eternal life (vv. 22-23).

We must recognize one other fact about this freedom and slavery: at the point of salvation, the slave to sin is not simply set free. This is important because of the nature of freedom from slavery in Roman society and law. One student of Roman slavery observed that the newly freed slave still had obligations to his old master: "As a condition of release from servile status the freedman might find himself bound to his patron by a nexus of obligations, summed up in the legal term *opera* [works!], as a result of which he continued to discharge various services for the patron for a certain length of time."[15] The freed slave in Roman society remained responsible to his former master for service. Therefore, when Paul addressed the believer's freedom from sin, he made it, not a manumission, but a new slavery—a slavery to righteousness. We are never finally freed. We remain in bondage all our lives. So it is indeed true for humanity that the only true freedom is in bondage.

When we enter our new slavery to righteousness, we are free from sin. We owe it no further "works" (*opera*!). We are no longer its slaves. This is similar to the position in which God Himself lives. He is free from sin and "enslaved" to righteousness. (In 6:19 Paul explained that he spoke in human terms: **I am using an example from everyday life because of your human limitations.**) Freedom for God is the ability to do what is right, but God is absolutely bound to do what is right! Thus, in a sense, He is utterly enslaved to righteousness. However this "slavery" is no failing or limitation at all in God. For Him the inability to sin is His absolute freedom. In fact, the ability to sin is no freedom at all; that is, it is the greatest bondage, the worst kind of slavery. The ability to sin is the most despotic form of limitation. Only the inability to sin is freedom. Therefore, when I am most the slave of righteousness, when I am most under the dominion, the reign, the lordship of righteousness, I am most free. So as I become more deeply enslaved to righteousness, I am becoming more like God.

This also is sanctification. Sanctification is not primarily our obedience to the commandments of Scripture, though it ultimately produces obedience. That idea is not an error of doctrine. Rather it is a misplaced emphasis. Sanctification is primarily becoming more and more like our God. Through sanctification, additionally, we do not become more righteous. We show more and more of the righteousness that we are through the justifying decree of God. We do not await some mystical experience that will immediately bring us into the blissful state of sanctification. We simply act out our identity in Christ, or as Paul said in verse 19, **offer yourselves as slaves to righteousness leading to holiness.** This is our freedom. This is our way to sanctification. This is the life of the justified.

The marvelous thing about all this is that this new freedom produces **eternal life.** We have usually thought of eternal life as endless life stretching on into the undefined future. Yet we must take a different perspective on eternal life. Eternity is not primarily endless existence. All humanity has endless existence. Even the lost at the great white throne judgment will receive bodies suited to endless existence in torment (see Rev. 20:11-15). So eternal life must refer to the quality of life we will live.[16] Some have pointed out the relation between the Greek adjective translated **eternal** (*aionios*) and the noun from which it comes (*aion*, "age"). The point of this relation is to say that the word eternal means "of or pertaining to an age." While this particular usage of the word does not appear in the New Testament, the idea is defensible. The life we receive as the goal of our slavery to righteousness is the life of the age to come, of the kingdom. It is the life of the age in which righteousness dwells (2 Pet. 3:13). This means that we who are free by faith, enslaved to righteousness, are free to live the life of the coming kingdom of God. We may live it already in this present evil age. Paul returned to this idea in Romans 13:11-14.

So this is how Paul described our freedom from sin. We are no longer its slaves, for we have moved into a new slavery to righteousness. He explained in Romans 7:1-6 how we have changed from one slavery to the other and the implications of the change.

Notes for Romans 6

[1]This statement identifies me as an immersionist. I follow that mode because it fits the Bible's imagery and data best. If you sprinkle or pour, you may skip this section—but I hope you won't!

[2]Brevard S. Childs, *Memory and Tradition in Israel*, p. 85.

[3]Helmer Ringgren, *The Faith of the Psalmists*, p. 100.

[4]Martin Noth, "The 'Representation' of the Old Testament Proclamation," pp. 76-88 in *Essays in Old Testament Hermeneutics*.

[5]R. C. Dentan, *The Knowledge of God*, p. 86.

[6]Childs, p. 83.

[7]Noth, p. 81.

[8]*Passover Haggadah*, p. 25.

[9]Alfred Edersheim, *The Life and Times of Jesus the Messiah*, 1:745-46.

[10]Jerry Bridges, *Trusting God*, p. 52.

[11]K. R. Bradley (*Slaves and Masters in the Roman Empire: A Study in Social Control*, p. 82) quoted Epictetus and provided a good background for Paul's ideas here. It refers to the difficulties the freed slave had to face: "Then he (the slave) is emancipated, and forthwith,

having no place to which to go and eat, he looks for someone to flatter, for someone at whose house to dine. Next he either earns a living by prostitution, and so endures the most dreadful things, and if he gets a manger at which to eat he has fallen into a slavery much more severe than the first; or even if he grows rich, being a vulgarian he has fallen in love with a chit of a girl, and is miserable and laments, and yearns for his slavery again. 'Why, what was wrong with me? Someone else kept me in clothes, and shoes, and supplied me with food, and nursed me when I was sick; I served him in only a few matters. But now, miserable man that I am, what suffering is mine, who am a slave to several instead of one!' (Epict. *Diss.* 4.1.35-37, Loeb translation)." Indeed it is not enough merely to avoid the old master. There must be some change of life, some change of loyalties, so that there is no desire for the old master and the old slavery.

[12]Other interpretations of this verb are possible. Some have interpreted it as an imperative (like the Ten Commandments) and have translated, "sin must no longer control you" (Goodspeed). Cranfield rejected this interpretation "on the grounds that the sentence would then be a lame repetition of the substance of v. 12, which would be quite out of place at this point" (1:319). Others have taken the statement as a "promise that those whom Paul is addressing will never again yield to sin" (Cranfield, 1:319). Lloyd-Jones took the statement eschatologically, that sin will one day not dominate Christians (*Romans: An Exposition of Chapter 6 The New Man*, 180-81). Finally, D. J. Moo (*Romans 1–8*, 404) listed the conditional interpretation (which he attributed to C. H. Dodd), which says that "if you stop letting sin reign (v. 12), it will have no mastery over you."

[13]Lloyd-Jones, p. 4.

[14]*Webster's Encyclopedic Unabridged Dictionary of the English Language*, 1989 ed., s.v., "freedom," p. 565.

[15]Bradley, p. 81.

[16]Louw and Nida (67.96) said, "In combination with [*zoe*, "life"] there is evidently not only a temporal element, but also a qualitative distinction."

¹Do you not know, brothers and sisters—for I am speaking to those who know the law—that the law has authority over someone only as long as that person lives? ²For example, by law a married woman is bound to her husband as long as he is alive, but if her husband dies, she is released from the law that binds her to him. ³So then, if she has sexual relations with another man while her husband is still alive, she is called an adulteress. But if her husband dies, she is released from that law and is not an adulteress if she marries another man.

⁴So, my brothers and sisters, you also died to the law through the body of Christ, that you might belong to another, to him who was raised from the dead, in order that we might bear fruit for God. ⁵For when we were in the realm of the flesh, the sinful passions aroused by the law were at work in us, so that we bore fruit for death. ⁶But now, by dying to what once bound us, we have been released from the law so that we serve in the new way of the Spirit, and not in the old way of the written code.

Romans 7:1-6 completes Paul's discussion of the question raised in 6:15. The paragraph gives his final summary of his answer, using the imagery of marriage and especially the Mosaic legislation on marriage. Moses had taught that a married woman may only marry again if her husband dies, in which case she is not **an adulteress.** Applied to the life of the justified, we must change Paul's illustration somewhat. First, it is not the husband who dies, as in his illustration, but the wife, that is, the believer. Thus the believer's relationship to the old husband, the law, comes to an end. Second, the wife-believer marries a new husband, **him who was raised from the dead.**

Here is the importance of Paul's teaching on the death and resurrection of the believer. Because we have died with Christ and arisen with Him, any relationship we might have had to the law has ended.

Now we are united with Christ. In the Bible, marriage has the purpose of **bearing fruit,** offspring. The Bible does not conceive that people would marry without attempting to have children. Indeed, children are God's blessing on a marriage. Therefore, our marriage to Christ can have only one result. There must be offspring for the union, that is, we **must bear fruit to God.** Paul expresses a similar idea to the Colossian believers, that they would "bear fruit in every good work" (1:10). The only offspring we can possibly bear to our new Husband is the offspring of righteousness. He does not, He cannot, bear fruit to sin. Therefore, since through death God has freed us from the law and has married us to Christ, we serve in **the new way[1] of the Spirit.** The **old way of the written code** is over and has ended.

In verse 5 Paul introduced for the first time in Romans the theological concept of the flesh. The Greek word for **flesh** (*sarx*) has appeared five times in the letter already (1:3; 2:28; 3:20; 4:1; 6:19), but not the theological concept. Until now it has always referred to the general human condition as living in fleshly substance. Here Paul contrasted our condition as married to Christ and enslaved in the freshness of the Spirit with our condition when we were **in the realm of the flesh,** (literally, "in the flesh"). We usually think of flesh as indwelling sin, and the New International Version of the Bible often translates this idea as "sinful nature." It is certainly true to see indwelling sin as a key element in the meaning of the word. But it is not enough, since flesh, law, and obedience appear together in pivotal relationships. Since the term is so important in the following context in Romans, I think it would be helpful to discuss it more fully.

One key place for defining "flesh" is Galatians 3:2-3. The book of Galatians is important because it deals with the same subject matter as Romans, namely justification by faith and living by faith. Paul asked, "I would like to learn just one thing from you: Did you receive the Spirit by the works the law, or by believing what you heard? Are you so foolish? After beginning by means of the Spirit, are you now trying to finish by means of the flesh?" We can interpret these verses in at least two ways: one sees four ways to live the Christian life; the other sees only two ways of life. The works of the law, the hearing of faith, the Spirit, and the flesh may be four unrelated ways for believers to live their lives before God. On the other hand, they certainly relate to one another in Paul's mind. If they do relate to one another, he has given us two paired ways of life. One way of life he calls the hearing of faith linked with the Spirit. He calls the other the works of the law linked with the flesh. But what would such a pairing imply?

The implication of pairing Spirit with hearing of faith is that the Holy Spirit is the one who teaches us to live by faith. That is precisely Paul's point in Romans 8, where those who walk by the Spirit fulfill the righteous decree of the law (v. 5). Those who walk by the flesh do not. In Romans, walking by the Spirit cannot simply refer to obedience, for obedience is not the primary point. In fact every self-righteous Pharisee sought obedience and aimed at fulfilling the law. But Romans says that no mere Pharisee can fulfill the law. The Pharisee faced an impossibility through the weakness of his flesh. Walking by the Spirit must refer to living by faith, for only faith can fulfill the law. Paul said this as well: "Do we, then, nullify the law by this faith? Not at all! Rather, we uphold the law" (3:31). Paul also said that "those who are led by the Spirit of God are the sons of God" (8:14). What does the Spirit lead them to do? Does the Spirit lead them to buy Pepsodent toothpaste instead of Crest? In the context, it must mean that the Spirit leads them to live by faith and not by law. For the Spirit's leading does not bring us to fear, as a life of law obedience would, but to an attitude of sonship. This is how we know our Father's intimate care for us. Thus, the relationship in Galatians 3:2-3 between Spirit and faith is that the Spirit leads us to live by faith.

But what is the relationship between flesh and works of law? I would suggest that it is the same as between the Spirit and faith. The flesh is what leads us to live by law. Notice what Paul said in Romans 7:5, "When we were in the flesh, the passions of sins which are through the law were at work in our members to bear fruit to death" (my own translation). It is this element of flesh that we have not fully recognized, for flesh is not simply indwelling sin. It is also what we might call "desire for law-righteousness."

Calling this aspect of the flesh a "desire for law-righteousness" might lead to a misconception. It might suggest that all who are in the flesh wish to please God by keeping His law. That notion is certainly not true. Rather every human being and every human society have always placed proper behavior high in any priority list for getting on in the world. Every religion in human history has offered its adherents blessing if they obey the rules of its deity and cursing if they do not. Every human society in the world has offered promotion in its ranks to those who achieve the society's ideals. They also demote or exclude those who do not. Even criminal societies have rules that their members must obey. Why does humanity fixate on behavioral rules? If God is preeminently interested in faith, why is humanity so interested in works?

God created humanity to desire to keep His commandments. Genesis 2 recounts God's creation of man and woman to live upon the earth. We might conceive of God reasoning with Himself this way: "Now I'm going to create a human and place him on the earth. I'm going to give him a commandment. Shall I give him any desire to keep the commandment or not?" Is it possible that a just and holy God, a God supreme in goodness and righteousness, would not give His creature a desire to please Him? That is unthinkable. So when He gave His creature a desire to please Himself, He gave him a desire to keep His law. (The command not to eat the fruit has all the characteristics of law that we have already seen.) The commandment has a demand for obedience and a threat for disobedience. We might call this desire to please a desire for law-righteousness. Now before sin entered into the world, desire for law-righteousness would be good. But once sin entered the world and the heart of mankind, it corrupted every desire for law-righteousness.

Linking desire for law-righteousness with indwelling sin produces every kind of lawlessness, every kind of sin. It produces every kind of wickedness known to man. It was those who wished to abide by the law who handed Jesus over to the Romans for crucifixion. It was the church that taught the need for obeying the law of God that led the Crusades and the Inquisition. Indeed, in Romans it is the self-righteous, those who make their boast in the law, who through their transgression of the law dishonor God (2:23). Every person on the face of the earth wants to do something that will make himself or herself worthy, indispensable, and accepted in the group to which he or she belongs. This is part of the scandal of the gospel, that people can do nothing that will commend them to God. Most of us remember the old song "At the Cross." In it there used to be a line that read,

"Would He devote that sacred head for such a worm as I?" Some of our hymnals have changed the song to read, "Would He devote that sacred head for sinners such as I?" The story goes that pastor D. B. Barnhouse made the comment that the song was changed because "man must preserve some shreds of dignity." Both terms are degrading for us proud human beings—though "sinner" is perhaps less so—but both are accurate since we are tormented by indwelling sin.

The point we are trying to make is that flesh has two sub-concepts associated with it. In the flesh are indwelling sin and a desire for law-righteousness, as suggested in Galatians 3:2-3. If the Spirit leads us to live by faith, then the flesh leads us to live by law. It makes no difference which law. God tells mankind that we cannot be right in His eyes by keeping the law, but man shakes his fist, sullied by sin, in God's face and says, "Oh yes I can. Just You watch!" Man does not seek to keep God's law. He offers laws of his own making to God as a means of righteousness with Him. Jesus said: "Isaiah was right when he prophesied about you hypocrites; as it is written: 'These people honor me with their lips, but their hearts are far from me. They worship me in vain; their teachings are merely human rules'" (Mark 7:6-8). Our fleshly desire for law-righteousness drives us to find some standard that we can keep to be acceptable.

Notice what Paul said about being in the flesh: **the sinful passions aroused by the law were at work in us** (Romans 7:5). This statement highlights another fact about the flesh. Because of its desire for law-righteousness, it longs for law. It seizes law wherever it can find law, because it yearns for a righteousness it can do. But because flesh also includes indwelling sin, flesh cannot accomplish its desire. Indwelling sin becomes active by law. Later in this chapter we find that law is the food on which indwelling sin lives, and flesh hungers for law because of its desire for law-righteousness.

The final observation we must make on this verse relates to the opening clause of the verse: **when we were in the realm of the flesh.** The idea here appears again in 8:9-10. Those who have died and risen with Christ are not in the flesh. We have died to the power of indwelling sin. Paul has already said (6:6) that all that we were in Adam died in our crucifixion with Christ. The result is that our co-crucifixion with Christ has made the body of sin (the flesh) powerless.

That means that we are no longer slaves to sin. Sin will not be lord over us who are not under law but under grace (6:14). We have died as Christ died, which was "to sin once for all" (6:10). We have risen as Christ rose, and we live to God. We are no longer in the flesh.

The meaning of this statement will only become fully clear as we proceed through the rest of chapter 7 and chapter 8. But here is the summary. Being no longer in the flesh has two consequences. First, we have come to know peace with God through faith in Jesus, resting in the righteousness He gives. Paul made the same point in Philippians 3:9, where he expressed what drove him in life: "and be found in him, not having a righteousness of my own that comes from the law, but that which is through faith in Christ—the righteousness that comes from God on the basis of faith." We are no longer in the flesh. This means that we have despaired of our works and placed all our hope in Christ. It means that we seek acceptance with God—not through our works—but only through relationship with Jesus Christ. Obeying commands is not the means of life for us. The means of life, life itself, is simply Christ, knowing Him, loving Him, relating to Him.

Second being no longer in the flesh means that we have despaired of our ability to overcome sin. When we were in the flesh, indwelling sin bore fruit for death through the law. But in Christ, by His Spirit, that is, by faith, the body of sin becomes powerless. We are "married" to Christ, and we bear fruit to God. Thus we serve not through the obsolete letter but through the new way of the Spirit.

e. The law is not itself sin, but sin can only exercise its dominion in a world of law (7:7-12).

⁷What shall we say, then? Is the law sinful? Certainly not! Nevertheless, I would not have known what sin was had it not been for the law. For I would not have known what coveting really was if the law had not said, "You shall not covet." ⁸But sin, seizing the opportunity afforded by the commandment, produced in me every kind of coveting. For apart from the law, sin was dead. ⁹Once I was alive apart from the law; but when the commandment came, sin sprang to life and I died. ¹⁰I found that the very commandment that was intended to bring life ac-

tually brought death. [11]For sin, seizing the opportunity afforded by the commandment, deceived me, and through the commandment put me to death. [12]So then, the law is holy, and the commandment is holy, righteous and good.

Romans 7:7-25 contains one of the most controversial passages of Romans. The following is a brief review of the interpretations offered for this passage, though there are many others.[2] I have pursued the road less traveled in interpreting the passage. Two views of the passage have commanded wide assent. One view is perhaps the most common view in the evangelical community. This view interprets the passage as describing the struggle with the sin nature, and all Christians who have not appropriated the filling of the Spirit experience it. Many who have taken this position argue that no lost man delights in God's law (see 6:22). They claim that only saved people would want to do what is good (see 6:19), even though they are not entirely able to do it. This certainly seems to be the condition of the Christian. Christians delight in God's law in the inward man but find sin constantly present within them (see 6:22). Further, the present tenses of verses 14–25 seem to suggest that the passage describes Paul's present Christian experience. Since Romans 7 comes amid a discussion on the Christian life that began in chapter 5, it would appear most reasonable to relate this passage to Christian living. Indeed, it is the testimony of many Christians in the history of the church that they have struggled regularly with sin. Finally, other passages that teach the same idea (e.g., Rom. 8:23; Gal. 5:17) seem to support this view.

A second view sees the passage as describing the struggle with sin experienced by the lost man who has never come to know Christ. Shedd recommended this view[3]. Supporters suggest that we should visualize Paul as a child growing up in a home that read and honored the Bible. His parents taught him the great stories of Abraham, Joseph, Moses, David, Elijah and the rest, and he delighted in them all. For him in those early years, God was the mighty, loving benefactor of Israel. He deserved nothing less from His people than their total love and allegiance. His child's heart burst with pride and admiration of his God. As he grew he came under instruction from God's law. As the law met him, he felt more and more distanced from the God of his childhood. Finally, in the study of the law, he awakened to his own responsibility for obedience. He found that the law had robbed him of the intimacy he had felt for God. As time passed he found that the law stirred up within him a force that he had not recognized, the power of sin. The life he had known with God was dead forever. The law had stirred up sin within him, and by it killed him (see vv. 8-11).

The supporters of this view have given the following evidence. While some say that no lost man ever delights in God's law, all Pharisees did (and do) delight in it. Further, Paul describes himself peculiarly in verse 14, especially considering what he had already said in chapter 6. Paul was sold under sin and characterized himself by the cry "wretched man" (v. 24). He was in slavery to the law (v. 25), dead under law (vv. 9-11), unable to practice righteousness (vv. 15-16), and a captive to the law of sin (v. 23). Each of these descriptions is difficult if Paul viewed himself as saved in this passage. But the proponents of this view suggest that the past tenses of verses 7-13 support their position. Proponents also point out that this view provides a proper contrast with the "now" of 8:1.

John Murray championed a third view, which sees the passage as describing the struggle with sin experienced by both the lost and the saved. Verses 7-12 describe the condition of the lost person, while verses 13-25 describe the saved person's struggle with sin.[4] The support for this view appears in the support for the other two views.

However, problems exist with each of these views—problems that arise because they conflict with the context. The first view, that Paul described the Christian's struggle with sin, contradicts each of chapters 5–8, and 5:21 is particularly difficult for this view: "as sin reigned in death, so also grace might reign through righteousness to bring eternal life." It is difficult to see how grace reigns through righteousness when the believer cannot do the good that he wants to.

This view creates problems in several places in chapter 6. In verses one to five believers are dead to sin and alive to God in Christ (vv. 1-55), but this interpretation of chapter 7 makes sin seem remarkably alive. Paul said that we were crucified with Christ (v. 6), and the body of sin is now powerless and we are no longer slaves to sin. But Paul described himself as sold under sin (7:14) and the slave of sin (7:25)! Paul made quite a case in 6:7-9 that we share Christ's condition—that He died once to sin and now lives to God. How could this possibly be the condition of believers who cannot overcome sin, who cannot do the good that they want to do? Can this be the condition of one who finds "the law at work: Although I want to do good, evil is right there with me" (7:21)? How can this be the condition that we share with Christ? How can it be true that we can control sin's reign in our lives through our death with Christ (6:12) when we cannot control the outbreak of sin in our lives? How can we be slaves to sin when Paul has so decisively declared that sin will not be lord over us since we are not under law but under grace (6:14)? Finally, how could Paul say that we are free from sin's dominion (6:18, 22), when he affirmed of himself that he is a slave to sin?

Problems also arise in the earlier part of chapter 7. In verse 4 Paul said that we have married Him who was raised from the dead to bear fruit to God. Is the work of Christ in our lives so fruitless, so ineffective, that sin overcomes it? And in verse 6 he said that we are free from the law since we died to it (see 6:9-10). He affirmed that we are no longer in the flesh; instead, we bear fruit to God.

Finally, problems with this view arise in chapter 8. First, this chapter begins with "therefore," which introduces conclusions that are valid because of preceding information. But the idea that sin masters us cannot be the background for the idea that "there is now no condemnation for those who are in Christ Jesus" (v. 1). If anything, sin's mastery over us should bring us *into* condemnation. Second, Paul declared that the "law of the Spirit who gives life has set you free from the law of sin and death" (v. 2). But Paul also said that he was a slave to the law of sin (7:25). How can both be true? Third, those who live by the Spirit fulfill the righteousness of the law (8:4). It is not impossible for them. So how was Paul was so overcome by sin in chapter 7?

The sum of what we have been saying is this. This first proposed interpretation contradicts Paul's teachings in Romans 5–8. Since the Bible is the Word of God, it cannot contain any errors or contradictions. So any interpretation that imposes contradictions in the text must, by definition, be an incorrect interpretation. For the reasons we have set out above, I have rejected this interpretation. We must seek some other way to understand the text that does not contradict some other passage in Romans.

The second view sees Paul as describing his experience growing up in a Jewish home. The main problem with this view is that at this point in Romans it is out of place. While discussing the life of the justified by faith, why would Paul discuss again the lost man's powerlessness in sin? While one might devise some way of answering this objection, it would be important to seek a closer tie to the immediate context than this view makes possible.

The third view is that verses 7–12 describe the experience of the lost man confronted by the demands of law, and it is not the Mosaic law but law in general that is meant. But verses 13–25 describe the experience of the saved man. Although no less a scholar than John Murray promoted the view, it does not do justice to the passage. It runs afoul of the same objections as the previous alternatives have. Indeed, to hold this view requires a redefinition of law, a redefinition that is unwarranted in the context. For if Paul was not referring to the Mosaic law, as Murray claimed, then the apostle has chosen a very strange way of expressing himself. As a result, we must seek some other way of dealing with the interpretation of Romans 7.

My view is similar to the one Lloyd-Jones suggested (see above). The issue raised in chapter 7 is whether anyone can live before God by law. The answer is that law only stirs up sin. Thus we can only live life before God by grace. Otherwise sin will dominate us, even against our will. Thus the passage is not primarily discussing anyone's struggle with sin. It is raising the issue of the impossibility of living before God by law, the issue under discussion since chapter 1. The issue in 7:7-12 is that law, while not evil in itself, becomes the tool of our indwelling sin to produce acts of sin. The issue in 7:13–25 is that law, while it is not itself the cause of our death, is the means of keeping us under sin's dominion. Therefore, we cannot do the good that we desire. These are the only questions Paul asked, and his answers are only for these two questions. Any other questions are extraneous to his point.

Since Paul said that sin will not be lord over us because we are not under law but under grace, someone might conclude that the law is itself sin (7:7). Paul's response to that question is a categorical denial. Indeed, as he concluded this paragraph, he said that **the law is holy, and the commandment is holy, righteous and good.** It is not the law that causes sin to be lord over people. It is not the law that is the problem. Human sin is the problem. A car is a wonderful tool, even though it can be abused and misused. Yet we do not conclude that cars are evil because some people misuse them. Similarly, the law is good, but sin can and regularly does misuse the law, as explained in verses 7-11. As already shown, the flesh includes two dynamic impulses: one, a desire for law-righteousness; the other, indwelling sin. It is this indwelling sin that lies in wait for law, since indwelling sin feeds on law and becomes powerful by law. This is precisely what Paul here (v. 8) affirmed: **For apart from the law, sin was dead**; and again, **when the commandment came, sin sprang to life.**

Indeed, Paul said that he would not even have known sin except through the law (v. 7). Some of the translations deal with this passage in a way that is inconsistent with this paragraph. They are hesitant to make the point Paul clearly made here. Law feeds indwelling sin and brings it to life in us. They want Paul's knowledge of sin to be nothing more than a recognition of what sin is.[5] Verse 8 illuminates the meaning of verse 7 here in a way that should not lead us astray: **But sin, seizing the opportunity afforded by the commandment, produced in me every kind of coveting.** Paul's knowledge of sin is not merely mental recognition that an act is sin. The knowledge of sin in Romans 7 is much the same as the knowledge of good and evil in Genesis 3. It is the experience of what sin is. Paul fixed on covetousness as the sin that caught him.[6] The law came to him with the commandment, **You shall not covet.**[7] Indwelling sin laid hold of it to produce coveting in his life. **Without the law, sin is dead,** so indwelling sin cannot act and cannot exercise power in our lives without law. Law is its food; it is the air it breathes. When Paul said in verses 9-10 that when **sin sprang to life and I died,** his point is that under the law he became spiritually powerless and sin regained its dominion over him. So the law is not at fault. Law, as I have said, is in itself wonderful. But it is not adapted to help people struggling with indwelling sin to become holy. It is itself **holy, righteous and good.** But all the law can do is stir up sin and make it active in the life of anyone who uses it. The fault lies not with law, but with indwelling sin. It was sin that took advantage of the law. It was sin that deceived Paul by the law. It was sin that by the law killed Paul (v. 11).

> f. The good law did not become death for Paul, since
> indwelling sin uses the law to produce acts of sin that
> he hates (7:13-25).

[13]Did that which is good, then, become death to me? By no means! Nevertheless, in order that sin might be recognized as sin, it used what is good to bring about my death, so that through the commandment sin might become utterly sinful. [14]We know that the law is spiritual; but I am unspiritual, sold as a slave to sin. [15]I do not understand what I do. For what I want to do I do not do, but what I hate I do. [16]And if I do what I do not want to do, I agree that the law is good. [17]As it is, it is no longer I myself who do it, but it is sin living in me. [18]For I know that good itself does not dwell in me, that is, in my sinful nature. For I have the desire to do what is good, but I cannot carry it out. [19]For I do not do the good I want to do, but the evil I do not want to do—this I keep on doing. [20]Now if I do what I do not want to do, it is no longer I who do it, but it is sin living in me that does it.

[21]So I find this law at work: Although I want to do good, evil is right there with me. [22]For in my inner being I delight in God's law; [23]but I see another law at work in me, waging war against the law of my mind and making me a prisoner of the law of sin at work within me. [24]What a wretched man I am! Who will rescue me from this body that is subject to death? [25]Thanks be to God, who delivers me through Jesus Christ our Lord!

So then, I myself in my mind am a slave to God's law, but in my sinful nature a slave to the law of sin.

But now it appears that Paul has made another almost heretical statement about the law. He said in verse 10: "I found that the very commandment that was intended to bring life actually brought death." This raised another question: **Did that which is good, then, become death to me?** But Paul emphatically declared that the law did not become death for him: **By no means!** The reason is that indwelling sin used law to produce acts of sin bringing death, and sin brought death by the good law to prove how sinful sin is (v. 13b).

Observe the prominence Paul gave to the law in this verse. The sinfulness of sin becomes clear through the commandment.

In verses 14-20, Paul denied that he complied fully with sin. As a whole person, he is not the source of his sins, for his sins come from indwelling sin. He was **sold as a slave to sin.** This means he was fleshly, and so are we. That condition means that we have indwelling sin and desire for law-righteousness. In that condition Paul could do nothing but sin. He was convinced of the law's spirituality, but he found himself committing the sin he hated. Indeed, he did not even understand[8] all that he was doing (v. 15). He wanted to do what was right, but he consistently found himself doing what he hated. He knew the desire to do what was right, but he also knew nothing of doing it (v. 18). Amid his spiritual perplexity, he could say **in my inner being I delight in God's law,** which shows that he did not fully endorse his sin. These ideas require us to discuss two related subjects.

First, it seems that Paul was trying to excuse his sin, which he wasn't. Such a reading of this passage is seriously mistaken. Paul was explaining exactly where his sin originated. Though he as a whole person did the sin, the "organic" cause of his sin is his flesh, his indwelling sin. We may illustrate his point by reference to sight. When I see something, I as a person do the seeing. It is not my eye or my brain that sees. That fact is clear. If you took my eye or brain out of my head and laid it on the table, no sight could occur. But when we want to locate the function of sight, we may say that the eye "sees." I must give my eye the proper conditions under which to operate, but it is the organ that allows sight to occur for me. Just so, Paul located here the function of sinning: it is an act of the whole person, and the whole person provides the proper conditions under which sin may operate. But the function of sin is located "in my flesh" (v. 18; NIV, "in my sinful nature"). It is the flesh, indwelling sin (see vv. 17, 20) that "sins." So under what conditions can indwelling sin go to work to produce acts of sin?

Second, we need to understand the role the law plays in this passage. Paul recognized its spiritual quality (v. 14) and connected it with that his condition of being sold under sin. Further, in verse 16 he testified that he delighted in the law of God. Considering what we saw in 6:1–7:12, we ought to conclude that the source of his bondage is this very delight in the law of God. Paul said that we are no longer slaves to sin as a result of crucifixion with Christ (6:6), and that sin will not be lord over us since we are not under law (6:14). This means that if we try to live by law, sin will be lord over us. We have died to the law through Christ's body and have married Him to bear fruit to God (7:4). Thus we serve no longer in the outdated way, the letter of the law, but in the freshness of the Spirit. Finally, in 7:7-11 he stated five times that indwelling sin becomes active under the influence of the law.[9] The problem that Paul described in 7:14-20 became possible because of his commitment to the law. The flesh hungers for law because of its desire for law-righteousness. When we feed it law, it must stir up indwelling sin that lives in the atmosphere of law. So it is no wonder that Paul did not understand his lifestyle. He desired and delighted in the righteousness of the law, but he watched himself producing the very sin the law condemns. Thus, he was not a fully compliant slave in committing sin.

Therefore, as long as Paul delighted in the law of God inwardly, evil was constantly present with him. It was at odds with **the law of my mind,** he said. It shamefully imprisoned him to the law of sin in his being (7:21-23). Here is abject slavery, the very slavery from which Paul has taught us to believe we are free (6:15–7:6). He delighted in the law inwardly (7:22), but watched, almost as a bystander, as **another law at work in me** took him captive (v. 23). Cranfield concluded that this other law is in contrast with the law of God, so it cannot be the law of God. He identified this law as the power and authority expressed by sin in Paul's life.[10]

While this interpretation is possible, another interpretation seems better in context. This law is not **another** in the sense of having nothing to do with the law of God but simply views the same law from a different perspective. The words **God's law** describe the law as it reveals God's holy will and righteous demands. The end of the verse further defines the phrase **another law at work in me** as **the law of sin at work within me.** The **law of sin** in this case is the law that stirs up sin.[11] This interpretation views the law of God, now not in its revealing capacity, but in its capacity of food for indwelling sin. What could be a more wretched life than this, delighting in God's law but enslaved through it to sin?

Therefore, Paul cried out, **What a wretched man I am! Who will rescue me from this body that is subject to death?** The first part of the verse (7:25a) is a parenthetical statement. It reviews chapters 3–4 and anticipates chapter 8. Thus Paul reminded us that deliverance from sin is not by obedience.[12] Our deliverance is only **through the Jesus Christ our Lord.** It is His atoning work that delivers us from the penalty of sin. It is His righteousness that delivers us from the need to earn God's favor. It is self-abandoning faith in Him that lays hold of it all, and by faith God frees us from sin and the law.

In the rest of verse 25 Paul finally summarized the ground of his plight: **So then, I myself in my mind am a slave to God's law, but in my sinful nature** ["flesh"] **a slave to the law of sin.** As long as we are slaves to God's law with our minds, we will remain slaves to the law that produces sin. We can never live life before God, all that God intended life to be, by law or obedience. Jesus said, "I have come that they might have life, and have it to the full" (John 10:10). Abundant life comes from Him, for He alone is life (John 11:25; 14:6). We live life by God's grace and by faith in Jesus Christ alone. No obedience can enhance it. Obedience is only its effect, not its cause. He is life.

Notes for Roman 7

[1]Louw and Nida (58.70) defined the Greek word used here as "the state of being new and different, with the implication of superiority." They add a footnote that the word implies a contrast with what is obsolete.

[2]C. E. B. Cranfield (*A Critical and Exegetical Commentary on the Epistle to the Romans*, ICC [Edinburgh: T&T Clark, 1975], 1:344) listed the following options for interpretation:

(i) that it is autobiographical, the reference being to Paul's present experience as a Christian;

(ii) that it is autobiographical, the reference being to his past experience (before his conversion) as seen by him at the time referred to;

(iii) that it is autobiographical, the reference being to his pre-conversion past but as seen by him now in the light of his Christian faith;

(iv) that it presents the experience of the non-Christian Jew, as seen by himself;

(v) that it presents the experience of the non-Christian Jew, as seen through Christian eyes;

(vi) that it presents the experience of the Christian who is living at a level of the Christian life which can be left behind, who is still trying to fight the battle in his own strength [cp. Charles Hodge, *Epistle to the Romans* [Eerdmans, 1950], p. 213)];

(vii) that it presents the experience of Christians generally, including the very best and most mature.

An eighth view was expounded by F. L. Godet (*Commentary on Romans* (Grand Rapids: Kregel Publications, 1977; reprint), p. 273-274), who interpreted the passage as dealing with the experience of the "carnal heart of man" trying to be sanctified by keeping the law.

Cranfield believed the best interpretation is a combination of (i) and (vii), leading him to interpret the passage in terms of the "losing" battle that all Christians fight with sin throughout their lives. He cited other writers who have supported this interpretation: Methodius, Ambrose, Ambrosiaster, Augustine, Aquinas, Luther, Calvin, Barth, Nygren, Barrett, and Murray.

[3]William G. T. Shedd, A Critical and Doctrinal Commentary upon the Epistle of St. Paul to the Romans (New York: Charles Scribner's Sons, 1879), 178.

[4]John Murray, *Romans*, p. 255.

[5]Compare *The Twentieth Century New Testament*, "On the contrary, I should not have learnt what sin is, had it not been for Law;" or Phillips, "But it must in fairness be admitted that I should never have had sin brought home to me but for the Law;" or the Living Bible, "No, the law is not sinful but it was the law that showed me my sin."

[6]I have often wondered, though it cannot ever be proven, whether Paul was the rich young ruler, for his was the same sin. The rich young ruler and Paul are much alike in their background.

[7]This is what demonstrates that this passage deals with the law of God, the Mosaic law, and not with some abstract principle of law. Murray's view is that Paul discussed the latter, especially in 6:14. "'Law' in this case must be understood in the general sense of law as law. . . Law must be understood, therefore, in much more general terms of law as commandment" (Murray, pp. 228-29).

[8]Cranfield (1:358) suggested that this word might better be translated "acknowledge," meaning Paul was denying his full complicity in the acts that indwelling sin produced in his life.

[9]Consider the following statements from that passage: "I would not have known what sin was had it not been for the law" (v. 7); "But sin, seizing the opportunity afforded by the commandment, produced in me every kind of coveting" (v. 8); "For apart from the law, sin was dead" (v. 8); "but when the commandment came, sin sprang to life and I died" (v. 9); and "For sin, seizing the opportunity afforded by the commandment, deceived me, and through the commandment put me to death" (v. 11).

[10]Cranfield, 1:364. Moo (p. 491), however, pointed out that there is a new identification of "another law" gaining ground, which is that all the references to the law in 7:22-25 "refer to the Mosaic law or. . . to the law of God generally." He rejected this view on the basis of the other law mentioned in v. 23.

[11]For the "Greeked" (those who have studied Greek), this would be the genitive of product. Martin Luther held a similar view. In his Heidelberg Disputation, Thesis 1 (see Timothy F. Lull, ed., *Martin Luther's Basic Theological Writings*, pp. 34-35) he said, "The law of God, the most salutary doctrine of life, cannot advance man on his way to righteousness, but rather hinders him." Then in explanation of his thesis, he said, "This is made clear by the Apostle in his letter to the Romans (3 [:21]): 'But now the righteousness of God has been manifested apart from the law." St. Augustine interpreted this in his book, *The Spirit and the Letter (De Spiritu et Littera):* 'Without the law, that is, without its support." In Romans 5 [:20] the Apostle states, "Law intervened, to increase the trespass," and in Romans 7 [:9] he adds, 'But when the commandment came, sin revived.' For this reason he calls the law a law of death and a law of sin in Romans 8 [:2]. Indeed, in II Cor. 3[:6] he says, 'the written code kills,' which St. Augustine throughout his book, *The Spirit and the Letter,* understands as applying to every law, even the holiest law of God."

[12]Cranfield made an amazing statement for such an insightful commentator (1:360) regarding v. 17: "God requires not ineffectual sentiments but obedient deeds."

ROMANS 8

Beginning in 8:1, Paul finally moved on to explain the fullness of life that God has given us in Christ. The chapter divides into two basic parts: verses 1-17, and verses 18-39. In verses 1-17, Paul explained our freedom from condemnation and our experience of God's intimate fatherly love for us, which makes us joint heirs with Christ. Verses 1-17 can be divided into three parts: verses 1-4 explain our freedom from condemnation through faith; verses 5-11 demonstrate the life of the Spirit; and verses 12-17 explain that the Spirit calls and teaches us to live by faith and not by law. The Spirit teaches us to know God's fatherly love that has made those who suffer with Christ joint heirs with Him. Verses 18-39 raise the issue of Christian suffering that Paul had already introduced in chapter 5. Suffering plays a significant part in the Christian life, the life of faith. We as believers are righteous in God's eyes and joint heirs with Jesus Christ. Yet we must suffer, for suffering is the condition of gaining the inheritance with Him. Suffering proves our faith as fire proves gold. While it causes us to groan as we await our redemption, suffering brings great hope for us since we know that God has eternally planned everything to conform us to Christ (vv. 18-39). This section further divides into four parts: verse 18, verses 19-27, verses 28-30, and verses 31-39. Verse 18 poses the basic point that our necessary suffering should not deter us from the life of faith. Indeed, it is not worth comparing with the glory that will be revealed in us. Verses 19-27 show the greatness of that glory—from the groanings of nature as it awaits our revelation as the children of God, from our groanings as we await the redemption of our bodies, and from the groanings of the Holy Spirit as He intercedes for us. Verses 28-30 tell us that all possible sufferings produce something good for us. God has included all our sufferings in His eternal plan to make us like Christ. Verses 31-39 conclude Paul's whole discussion of the life of faith. From all he has said, we can conclude that we are indeed at peace with God. He has freely given us everything. Nothing can separate us from the love of God. Here is the life of faith-righteousness.

> g. **Therefore, we who live by faith in Christ are not condemned, but we live the life of the Spirit of God who will raise us from the dead, giving us His fatherly love as we suffer with Christ, showing that we are joint heirs with Him (8:1-17).**
>> (1) **There is no condemnation for those in Christ Jesus since He gives us His Spirit to fulfill the requirement of the Law through faith, not through works (8:1-4).**

[1]Therefore, there is now no condemnation for those who are in Christ Jesus, [2]because through Christ Jesus the law of the Spirit who gives life has set you free from the law of sin and death. [3]For what the law was powerless to do because it was weakened by the flesh, God did by sending his own Son in the likeness of sinful flesh to be a sin offering. And so he condemned sin in the flesh, [4]in order that the righteous requirement of the law might be fully met in us, who do not live according to the flesh but according to the Spirit.

Because of our faith in Christ, God has set us free from all **condemnation** since He has set us free **from the law.** The law brings about wrath, but having died to the law, having died to sin, having the penalty paid for our sins in Christ's crucifixion, we are no longer under condemnation. Our condition of being free from condemnation is clear because of the Spirit He has given us. We now have **the Spirit of life** who has set us free from the law of Moses. It stirred up sin (7:7-12) and imposed death (7:13-25) as a penalty for sin (4:15). Faith, which is **the law of the Spirit who gives life,** has come to accomplish in us what the law of Moses itself could never do. First, faith (not he, referring to God, as in the NIV) **condemned sin in the flesh** (8:3), and second, faith fulfilled (**fully met**) in our lives the righteousness that the law of Moses required. Here is the paradox of the life of faith-righteousness. Only those who despair of obedience as a way of life can achieve the obedient lifestyle the law required. Such an idea is contrary to everything we have thought. As already stated, we tend to think that good people, given good laws, will be more obedient people. Yet the law faced an impossibility because of its weakness in dealing with our flesh (indwelling sin and desire for law-righteousness). For this reason, God instituted an entirely new way of living out the righteousness of the law, but the law is not part of it. Only those who **live** (literally "walk") **according to the Spirit** can fulfill the law. Those who walk **according to the flesh** never will. Paul explained this further in verses 5-11.

> **(2) Life in the Spirit means that one is not in the flesh but lives by faith in God who will raise such people with Christ (8:5-11).**

[5]Those who live according to the flesh have their minds set on what the flesh desires; but those who live in accordance with the Spirit have their minds set on what the Spirit desires. [6]The mind governed by the flesh is death, but the mind governed by the Spirit is life and peace. [7]The mind governed by the flesh is hostile to God; it does not submit to God's law, nor can it do so. [8]Those who are in the realm of the flesh cannot please God.

[9]You, however, are not in the realm of the flesh but are in the realm of the Spirit, if indeed the Spirit of God lives in you. And if anyone does not have the Spirit of Christ, they do not belong to Christ. [10]But if Christ is in you, then even though your body is subject to death because of sin, the Spirit gives life because of righteousness. [11]And if the Spirit of him who raised Jesus from the dead is living in you, he who raised Christ from the dead will also give life to your mortal bodies because of his Spirit who lives in you.

My definition of **flesh** in chapter 7 states that it consists not only of indwelling sin but also of the desire for law-righteousness. These ideas are critical for our present discussion, since this entire passage depends on the meaning of flesh. If we understand flesh only to include indwelling sin, we will draw the wrong conclusions. We will think that Paul's contrast is between the lifestyle of those who pursue sinfulness and that of those who pursue righteousness. The pursuit of sinfulness is not even a part of this book. In this book, Paul addressed people who were trying to be righteous. They were not pursuing sinfulness as a goal. Read again chapters 2 and 14. Paul's problem in this epistle was not with people who were trying to be sinful; it was with those who were trying to achieve righteousness by their works. They judged and condemned others who did not measure up to their rules. Thus, an incomplete understanding of flesh leads to a misinterpretation of verses 5-11. Let me repeat: flesh includes both indwelling sin and the desire for law-righteousness, and these two elements are foundational for understanding this chapter.

Those who walk **according to the flesh have their minds set on what the flesh desires.** Many people try to gain righteousness by their obedience to the law. But Paul provided a basic principle in verse 5: worldly concerns dominate people who live by works, while spiritual concerns dominate those who live by faith. Notice how Paul described those who are **according to the flesh** in verses 5-11: they set their minds on the things of the flesh (v. 5); the mind of the flesh is death (v. 6); it is hostile to God and unable to subject itself to the law of God, unable even to please God (vv. 7–8). Here is the type of person who sets out to gain God's favor through obedience.

But someone may wonder how these statements can characterize those who pursue law-righteousness. Let's consider each in turn. First, Paul said that they set their minds on the things of the flesh. Is this true of legalists? Only a little reflection will suggest that it is indeed true. What were the dominating concerns of the legalists, the Pharisees, of Jesus' day? Were they concerned with matters of the spirit and the heart, or with externals? We have considered this already in chapter 2, where we looked at the negative side of this discussion. Now we must consider the more positive side. In dealing with the law in which they took such pride, the Pharisees cut away its very heart. In the Sermon on the Mount, Jesus attacked their prayer lives and practices: "And when you pray, do not be like the hypocrites, for they love to pray standing in the synagogues and on the street corners to be seen by others" (Matt. 6:5). Jesus said of them elsewhere, "Woe to you, blind guides! You say, 'If anyone swears by the temple, it means nothing; but anyone who swears by the gold of the temple is bound by that oath'" (23:16). Again, He said, "Woe to you. . . You clean the outside of the cup and dish, but inside they are full of greed and self-indulgence. Blind Pharisee! First, clean the inside of the cup and dish, and then the outside also will be clean. Woe to you. . . You are like whitewashed tombs, which look beautiful on the outside but on the inside are full of the bones of the dead and everything unclean. In the same way, on the outside you appear to people as righteous but on the inside you are full of hypocrisy and wickedness" (vv. 25-28). Again Jesus said, "You have a fine way of setting aside the commands of God in order to observe your own traditions! For Moses said, 'Honor your father and mother,' and, 'Anyone who curses his father or mother must be put to death.' But you say that if anyone declares that what might have been used to help their father or mother is Corban (that is, devoted to God)—then you no longer let him do anything for their father or mother. Thus you nullify the word of God by your tradition that you have handed down. And you do many things like that" (Mark 7:9-13). Consider the obscene spectacle of the religious leaders of Jesus' day standing outside Pilate's residence, offering a righteous man as a criminal, but "to avoid ceremonial uncleanness they did not enter the palace, because they wanted to be able to eat the Passover" (John 18:28)! Here is the offense of legalism. It seeks an outward righteousness without concern for the inner man.

From other sources, we know the Pharisees were concerned about such spiritual matters as how far one might walk on the Sabbath.[1] They prohibited anyone from eating more than an olive's bulk of un-tithed grain.[2] One whole section of the rabbinic commentary on the Mosaic law concerns itself with "Peah," that is, the corners of the field. The law of Moses stipulated that whenever a farmer harvested he must leave the corners of the field unharvested (Lev. 19:9-10; 23:22). This permitted the poor and the landless to gather food. Any law abiding Israelite would, of course, want to know. . . "How big is the corner?" For a spiritual man, the answer would lean toward generosity. The Old Testament consistently presents the spiritual man as generous. But the man who is intent only on keeping the law would not be satisfied with generosity. The rabbis determined the corners of the field constituted one-sixtieth of the field.

The Pharisees contended with Jesus' disciples for plucking grain on the Sabbath day (Mark 7:1-5). The rabbis taught that one may pluck only as much as an olive's bulk of grain without it being considered "harvested." They taught that it was unlawful to administer medical aid to one who was not in mortal danger on the Sabbath. On the other hand, they taught that they might rescue an animal from a pit on the Sabbath (Matt. 12:11).[3] Therefore, they grew angry when Jesus healed a man with a withered hand on the Sabbath, though in fact He applied no medicinal aid to the man! Are these the cares of those who have fixed their minds on the flesh or on the Spirit? This is the very position Paul attacked in the Book of Romans.

Now consider Romans 14:17: "For the kingdom of God is not a matter of eating and drinking, but of righteousness, peace and joy in the Holy Spirit." These are the concerns of the kingdom. The trouble with these matters, though, is that we cannot measure them. I cannot look at you and see that you are practicing righteousness or peace or joy. But the legalist is unhappy with that arrangement, thinking that what cannot be measured does not exist. The legalist is happy only with what he can see. He has his mind set on the flesh, on externals.

This is why Paul said the mind set on the flesh is hostile to God. God has said that "no one will be declared righteous in God's sight by the works of the law" Rom. 3:20). But the mind of the flesh says, "Oh yes I can! Just watch me do it, God." The mind of the flesh calls God a liar. The mind of the flesh sets out to do what God has said cannot and must not be done. They are like Israel at Kadesh Barnea. When God told them to enter Canaan and take it, they said that they could not. Then when He told them to turn back to the desert, they determined to go on in to take the land (Num. 14:1-4, 39-45). They set themselves as God's enemies, and they died as God's enemies at Hormah (v. 45). This proper noun is a wordplay on the Hebrew term translated elsewhere "totally destroy." It is a description of what God commanded Israel to do to the Canaanites, indicating that they died under God's wrath. Such a mind set on the flesh is hostile to God: **it does not submit to God's law of God, nor can it do so. Those who are in the realm of the flesh cannot please God.**

The alternative to hostility to God is to walk according to the Spirit. This phrase might describe some condition of life that is beyond the norm for Christian living. Yet nothing in the context has prepared us for that. The context suggests that living according to the Spirit means to live by faith. It means to live on the basis of the grace offered in the Lord Jesus Christ. Earlier Paul mentioned people who live by the Spirit and contrasted such a life with life by law (2:29). Such people are circumcised in the heart, by the Spirit, and have praise from God. This circumcision is contrasted with circumcision by the written code. Those who are circumcised by the Spirit have their praise from God. And then Paul contrasted those who live by the flesh with those who now "serve in the new way of the Spirit, and not in the old way of the written code" (7:6). Therefore life in the Spirit is opposed to life according to works of law. Indeed, life in the Spirit is life lived while enjoying the peace of God (5:1), boasting in the hope of the glory of God (v. 2) and in sufferings, since in them we come to experience God's love poured out in our hearts through the Holy Spirit (v. 5). Further, it is the law of the Spirit of life that has set us free from the law of sin and death (8:2). But all of this comes to those who are justified by faith, who live by faith, who look only to the Lord Jesus to satisfy all of God's demands. That is, all of this is for those who live by grace (the Spirit), not law.

Those who live according to the Spirit set their minds on the things of the Spirit: **The mind governed by the flesh is death, the mind governed by the Spirit is life and peace.** It is life and peace because it's constantly enjoying the peace that Jesus Christ has provided in justifying us by faith (5:1). It is the life that God gives as He raises believers from the dead and gives them resurrection life. Paul's point is that the only way to live before God is to live by the Spirit. It means to live by faith in Jesus Christ, to find one's acceptance before God, one's righteousness, all one's hope, in Him alone. This is the life of faith that Paul has been describing since chapter 5.

Paul reminded us that those of us who are right with God by faith are not in the flesh. In 7:5 Paul implied that we are not in the flesh, for he speaks of that condition in the past tense. Here he openly affirmed that truth: **You, however, are not in the realm of the flesh but in the realm of the Spirit, if indeed the Spirit of God lives in you.** On the basis of this verse, we must conclude that it is not possible for us to pop back and forth between the flesh and the Spirit. If we are indwelled by the Spirit, we are in the Spirit. If we are not in-dwelled by the Spirit, we are in the flesh. No in-between state exists. The only proper way to live, then, is to live by faith without works of law. As Paul explained elsewhere: "just as you received Christ Jesus as Lord, continue to live your lives in him" (Col. 2:6). We began the spiritual life by faith. Therefore, we cannot complete it by works. In Galatians 3:2-3 Paul made this very point: "I would like to learn just one thing from you: Did you receive the Spirit by the works of the law, or by believing what you heard? Are you so foolish? After beginning by mean of the Spirit, are you now trying to finish by means of the flesh?" If we want to please God, we can only live this life by faith.

While we live by faith, we are not fully enjoying all that we will since we still drag around this old dead body. The body is in some way related to sin, for sin occurs while we are in the flesh. In fact, Paul said that **the body is subject to death because of sin.** We await our physical resurrection with Christ, which is the redemption of our bodies (v. 23). But because we have the Spirit of Christ and belong to Him, our spirits are life! The King James verbiage ought to be retained at this point, for it rightly preserves the strength of the Greek text. The verse does not say that our spirits are alive, but that our spirits are *life* **because of righteousness.** For although we await physical resurrection, we have come to participate in a spiritual way in Christ's physical resurrection. Thus we are not under law but under grace (6:14).

Paul described the life that we now are by the expression **because of righteousness.** The nature of life for us is to express itself in righteous behavior that reveals our identity as the children of God. Life shows itself through actions. Under law I die, that is, I lose capacity to live righteously. Under grace I live, that is, I gain the ability to live righteously. But the only way I can achieve life is by faith. This leads to the conclusion of the paragraph where Paul explained the way of life for those who by faith are in the Spirit.

> **(3) This all means that we are called and taught by the Spirit to live by faith and not law, and to know God's fatherly love that has given those who suffer with Christ the role of joint heirs with Him (8:12-17).**

¹²Therefore, brothers and sisters, we have an obligation—but it is not to the flesh, to live according to it. ¹³For if you live according to the flesh, you will die; but if by the Spirit you put to death the misdeeds of the body, you will live.

¹⁴For those who are led by the Spirit of God are the children of God. ¹⁵The Spirit you received does not make you slaves, so that you live in fear again; rather, the Spirit you received brought about your adoption to sonship. And by him we cry, "Abba, Father." ¹⁶The Spirit himself testifies with our spirit that we are God's children. ¹⁷Now if we are children, then we are heirs—heirs of God and co-heirs with Christ, if indeed we share in his sufferings in order that we may also share in his glory.

We as believers have no **obligation. . . to the flesh.** Instead, we are to live **by the Spirit** and thus **put to death the misdeeds of the body.** This does not refer to fasting regularly or praying for hours each day. Such ideas are completely foreign to the context of Romans 8. The context refers to learning not to succumb to the impulses of the flesh, that is, living by law. Paul referred to the same ideas in Galatians 5:17-21, where he commanded his readers to "walk by the Spirit" so as not to "gratify the desires⁴ of the flesh." But what are the desires of the flesh? Are they not the works of the flesh that Paul listed in verses 19-21? Based on Galatians 3:2-3, the answer is no. What the flesh desires is to accomplish the righteousness of the law. But Paul also said that the flesh is at war with the Spirit. People often assume that the enmity between the flesh and the Spirit means that the flesh wants to be evil. This is not the background of Galatians or of Romans. Both letters were written to people who believed that their works made them more acceptable to God. The reason the flesh and the Spirit are opposed to one another is that the two seek entirely different means of righteousness. The flesh seeks to gain God's approval by its obedience, while the Spirit teaches us that we attain God's approval through faith and by grace.

So what the flesh aims to do is not what it does. The flesh actually accomplishes only breaking the law, the deeds listed in verses 19-21. In verse 20, Paul listed seven sins that the flesh accomplishes that cause disharmony: "quarrels, a contentious temper, envy, fits of rage, selfish ambitions, dissensions, party intrigues."[5] Such is always the production of the flesh, and such is what law produces in anyone's life. Therefore, living by law actually makes us debtors to the flesh, debtors to sin, and it will certainly kill us. It kills us, not by taking away spiritual life so we lose our salvation, but it kills us by taking away our ability to practice righteousness.

However, the Spirit leads us to live by faith, proving that we are sons of God. What is it that the Spirit does to show that we are sons of God? Romans 8:14 that the Spirit guides us. Many have concluded from such statements that the Spirit's guidance is necessary for making the daily decisions of life: where to live, where to go, what brand of toothpaste to buy. Again, these ideas are not in the context. One of the basic rules of interpretation is that all meaning comes from context. How does our context suggest that the Spirit leads us? First, He leads us to live by faith. This is the teaching of Romans 3–8. We have seen (Rom. 6; 8:4) that the life of faith actually does produce the righteousness that God revealed in the law (Rom. 6:1-14; 8:4). The irony and paradox of Christian living is that no one can ever fulfill the law by trying to obey the law.

The only way we can produce the righteousness of the law is to give up on obedience and pursue faith and grace alone. We must pursue the righteousness bought for us by Jesus, what we have been calling faith-righteousness. Paul called this lifestyle "the fruit of the Spirit" (Gal. 5:22-23). It is interesting that Paul called it fruit. If it is indeed the fruit of the Spirit, then we do not have to labor to produce it. Vines do not strive to produce their fruit. Apple trees are not weary at the end of the day from producing apples. What wearies us so much in the Christian life is that we are working to produce the fruit of the Spirit. We have not learned simply to trust Jesus to produce in us, by His Spirit, the fruit that proves our divine sonship. Carefully consider the list in Galatians 5:22-23. If we were reading a theology book and ran across a list like this, whose characteristics would they be? Would we expect to find this list in a description of the attributes of God? Indeed, we would, for these are His characteristics.

Let me give a personal illustration. When I cough, I sound just like my father! Who would ever try to imitate someone else's cough? My family tells me that I walk just like my grandfather who died when I was ten. Why would a little child try to imitate his grandfather's walk? Then why do I have these characteristics? The answer is that I am genetically related to my father and my grandfather. My throat and my legs are built like theirs. I show my relationship through the way I live. I don't work at it. I just do it because of my identity and my natural relationship to them.

This illustration may help us to understand what Paul has been talking about. Why do people of faith produce the righteousness of the law? Why do people of faith produce the fruit of the Spirit, that is, the attributes of God? It is because they are God's sons.[6] They have died to sin, and He has raised them from the dead. They are married to Him who rose from the dead. Therefore, He produces through them fruit for God (Rom. 7:4), the fruit of the Spirit (Gal. 5:22-23), the character of their Father. It is the character of the Father in the lives of the children that shows who their father is. Jesus said, "If God were your father, you would love me, for I have come here from God. . . You belong to your father, the devil, and you want to carry out your father's desire" (John 8:42, 44). The character of the father shows in the life of his sons. Therefore, what the Spirit leads us to do is to live the life of the Father.

In one very restricted sense, God does not care where we live, where we go, or what brand of toothpaste we buy. In one very restricted sense, God does not care whether we become pastors, or what church we pastor, or whether we become missionaries, or where we serve as missionaries. God cares about holiness, not geography. If God wants you somewhere else, He can do to you what He did to Philip in Acts 8. It is simple for Him to snatch you from where you are and place you where He wants you. More to the point, He knows that if His Spirit is producing in us the life of faith, where we are is right. If we live by grace, producing the fruit of the Spirit, we are right. Where we go is right. What we buy is right. The ministry we pursue is right. One who has the fruit of the Spirit will not be a pimp or a drug dealer or a drunk. The Spirit leads us to act like God acts, and the way God acts is always right.

Romans 8:15 adds something very important to our discussion of the Spirit's leading: **The Spirit you received does not make you slaves, so that you live in fear again; rather, the Spirit you re-**

ceived brought about your adoption to sonship. And by him we cry, "*Abba,* Father." The Spirit does not lead us to live by law with its condemnation and wrath. Rather, the Spirit produced our **adoption to sonship**[7] and through Him we cry out, **"*Abba*, Father."** This experience is our birthright as children of God, and law has robbed us of it. This experience allows us to know the fatherly intimacy of God's loving relationship with us. The word *Abba* is an Aramaic term that a little child would use for his daddy.[8] The term, as Jesus used it during His days on earth, may have sounded disrespectful to His hearers. "In other words, He uses the simple 'speech of the child to its father.'"[9] God's Spirit comes to us to lead us to know and experience this intimate father-child relationship. It is not a spirit of fear that binds us. It is the Holy Spirit of God who sets us free in this new relationship.

Unfortunately, many people's fathers were intimate with them but in a way that they dreaded. For some of us, a father was a person who, at best, was unconcerned in our lives, present in body, but absent in spirit. Some of us grew up assuming that our Father-God was just like our human fathers. It is only by the gracious working and leading of God's Spirit that we grow beyond this. Only by His grace will we no longer think of God according to the pattern set by our human fathers. The privilege God has given us, our birthright from God, is to address Him as Abba. He has given us the privilege of feeling toward Him as a little child does toward his mother or father. If we have a God of law, then He stands with a club ready to beat us down. This is the spirit of fear that leads again to bondage. But if we have a God of grace, then He stands with His arms wide open, ready to receive us. As we come to experience this sonship, then **the Spirit himself testifies with our spirit that we are God's children.** What we need to cultivate in ourselves and for each other is this attitude of the intimacy of the family.

We must understand that we have Abba sitting on the throne of the universe. Abba, our Father, is the One who created the universe, who holds the earth's waters in the palm of His hand, who measures the heavens with the span of His hand, who weighs the nations like fine dust that is so light that we do not even dust the scales, since they make no difference to Him whatever. This is my Abba, your Abba, our Abba. When the Spirit leads us to call God Abba, He does not lead us to be afraid of Him. Then we cannot impose on one another such a relationship. We must learn within the fellowship of the church to live out the character of our Father. He does not give a spirit of fear, so we must not. He gives the Spirit of sonship, acceptance, love, and intimacy. This will be the atmosphere of our churches when we practice grace, when we receive one another as Christ received us, for the glory of God.

Is it any wonder that our gospel presentation is so weak when we in the family of God do not even believe it? We preach grace. We preach that God saves by faith without works of law. But in our fellowships we practice condemnation, the bondage of works, divisiveness, strife, envy, hatred. Many churches have two doctrinal statements—they preach one and practice the other. The one we practice allows the world to see that we do not believe the one we preach. It is the one we practice that is a bondage to slavery that leads to fear. In fact it is the one that we practice that suggests that our gospel is false. Until our practice becomes marked by love, by the grace that God has showered on us, we will never have any power in our gospel. The world watches our guilt and our fear of God and concludes, rightly, that our gospel is false.

Romans 15:7 says that I must accept other believers in the same way that Christ accepted them for the glory of God. What sin is there that is so great that I can't accept another believer? What experience of life is so traumatic, so horrible, so terrifying, that I can't do that? How did God accept us? What sin is so wicked, so horrifying, so vile, that God doesn't accept the sinner? We work so desperately to hide ourselves from one another, and why? It is because we don't receive grace from each other. We do not know the grace of God, and we do not express His grace to each other. The two are not unrelated. They are directly related. Only as the recipients of God's grace understand the grace of God will we finally learn to receive each other by grace.

This has implications for our evangelism. People who know God's grace do not worry when lost people act like sinners. What else could they do, after all? Their unbelief is the greatest possible sin they can commit. All the rest of their behavior, distasteful as it may be, is less serious than their unbelief. Yet as we look at the sinners of the world, we transfer our disgust at their behavior to their persons. We lose sight of the gracious heart of God as we recoil at their sin. What grace is there in this response? "Oh no! I don't like you because you used my Savior's name in vain!" A sinner doesn't care that he is reviling God. He expects God to condemn him. He feels that God is his enemy. What the sinner needs to know from you is whether this God whom he reviles, whom he hates, whom he fears, has anything for him other than the darkness and despair of eternal condemnation. People of grace don't walk around with "evangelism Bibles." That is a Bible so big that if they won't submit to the gospel, they will submit to the Word crashing down on their heads. People of grace weep at sin. People of grace grieve over the sinner's hostility to God. People of grace know how to accept the sinner without adding condemnation. People of grace are winsome and attractive as they deal with the lost. They win a hearing for the gospel by their gracious ways and words. And when sinners reject their message, they have rejected the message itself, not the obnoxious ways of the witness. O holy Father, cover us with Your grace!

We are not simply God's children, led by the Spirit to experience the intimate loving relationship of a Father to His beloved children. Paul declared that as children of God we are also **heirs of God.** Under Roman law the heir is one who, because he is a son of the family, already has co-ownership of all the father's estate, shared with the father. The heir has not yet gained the right of full use of all that he owns. The father "has the controlling interest, to use a modern analogy, but ownership is, in a sense, joint."[10] Thus the fullness of possessing the inheritance awaits a time set by the Father, but we are now heirs of God. If, as Paul says, we are **heirs of God,** we are also **co-heirs with Christ.** There is a community of property. We stand to inherit all that Jesus owns, and not only a fraction of it. We are His co-heirs. All of us own all of it jointly.[11]

All this is wonderful, and it would have been wonderful if Paul had just left it there. But he added a condition at the end of verse 17. We are **heirs of God and co-heirs with Christ, if indeed we share in his sufferings in order that we may also share in His glory.** That word **if** is emphatic because of a suffix that Paul added to it.[12] We will share in Christ's inheritance, but emphatically only on the condition that we suffer with Him. I suspect that among Christians in our day it is normal to think that those who are living life as God intends it will never suffer. But Paul clearly stated here that not only should we expect to share in Jesus' messianic glory, but we should also expect to suffer in Jesus' messianic suffering. Jesus said much the same thing: "Whoever wants to be my disciple must deny themselves and take up their cross daily and follow me. For whoever wans to save their life will lose it, but whoever loses their life for me will save it" (Luke 9:23–24). Those who would reign with Christ must share the life Jesus had. Jesus will come to the throne through suffering. It was, in fact, God's will for Him to suffer (Luke 24:46). Therefore, His co-heirs will come to their glory through suffering as well. It cannot be otherwise. It must be. In a world of sinful hostility to God, those who walk the path of the Messiah, those who seek His kingdom, must suffer as He did. Paul himself suffered, filling up in his flesh, as he said, "what is still lacking in regard to Christ's afflictions" (Col. 1:24). Indeed, Paul affirmed that all Christians will suffer (Phil. 1:29; 2 Tim. 3:12). But what is the suffering that we must endure? In the passage that follows, Paul explained the extent and kind of suffering he meant here. His conclusion regarding the life of those justified by faith reveals the biblical role of suffering in the Christian life (8:35-39).

h. But suffering, while it causes us to groan as we await our redemption, is bringing great hope for us since we know that God has eternally planned everything to conform us to Christ (8:18-30).

Romans 8:18-30 can be divided into three parts. Paul first stated his general principle about suffering in verse 18, that the glory that awaits us is incomparable to our suffering. Then in verses 19-27, he explained that principle, especially giving us insight into the greatness of that glory. Since the glory that will come is essentially inconceivable (1 Cor. 2:9), he explained the glory by describing those who long for its revelation. Finally, in verses 28-30, Paul showed how suffering can in fact produce good for us. It is in this passage that Paul made the seemingly far-fetched statement that "God causes all things to work together for good" (v. 28; NASB).

(1) The sufferings of our lives are not worth comparing with the glory that will be revealed in us (8:18).

[18]I consider that our present sufferings are not worth comparing with the glory that will be revealed in us.

Paul realized that no normal, healthy person enjoys **our present sufferings.** So he established a principle about suffering in verse 18. If Christians in America made this statement, other Christians might have reason to doubt its validity. For the most part, American Christians have not suffered for the cause of the Messiah. But it was the apostle Paul who made the statement. To understand his meaning it may be helpful to recall some of his sufferings. Fortunately, Paul provided a resume of some of his sufferings in 2 Corinthians 11:23-28:

> Are they servants of Christ? (I am out of my mind to talk like this.) I am more. I have worked much harder, been in prison more frequently, been flogged more severely, and been exposed to death again and again. Five times I received from the Jews the forty lashes minus one. Three times I was beaten with rods, once I was pelted with stones, three times I was shipwrecked, I spent a night and a day in the open sea, I have been constantly on the move. I have been in danger from rivers, in danger from bandits, in danger from my own fellow Jews, in danger from Gentiles; in danger in the city, in danger in the country, in danger at sea; and in danger from false brothers. I have labored and toiled and have often gone without sleep; I have known hunger and thirst and have often gone without food; I have been cold and naked. Besides everything else, I face daily the pressure of my concern for all the churches.

This is the apostle who considers our present sufferings so lightly. How did Paul survive such great suffering? What made it possible for him to bear shipwreck, prison, stoning, and hardship? More particularly, how can we, how can I, make it when God calls us to undergo such sufferings? We will surely not survive by some dogged reliance on obedience and rules! The only way we can survive is by a growing love for the Savior and by the hope that He extends to those who bear His sufferings with Him. This is how Paul survived. Indeed, he also said, "For our light and momentary troubles are achieving for us an eternal glory that far outweighs them all" (2 Cor. 4:17).

But these are not the only sufferings that are producing **glory** for us. Paul provided some idea of what the sufferings are and how great the glory is in verses 19-27.

> **(2) The greatness of the glory is shown by the longing of creation for our revelation as children of God, and by the Spirit's own groanings in His intercession for us, all leading us to hope (8:19-27).**

[19]**For the creation waits in eager expectation for the children of God to be revealed.** [20]**For the creation was subjected to frustration, not by its own choice, but by the will of the one who subjected it, in hope** [21]**that the creation itself will be liberated from its bondage to decay and brought into the freedom and glory of the children of God.**

[22]**We know that the whole creation has been groaning as in the pains of childbirth right up to the present time.** [23]**Not only so, but we ourselves, who have the firstfruits of the Spirit, groan inwardly as we wait eagerly for our adoption to sonship, the redemption of our bodies.** [24]**For in this hope we were saved. But hope that is seen is no hope at all. Who hopes for what they already have?** [25]**But if we hope for what we do not yet have, we wait for it patiently.**

[26]**In the same way, the Spirit helps us in our weakness. We do not know what we ought to pray for, but the Spirit himself intercedes for us through wordless groans.** [27]**And he who searches our hearts knows the mind of the Spirit, because the Spirit intercedes for God's people in accordance with the will of God.**

This passage lists three groanings, and those who groan show the greatness of the glory awaiting us. Knowing the greatness of this glory gives us the ability not only to endure, but even to flourish in the midst of sufferings. Creation itself urgently longs for release from its God-imposed fruitless existence, its bondage to corruption, into **the freedom and glory of the children of God.** Paul described the profound desire of the creation to see **the children of God to be revealed.** Who are we, and what will we be that even the creation longs for our revelation? The answer is not yet clear. But we can know certainly that when God reveals us in our glory, the creation itself will join us in our **freedom and glory.** For God subjected the creation to **frustration** (or "decay," Confraternity Version; or "futility," Berkeley Version). He did it because of our sin. In our freedom creation will achieve freedom also. Paul deepened our understanding of creation's yearning for our revelation by describing creation as if it is experiencing **the pains of childbirth.** Creation's groaning is the first of the groanings that demonstrate for us what is the greatness of our future glory with Christ.

Not only does the creation groan, but **we ourselves. . . groan inwardly.** We do indeed have the indwelling Spirit as the firstfruit of God's promises. But we groan within ourselves since we await **our adoption to sonship,** the day when God accomplishes **the redemption of our bodies.** We live in our old dead bodies, as Paul described them earlier in this chapter (see v. 10). We know what life is because God has given us His Spirit as the down payment on all His promises (Eph. 1:14). He lives in us, leading us to live by faith. He fulfills in us the righteousness demanded by the law. He leads us to know the intimate love of God. But we still drag around this old body, dead because of sin, subject to the influences of indwelling sin and law. Mortality stares at us from the mirror each morning as we rise to face another day. For though Christ has redeemed us from the curse of the law (Gal. 3:13), His redeeming work has not yet reached our bodies. We wait for that day with a holy greed, a heavenly lust. We know that then, and only then, will Christ's redeeming work come to completion.[13] Our own groaning shows that we have not yet received the completion of the promises.

It is here that Paul began to expand our understanding of our sufferings. Not only does this include the suffering we bear for the cause of Christ as Christians, but it also includes all the physical sufferings that we endure so that we may be glorified with Him (v. 18).

Those sufferings are of two kinds. They are, first, the physical sufferings of the body, the pains and ills each of us knows from our daily lives. What a comfort! It is possible for every pain to be part of the ministry we bear for Christ. But second, our sufferings in this unredeemed body include what Paul discussed in chapter 7, the suffering that we bear as we struggle with indwelling sin. We find nothing in this life in which to place our confidence. Life for us only has confidence as we keep in mind the future we will share with Christ. This is our unseen but exceedingly certain hope (vv. 24-25). Paul introduced these ideas in chapter 5, where he spoke of suffering as the first link in the chain of the Christian life (vv. 3-5): suffering produces patience, which produces approved character, which in turns produces hope—and this is the confidence of which we speak: "hope does not put us to shame, because God's love has been poured out into our hearts through the Holy Spirit, who has been given to us." We have confidence about the future, but not because of the suffering we undergo now. We have confidence about the future because of our experience of our Father's love. We have not seen Him. We have not seen the glory that awaits us either. Therefore, we wait patiently in hope of what God has promised us. All of this comes to us demonstrating that God's Word is true, and we gain confidence in our sufferings. Through them we come to know our Father.

The Holy Spirit also groans. Paul began verse 26 with **In the same way.** As the creation groans and we groan, **the Spirit himself intercedes for us through wordless groans** ("with sighs too deep for words," Berkeley Version). Christian leaders like to give prayer conferences. But Paul said that **we** (which included the apostle himself) **do not know what we ought to pray for.** We stumble around in our weakness, ignorant of proper prayer. But as we struggle in the midst of our sufferings, we can take confidence because the Holy Spirit Himself helps our weakness[14] by interceding for us. Verse 27 shows the splendid comfort of His intercessory ministry: the Spirit knows the mind of God and always intercedes in a way that fits God's will for us. Now it should be clear that the Holy Spirit has never voiced a prayer that the Father has turned down! The Father always answers His Spirit's prayers, granting Him the exact requests He has made.

161

This third groaning, of all the groanings in our passage, suggests the most about our future glory. I might groan only selfishly, longing simply for release from difficulty. But the Spirit's groanings are the deep longings of God's Spirit to complete in us the work He has begun. I might pray for release from pain, but He always prays for my glorification. I might pray for release from difficulty. But if God granted every one of my prayers, I would never grow in patience and character. I would never grow in hope. Thus I would experience neither God's love in the present nor the sharing in Christ's inheritance in the future—the glory of God.

> **(3) We know that whatever comes to us comes from God who has purposed for us to become conformed to the image of Jesus, as the purpose of His age long plan (8:28-30).**

[28]And we know that in all things God works for the good of those who love him, who have been called according to his purpose. [29]For those God foreknew he also predestined to be conformed to the image of his Son, that he might be the firstborn among many brothers and sisters. [30]And those he predestined, he also called; those he called, he also justified; those he justified, he also glorified.

Sometimes Christians will unintentionally use Romans 8:28 as a club on those who are suffering. We think that somehow once we have repeated it, the suffering all becomes easier. At other times we read the verse as if it means that nothing really bad will ever happen to Christians. The value of verse 28 lies in neither of these views. This verse provides insight into the way God governs the universe so we can be ready to handle whatever comes to us.

But verse 28 must be one of the most outlandish statements in the whole Bible. All things work together for good? We must ask what that word **all** means, for it does not always mean all in the absolute sense. Most of us as teenagers came home late from a date at least once. Our parents met us at the door with the inevitable question, "Where have you been?" We answered, "Well, everyone was going to the movies, so I went." Our parents may have responded, "Everyone in town was going to the movies? No one remained in any of the restaurants. All the houses were empty. The streets had no one in them, because everybody was going to the movies? Is that what you're saying?" Then we had to admit that what we really meant was that all of our friends, or better, those in the group we were with, were going to the movies. So "all" does not always mean "all without exception." What does Paul mean when he said all things work together for good?

First, we must define any word by its context. **All things** must refer to the things the author has mentioned in the context. In the context Paul's point is that suffering has a key role to play in the Christian life (see especially v. 17). Unfortunately, this point of view is not welcome in most circles. Therefore, Paul must justify his statements about suffering. Verses 28-30 shows that all suffering produces good for those who love God, who are called according to His purpose. It is for them alone. It is this that is so outlandish, that suffering could in any way be useful and helpful, and that all suffering produces good. The human mind rebels against such an idea. But here it is in inspired words. Two questions face us that we must answer before we leave these ideas. First, Paul said that **we know** these things. Second, he said that what we know is that all things work for **good.** We need to know the meaning of each of these terms to understand Paul's meaning. I believe he explained what he meant by **good** in verse 29. In verses 29-30 he explained how we know that all things work together for good.

Verse 29 opens with the word **for,** indicating that what follows provides the information we need to understand Paul's certainty about suffering, which gives us the same certainty. The reason for Paul's certainty involves five things he knew about God. First, he says that **those who love him** are **called according to His purpose**, and they are the ones **God foreknew.**

God's foreknowledge has been subject to much discussion over the centuries. Some have held that the word primarily relates to God's previous knowledge of who will believe in Jesus Christ. The word can appear with such a meaning. Acts 2:23 uses the noun "foreknowledge" in reference to a personal object that indicates relationship, not just temporal knowledge. But when "know" appears with a personal object, it normally has a relational sense. I may tell you that I know Harry S. Truman. He came to my hometown in about 1954 or 1955, and I met him then. However, you might doubt my claim to know him. For you might know that at the time I was in the first or second grade, and I met him in a group from my school. I met him, and I might be able to tell you several facts about him, but you would not agree that I know him. To meet someone or to know facts about a person is not the same as knowing him. Observe in our verse that it is not facts about people that God foreknows. He foreknows the people themselves: **those God foreknew.** Everywhere in the Bible, when the verb "know" appears with a personal direct object, it refers to relationship, not to facts about someone.

Three passages can help us understand this concept. First, Genesis 4:1 says, "And Adam knew Eve his wife, and she conceived" (KJV). But what really happened is this. One day Adam came walking out into a clearing and saw Eve standing there. In his amazement and delight at seeing her, he shouted, "I know you! You're Eve!" Immediately she conceived a child. Right? No, the knowledge that Adam had of his wife was the most intimate kind of relationship known to mankind—the NIV translates the verb "know" here as "made love." From this first reference we learn that "knowledge" can have the implication of intimate relationship.

Second, God addressed the Northern Kingdom in Amos 3:2, "You only have I known of all the families of the earth" (KJV). Now either God is woefully ignorant or "know" does not always refer to facts in the brain. The NIV correctly translates the verb as "chosen" in this verse. The point God made in Amos 3:2 is that Israel is the only human family on earth with whom He has formed a relationship as a family. He has not determined to establish a relationship with the Smith family, as such, or the Jones family, as such; only with the Jacob family. So God's knowledge refers to relationship, not to facts in the brain. The verb "know" has a significant relational aspect to its meaning, in addition to the cognitive aspect we usually associate with it.

The third passage is perhaps the most significant one. Acts 26:5 uses the very word that appears in Romans 8:29. In his speech to King Agrippa, Paul said of the Jews who were there with him that "They have known me for a long time." Notice that the same Greek

164

word (*proginosko*, "foreknow") appears in a relational sense, not in a cognitive sense. Therefore "foreknow" means to have a prior existing relationship with someone. The same sense appears in Romans 11:2 where Paul used it to describe the relationship God has with Israel.

The first of the five things Paul knew about God that gave him such certainty is that God foreknew His people. We may draw the following conclusion from the usage of the words know and foreknow. God determined to establish a relationship with all the justified before they came into existence. The relationship He established was one of intimate affection and exclusive union.[15]

The second one is that **those God foreknew he also predestined.** Christians as a rule do not like this word any more than the previous one. The verb itself means "to decide beforehand, to determine ahead of time."[16] We need to recognize that God's affection (His foreknowledge) leads Him to set a goal for us. Paul revealed that goal in the rest of the clause: **to be conformed to the image of His Son.** Paul has not yet given us enough information to be able to conclude when this happened. We do know, however, that in some past time God determined to make those He loves to be like Christ.

Is it possible for us to conceive that God would establish a purpose that might fail? While we might fail in our purposes, it is not possible that God's purposes should fail. A plan might fail for only a few possible reasons. A plan might fail because the person who made it did not know enough about what he is planning to make a good plan. But God, who is perfect in knowledge (Job 36:4), cannot fail for lack of knowledge. A plan might fail for lack of wisdom, that is, the planner might not be able to plan well enough to make his purpose succeed. But God is infinitely wise (Job 9:4) and cannot fail for lack of wisdom. A plan might fail for lack of strength, for the planner may be incapable of carrying out his plan. But God is almighty (Rev. 1:8). He will never fail to carry out His plans because of lack of strength. A plan might fail for lack of goodness or faithfulness. The planner may promise us that he will do something, but because he is not good, he may lie. If he is not faithful, he may refuse to carry out his plan. But God is the definition of goodness and faithfulness (see Ps. 136). A plan may fail because the planner may not have the authority to carry it out. But God has no authority to which He is accountable, no one whom He must obey. This is the lesson Nebuchadnezzar learned when he proclaimed "Then I praised the Most High; I honored and glorified him who lives forever. His dominion is an eternal dominion; his kingdom endures from generation to generation. All the peoples of the earth are regarded as nothing. He does as he pleases with the powers of heaven and the peoples of the earth. No one can hold back his hand or say to him: 'What have you done'" (Dan. 4:34-35). God said, "I make known the end from the beginning, from ancient times, what is still to come. I say: 'My purpose will stand, and I will do all that I please'. . . What I have said, that will I bring about; what I have planned, that will I do" (Isa. 46:10–11). No, God's plan cannot fail. If He has planned to make us like Christ, He will do it. The way He will do it is through our sufferings! So this is the "**good**" for which all things work together (v. 28). The good is that we should become like Christ. It will only come to fruition in the future. It will only be when God fully establishes His rule over our creation. But it will come.

It is God's purpose to make His people like His Son. The intention of this is **that He might be the firstborn among many brothers and sisters.** Significantly, the final reason for God's action is not to benefit mankind. Here is a difficult truth for us arrogant humans to learn. We are deeply involved in the plans and purposes of God, but we are not the center of them. In the seventeenth century Galileo astounded the religious world when he declared that the earth was not the center of the universe. He overturned the whole scholarly, scientific, and theological consensus of his day. The theologians were certain that since man was the crown of God's creation, the earth must be the center of the universe. With the audacity born of truth, Galileo declared that the sun was the center of our solar system. He declared that the earth was only one small part of the whole of God's creation. We modern Christians, while our cosmology is more scientifically correct, have a Copernican view of our importance. We believe that what God does, He pretty much does so for our benefit.

But verse 29 indicates that what God does He does for His own sake. Ezekiel 36:22 is similar: "It is not for your sake, people of Israel, that I am going to do these things, but for the sake of my holy name." Isaiah 48:9-11 is similar, "For my own name's sake I delay my wrath; for the sake of my praise I hold it back from you, so as not destroy you completely. See, I have refined you, though not as silver; I have tested you in the furnace of affliction. For my own sake, I do this. How can I let myself be defamed? I will not yield my glory to another." In 1 Corinthians 1:30 Paul said, "It is because of him that you are in Christ Jesus," and in Philippians 1:29 he said, "it has been granted to you on behalf of Christ not only to believe on him but also to suffer for him." It is for the sake of His own honor that God acts, not for the sake of humanity. Therefore, as He foreknows and predestines those who love Him, He does it for the sake of His Son. He has purposed for Him to be the firstborn among many brothers.

You may remember that we are studying a list of five of God's works. They give Paul certainty that all things work together for good to those who love God. The third of those five things appears in verse 30: **And those he predestined, he also called.** Calling is a concept that the theologians have divided into two subcategories. One is general calling, the call that God issues to all humanity through creation, the conscience, and the proclamation of the gospel (see John 12:32; Matt. 22:14). The special or effectual call is the call that surely and always issues in faith and salvation (1 Tim. 1:9). The calling in Romans 8:30 is the second type, a special calling. We know this because God's foreknowledge and predestining precede it, and His justifying and glorifying follow it. As God brings His people to glory and into the image of His Son, He leaves nothing to chance. He sees to it that all the foreknown are predestined, and that all the predestined are called. He takes the initiative, leaving nothing to luck.

Then **he also justified** all whom He had foreknown, predestined, and called. It is at this point that we begin to get enough information to determine the timing of these magnificent deeds. When did God foreknow us? When did He predestine us? The answer must be that He did His work before He justified anyone! Who do we know in Romans whom God has justified. If you said Abraham, you would be right. That means that all of God's foreknowing and predestining came before Abraham's justification. But can we be more precise in our answer? Is there any one else in Bible history whom we know to have been a believer, and thus justified by faith? Hebrews 11 says that Abel was a man of faith. Then God's foreknowing and predestining work occurred before Abel's day. Now Abel lived very early in human history. Some of us believe that Adam and Eve themselves responded by faith in God, and thus that they were justified people too. That would mean that God accomplished His foreknowing and predestining work before their existence.

Paul said that God "has saved us and called us with a holy calling, not according to our works, but according to His own purpose and grace which was granted us in Christ Jesus from all eternity" (2 Tim. 1:9, NASB). How much clearer could it be? God, in eternity past, set His affection on us, not for anything He knew about us. The only relevant facts about us were that we would be lost, defiled, hateful, sinners in open rebellion against His rule. He set His affection on us and marked us out to become like His Son Jesus Christ. Then He planned and carried out our calling so we would indeed come to faith (faith He Himself supplied). Now He has **justified** us, that is, He has declared us righteous because of the righteousness of Jesus Christ. Finally, in eternity past, He planned in the end to bring us to glory, so we would indeed share in the divine nature (2 Pet. 1:4).

The tenses of the verbs we are discussing in this passage are significant. Verses 29-30 have five verbs: foreknew, predestined, called, justified, and glorified, and each one is in the past tense (Gk aorist). Most of the verbs are understandable in the past tense, but not the verb "glorified." What could Paul have meant when he used this tense of the verb? First, we must understand something about God. God is eternal. This is an axiom of Christian teaching. Yet we often mistake its meaning. Eternity does not refer to an endless extension of time; rather it refers to timelessness. When we say that God is eternal, we are saying that He exists outside of time altogether. All time and all events are equally present to Him. We know the truth of God's omnipresence, that God fills the universe with the whole of His being and transcends it by infinity. As God is omnipresent in space, so is He in time. Therefore, God may describe things that are in our future as having already occurred. Such a description communicates as strongly as possible the utter certainty of those future events.

Paul used these ideas elsewhere in his writings. "And God raised us up with Christ and seated us with him in the heavenly realms in Christ Jesus" (Eph. 2:6). From God's point of view, those who are in Christ—those whom He foreknew, predestined, called, and justified—are already seated with Christ in heavenly places. God is not waiting for our glory. Glory is already achieved. The future is not some dark unknown right now—certainly not for God and no longer for us. When we step into the future, we step into the presence of our God. He has been patiently waiting for us to catch up with what He has already been doing!

This is how Paul can know so certainly that all things do in fact work together for good to those who love God, who are the called according to His purpose. God has included all events of our lives, fashioning them precisely to make us like Christ. Every suffering that comes our way will and must make us like Him. For every suffering is part of an eternal plan. In His wisdom and omniscience, He has left nothing out to insure that we will reach the goal He has set for us. In His sovereignty, He has no one to whom He must give account of His actions. He has no higher will that may veto His purposes. In His omnipotence He bends all things, all wills, to His purpose to achieve in us "an eternal glory that far outweighs" all our sufferings (2 Cor. 4:17). In His goodness and faithfulness to us, indeed to Himself and His Son, He surely will carry out His plan. Therefore, nothing will stand in God's way for achieving His grand plan in our lives.

This means that we must spend some more time discussing what kinds of suffering Paul has in mind. We have already seen that physical suffering is involved (8:23), and the suffering we undergo as we struggle with indwelling sin (chap. 7). Later in the chapter, Paul showed that other kinds of suffering face us too. Verse 35 lists several kinds of suffering we might undergo: trouble, hardship, persecution, famine, nakedness, danger, and sword. Each of these is what God sent against Israel for breaking His covenant with them. The curses proved that Israel had sinned and that He was dealing with them in wrath. We will say when we get there that these are sufferings that come upon sinners. But Paul says that even suffering for sin cannot separate from the love of God. Then neither can sin. What a marvel, that God has even included sin, our sin, in His eternal plan for us. Sin itself has a role to play in the Christian life. When we fall into sin, God sends His ministers to buffet us so that we will surely come into the image of Christ and be glorified with Him in the last day! If even sin works together for our good, to make us like Christ, all things work together for good. If God is sovereign over sin, He is sovereign over everything. Here is powerful confidence before God. Paul cried out, "Therefore, there is now no condemnation for those who are in Christ Jesus" (8:1) And now we can understand more fully what he meant when he said that we have not received a spirit of bondage leading again to fear but the Spirit of adoption to sonship by whom we cry out Abba, Father (v. 15).

> ### i. Therefore, we are indeed at peace (see 5:1) with God who has freely given us everything, so that nothing at all can separate us from the love of God that is in Christ Jesus our Lord (8:31-39).

[31]**What, then, shall we say in response to these things? If God is for us, who can be against us?** [32]**He who did not spare his own Son, but gave him up for us all—how will he not also, along with him, graciously give us all things?** [33]**Who will bring any charge against those whom God has chosen? It is God who justifies.** [34]**Who then is the one who condemns? No one. Christ Jesus who died—more than that, who was raised to life—is at the right hand of God and is also interceding for us.** [35]**Who shall separate us from the love of Christ? Shall trouble or hardship or persecution or famine or nakedness or danger or sword?** [36]**As it is written:**

> **"For your sake we face death all day long;**
> **we are considered as sheep to be slaughtered."**

[37]**No, in all these things we are more than conquerors through him who loved us.** [38]**For I am convinced that neither death nor life, neither angels nor demons, neither the present nor the future, nor any powers,** [39]**neither height nor depth, nor anything else in all creation, will be able to separate us from the love of God that is in Christ Jesus our Lord.**

Is it any wonder that Paul followed these ideas up with the question, **If God is for us, who can be against us?"** This question is no less surprising than what Paul said in verses 28-30. Norlie's translation of this verse expresses well Paul's point: "If God is for us, what does it matter who may be against us?"[17] While the NIV gives an adequate translation, Norlie's is a little closer to the point. God is for us, and He has planned everything to produce in us Christlikeness. This means that everything and everyone—even all enemies, actual and possible—become tools in God's hand to shape us so that we might become like Christ. No one is against us. Satan himself—though he opposes us at every turn and is the accuser of God's people—only succeeds in supporting God's eternal plan. We face no more wrath, no condemnation. The consequences of sin are very real. But God's sovereign power turns them into means of shaping us into the image of Christ. So if God is for us, no one and nothing are against us. An old song asks, "Is this vile world a friend of grace to lead me home to God?" It seems to suggest that the answer is no, but our text tells us that the world in the end does lead us home to God. God has planned it so. God is for us! **He did not spare his own Son** in redeeming us. Therefore, He will withhold nothing from us now that we are His.

It is God who justifies. He has declared us righteous because of Jesus alone. No one can ever bring a charge against God's people that will stick (v. 33). No accusation can ever bring us into condemnation. The Judge before whom anyone might make such an accusation has already pronounced the verdict, and He has pronounced us righteous—in right relationship with Him. No one would dare stand in His face and bring charges against God's people now. The Eternal Supreme Court has already spoken, and no legislature or executive branch can check or balance His rule.

Paul asked another question in verse 34: **Who then is the one who condemns?** (See "no condemnation" in v. 1.) The answer must be, **No one.** Nothing less than Christ's death (**Christ Jesus who died**) and resurrection (**who was raised to life**) were necessary to accomplish this, and now he **is at the right hand of God and is also interceding for us.** So how can anyone condemn us now? They can't. He bore our penalty and triumphed over it. That is the meaning of the resurrection. It is no longer possible to assess the penalty of sin against us. Christ paid the penalty in full. Now He pleads His own work on our behalf before His Father. We have the Holy Spirit interceding for us (vv. 26-27), and we have the risen Christ interceding on our behalf and pleading His atonement. No one can ever condemn us again. Indeed, "there is now no condemnation for those who are in Christ Jesus."

Therefore, no suffering, even if it appears to thwart our whole ministry, can ever **separate us from the love of Christ.** Not even suffering for sin can separate us from the love of Christ. Many years ago I sat on the platform of our church preparing to preach this passage. Just moments before I was to begin my sermon, a significant question occurred to me. Why would anyone have thought that the seven items in verse 35 (**trouble or hardship or persecution or famine or nakedness or danger or sword**) could possibly separate us from God's love? I certainly never thought that a sword might separate me from God's love. Then it occurred to me that it was possible that these items are related to the covenant curses in the Old Testament. If they were covenant curses, they would demonstrate that people who suffered them were separated from God's love. Deuteronomy 28 states:

> All these curses will come on you. They will pursue you
> and overtake you until you are destroyed, because you did
> not obey the LORD your God and observe the commands
> and decrees he gave you. They will be a sign and a wonder
> to you and your descendants forever. Because you did not
> serve the LORD you God joyfully and gladly in the time of
> prosperity, therefore in hunger and thirst, in nakedness
> and dire poverty, you will serve the enemies the LORD
> sends against you. He will put an iron yoke on your neck
> until he has destroyed you. . . Just as it pleased the LORD
> to make you prosper and increase in number, so it will
> please him to ruin and destroy you. You will be uprooted
> from the land you are entering to possess (vv. 45-48, 63).

This is the wrath of God. Anyone under the Mosaic covenant who broke or despised the covenant came under God's wrath: "The LORD will never be willing to forgive them; his wrath and zeal will burn against them. All the curses written in this book will fall on them, and the LORD will blot out their names from under heaven"

(Deut. 29:20). Therefore, items listed in Romans 8:35 come from the covenant curses in the Mosaic covenant. This shows that they were signs that those who suffer these curses were indeed separated from the love of God.

Later in the week I got the opportunity to pursue that question a little farther. I found that the Greek words Paul used occurred in the LXX in passages dealing with covenant curse: **trouble** (Deut. 28:5); **hardship** (Deut. 28:53; both of these appear in 28:55, 57); **persecution** (Deut. 28:22, 45); **famine** and **nakedness** occur together (Deut. 28:48). The word **danger** does not appear in the covenant curse lists in either Deuteronomy 28 or Leviticus 26, but the idea of danger pervades both contexts. Covenant disobedience brought danger to every aspect of the ancient Israelites' lives (see the general statement in Deut. 28:15-29). Finally, **sword** appears in the covenant curses in Leviticus 26:36-37. The sword speaks of conquest by a foreign enemy and death, the final stages of covenant curse (Deut. 28:49-52, 64-68).

All of this is important for the following reasons. Since these sufferings appear in the covenant curses, they are things that under the old covenant separated the sinner from the love of God. Yet now, with Jesus' work on the cross and at the right hand of God, they cannot separate us from God's love. In the outworking of God's plan, He has by His power turned the signs of wrath into means of grace. They bring us into the image of Christ. Indeed, all things work together for good to those who love God. God has turned covenant curse into covenant blessing.

We wish that we could say that no Christian ever suffers such things. But we read about these very things in Hebrews 11, though we lose sight of them in the chapter. We like to read the verses 1-34 since they are full of victory and triumph. We do not like the verses 35-38 quite as well. There we read about torture, flogging, imprisonment, stoning, destitution, persecution, and homelessness for people of faith. Considering church history, it is this group that has been the larger. Suffering is the way of the kingdom. In fact, we may even go so far as to say that God sets suffering in our path to hinder us on our way. He makes promises to us. To build our faith, he sets obstacles in our way that seem to make it impossible for His promises to reach fulfillment.

Consider Abraham. In Genesis 12 God promised to make Abraham's name great and to give him the land of Canaan. But then a famine arose in Canaan that made it impossible for Abraham to live there. As far as he could see, if he stayed in Canaan, he would die. If he left Canaan, he would lose the land. Who brought the famine? In chapter 13 he returned from Egypt with enormous wealth, but the land could not support both him and Lot. How could it support his numberless descendants when it could not even support those two families? In chapter 15 God promised Abraham a numberless offspring, but he had married a barren wife. Who kept Sarah's womb from conceiving? Abraham and Sarah struggled with the problem of barrenness until chapter 21. Finally, in chapter 22 God commanded Abraham to offer his son as a burnt offering. God placed these obstacles in the path of Abraham's faith. God intended each of them to produce godliness in Abraham's character, and indeed we watch with joy as his faith grows and triumphs. But it triumphs because of suffering.

Paul wanted believers to understand the role of suffering in their lives. He quoted Psalm 44:22 to help us see the part played by suffering: **For your sake we face death all day long; we are considered as sheep to be slaughtered.** The psalm is difficult. The psalmist claimed that Israel had been faithful to the covenant, but that God had abandoned them in battle. They were experiencing covenant curse even though they were obedient to the covenant! Of course, this raised all sorts of questions in the psalmist's day, and no fewer in ours. Can it really be that Israel was faithful to the covenant? It is hard for us to find a time in Israel's history when we could believe such a claim. To make the problem even more difficult, the psalm gives no information about its historical setting, except that they have suffered defeat in battle. One commentator on this passage took the position that Israel's claims to be faithful to God are simply wrong. He believed that in the Old Testament people had a view of sin that permitted them to claim that they did not deserve to suffer, but we have a more complete view of sin. According to this commentator, we now know that we can never be free of sin; we know that we do deserve suffering as punishment for our sins.[18]

On the other hand, the psalmist calls God as a witness that they have been faithful to the covenant. Could it be that the psalm itself is

God's testimony that the psalmist was telling the truth? We already have illustrations of righteous sufferers in Abraham and Job. They endured much suffering that their lifestyles did not warrant as punishment for sin. Furthermore, in Romans we have been learning that there is now no condemnation for those who are in Christ Jesus. We are learning that the path of suffering is the path by which we come to the kingdom. Could it be that in their history God subjected Israel to the same kind of thing? I suspect that this is exactly what happened as recorded in Psalm 44. In fact, verse 22 is extremely important for the interpretation of the whole psalm. This verse gives us some insight into the particular situation they were facing. They had been involved in warfare. This verse tells us that they were involved in "the wars of the Lord." In the covenant God made with Israel, He commanded them to extend His rule among the nations by warfare. Furthermore, their warfare would be one of the key means for them to show that they loved God with all their hearts (see Deut. 6:4-5). In the rest of chapter six Moses explained some hindrances to such love. But he did not explain to them how to show their love for God until chapter 7. The very first command He gave them in that chapter was to carry out warfare to expand the kingdom of God (vv. 1-6). He expanded on that commandment in chapter 20. Israel was involved in war for the Lord's sake. The conclusion is clear that they were being faithful to the covenant.

Then why did God fail to go out with their armies? He did to them what He did to Abraham, what He did to Jesus, and what He does to us. He set obstacles in the way of their faith. Those obstacles appeared to make it impossible for them to fulfill their God-given ministries. They suffered profoundly in the face of the obstacles, but the obstacles did not weaken their faith. Psalm 44:1-8 shows how committed these Israelites were to God (esp. vv. 6-8). Despite the losses and defeat of the previous days, they intend to return to the battle. They thoroughly expect to see victory, because no matter the sufferings they have undergone for the sake of God's name, they trust their God. Suffering was not the end of their ministry or of their hope. They did not understand it; it did not seem consistent with God's self-revelation. But they did not give up. This is the life to which God has called all of His people today.

A joke made the rounds during the Civil War. The soldier said, "When the battle is hottest, you'll find me where the shells are thickest: under the ammunition wagon."[19] No battle was ever won in the rear area. The army that wins the war is the one that stays in the place of pain and suffering and death the longest. We are in a battle. Jesus, our Brother, has already won the war, and we are in the mopping up phase. The only way to come through to the end is to endure the suffering of battle. Indeed, all that God asks of us is that we endure. Many know 1 Corinthians 10:13 by heart, but too often we fail to take the latter part of the verse into account. "No temptation has seized you except what is common to mankind. And God is faithful; he will not let you be tempted beyond what you can bear. But when you are tempted, he will also provide a way out so that you can endure it." We must not stop before we get to the end of the verse: "so that you can stand endure it." James 1:12 says, "Blessed is the man who perseveres under trial because, having stood the test, that person will receive the crown of life that the Lord has promised to those who love him." Paul said to Timothy, "Join with me in suffering, like a good soldier of Christ Jesus" (2 Tim. 2:3). Endurance is what God seeks from us. Endurance is what God rewards with the crown of life. We can endure if we know that all things work together for our good.

Suffering for us does not mean that we have been evil. It means that we are God's sons, and He is dealing with us by His love. It is His love that motivates His discipline (Heb. 12:5-6), and suffering is the means of His discipline. God's loving discipline always results in sharing His holiness, in Christlikeness. Therefore, when God sets obstacles in our way, painful hindrances to our lives and ministries, we need not lose heart. Even more, we need never heap guilt on our brothers and sisters for the suffering they bear. Sin does bring consequences, but God has changed the nature of the consequences. They once were the means of God's wrath. Now they are the means of His love and grace to bring us into the image of Christ. Once their purpose was solely to satisfy justice. Now their purpose is to make us like God's Son. If, therefore, we practice the teaching of the Book of Romans, to receive one another as Christ received us (14:7), we cannot deal in guilt with our brothers and sisters in Christ. We can extend them hope. We can offer them acceptance and love. We can support them as they go through difficult times, times they do not even understand. We can be instruments of God's grace.

This teaching about suffering offers hope for those who suffer because of sin. Rather than extending only the consciousness of guilt to the sufferer, we can offer the love and grace of God. We can encourage them to see that the suffering they are undergoing, caused by their own sin, will produce in them a new measure of Christlikeness. In fact, we can reassure them that no present suffering can ever compare with the glory that God will reveal in us (v. 18). Further, we can and must offer them support through their sufferings, for in this key way they will come to know the grace of God. We need to allow the body of Christ to show the attributes of God in action.

What we are saying here is not only for Christian sufferers. We need to learn to offer the same love and support to sufferers outside the body of Christ. We are the temple of God. A temple has at least two functions. First, a temple is a place of communion between the deity and mankind. Second, a temple is a place for the fullest possible revelation of the glory or attributes of the deity. As the temple of God on earth, the church has these two key roles to fulfill. We have done a good job in communicating to the world God's distaste and disgust at sin. But we have not communicated well His love and grace to the world. If strangers were to come into many of our churches, we would welcome them only because they are potential members for our organization. We express little true love and very little grace. When we are at each other's throats, we certainly show no grace to the world. Paul warned us against this: "If you bite and devour each other, watch out or you will be destroyed by each other" (Gal. 5:15). When we condemn one another, we show no gospel of grace to the world, but the old message of the law. We have nothing to offer beyond condemnation and hopelessness. Is the character of our God so cruel? We have forgotten the message that we become like the deity we worship (Ps. 135:15-18). The tragedy is that we have already become like the deity we worship. When we live in condemnation, we are worshiping the wrong god, not the God of the Bible.

All of this means that we need to learn to "accept one another, then, just as Christ accepted you, in order to bring praise to God" (Rom. 15:7). We will suffer. God will send us difficulties, as Psalm

44:22 indicates. These difficulties will hinder our ministries, and even make it seem that God is our enemy. But He has given us the marvelous resource of the body of Christ to reveal His character so that we may survive those times. Our response as the body of Christ, accepting the sufferer with grace, will show the nature of the God we worship. It will draw sinners to the Savior, because they will see the gospel lived, not merely preached. It will make us all **more than conquerors through him who loved us."**

This is the way to the glory of the kingdom. This is the path Jesus trod. This means it is the path of victory. God our Father holds out no mere distant future of hope. Through the body of Christ and through the mystical workings of the Holy Spirit who indwells us, we come to know the love of our God during our sufferings. Thus we become **more than conquerors.** We are already experiencing the final victory of our Lord Jesus Christ.

Thus we come to the same settled persuasion that Paul had when he wrote Romans 8:38-39. The list that confronts us in these two verses illustrates a figure of speech by which the author tells us how to read the list. There are several conjunctions in the list, which indicates that we should stop and consider each item in the list since each one is critical.[20]

Paul is **convinced that neither death nor life. . . will be able to separate us from the love of God that is in Christ Jesus our Lord.** I suspect that none of us were particularly concerned that life would separate us from God's love. On the other hand, large numbers of Christians who face death personally or in a loved one feel that death certainly does separate us in some way from God. How many Christians fear death? Yet death should hold no terror for the Christian. It is the means by which God brings us finally and most directly into His presence—the very presence of our Father who set His affection on us in eternity past! How can that hold any dread for us? If the "sting of death is sin" (1 Cor. 15:56), and if in Christ there is now "no condemnation for those who are in Christ Jesus," then death should hold no terror. The death of a Christian loved one, of course, causes us terrible sorrow because of the parting, but the parting is only temporary. It brings no cause for fear. God will reunite us and then there will be no parting. Death is among those "all things" that work together for good to those who love God, who are called according to His purpose. It is painful, but it is not worth comparing with the glory it will produce in us. Death cannot **separate us from the love of God that is in Christ Jesus our Lord.**

Paul also stated that **neither angels nor demons** can separate us from God's love in Christ. Again, I suspect that none of us has expected Gabriel or Michael to try to separate us from God's love. Hebrews 1:14 teaches us that the angels are God's ministering spirits whom He sends to serve those who are about to inherit salvation. But what about **demons** ("principalities," KJV) and **powers**? Ephesians 6:12 states: "For our struggle is not against flesh and blood, but against the rulers, against the authorities, against the powers of this dark world and against the spiritual forces of evil in the heavenly realm." Satan and his demons are set to oppose us. They seek to harm and obstruct us. But what have we learned in Romans 8? We have learned that all things work together for good to those of us who are called according to God's purpose. Then even Satan himself and all his dark authorities cannot separate us from the love of God. They, like death, can cause us pain. They can cause us sorrow. They have no intention of doing us good. But because of the sovereign, eternal plan of our loving Father, all they can do is help us to become like our Savior. Demons cannot **separate us from the love of God that is in Christ Jesus our Lord.**

Paul says further that he is persuaded that **neither the present nor the future** can separate us from God's love in Christ. The only events in life that might conceivably separate us from the love of God are our sins. But we have seen that even sin cannot separate us from God's love. God lovingly disciplines us so we will share in His holiness (Heb. 12:10). This must be the case if indeed Jesus has paid the penalty for all of our sins. In the nature of the case, He could not bear the penalty only for our past sins, since to Him all of our sins were future. He must have paid all that God's just wrath could impose as payment for sin. God can impose on us no further payment for sin, since He has already exacted all that justice can require. Discipline is an act of God's love. No discipline is pleasant at the time we experience it. In the long run, however, it produces a harvest of righteousness and peace for those who have been trained by it (Heb.

12:11). It causes us pain and sorrow. But the pain and sorrow are not worth comparing with the glory that God will reveal in us. Nothing we can do at present and nothing we can do in the future will in any way separate us from God's love.

No **powers** can separate us from the love of God that is in Christ Jesus. What precisely these **powers** are is unclear. Paul used the term elsewhere for miracles (1 Cor. 12:10, 28-29; 2 Cor. 12:12) and to describe spirit beings (1 Cor. 15:24; Eph. 1:21). The context of Romans 8 does not specifically help define the meaning of this word. Because the word appears with **the present** and **the future,** it seems likely that miracles are in view. Paul used the term once for Satan's miracles performed through the man of sin (2 Thess. 2:9). It may be that here he refers to deceptive miracles of Satan. But even they will be unable to separate us God's love.

Neither height nor depth can separate us from God's love. We might wonder why Paul added these as possible hindrances to God's love. Paul likely included this pair of terms and the next one as a final scraping of the galaxy—nothing in the universe can separate us from God's love for us in Christ! Moo added a comment on the last element in the list, which is **nor anything else in all creation**: "Lest a picky reader think that Paul has omitted something that could threaten the believer's security in Christ, Paul concludes with the comprehensive 'any other creature.'"[21] Some people believe that Christians can lose their salvation. They agree that nothing will be able to separate us from God's love. But they believe that we can separate ourselves from His love by our willfulness. This last element in Paul's list should prove that such an idea if false. Nothing at all, no created thing, including ourselves, can **separate us from the love of God that is in Christ Jesus our Lord.**

Those who have been justified by faith have peace with God (Rom. 5:1), and for them there is no condemnation because they are in Christ (8:1). Here is the hope we have. Here is our peace with God. Here is the life free from condemnation. Here is the Spirit of sonship by which we cry out, "Abba, Father." Here is the possibility of rejoicing, indeed boasting in suffering. Here is why we must learn to receive each other by grace, as Christ received us. None of us deserves what God has done, is doing, or will do for us. We all stand before God without works of law, solely by the meritorious right-eousness of Jesus Christ. He makes no demands on us that He does not Himself provide to us. Then in our relationships with our broth-ers and sisters in Christ, we must demonstrate grace. The "must" of grace is not one of law: Do it, or die. The "must" of grace is the obli-gation of nature. The oak tree does not produce acorns out of obliga-tion. The oak tree produces acorns because that is its nature. Nothing else is possible. So also for the recipients of grace. Grace is the neces-sity of our lifestyles and our interrelationships. Nothing else is possi-ble. If people do not live grace, we must ask whether they have re-ceived grace. Paul wrote these eight chapters of the Book of Romans to confront his readers with their judgmental lifestyles. He longed for them to extend to one another the hope, grace, and love they have received in Christ, lest, as he tells the Thessalonians, "our efforts might have been useless" (1 Thess. 3:5).

Christians need to learn the grace of God. We must not allow the grace of God to be vain in our lives. If we do in fact become like the God we worship, how critical it is, both for our own well-being as Christians, and for all our ministries, that we learn to live God's grace. Receive one another, as Christ received you, for the glory of God.

Notes for Romans 8

[1]There is a whole tractate of the Jewish discussions of the Law on "borders," called Erubin. Concerning these laws, Blackman says, "If one happens to be in a town it is permitted to walk for any dis-tance in the town itself—however large it may be—up to a line 70 2/3 cubits beyond the last houses on the outside of the town. . . If it is desired to go on the Sabbath beyond this limit an [extension of the limit] is prepared on the Friday preceding, thus: food sufficient for two meals is deposited on the Friday before dusk at a convenient spot where the ordinary [sabbath limit] ends, with the appropriate *Blessing ... Blessed are Thou O Eternal our God King of the Universe Who hast hallowed us with His commandments and hast commanded us concerning the commandment of the Erub* [extension], followed by ... *In virtue of this Er-ub it is permitted to me to walk from this place for two thousand cubits in every direction on this Sabbath...* and by this symbolical act one acquires a

[resting place] a new [Sabbath limit] from that point to a distance of 2000 cubits in all directions; the deposited food must be eaten on the third Sabbath meal (before nightfall) where it has been deposited. Should the line of the new [Sabbath limit] cut into another town the whole of that town whatever its extent … is included therein" (Philip Blackman, *Mishnayoth*, 2:99-100.

²Makkoth 3.2. Those who violate this rule are to be scourged.

³Compare CD 10:14–11:17. The text: "*14* Concerning the sa[bba]th, to observe it in accordance with its regulation. *Blank* No-one should do*15* work on the sixth day, from the moment when the sun's disc is*16* at a distance of its diameter from the gate, for this is what he said: *Deut 5:12* «Observe the*17* sabbath day to keep it holy». And on the day of the sabbath, no-one should say a*18* useless or stupid word. He is not to lend anything to his fellow. He is not to take decisions with regard to riches or gain.*19* He is not to speak about matters of work or of the task to be carried out on the following day.*20 Blank* No-one is to walk in the field to do the work which he wishes «on»*21* the sabbath «day». He is not to walk more than one thousand cubits outside his city.*22 Blank* No-one is to eat on the sabbath day except what has been prepared; and from what is lost*23* in the field *Blank* he should not eat, nor should he drink except of what there is in the camp.

"*Col.* xi (= 4Q270 6 v; 4Q271 5 i)*1* On the road, if he goes down to bathe, he should drink where he stands. *Blank* But he is not to draw (water) with*2* any vessel. He is not to send a foreigner to do what he wishes on the sabbath day.*3 Blank* No-one is to wear dirty clothes or (clothes) which are in a chest, unless*4* they have been washed with water or rubbed with incense. *Blank* No-one should intermingle voluntarily*5* on the sabbath. *Blank* No-one should go after an animal to pasture it outside his city, except for*6* two thousand cubits. *Blank* He is not to raise his hand to strike it with the fist. *Blank* If*7* it is stubborn, he should not bring it out of his house. *Blank* No-one should remove anything from the house*8* to outside, or from outside to the house. Even if he is in a hut, he should remove nothing from it*9* nor bring anything into it. He is not to open a sealed vessel on the sabbath. *Blank* No-one should wear*10* perfumes, to go out «or come in» on the sabbath. *Blank* In his dwelling no-one should

lift*11* a stone or dust. *Blank* The wet-nurse should not lift the baby to go out or come in on the sabbath.*12 Blank* No-one should press his servant or his maidservant or his employee on the sabbath. *Blank* {Not} No-one should help an animal give birth on the sabbath day. *Blank* And if «it falls» into a well*14* or a pit, he should not take it out on the sabbath. *Blank* No-one «should stay» in a place close*15* to gentiles on the sabbath. *Blank* No-one should profane the sabbath for riches or gain on the sabbath.*16 Blank* And any living man who falls into a place of water or into a «reservoir»,*17* no-one should take him out with a ladder or a rope or a utensil."
Florentino García Martínez and Eibert J. C. Tigchelaar, *The Dead Sea Scrolls Study Edition (translations)* (Leiden; New York: Brill, 1997–1998), 569.

[4]The *Twentieth Century New Testament* translates this word well as "cravings." The word itself is neutral, neither positive nor negative (whereas lust is only negative). Jesus used the word about His desire to participate with His disciples in the Passover in Luke 22:15.

[5]*The New English Bible.*

[6]I hope Christian women who are reading this will recognize that Paul was not hostile to women. Rather, he meant that God has extended to all of us the highest possible status in His household. There are no second-class citizens in the family of the King.

[7]Douay-Rheims, which reads "a spirit of adoption as sons," agrees with this translation. Schweizer (*TDNT*, s.v., "[*huiothesia*]" 8:399) treated the word in the same way, always, however, remembering that the state of sonship rests on God's free grace.

[8]Joachim Jeremias, *The Parables of Jesus*, p. 191.

[9]Gerhard Kittel, "[*Abba*]" *TDNT*, 1:6.

[10]Francis Lyall, *Slaves, Citizens, Sons: Legal Metaphors in the Epistles*, p. 111.

[11]Lyall, p. 115.

[12]Louw and Nida, 89.66: "an emphatic marker of condition."

[13]This means that the proper answer to the question, "Are you redeemed?" is yes and no. Christ has already redeemed us from sin (Gal. 3:13; 1 Pet. 1:18), but the completion of redemption awaits that day when God will glorify even our mortal bodies to resemble Christ's own resurrection body.

[14]God has expected and planned for our weakness. He doesn't expect us to be strong.

[15]The Williams translation of the New Testament renders the first part of v. 29, "For those on whom He set His heart beforehand." This well represents the point of the expression.

[16]Louw and Nida, 30.84.

[17]*The New Testament, A New Translation*, by Olaf M. Norlie (1961).

[18]J. J. S. S. Perowne, *The Book of Psalms*, 1:364. I am uncomfortable with such an approach because it seems to suggest that God was not working to convict of sin as fully in the Old Testament as He does in the church. Furthermore, it makes a whole psalm into a truthfully recorded (that is, an inspired) lie to fit a preconceived notion of what was possible in Old Testament times. For these reasons I reject Perowne's interpretation.

[19]To understand this joke well, you need to know they often kept the ammunition wagons as far as three miles behind the battle line.

[20]The figure is polysyndeton. Its opposite is asyndeton, where the author uses fewer conjunctions than are normally used. That figure instructs the reader to go on to the end of the list, since the author makes his point there. The list as a whole is more important than the individual members of the list. Another example of asyndeton is in Romans 1:29-32.

[21]Moo, p. 589.

Chapter 8 completed the first major subsection of Romans. In chapters 1–8 Paul showed that righteousness is by faith alone and what the life of faith is like. What he said in those chapters might seem terribly radical to any Jewish listener. All the rabbis had taught that righteousness is by works. But Paul taught that righteousness is by faith. While he has made a good case for his doctrine from the Old Testament, one question remained that he needed to answer. One of Paul's Jewish listeners might have asked, "Paul, if this really is the way of righteousness that God has always intended, why didn't Israel accept it? What does this mean for Israel?" Chapters 9–11 answer these questions. Ultimately, the Jews, like the Gentiles, receive life by faith alone.

Israel's unbelief calls the very purposes of God into question. For Paul himself has said that the gospel is for the Jew first. So if the promises to Israel failed, what hope do Gentiles have? If their unbelief has frustrated the purpose of God, then that would "call in question the very reliability of God Himself."[1] Therefore, Paul must deal with Israel's unbelief, showing how it fits into God's purposes.

B. Israel, like the Gentiles, will receive life by faith alone (9:1–11:36).

Paul's response to the issue of Israel's unbelief has five parts: (1) God has hardened unbelieving Israel (9:1–29). (2) The reason God has hardened Israel is that Israel rejected God's righteousness (9:30–10:21). (3) For Israel, God is never satisfied to have wrath as the final word, so even in these days of hardening God has preserved a remnant chosen by grace (11:1-10). (4) God has given the promises to the Gentiles through faith (11:11-24). (5) Through the Gentiles' faith, God will stir Israel to jealousy, bringing them to salvation through faith (11:25-32). This entire section takes up the ideas Paul had introduced earlier at the beginning of chapter 3, so here he returned to discuss those ideas, namely, the advantages that accrue to Israel (the Jews).

Romans 9–11 contains some of the most difficult material in Romans, particularly chapters 9 and 11. The language is not so hard, but the ideas Paul presented are difficult for people to grasp. Some Christians have struggled for years with the meaning of chapter 9 especially. Not everyone who reads my interpretation of these chapters will agree with everything I say. Indeed, I do not even like everything that I say here. Nonetheless, I feel compelled to say what I believe the passage teaches. As I teach and handle the Word of God, I become more and more convinced how essential it is to follow Paul's warning in 1 Corinthians 4:6, where he said that in interpreting the Scriptures we must "not go beyond what is written." It is my aim to cause as little pain as possible to my readers, but to remain faithful to what I see in the text. I also understand that my interpretation of the passage is not equivalent in authority or accuracy with the Scriptures. The Scriptures remain true and authoritative, and I know that my Christian brothers and sisters who disagree with me accept the Scriptures as such whether they accept my interpretation or not.

The interpretation that I give here falls into that branch of theological study called Calvinism. If I could find some other way to interpret the passage, I certainly would. But at this point in my understanding, this is the interpretation that best fits the particulars of the passage. So I ask my readers to give a hearing to what I have written. If, after carefully considering this approach, you decide that it is inadequate to deal with the passage, reject it. But please do not reject it because it is painful for you or contradicts some presuppositions you hold. If we can read the Bible for years and it never confronts us or challenges anything we think, have we really been reading the Bible? Or are we not really reading our own thoughts into the Bible?

This portion of the letter also relates closely to the purpose we have suggested. Paul was calling Jews and Gentiles in the church at Rome to receive each other by grace. If the Jews have no special standing before God because of their obedience, then they cannot judge or condemn their Gentile brothers. Likewise the Gentiles stand contrary to nature in the "olive tree" because of faith, holding the Jews' position before God, so they cannot despise the Jew who is in

Christ. Both Jew and Gentile must learn to receive one another as Christ received them. Cranfield has a helpful comment:

> It is only where the Church persists in refusing to learn this message, where it secretly—perhaps quite unconsciously!—believes that its own existence is based on human achievement, and so fails to understand God's mercy to itself, that it is unable to believe in God's mercy for still unbelieving Israel, and so entertains the ugly and unscriptural notion that God has cast off His people Israel and simply replaced it by the Christian Church. These three chapters emphatically forbid us to speak of the Church as having once and for all taken the place of the Jewish people.[2]

God's purposes cannot fail, even because of unbelief. If this is the case with unbelieving Israel, then we should treat one another in the church, the body of Christ, with grace.

1. God has hardened unbelieving Israel (9:1-29).

The first part of Paul's answer to the questions posed above consists of five parts (9:1-5, 6-13, 14-18, 19-21, and 22-29), and verses 1-5 provide an introduction to the entire section. In the past few decades it has been fashionable in some circles to charge Paul with anti-Semitism, especially on the basis of passages such as Romans 9–11. Verses 1-5 are strong evidence that Paul was not anti-Semitic. On the contrary, he loved his people. Anti-Semitism has no place in the Christian community, for all racism is simply and purely sin. Failure to receive a brother in Christ, any brother in Christ, is a denial of the position God has granted us in Christ. Thus, racism is just as much out of place in our churches as it was for the apostle Paul.

a. Paul longs for the salvation of his Israelite kinsmen who have incredibly great blessings from God (9:1-5).

[1]I speak the truth in Christ—I am not lying, my conscience confirms it through the Holy Spirit— [2]I have great sorrow and

unceasing anguish in my heart. ³For I could wish that I myself were cursed and cut off from Christ for the sake of my people, those of my own race, ⁴the people of Israel. Theirs is the adoption to sonship; theirs the divine glory, the covenants, the receiving of the law, the temple worship and the promises. ⁵Theirs are the patriarchs, and from them is traced the human ancestry of the Messiah, who is God over all, forever praised! Amen.

Paul's introduction to the deep subject he must treat in these chapters reminds his readers of his deep love for Israel. He had **great sorrow and unceasing anguish** for his kinsmen. Even further, he said, **I could wish that I myself were cursed and cut off from Christ for the sake of my people, those of my own race.** Here is the depth of his concern for them. The word "curse" appears in the Old Testament to describe the Canaanites and everything that belonged to them. Paul was willing, if it would have helped Israel, to suffer covenant curse, the fate of the accursed Canaanites, to bring Israel to salvation.

Besides his natural affection for his own countrymen, the reason for his deep love appears in verses 4-5. Israel had enormous privileges that Paul yearned for them to enjoy fully. They were **the people of Israel,** a name of honor they had held ever since God Himself renamed their ancestor Jacob. Paul continued:

> **Theirs is the adoption to sonship; theirs the divine glory, the covenants, the receiving of the law, the temple worship and the promises. Theirs are the patriarchs, and from them is traced the human ancestry of the Messiah, who is God over all, forever praised!**

These privileges were true of no other nation on earth and eventually culminated in the coming of Jesus Christ—the Savior for Jews and Gentiles.

> **b. In every generation of Israel, God has made a distinction between the seed of promise, chosen by grace, and the seed of the flesh (9:6-13).**

⁶It is not as though God's word had failed. For not all who are descended from Israel are Israel. ⁷Nor because they are his descendants are they all Abraham's children. On the contrary, "It is through Isaac that your offspring will be reckoned." ⁸In other words, it is not the children by physical descent who are God's children, but it is the children of the promise who are regarded as Abraham's offspring. ⁹For this was how the promise was stated: "At the appointed time I will return, and Sarah will have a son."

¹⁰Not only that, but Rebekah's children were conceived at the same time by our father Isaac. ¹¹Yet, before the twins were born or had done anything good or bad—in order that God's purpose in election might stand: ¹²not by works but by him who calls—she was told, "The older will serve the younger." ¹³Just as it is written: "Jacob I loved, but Esau I hated."

This introduction seems to indicate that God gave Israel significant privileges that have failed, that **God's Word had failed.** This idea Paul could not endure. He acknowledged that God has always made distinctions within the family of Abraham, and not only in the early generations of the family. This is the point he made in that somewhat enigmatic statement in verses 6-7: **For not all who are descended from Israel are Israel. Nor because they are his descendants are they all Abraham's children.** The point here is that descent from Abraham through Jacob/Israel is no guarantee of being a child of Abraham. God's Word cannot fail. Rather, in each generation God separated the seed of Abraham from those who are not of the promise. This truth Paul proved in verses 7-13. Abraham had two sons, Isaac and Ishmael. But only Isaac, the one born of promise through Sarah, was the seed or **offspring,** just as God had promised. God made a distinction between Isaac and Ishmael, giving the promised blessing only to Isaac. Why did God not give the blessing to Ishmael? Why did He separate Ishmael from Isaac? They were both sons of Abraham. The answer is natural descent from Abraham guarantees nothing so far as inheriting the blessing. Rather, the blessing goes to faith. The one fact we should learn about Ishmael and his birth is that Ishmael's birth required no faith. Abraham was scheming, trying to solve the problem of Sarah's barrenness, to fulfill God's promise. In fact, the promise ruled him out, for God promised the blessing to the son born from Sarah. From the very beginning God's promise ruled out Ishmael and his descendants as heirs of the blessing.

The perceptive reader will already have conceived an objection to the analysis we have made of God's choice between Ishmael and Isaac. These boys did not have the same mother. Then it is no wonder that God made a distinction between them. As Paul pointed out elsewhere, Ishmael was born to the slave woman, while Isaac was born to the free (Gal. 4:21-23). That objection might in part explain the choice in that first generation, but it can have no role in explaining the second generation. For Isaac also had two sons, Esau and Jacob, but these boys were twins with the same mother. Here again the Word of God determines from the beginning who would receive the promise. The time when God spoke to Rebekah proves that the boys had no merit. The human situation prompted God in no way to make His choice. For God declared that Jacob would be the heir before their birth. Paul explained the implications of God's timing in verses 11-12. **Yet, before the twins were born or had done anything good or bad—in order that God's purpose in election might stand: not by works but by him who calls—she was told, "The older will serve the younger."** This proves again the principle that mere descent from Abraham carries with it no guarantee of inheriting the promises to Abraham.

At this point someone might object that God chose Jacob over Esau because He saw what Jacob would become, or that God saw ahead of time the faith that would be in Jacob.[3] For those who take this position, we would recommend a rereading of the stories of Jacob and Esau in Genesis. The New Testament says Esau was "godless" (Heb. 12:16). We may see clear evidence of Esau's spiritual and even mental dullness. Esau was a man of appetite who could not deny himself anything when it came to satisfying some physical desire. He did, after all, sell his birthright for a bowl of stew! On the other hand, it is difficult to see greatness of person or faith in Jacob. Before he encountered the Angel of the Lord at Peniel (Gen. 32), he was a miserable man—a liar and a cheat. He habitually practiced what

Genesis considers one of the most serious sins, breach of family loyalty. Some have called his encounter with God at Peniel his conversion experience. That may be so, but if it is, I, at least, like him less after Peniel than before.

After Peniel we rarely hear him say anything positive. When he was not trying to give away the blessing,[4] he was groveling before his brother. When he was not whimpering about how everyone opposed him, he was whining about his death and the misery of his life. Jacob had faith. Hebrews lists him along with the other faith heroes in chapter 11, but his faith is like gold—it's hard to find! The only reference Hebrews makes to his faith relates to the blessing he pronounced on his grandsons on his death bed. No, God did not choose Jacob for foreseen faith. In fact, that would be contrary to what Paul's in Romans 9. God made the choice in accord with His purpose, not of works. The reason for choosing Jacob appears in Romans 9:12: **not by works but by him who calls.** Therefore, God said that **the older will serve the younger.** This is consistent with what Malachi wrote later, **Jacob I loved, but Esau I hated.**[5]

Within each Israelite generation God chose to separate the spiritual seed from the merely physical descendants of Abraham. So Paul says in verse 8, **In other words, it is not the children by physical descent who are God's children, but it is the children of the promise who are regarded as Abraham's offspring.** This is the problem the Jews had in the days of John the Baptist. John had to say to them, "And do not think you can say to yourselves, 'We have Abraham as our father.' I tell you that out of these stones God can raise up children for Abraham" (Matt. 3:9). Mere descent from Abraham might place anyone with Ishmael or Esau, as well as with Isaac or Jacob. Then what is it that happened to Israel so they did not receive the gospel Paul preached? Has God rejected His people? Didn't He promise to show them mercy and to save them?

c. God is perfectly just in sovereignly dispensing His own compassion as He wills (9:14-18).

[14]**What then shall we say? Is God unjust? Not at all!** [15]**For he says to Moses,**

> **"I will have mercy on whom I have mercy,**
> **and I will have compassion on whom I have compassion."**
> **¹⁶It does not, therefore, depend on human desire or effort,**
> **but on God's mercy. ¹⁷For Scripture says to Pharaoh: "I raised**
> **you up for this very purpose, that I might display my power in**
> **you and that my name might be proclaimed in all the earth."**
> **¹⁸Therefore God has mercy on whom he wants to have mercy,**
> **and he hardens whom he wants to harden.**

What God promised was to show **mercy** and **compassion,** but He does so on His own terms (v. 15, quoting Ex. 33:19). From this point Romans 9 becomes terribly difficult. We would prefer to have God show mercy as we would. We don't expect Him to show mercy on any other ground than would be acceptable in a human context. But what we have already seen should have prepared us to realize that God does not act as humans would. We would show mercy to our friends and loved ones. We would show mercy to people who would increase the prestige of the church. This is not God's way. Again, a study of Genesis would go a long way to remedy our misconception. In virtually every generation where we can tell, God passed over the son whom man would choose, preferring the son whom man would normally pass over. Noah is not the firstborn of Lamech. Abram is not the firstborn of Terah. Isaac is not the firstborn of Abraham. Jacob is not the firstborn of Isaac. We know that Abraham longed for Ishmael to live under God's blessing (Gen. 17:18). We know that Isaac much preferred Esau to Jacob (27:2-4). But the sovereign God of mercy chose the men whom no one else would have chosen to be the bearers of His blessing for future generations. Would you really want your daughter to choose a man like Jacob to marry?

In all of this God is not unjust in reserving to Himself the right to dispense His own compassion. One reason we have such a problem with this idea is that we misunderstand not only God's mercy but also human nature. In human affairs it would be wrong, the worst kind of bias and injustice, for an official to pass over one citizen to give benefits to another simply because of personal preference. All citizens who are not felons are to be equal before the government and in the eyes of the law. The problem is that we bring this same attitude to our relationship with God. We think that all subjects of the divine rule are basically equal before God, and thus all are equally worthy of His benefits. If by this point in Romans we are still thinking that way, we have learned very little from Romans. Paul spent chapters 1–4 showing that no one is acceptable before God. This is what he said in 3:10-20:

> There is no one righteous, not even one; there is no one who understands; there is no one seeks God. All have turned away, they have together become worthless; there is no one who does good; not even one. Their throats are open graves; their tongues practice deceit. The poison of vipers is on their lips. Their mouths are full of cursing and bitterness. Their feet are swift to shed blood; ruin and misery mark their ways, and the way of peace they do not know. There is no fear of God before their eyes.

> Now we know that whatever the law says, it says to those who are under the law, so that every mouth may be silenced and the whole world held accountable to God. Therefore no one will be declared righteous in God's sight by the works of the law; rather, through the law we become conscience of our sin.

With such an estimate of the human race, no one could doubt that all need mercy. But no one deserves anything from God but His wrath. Mercy is not something that any one deserves. It is not something that God is obligated to give to any human being. It is true that if God saved no one at all, He would be just. God retains the right to dispose of His own mercy and compassion as He desires, completely disregarding any other will outside His own. After all, He is the sovereign God, and it is entirely improper to charge Him with injustice. Or is God the only person in existence who has no right to dispose of His gifts as He desires?[6]

Paul quoted Exodus 33:19 to prove the principle that God shows His mercy sovereignly. This verse occurs at a crucial point in Exodus, crucial especially for our discussion, for it appears during the golden calf episode at Mount Sinai. It occurs at the beginning of the story where God reveals His glory to Moses. Israel was expected to live under this standard of God's relationships. Just a few days before God made this powerful statement, three thousand Israelites died because of their sin with the golden calf. They had in their own experience seen what it means when God says, **I will have mercy on whom I have mercy, and I will have compassion on whom I have compassion.**

Therefore, God's choice depends entirely upon His own will and purposes. Paul says (9:16), **It does not, therefore, depend on human desire or effort, but on God's mercy.** God's choice does not depend on **human desire,** that is, human will. This should be evident since Paul has already told us that none of humanity ever seeks for God (Rom. 3:11). If God left it to the human will to seek Him, no one would ever come to salvation. No one would receive God's mercy or compassion. In fact, if God did leave everything to the human will, He would have no opportunity to show His mercy, for any favor He would show would be fully deserved. It would not be compassion; it would be justice he would give the seeker.

Furthermore, Paul says, God's choice does not depend on human **effort.** This should also be clear. If anyone has ever striven to gain the blessing of God, it was Esau; but he "could bring about no change of mind, though he sought the blessing with tears" (Heb. 12:17). If human effort brought the sure means by which we gain the mercy of God, then God's mercy would again go to the deserving. But God deals with the undeserving. It is often the case that when a man wants something and tries to get it, it is usually appropriate to give it to him. But God gives His blessing to those whom no one else would choose, proving that He deals in grace, not in works.

God's mercy goes to those to whom He wills to give it. This sounds arbitrary. The arbitrariness is altogether on our side of the understanding, not on God's. He has not fully revealed the reasons for His actions, but that does not make them capricious or unjust. The final justification for God's action remains the character of God. He alone is unchangingly just. He alone is immutably wise, gracious, and loving. The very holiness of God is our guarantee that He is not irresponsible and undependable, that He is not unfair in His dealings.

In verse 17, Paul began to provide some help so we can see that He acts justly. The supreme demonstration of the principle we are studying is Pharaoh. Here Paul emphasized—not God's conferring of mercy but the opposite of His mercy—His just wrath. He does this because he is stressing in this chapter God's rejection of Israel as a whole. Again, within Paul's generation, as at the beginning of His dealings, God has separated the seed from the natural descendants of Abraham. He will now explain the principle on which God works from the experience of Pharaoh.

God said concerning Pharaoh: **I raised you up for this very purpose, that I might display my power in you and that my name might be proclaimed in all the earth** (quoting Ex. 9:16). God raised Pharaoh up for one purpose, to demonstrate His own character in him. The statement **I raised you up** is difficult. We might interpret the statement in one of two ways. It could mean that God gave Pharaoh physical existence, or that God brought Pharaoh to the throne of Egypt—though neither has much evidence. The latter may find support in Zechariah 11:16 and Isaiah 41:2. In those passages the word appears in contexts of appointing rulers to rule. The only reason that particular Pharaoh ever sat on the throne is that God put him there. God put him there only to show His divine power and to proclaim God's name in the earth. The God of Israel is the one who exalts kings and deposes rulers (Ps. 105:14; Isa. 41:2; 45:1). Luke 1:52 says, "He has brought down rulers from their thrones, but has lifted up the humble." And Daniel 4:17 says that God humbled Nebuchadnezzar "so that the living may know that the Most High is sovereign over the kingdoms of men and gives them to anyone He wishes, and sets over it the lowliest of men." The Most High God rules over the affairs of earth, and Nebuchadnezzar had to learn this difficult lesson. Eventually, he declared, "All the peoples of the earth are regarded as nothing. He does as he pleases with the powers of heaven and the peoples of earth. No one can hold back his hand or say to him: 'What have you done?'" (v. 35). Pharaoh thought himself a god, but the God of the universe gave him his position to show His own glory. God acts in perfect freedom in disposing even of kings without consulting any other will than His own. No one can call Him to account. The final explanation of world history is God's character. The final justification and rationale for all events is the glory of God. Everything functions to declare what sort of God He is.

So far as I know, all Christians hold to the sovereignty of God. The main question that perplexes us is how God exercises His sovereignty. Our passage seems to say that God established Pharaoh only to destroy him. We are in a passage dealing with Israel's unbelief. Pharaoh is a pattern for understanding what it is that God has done with Israel. So was Pharaoh a mere pawn in God's hand? Did he have free will to reject God, or did God force him to do what he would not otherwise have done?

The answer to these questions should be obvious. The first part of the answer will be clear if we think a bit about Pharaoh himself. Pharaoh believed, as all the Egyptians did, that he was a god, the offspring of the Sun god. Here was the wild man Moses coming from the desert to Pharaoh's throne room to demand that he release Yahweh's people to worship in the desert. Was any other response possible for Pharaoh? Could he have said anything other than he did? Can we conceive Pharaoh responding in this way? "Moses, Moses! How I have missed you, Moses. Where have you been all these years? Now you come to me demanding the release of your people. You know how I love you, don't you, Moses? You know I would do anything I could for you. I want to release them so badly, but I can't. God won't let me!" Is such a response possible? You will surely agree that it isn't possible. This god of Egypt could respond in no other way than he did, when he said (Exod. 5:2), "Who is the LORD that I should obey him and let Israel go?" (Ex. 5:2). God did not force Pharaoh to do something he did not want to do. As we read in Romans 1, God handed him over to his own sin. He made it possible for Pharaoh to do exactly what he wanted—to reject Yahweh and His word, to rebel against His command. So it was with Israel, and this is the second part of the answer. Israel rejected God's righteousness (see Rom. 10:3). Therefore, God gave them full opportunity to do just what they wanted—to rebel against His command, to reject their God and His word. So Paul drew the conclusion in verse 18, **Therefore God has mercy on whom he wants to have mercy, and he hardens whom he wants to harden.**

> **d. No one may legitimately call God's justice into question in this, since he may do with His creatures as He wills (9:19-21).**

[19]One of you will say to me: "Then why does God still blame us? For who is able to resist his will?" [20]But who are you, a human being, to talk back to God? "Shall what is formed say to the one who formed it, 'Why did you make me like this?'" [21]Does not the potter have the right to make out of the same lump of clay some pottery for special purposes and some for common use?

The ideas Paul has presented raise serious questions in our minds, questions that Paul had apparently already received, as verse 19 seems to indicate. If God hardens whom He will, and if He has hardened Israel, **Then why does God still blame us? For who is able to resist his will?** We should recognize in Paul's response to these questions that they are not legitimate questions as posed. They grow from unbelief, not from faith. The sovereignty of God can never furnish the breeding ground for sin and rebellion. His dominion uses sin; it does not excuse it.

Paul responded with indignation to these questions. **But who are you, a human being, to talk back to God?** He illustrated the folly of such questioning by the illustration of **the potter** and **a lump of clay.** A potter does not consult the clay before determining what to make out of any lump. In fact, the same lump of clay may furnish material for a beautiful vase or for a chamber pot. The vessel will not question the potter about his plans and purposes. What folly! Then why do men intrude into God's creation purposes? The difference, of course, between Paul's illustration and our interest in God's purposes in creation is that we are dealing with rational beings, not lumps of clay. For this reason, we feel we have the right to challenge God's work. But God is as far above us as the potter is above the clay, so our objections melt into nothingness. God's infinite greatness renders meaningless any challenge to His right to create and use as He will.

Does this imply an arbitrary capricious will in God? Not at all. We have seen too much of the character of God already in Romans to conclude that God is capricious and arbitrary. We may not always be able to explain the rationale of God's actions, but we can always know that God does only what is good and fair and just. Sometimes the actions of God appear capricious. Sometimes they seem arbitrary. The very appearance of caprice places demands on us in two ways. First, God's apparent caprice calls us to greater faith. We must be content to allow God to be God. We must allow Him to do what we cannot understand. We will be able to trust Him when we have come to know Him. Second, the apparent caprice of God challenges us to learn something very important about humanity. (1) We must learn that human beings are not the center of God's attention or thought. The Babylonian king Nebuchadnezzar learned this lesson (Dan. 4:35). Why have so few Christians learned it? God humiliated Nebuchadnezzar severely to teach him this lesson. God owes absolutely nothing to His creatures. His creatures are just that, His creatures. By right of creation He retains over them absolute right of disposition. While He always acts rationally, He does not owe them even an explanation of His actions. (2) We must remember the lessons about humanity we learned in chapters 1–3. All men—whether Pharaoh, Israelites, or Gentiles—are sinners who deserve from God nothing but His eternal wrath.[7] When God hardens a sinner so that he goes deeper into his sin and rebellion, is there injustice with God? The answer must be no, because what God does is perfectly just. To harden the sinner is right. To save the sinner is mercy and grace. Grace is undeserved; it is favor shown to those who have forfeited all claim on God's favor. If God gives grace, it is to the undeserving. They have no claim on God. They cannot charge Him with injustice for showing them grace. Indeed, so far as saved sinners are concerned, God's actions involve no justice. He saves them justly, but He saves them without regard to what is justly due them. Therefore, we cannot complain if God shows justice to the undeserving. Lost sinners deserve nothing but the eternal wrath of God. John tells us that God's wrath already abides on those who have no faith in Jesus (John 3:36).

God sovereignly reserves the right to dispense compassion and hardening. He does so for sufficient reasons but without consulting any will outside His own. Romans 9 is not the only place where such ideas occur. Christians are often surprised to find the same idea in the first chapter of John. People are familiar with John 1:12, but often fail to understand verse 13: "Yet to all who did receive him, to those who believed in his name, he gave the right to become children of God—children born not of natural descent, nor of human decision or a husband's will, but born of God." God as Father begets the children whom He wills. He does not, in the fullest sense, ever consult the will of man in the begetting. Teenagers have said, "I didn't ask to be born!" This is true in human birth, so how much more so in birth from God? Spurgeon supposedly spoke of a good piece of theology that Jonah learned "in a strange college." That good piece of theology is, "Salvation comes from the Lord" (Jonah 2:9).

> e. God has sovereignly hardened unbelieving Israel, but He has called out believers from both Jews and Gentiles, as the prophets said He would (9:22-29).

²²What if God, although choosing to show his wrath and make his power known, bore with great patience the objects of his wrath—prepared for destruction? ²³What if he did this to make the riches of his glory known to the objects of his mercy, whom he prepared in advance for glory— ²⁴even us, whom he also called, not only from the Jews but also from the Gentiles? ²⁵As he says in Hosea:

> "I will call them 'my people' who are not my people;
> and I will call her 'my loved one' who is not my loved one,"

²⁶and,

> "In the very place where it was said to them,
> 'You are not my people,'
> there they will be called 'children of the living God.'"

²⁷Isaiah cries out concerning Israel:

> "Though the number of the Israelites be like the sand by the sea,
> only the remnant will be saved.
> ²⁸For the Lord will carry out
> his sentence on earth with speed and finality."

²⁹It is just as Isaiah said previously:

**"Unless the Lord Almighty
had left us descendants,
we would have become like Sodom,
we would have been like Gomorrah."**

God as a potter has the sovereign right over a human as clay to make one vessel for honor and another for dishonor. Why does He do this? Verses 22–23 give us God's reasons for acting in this way. On the one hand, He wishes to show His **power, great patience,** and **wrath**; on the one hand, He wishes to show and demonstrate His **glory** and **mercy.** Verse 22 contains some of the most difficult statements in Romans. Paul introduced a question that extends through verse 23. But verse 22 contains one painful idea that centers around the word **prepared.** In Greek the word could be mean that the vessels of wrath have prepared themselves for destruction (middle voice). Or it could mean that someone else has prepared them for destruction (passive voice). With this particular form context must decide which is the proper interpretation. Because of the context of verses 17-20, I have concluded that Paul meant the latter. Someone else has **prepared** the vessels of wrath for destruction, and that someone is God Himself. He is the potter who makes of the one lump of clay one vessel for dishonor. The implication of this statement is unwelcome to many Christians. God, from eternity past, set His affection on certain people, determining to bring them into Christ's image through calling, justification, and suffering. Similarly, He has determined from eternity past to harden some sinners so they will not be able to come to the knowledge of the truth.

This is not the only passage of Scripture which discusses God's hardening of sinners. Proverbs 16:4 says, "The LORD works out everything to its proper end—even the wicked for a day of disaster." Our God has included all things that come to pass in a plan (Eph. 1:11) so even the wicked who oppose His will fit within it. They carry out His purposes. In Genesis 15:13-14 God promised to judge the nation that would enslave Israel. It was not solely His foresight that was at work in this declaration. He decreed that they would enter slavery. It was His purpose for Israel, and it was His purpose for Egypt to enslave them. Then it was equally His purpose to condemn Egypt. In Joshua

11:18-20 the Holy Spirit informs us of God's intent for the Canaanites. "For it was the LORD himself who hardened their hearts to wage war against Israel, so that he might destroy them totally, exterminating them without mercy, as the LORD had commanded Moses" (v. 20). Here is God's sovereign intent to judge sinners. Here is God's intent to destroy, based on His own purposes, those whom He wills.

If we object that we cannot accept such a view of God, should we not rather understand that our minds must be subject to the Word of God? Will we subject His Word to our reason?[8] We should remember what Peter said. The lost consider Jesus "a stone that causes people to stumble and a rock that makes them fall. They stumble because they disobey the message—which is also what they were destined for" (1 Pet. 2:8). Also, "these people blaspheme in matters they do not understand. They are like unreasoning animals, creatures of instinct, born only to be caught and destroyed, and like animals they too will perish" (2 Pet. 2:12). Similarly, Jude 4 says: "For certain individuals whose condemnation was written about long ago have secretly slipped in among you. They are ungodly people, who pervert the grace of our God into a license for immorality and deny Jesus Christ our only Sovereign and Lord."[9]

God has justly and in prolonged forbearance made some vessels for dishonor to show His wrath and power. His justice stands above all question (v. 22). He has also made other vessels of mercy for glory to reveal the wealth of His own glory. Certainly here no one would question His justice (v. 23). Paul expressed God's overall purpose in these verses. It is basic to our understanding of God's purposes that what He does is to reveal His own character. Of necessity, this must be the highest purpose for such a being as God is. For the most perfect being, the only purpose that is fitting and proper is the purpose of showing the extent of His perfection. He ought to help His creatures understand how great He is. Therefore, what God does with both sinful humanity and with the vessels of mercy, He does to show His perfection.

We must not think, therefore, that somehow God has simply made creatures to destroy them. He has endured them with great longsuffering. He has tolerated their rebellion and sin through protracted centuries. Thus, when He finally does bring them to their well-deserved end, He will show the justice of His wrath and His power. Indeed, the demonstration of wrath is essential to the revelation of grace. If God showed favor to all sinners equally, we would only know that favor as mercy since we would have no sign of the depth of sin He has saved us from. It is only when God exercises His wrath that we can clearly see grace for what it is—God's favor shown to those who have forfeited all claim on His favor. So God has set out in our creation peculiarly to show His wrath and His grace. He does it through the vessels of wrath fitted for destruction and the vessels of mercy whom He prepared for glory.

Considering the purpose of Romans expressed in 15:7, these ideas ought to challenge us to the depths of our lives. God has determined to harden some and to give faith to others. Then how shall we in the church respond to His sovereign purpose accomplished in our lives?

First, we must recognize that the vessels of mercy include those He called from both Jews and Gentiles. Then Jew and Gentile must learn to accept each other by grace in the church's fellowship. The Jewish Christian whom the Gentile Christian despises is a vessel for honor, a vessel of God's mercy, whom God has prepared for glory. Who can despise such a work of God? Conversely, the Gentile Christian is likewise a vessel of honor. Who is the justified Jew to condemn one whom God has declared righteous? God determined from eternity past to save Jews and Gentiles on the same basis—through faith in Jesus Christ. Both stand before God by faith. Both stand before God by the merit of Jesus Christ. Both stand before God because of the propitiation and the redeeming work of Christ. Then neither has ground for despising or condemning the other. All of this calls Christians to express God's grace to one another.

Second these truths ought to astonish and delight us, for God has included us who believe in His plan. He might have made us vessels of wrath, but He has given us the Spirit of sonship by which we cry out Abba, Father! God has set His affection on us! God has made us His sons. John reminded us that "everyone who loves the father loves his child as well" (1 John 5:1). If we have come to know the eternal love of God as our Father, we will be people who love one another with the same love. It is the mark of family relationships that the members of God's family love one another. John also said, "Dear friends, let us love one another, for love comes from God. Everyone who loves has been born of God and knows God. Whoever does not love does not know God, because God is love. . . Dear friends, since God so loved us, we also ought to love one another" (1 John 4:7-8, 11).

Third, these truths ought to humble us, for we stand in this honored position before God, not by works of righteousness which we have done, but by His mercy and grace. Pride is one of the besetting sins of those who hold strongly to the doctrine of the sovereign, electing love of God. Somehow such people feel themselves superior to others, even to other Christians who do not agree with them doctrinally. This doctrine contains no room for pride. It ought to banish it. It ought to drive it from the heart. We have nothing of which to boast except the monumental privilege of knowing the living God. Jeremiah said, "but let him who boasts boast about this: that that they have the understanding to know me" (9:24).

Fourth, these truths ought to encourage us to evangelism, for God everywhere and in every generation has those who are His. His is the work of creating and arousing faith in the lost. To us He has granted the right to proclaim the marvels of God's saving grace. When we proclaim the truth, then, He will honor His Word, using us to bring new children to birth in the family. In fact, Paul closed the first part of chapters 9–11 with this very truth, for in verses 24-29 he quoted five Old Testament prophecies demonstrating the hardening of Israel and the hope that hardening gives to the Gentiles.

Paul introduces the quotations as part of his demonstration that the rejection of Israel is in the plan of God. He quotes from Hosea (2:23; 1:10), and Isaiah (10:22-23; 1:9). All the citations confirm that God has planned to reject Israel, even though that rejection is not final. The verses from Hosea reminded Paul's Jewish readers that God had planned centuries before to reject their nation as a nation. The remnant that his readers represent are a type of the future remnant whom God will save when He fulfills all the promises. Furthermore, when the Lord does these things, bringing them to completion and to an end, it will be as Isaiah said when he spoke of the remnant God would leave. Isaiah used the imagery of Sodom and Gomorrah to ex-

plain the judgment he foresaw for his people. Yet even so, the Lord of
Hosts left them a remnant. The judgment that fell on Israel in Paul's
day was as terrible a disaster as that which overtook Sodom and Gomorrah. God judged Israel as He said He would.

In conclusion, Romans 9:1-29 declares that God made a separation in the Israel of Paul's day, as He had in the days of the patriarchs. The seed, the Israel of faith, received the promises. But God
sovereignly hardened the rest and has included the Gentiles in the
inheritance promised to Abraham. The next section (9:30–10:21) explains why God hardened Israel. His hardening was not an arbitrary
decision; it took place for proper reasons.

2. Israel rejected God's righteousness (9:30–10:21).

This section explains that God hardened Israel because they rejected
the offer of faith-righteousness. They should have understood this
righteousness of God from their own Scriptures and from the divinely appointed messengers who proclaimed it to them. The passage
consists of four subsections. In 9:30-33, Paul said that the Gentiles
who were not seeking righteousness found faith-righteousness. Israel,
on the other hand, while seeking law-righteousness, did not achieve it
because of their unbelief. He expressed some of the longing he feels
for Israel's salvation in 10:1-3. Yet he showed that they rejected
God's righteousness while seeking to establish their own. The reason
they rejected God's righteousness (10:4-13) is that they stumbled
over Christ who is true righteousness. They refused to call upon Him
as the God who is mighty to save. Finally, he showed in 10:14-21 that
they did in fact know the message from the prophets. They remained
obstinate in their unbelief, but they knew the message.

a. The Gentiles by faith received what Israel rejected, who stumbled over Christ the rock in unbelief (9:30-33).

**[30]What then shall we say? That the Gentiles, who did not
pursue righteousness, have obtained it, a righteousness that is
by faith; [31]but the people of Israel, who pursued the law as the**

way of righteousness, have not attained their goal. [32]Why not? Because they pursued it not by faith but as if it were by works. They stumbled over the stumbling stone. [33]As it is written:

> "See, I lay in Zion a stone that causes people to stumble
> and a rock that makes them fall,
> and the one who believes in him will never be put to
> shame."

The rhetorical question that begins this paragraph usually introduces the conclusions appropriate to what has preceded. Here it introduces the conclusion to Paul's evidence that God has hardened Israel: the Gentiles have obtained faith-righteousness—**a righteousness that is by faith.** They did not even seek it; they received it by faith, which is to say that they received it by grace (see 11:6). On the other hand, the Israelites, though they sought righteousness (even if it was the righteousness of the law), failed to achieve it. They failed because they sought to achieve righteousness by their own works. They did not seek it **by faith.**

Instead, **They stumbled over the stumbling stone.** Cranfield suggested that the contextual meaning of Isaiah 28:16 (quoted in v. 33), was that, "in contrast with the false security which the rulers of Jerusalem had thought to establish for themselves, God was establishing true and lasting security in Jerusalem for those who trusted in Him."[10] This is the least it could mean in context. Certainly this meaning is appropriate to Paul's discussion. The Israelites had sought to establish their own security by obedience to the law, but they did not understand that only the **rock** that God founded would provide true security for them. Only in Christ and in the righteousness He provides through faith can anyone find true security. Therefore, they did indeed stumble at the stone of stumbling—Christ. Therefore, they will suffer shame since their assumed object of hope, their law-righteousness, will ultimately fail them in the extreme. God has rejected it, and He has rejected all who trust in it. He has declared that Christ is the only way to righteousness and security before Himself, and the Israelites have rejected His way. This double rejection leads to Paul's deep desire for Israel's salvation, the desire he expresses in 10:1-3.

Notes for Romans 9

[1]Cranfield, 2:448.

[2]Cranfield, 2:448.

[3]A story has been told about a troubled lady who approached Charles Haddon Spurgeon. She said, "Mr. Spurgeon, I have a great problem with the fact that God hated Esau." Spurgeon responded, "I can understand why God hated Esau. My problem is, how could God love Jacob?"

[4]In Genesis 33:11 the Hebrew reads, "Please accept my blessing." Jacob had robbed his brother Esau of the blessing. Was Jacob trying to give it back to Esau?

[5]We must not confuse the love and hate here with mere human love and hate. Was it not the same God who said, "Honor your father and mother," and "If anyone comes to me and does not hate his father and mother, his wife and children his brothers and sisters—yes, even his own life—he cannot be my disciple" (Luke 14:26)? To love someone is to choose that one in preference to another. Conversely to hate someone is to pass over that one in favor of another. In fact, since Isaac gave the blessing to Jacob, we could say, in biblical terminology, that he loved Jacob and hated Esau, even though we know that he preferred Esau to Jacob. It is the same when God chose Jacob over Esau. There is no emotional revulsion in God against Esau. God preferred Jacob by choosing him over Esau.

The same distinction appears in Deuteronomy 21:15-16 and Genesis 29:31. Concerning the former passage, Thompson commented: "The terms *love* and *hate* (*dislike*) in the context of polygamous marriage may not connote the clear distinction that is implied in English. The difference may range from the extremes 'love' and 'hate' to the contrast between 'more loved' and 'less loved' (though not 'hated'), i.e. one wife was preferred to the other (cf. Rachel was preferred to Leah, Gn. 29:30, 31; 1 Sa. 1:5)" (J. A. Thompson, *Deuteronomy: An Introduction and Commentary*, p. 229).

[6]Many who are troubled by these ideas struggle with them because of their understanding of free will. If God chooses whomever He wants, then people cannot have free will. This seems to be a valid conclusion. On the other hand, if man's free choice really does determine God's choice, then God is not sovereign at all; man is sover-

eign. I would much prefer to have God's will determining life than the will of man. Would you really rather have sinful man's will determine his eternal destiny, or God's?

[7]The point of this passage deals not with the eternal questions of the problem of evil, but with the temporal disposition of individual humans and peoples. The comments that follow are an attempt to deal only with the issues raised in Romans 9. The passage, and my comments, only push the question of the problem of evil back into eternity where the solution rests only in the person of God. Ultimately, He is the justification of the problem of evil, and that means that we will never fully understand the problems that the existence of evil poses—at least not in this life.

[8]A. W. Pink wrote to this point: "The trouble is that, nowadays, there are so many who receive the testimony of God *only so far* as they can satisfactorily account for all the reasons and grounds of His conduct, which means they will accept nothing but that which can be measured in the petty scales of *their own* limited capabilities" (*The Sovereignty of God,* p. 81). I remain painfully aware that my interpretation may be incorrect. I hope the reader will accept my interpretation as only one student's attempt to grasp the meaning of Scripture, and will continue to pray that God will lead us all into His own truth.

[9]Pink has a rational argument, not based directly on Scripture, for the doctrine that we are advocating: "God had a definite reason *why* He created men, a specific purpose why He created this and that individual, and in view of the eternal destination of His creatures, He *purposed* either that this one should spend eternity in Heaven or that this one should spend eternity in the Lake of Fire. If then He foresaw that in creating a certain person that person would despise and reject the Saviour, yet knowing this beforehand He nevertheless, brought that person into existence, then it is clear He designed and ordained that that person should be eternally lost. Again; faith is God's gift, and the purpose to give it only to some, involves the purpose *not* to give it to others. Without faith there is no salvation—'He that believeth not shall be damned'—hence if there were some of Adam's descendants to whom He purposed not to give faith, it must be because He ordained that *they* should be damned" (p. 82).

[10]Cranfield, 2:511.

b. Paul desires that Israel's zeal for God would bring them to faith, but they have rejected God's righteousness and have tried to establish their own (10:1-3).

¹**Brothers and sisters, my heart's desire and prayer to God for the Israelites is that they may be saved. ²For I can testify about them that they are zealous for God, but their zeal is not based on knowledge. ³Since they did not know the righteousness of God and sought to establish their own, they did not submit to God's righteousness.**

It is the very zeal Israel has for God that fuels Paul's strong passion for the Israelites to **be saved.** They were **zealous for God,** but it was **not based on knowledge.** They were ignorant of **the righteousness of God** that He offers and requires. Yet this ignorance is not a failure in mental capacity or a failure of information. The latter Paul proved in the rest of this chapter. The former Paul showed in verses 3-4.

To understand adequately what Paul meant we need to investigate Israel's ignorance. For us, ignorance refers to a person's low level of knowledge generally or the lack of information on a specific subject. But in the Bible ignorance is not a lack of information that one can solve with proper instruction. Ignorance is a condition of rejecting what one knows. That is, ignorance is a sin. Romans 10 gives enough evidence of that fact. Israel could have known **God's righteousness,** and they should have known it. But what they knew, they suppressed (see 1:18-21). As they suppressed their knowledge of God, they substituted a religion of their own creation. As we saw in Romans 1, people tend to substitute a religion of idol worship. Israel, especially in Paul's day, had substituted a religion based on human obedience. In either case, either in idolatry or in legalism, people substitute what man can do for what God does. Therefore, Israel's ignorance was a rejection of God's prescribed way of righteousness, faith-righteousness.

The Israelites would **not submit to God's righteousness,** and they refused to do so because they were trying to establish their own. They cared nothing about faith-righteousness. In our discussion in chapter 8 we described the flesh as consisting of indwelling sin and a desire for law-righteousness. Here we can see the flesh in its desire for law-righteousness and the spiritual effect it has in a person's life. When we give full rein to the flesh, we reject the righteousness of God, becoming vain in our imaginings (1:21-22) and ignorant of God's revelation. The flesh leads us to reject God's free grace while we try to earn righteousness with God.

> c. **Christ is the true goal of all righteousness that is offered to both Jew and Gentile who will call on Jesus as Yahweh, mighty to save (10:4-13).**

[4]**Christ is the culmination of the law so that there may be righteousness for everyone who believes.**
[5]**Moses writes this about the righteousness that is by the law: "The person who does these things will live by them."** [6]**But the righteousness that is by faith says: "Do not say in your heart, 'Who will ascend into heaven?'"** (that is, to bring Christ down) [7]**"or 'Who will descend into the deep?'"** (that is, to bring Christ up from the dead). [8]**But what does it say? "The word is near you; it is in your mouth and in your heart,"** that is, the message concerning faith that we proclaim: [9]**If you declare with your mouth, "Jesus is Lord," and believe in your heart that God raised him from the dead, you will be saved.** [10]**For it is with your heart that you believe and are justified, and it is with your mouth that you profess your faith and are saved.** [11]**As Scripture says, "Anyone who believes in him will never be put to shame."** [12]**For there is no difference between Jew and Gentile—the same Lord is Lord of all and richly blesses all who call on him,** [13]**for, "Everyone who calls on the name of the Lord will be saved."**

Verses 4-13 explain why Israel remained ignorant of God's righteousness. They rejected Christ. Therefore, since they did not submit to Christ, they did not submit to God's righteousness. Paul stated that **Christ is the culmination of the law so that there may be righteousness for everyone who believes.**[1] Some commentators struggle to show that law here refers to law as a general principle that places demands on people,[2] not to the Mosaic law. They argue that the law cannot be at an end since Paul shows in verses 5-13 that the law testifies to faith-righteousness. It is certainly true that Paul appealed to the law to prove to Israel the truth of his teaching that the law communicated faith-righteousness. But this does not prove the continuing validity of the law as a system of relationship with God.

Some commentators have fallen into a trap. They separate the beginning of relationship with God from the outworking of the relationship.[3] In the Old Testament, life with God began with faith, but it expressed itself by obedience to the Mosaic law. Therefore, we might think that the same pattern would hold in the New Testament, but that is simply not true (see Col. 2:6). The Christian life does not begin with grace and proceed by obedience. The Christian life begins with grace and proceeds only by grace. This is the substance of Romans 5–8. The problem confronted by most of the reformed writers who commented on this text is their view that the law provided a perfect pattern of life for the redeemed. They did not fully accept Paul's teaching that all righteousness for the Christian comes from Christ without works of obedience (Rom. 5). They did not recognize that the believer's righteousness derives altogether from our relationship to the death and resurrection of Christ (Rom. 6). They did not understand the role of the law in stirring up indwelling sin (Rom. 7). They did not see that the power of faith in accomplishing the righteousness is something the law could never and can never produce (Rom. 8).

But if we grant these truths, then we must come to two conclusions. First, we must conclude that when Paul referred to law here, he meant the Mosaic law. This is the only law he could have had in mind. None of his readers would have thought that the law of Rome could give them right relationship with God. Only God's law could even conceivably provide a right relationship with God. Israel did not reject Christ for some undefined principle of obedience. They rejected Jesus' disciples because they were a threat to the law of Moses (Acts 6:11,14). This is the charge even Christian Jews leveled against Paul (Acts 21:21; and so did non-Christian Jews, 18:13). In fact, when Paul described his ground of boasting under Judaism, he described it by law. He said that his deep longing was to "be found in him, not having a righteousness of my own that comes from the law, but that which is through faith in Christ" (Phil. 3:9). Indeed, the issue at the Jerusalem Council was whether to require the Gentiles to be circumcised and to keep Moses' law (Acts 15:5). The concern in the apostle's ministry was not with some vague principle of obedience, but with the Mosaic law's role in the church's life. Therefore, law here, as elsewhere in Romans, is the Mosaic law.

The second conclusion we must draw from these observations is that Christ is "the end of the law" (a more literal rendering of the Greek). Christ is not merely the consummation of the law (as in the NIV), nor the completion of the law (as in the Berkeley version). He is its end regarding righteousness. It can give no righteousness to the believer. All it can do is stir up sin. Only Christ can give righteousness, either in the beginning of the relationship or in its outworking.

Jesus has paid the penalty for our sins through His death. Through His obedience, He has bought for us complete righteousness before God, for in Him we have become the righteousness of God (2 Cor. 5:21). Therefore, the law no longer holds penalty over us; there is now no condemnation (Rom. 8:1). Furthermore, the law no longer provides the standard of relationship with God. Jesus has already set the standard and given it to us in His own righteousness. Therefore, Jesus is the end of the law for righteousness to all believers.

Even Moses taught the distinction between the way of the law and the way of faith. Verses 5-8 give quotations showing that distinction. In verse 5 Paul quoted Leviticus 18:5, showing that the way of the law is obedience to it.[4] But verses 6-8 give a patchwork of quotations from Deuteronomy. "Do not say in your heart" is a quote from the Greek translation of Deuteronomy 8:17 and 9:4. Cranfield stated: "It is significant that both these verses are warnings against a self-complacent, presumptuous boasting in one's own merit."[5] Even Moses warned against the dangers of exalting legal obedience above the grace of God.

But faith-righteousness assures its followers that achieving right standing with God is not a matter of spiritual feats but of believing the message God has authorized (10:6-8). This Paul established by quoting Deuteronomy 30:12-14 in verses 6-8. While the way Paul used the quotations is somewhat ambiguous, the point is clear. The covenant relationship for which Paul was acting as midwife was one that demanded faith, the love relationship that is at the core of faith. Paul quoted part of Moses' affirmation of this in Deuteronomy 30:14 ("No, the word is very near you; it is in your mouth and in your heart so you may obey it") when he said, **The word is near you; it is in your mouth and in your heart.** And what was that word? "See, I set before you today life and prosperity, death and destruction. For I command you today to love the LORD your God." It was their love for God that would lead Israel to keep His commandments. It was Israel's heart that God wanted, for if He captured their heart, He would receive their obedience. What Moses called for in his generation, Paul also taught in his. God looks for faith in Himself, but Israel rejected faith, preferring their own righteousness. They did indeed stumble over the stone of stumbling and the rock of offense. Paul showed in verses 9-13 that this is this very truth of faith in God that Israel rejected, because they rejected the deity of Jesus.

The good news that God has provided for both Jews and Greeks is faith that calls on Jesus as Yahweh, who alone is mighty to save (10:9-13). The message of faith calls for the believer to place loving trust in no less a person than God Himself. That was the message Moses proclaimed (Deut. 30:16), and that was Paul's message too. In fact, Paul summarized some of his preaching in Romans 10:9: **if you confess with your mouth, 'Jesus is Lord,' and believe in your heart that God raised Him from the dead, you will be saved.**

Unfortunately, this verse has been greatly misunderstood. Some have taken the position that this verse refers to walking the aisle at the end of a church service. They will tell us, "If you are not willing to walk to the front of the church before other people, you are not willing to be saved." Nothing could be farther from the truth. In the first place, the first century church had no aisle. In fact, it had no building. It is not the form that the confession takes that is important here. Rather, it is the content of the confession.

Again, some have used the verse to say that if one does not take Jesus as Lord, he does have Him as Savior. But the verse does not address this issue. The two main issues in the verse are the primacy of faith without works of law and the centrality of Jesus' deity to the gospel. Ever since chapter 3, the primacy of faith has been dominant to the message of Romans. All that needs to be said here is that adding anything to faith as a condition of the gospel, especially obedience, denies what we have already seen in the book. Further, it is to deny what we have learned about faith. I have particularly tried to show that faith is a love relationship. In a real love relationship, no one worries about obedience. We do things for the one we love because we love, not because we ought. We do obey. We do things our loved one wants. The difference is that in the realm of obedience, we keep track of what we have done; in the realm of love, we do not. Love keeps no record of obedience.

An illustration might help here. In Luke 7:36-50 Jesus described love by saying that the forgiven woman demonstrated "great love" (v. 47). Her love was a shameless love, for contrary to custom that sinful woman touched a rabbi in public. No self-respecting woman would ever touch a rabbi in public, but she wept over Jesus' feet and wiped them with her hair. She was not content to love Jesus in silence, for she kissed His feet repeatedly while He reclined at the table in Simon's house. Her love required her to demonstrate her love for Him. Finally, she loved Him extravagantly and wastefully, for she "wasted" her valuable myrrh by anointing His feet. This is the woman Jesus said had great love." Jesus Himself said that her great love was proof of how much He had forgiven her. She did not worry about obedience. She yearned simply to do something for the One who had forgiven her sins. This was not a mere intellectual grasp of the gospel. This was not cheap grace. On the other hand, she did not merely submit to Christ's lordship. She showed what faith is like. She demonstrated the depth of the love relationship that Paul has shown us that faith is. To miss this is to misunderstand faith.

The deity of Christ is also of central importance in Romans 10:9-13. To deal with this idea, it is necessary to show that the meaning of **Lord** in verse 9 is indeed "deity." This is clear from the Old Testament passage Paul quoted. The word **Lord** appears three times in the passage (vv. 9,12,13). The word in verse 12 refers to God Himself, not in the sense of His mastery over mankind, but in His capacity as the Savior of all who call upon Him. But verse 13 is a quotation from Joel 2:32, which occurs in a chapter describing how God will save Israel in the future. He will turn to His people to bring them salvation, and then **Everyone who calls on the name of the Lord will be saved.** English versions of Joel 2:32 normally render the Hebrew as LORD (all capitals). Now we know that when the word appears that way, it represents the Hebrew name God gave His people to refer to Himself—Yahweh.[6] It is Yahweh who will save His people Israel when they call upon Him, not some other god.[7] All meaning comes from context. The meaning of LORD in the quotation from Joel 2:32 determines its meaning in Romans 10:9. Thus, what Paul stressed here is that a person must publicly align or identify himself with Jesus who is Yahweh, God Himself, and that salvation comes only from one who is fully God.

This is not merely a matter of idle and insignificant doctrine. If Jesus is not full deity, He cannot save us. If He is merely a man, even a wonderful, exalted man, He has nothing to offer us. Consider these verses: "No one can redeem the life of another or give to God a ransom for him—the ransom for a life is costly, no payment is ever enough—that he should live on forever and not see decay" (Ps. 49:7-9). This passage teaches us an extremely important truth about our redemption. The redeemer cannot be merely a man. Sin demands an infinite payment as penalty, and only God has the resources to pay the ransom for a man's life "that he should live on forever." Unfortunately, as we have already seen, the ransom for a man's life demands death, and God cannot die. Therefore, not even God, in His full deity, can bear the ransom for the life of mankind. For these reasons Jesus, the Son of God, full Deity Himself, had to become a man. In this way, as God, He had the resources to pay the penalty, being Himself infinite. And as man, He could die for man's sins. Jesus' full deity is, therefore, central to the gospel. A Jesus who is not fully God cannot save.[8]

Those who hold to "lordship salvation"[9] use this passage as proof that the sinner must receive Christ as Lord to receive Him as Savior. John MacArthur, an eminent advocate of this position, said:

215

The two clearest statements on the way of salvation in all of Scripture both emphasize Jesus' lordship: "Believe in the Lord Jesus, and you shall be saved" (Acts 16:31); and "If you confess with your mouth Jesus as Lord, and believe in your heart that God raised Him from the dead, you shall be saved" (Rom. 10:9).... No promise of salvation is ever extended to those who refuse to accede to Christ's lordship. Thus there is no salvation except "lordship" salvation.[10]

MacArthur was reacting against a position suggesting that only intellectual faith is necessary for the salvation of the lost. This position says the lost only need to learn good doctrine to receive salvation.

The truth lies somewhere in the middle of the two extremes lordship salvation and mere intellectual faith. To review the position that I have taken in this book, a review of chapters 3–4 would be helpful. I do agree with my lordship salvation friends in some areas. I agree that "No one who comes for salvation with genuine faith, sincerely believing that Jesus is the eternal almighty, sovereign God, will willfully reject His authority."[11] But this statement does not prove that one must accept the lordship of Christ to be saved.[12] Again, I would agree with my lordship salvation friends who say:

Real salvation is not only justification. It cannot be isolated from regeneration, sanctification, and ultimately glorification. Salvation is an ongoing process as much as it is a past event. It is the work of God through which we are "conformed to the image of His Son" (Romans 8:29, cf. Romans 13:11).[13]

On the other hand, I disagree with lordship salvation advocates who seem to mistake works that *result from* faith with works that *are* faith.[14] The real problem, among those who support lordship salvation and those who oppose it, is to define faith properly. Faith is neither mere intellectual assent, nor is it simply equivalent to obedience. To stress obedience in faith is to sap faith of its vitality. We must conceive of faith as a love relationship. Emphasizing obedience forces Christians to focus on externals rather than the heart. Again, we find the specter of the flesh feeding on calls to behavior modification, using the demands of rules to stir up sin in our lives. But we should focus on helping people love Christ more deeply. Then, and only then, will they grow spiritually and manifest the lifestyle of the redeemed. Remember that few Jews in Jesus' day would resist an emphasis on obedience to God. Yet they rejected Jesus absolutely. Why? Not because He stressed obedience, but because He called for an internal righteousness of the heart, not an external righteous of the hands. People may not see the heart's righteousness; they did not see Jesus' righteousness. Romans 14:17 says, "The kingdom of God is not matter of eating and drinking, but of righteousness, peace and joy in the Holy Spirit." These are the authentic issues of the kingdom and of Christian living. But they are not obvious to the eye, and they cannot be measured. To focus on obedience puts us in the position of becoming agents of God's department of weights and standards. It raises again the ghost of self-righteously judging one another, offering each other no grace—only condemnation. Love does not condemn. Obedience cannot help but condemn. In fact, if righteousness and faith are simply obedience, then Paul would not have said what he did in Romans 10:4—Christ is the end of the law. Note that! The person of Jesus Christ is the end of the law. It is not faith in Christ that is the end of the law, but Christ Himself. It is not our obedience that is the end of the law, but Jesus Christ the Lord Himself.

Therefore, this discussion is critical to what Paul wrote in this chapter. Paul showed that Israel rejected the gospel of God's righteousness in Jesus. They wanted a righteousness of their own that comes through the law (v. 3). But they should have known about God's righteousness, that their love relationship with God was the essence of righteousness. Thus, when Paul or Jesus or Peter called a Jew to trust Christ for salvation, they called him to enter a love relationship with the very God who spoke in Deuteronomy—in the Mosaic law. It is the truth of the deity of Jesus that the Jews finally rejected. They wanted to love and serve God without loving and serving His Son. Jews must of necessity accept the truth of Christ's deity to be saved, as must Gentiles. This is crucial to the salvation God offers. People do not need to accept a new master, but to recognize who their God really is. Here is the centrality of Jesus' deity for the gospel.

Just as central to the gospel Paul preached, however, is the resurrection (Rom. 10:9). Paul had already referred to the resurrection in 4:25—Jesus rose from the dead "because of our justification." This means that if Jesus is still in the grave, we remain in our sins. Faith in Jesus' resurrection is basic to saving faith. Again, many of the Jews in Paul's day, as in ours, find the resurrection of Jesus a truth virtually impossible to receive. But if it is true, then the claims of Christ are true. If it is false, Christianity offers nothing but falsehood. The resurrection of Jesus is essential to the gospel.

Israel should have been ready to receive the doctrine of the resurrection. The Pharisees already held to the resurrection of the dead as an essential part of their basic belief system. The Old Testament taught the resurrection of the dead. It prefigured resurrection in historical events (see 2 Kings 4) and in word (see Dan. 12:1-2). The problem Israel faced with the resurrection is the problem Paul had faced. If indeed Jesus rose from the dead, then Pharisaism is obsolete as a religious system. The law is at an end. God has become incarnate and has paid the penalty for our sins. These truths they could not accept. Not knowing God's righteousness, and seeking to establish their own, they did not submit to the righteousness of God (Rom. 10:3).

d. But Israel has surely heard the message proclaimed constantly by the prophets and has obstinately disobeyed in unbelief (10:14-21).

[14]**How, then, can they call on the one they have not believed in? And how can they believe in the one of whom they have not heard? And how can they hear without someone preaching to them?** [15]**And how can anyone preach unless they are sent? As it is written: "How beautiful are the feet of those who bring good news!"**

[16]**But not all the Israelites accepted the good news. For Isaiah says, "Lord, who has believed our message?"** [17]**Consequently, faith comes from hearing the message, and the message is heard through the word about Christ.** [18]**But I ask: Did they not hear? Of course they did:**

"Their voice has gone out into all the earth,
their words to the ends of the world."
[19]Again I ask: Did Israel not understand? First, Moses says,
"I will make you envious by those who are not a nation;
I will make you angry by a nation that has no under
standing."
[20]And Isaiah boldly says,
"I was found by those who did not seek me;
I revealed myself to those who did not ask for me."
[21]But concerning Israel he says,
"All day long I have held out my hands
to a disobedient and obstinate people."

Someone might object that the reason Israel did not receive the gospel is that they did not know it (vv. 14-15,18). Jesus did not preach to the whole nation. The apostles might have obscured the message in some way. Isn't it possible, someone might ask, that Israel rejected the gospel because they did not know it? Verses 14–21 answer that question with an emphatic no.

Israel did indeed hear the gospel. The Old Testament proclaimed it to them. Verse 15 quotes Isaiah 52:7 to show that the prophets themselves proclaimed the message to the people.[15] In proof of this proposition, Paul quoted four Old Testament passages (Ps. 19:4 in v. 18; Deut. 32:21 in v. 19; Isa. 65:1 in v. 20; Isa. 65:2 in v. 21). It is this proclamation of the good news that brings faith: **faith comes from hearing the message, and the message is heard through the word about Christ.** God uses the proclamation of the gospel to create faith in its hearers. But what did God prophesy about Israel's reception of the gospel? Paul explained in verses 19-21 that Israel would reject it. God predicted that He would have to make them who were not a people **envious** (v. 19) and that those who did not seek Him would find Him (v. 20). But as for Israel, He said, **All day long I have held out my hands to a disobedient and obstinate people.** He knew from the beginning that they would reject Him.

So is there any hope for God's people? Has He cast them off forever? Chapter 11 answers these two questions.

Notes for Romans 10

[1]The NIV's translation is similar to many others: the Confraternity Version of the Bible, Goodspeed, the Twentieth Century New Testament, Knox, the Centenary Translation, Williams, Phillips, the New American Standard, and the King James Version. The Berkeley Version and Weymouth give other translations.

[2]So John Murray (*The Epistle to the Romans,* NICNT, 2:51) said, "Paul is speaking of 'law' as commandment, not of the Mosaic law in any specific sense but of law as demanding obedience, and therefore in the most general sense of law-righteousness as opposed to faith-righteousness." Cranfield's position is similar (2:515-20).

[3]So Murray said, "There is no suggestion to the effect that in the theocracy works of law had been represented as the basis of salvation and that now by virtue of Christ's death this method had been displaced by the righteousness of faith" (2:51).

[4]This very quotation further demonstrates that Paul speaks here about the Mosaic law, not about a general principle of obedience.

[5]2:523.

[6]This way of writing the name is the nearest guess scholars have been able to make to the original spelling and pronunciation of the name (see *ISBE,* s.v., "God, Names of," 2[1982]: 507, by Robert J. Wyatt).

[7]Notice that Joel 2:32 is in a context promising salvation to Israel in the future. Again, Paul selected quotations from the Old Testament that offered and promised salvation to Israel. Additionally, the passage in Joel promises salvation to Israel despite their rebellion, which required God to destroy them. Sin is no obstacle to the saving grace of God—not even future known sin.

[8]This is why it is so important for us, when dealing with the teachings of cults, to identify who they think Jesus is. The Jesus of the Mormons is the son of Adam-God, born to His celestial wife Mary. His spirit brother is Lucifer who became Satan. The Jesus of the Jehovah's Witnesses is the first and greatest creation of Jehovah. The Jesus of the Baha'is is one of a series of manifestations of divine wisdom, the seventh of which now lives and supersedes all who have gone before him. These Jesuses cannot save. They are not God. There is no hope in them.

[9]To be honest, some who hold the position we describe dislike the term "lordship salvation," but the term is useful for identifying this position.

[10]John MacArthur, *The Gospel According to Jesus*, p. 28. I have cited this book because of MacArthur's influence in evangelical circles. It is not necessarily the best defense of the position. Actually, I find it lacking in some logical and theological precision and in need of some serious reworking exegetically.

[11]MacArthur, p. 29.

[12]I would say the same thing about the virgin conception of Christ. Anyone who denies that doctrine denies the full deity of the Lord, and that prohibits such a person from salvation. No one who is not God can save. But the doctrine of Jesus' virgin conception is not central to the gospel presentation. It is not necessary for faith and regeneration. That is, believing in the virgin conception (as in being aware of it) is not essential to salvation, but DENYING it prohibits someone from being saved.

[13]MacArthur, p. 23.

[14]MacArthur, pp. 174-75: "Clearly, the biblical concept of faith is inseparable from obedience. 'Believe' is synonymous with 'obey' in John 3:36.... Commenting on this passage, the leading theological dictionary says, 'To believe' is 'to obey.' " This is a difficult statement to understand precisely. MacArthur may be saying "To believe *means* to obey," or he may be saying, "To believe *is the same as* to obey." But he also said, "True faith is humble, submissive obedience" (p. 140); and "True faith is never seen as passive—it is always obedient. In fact, Scripture often equates faith with obedience (John 3:36; Rom. 1:5; 16:26; 2 Thes. 1:8)" (pp. 32-33). But John 3:36 contrasts faith with disobedience, but it does not equate it with obedience. The other three verses are not really relevant to the discussion since they figuratively, not literally, identify faith and obedience. They do indeed say that obedience is faith, not that faith is obedience. Such statements are not reversible. Consider John's statement: "God is love" (1 John 4:8). The reverse of the statement would be heresy.

One key problem I have with MacArthur's position is his emphasis on "full commitment to Christ." He is even uncomfortable with the implications of his own position. On p. 140 he said, "[Faith] is an exchange of all that we are for all that Christ is. And it denotes implicit obedience, full surrender to the lordship of Christ." But later on the same page he backed off: "But a true believer has a desire to surrender." These are not equivalent statements. We know that a desire to surrender to Christ is not always matched by complete surrender. We grow in our understanding of all that a relationship to Christ means (as MacArthur acknowledged). But when and how do we know that we have fully surrendered ourselves to Christ. If that is what faith is, who has it?

[15]This chapter is just before Isaiah 53, a point Paul made in v. 16 by quoting Isaiah 53:1. If the gospel is anywhere in the Old Testament, it is certainly in Isaiah 53!

So far we have seen two parts of the answers to the questions posed in chapters 9–11, which discuss the role Israel plays in the plan of God and the problem presented by Israel's rejection of the gospel. First, God made a distinction between true Israel and fleshly Israel (9:1-29). Second, Israel rejected God's offer of righteousness, even though He had revealed it to them through their prophets (9:30–10:21).

Chapter 11 presents the other three parts of the answer. First, even though God has hardened the nation as a whole, He has preserved a remnant chosen by grace (vv. 1-10). Second, Israel lost their place in God's blessing so that blessing might come to the Gentiles (vv. 11-24). But Israel's displacement is not permanent. God will stir them up to jealousy through the Gentiles. Third, Israel will surely come to faith and salvation (vv. 25-32). Paul closed the chapter with a glorious doxology over God's wisdom in all He has done (vv. 33-36).

3. But God preserved a remnant chosen by grace (11:1-10).

¹I ask then: Did God reject his people? By no means! I am an Israelite myself, a descendant of Abraham, from the tribe of Benjamin. ²God did not reject his people, whom he foreknew. Don't you know what Scripture says in the passage about Elijah—how he appealed to God against Israel: ³"Lord, they have killed your prophets and torn down your altars; I am the only one left, and they are trying to kill me"? ⁴And what was God's answer to him? "I have reserved for myself seven thousand who have not bowed the knee to Baal." ⁵So too, at the present time there is a remnant chosen by grace. ⁶And if by grace, then it cannot be based on works; if it were, grace would no longer be grace.

⁷What then? What the people of Israel sought so earnestly they did not obtain. The elect among them did, but the others were hardened, ⁸as it is written:

"God gave them a spirit of stupor,
eyes that could not see
and ears that could not hear,
to this very day."
⁹And David says:
"May their table become a snare and a trap,
a stumbling block and a retribution for them.
¹⁰May their eyes be darkened so they cannot see,
and their backs be bent forever."

Even though God has hardened the nation Israel as a group, it is not true to say He has rejected the nation. Paul himself was **an Israelite, not because of his faith, but because he was a descendant of Abraham, from the tribe of Benjamin.** Therefore, **God did not reject his people, whom he foreknew.** In every generation, God preserves a remnant of His people, even in times of great apostasy. It was true in Elijah's day (1 Kings 19:10-18). Elijah felt abandoned by his generation. He believed that he alone remained who worshiped God. But God reminded him, **I have reserved for myself seven thousand who have not bowed the knee to Baal.** God never leaves Himself without a remnant that consists of those **chosen by grace.**

Verse 6 emphasizes the point that God's choice is by grace: **if by grace, then it cannot be based on works; if it were, grace would no longer be grace.** The grace of God's choice absolutely rules out any part for works. No human reason determines the choice God has made. Grace and works are polar opposites. They are as distinct as the north and south poles of the globe. Thus grace and works do not mix. Anyone who tries to mix them, even just a little, destroys both systems. Grace cannot remain grace mixed with even a little work, and work cannot remain work mixed with even a little grace.

This is an important observation for the point Paul made in his letter. We have been saying since the beginning of our study that Paul faced a problem in Rome between the Jewish Christians and the Gentile Christians. The Jews felt superior to the Gentiles because they kept the law of Moses. But here Paul showed them that they cannot plead their obedience. Their standing before God is exactly the same as the Gentiles' standing: by grace. Grace rules out faultfinding in our relationships. Jewish Christians have nothing by which to judge or condemn their brothers in Christ. They, like Paul, are a remnant according to the election of grace. Equally, the Gentile Christians cannot despise their Jewish brothers since Jewish Christians are the recipients of great blessings from God (see 9:1-5). The grace in their relationship with God structures their relationships with each other. Both groups need to learn their standing in grace. Works give them nothing. They undeservedly receive all they have because of God's grace.

The offshoot of these observations for Israel as a whole comes in verses 7-10. God has **hardened** Israel as a nation, in fulfillment of Scripture, while the remnant received the promise. Even though Israel sought the promises, they did not obtain them (though the elect did), but God hardened them.

Verses 8-10 give Old Testament quotations showing that God intended to harden His people. Verse 8 gives a composite quotation from Deuteronomy 29:4 and Isaiah 29:10[1] Even from the days of Moses and Israel's entry into Canaan, God had not given Israel **eyes** to see or **ears** to hear. They were unable to understand in Moses' day what God had done for them. Similarly, in Paul's day God gave them **a spirit of stupor** just as He had done in Isaiah's day. Isaiah preached continually to the people, but they rejected his word. Therefore, God reoriented Isaiah's ministry to Israel to be a ministry of hardening. Isaiah 29:10 occurs in a passage promising terrible, apocalyptic judgments on Israel. God judged Israel by withholding revelation from them. The result appears in verse 11: "For you this whole vision is nothing but words sealed in a scroll." Paul explained in Romans 1 that refusal to receive God's revelation brings darkness.

Verses 9-10 introduce a quotation from Psalm 69:22-23. This is an imprecatory psalm,[2] a psalm in which David prays for God's curse to fall on his enemies. He prayed in verse 4 for it to fall on "those who hate me without a reason." These psalms appeal to God to destroy the enemies of Israel's king, who are equally enemies of God's rule on earth. They present David as a type of Messiah, who Himself would face enemies who hate Him without a cause (see John 15:25). The petitions they bear indicate the destiny that awaits those who oppose God's Anointed. By using this quotation Paul meant that national Israel is now in the place of the enemies of the Messiah.

According to Anderson, the **table** that becomes **a snare** is a reference to the sacrificial feasts. Israel intended the feasts to honor God,[3] but, as **a snare** and **a trap,** their table will be an occasion to capture them in sin. Applied to Israel, even their worship would become occasions of sin, occasions to be **a stumbling block and a retribution to them,** since they have spurned their Messiah. Christ's enemies opposed him as God's Anointed. For this reason, David prayed that their eyes should grow blind (**darkened so they cannot see**) and that they would be in terror continually (**backs be bent forever**). Such is the fate of all who defy Messiah.

Why would God offer such tremendous promises and privileges to Israel in the Old Testament, about which we read in chapter 9, and then reject Israel? The answer to that question is the next step Paul took in dealing with Israel's place in God's plan and their response to the gospel.

4. God took the promises from Israel to give them to the Gentiles who received them by faith (11:11-24).

[11]**Again I ask: Did they stumble so as to fall beyond recovery? Not at all! Rather, because of their transgression, salvation has come to the Gentiles to make Israel envious. [12]But if their transgression means riches for the world, and their loss means riches for the Gentiles, how much greater riches will their full inclusion bring!**

[13]**I am talking to you Gentiles. Inasmuch as I am the apostle to the Gentiles, I take pride in my ministry [14]in the hope that I may somehow arouse my own people to envy and save some of them. [15]For if their rejection brought reconciliation to the world, what will their acceptance be but life from the dead? [16]If the part of the dough offered as firstfruits is holy, then the whole batch is holy; if the root is holy, so are the branches.**

[17]**If some of the branches have been broken off, and you, though a wild olive shoot, have been grafted in among the others and now share in the nourishing sap from the olive root, [18]do not consider yourself to be superior to those other branches. If you do, consider this: You do not support the root, but the root**

supports you. [19]You will say then, "Branches were broken off so that I could be grafted in." [20]Granted. But they were broken off because of unbelief, and you stand by faith. Do not be arrogant, but tremble. [21]For if God did not spare the natural branches, he will not spare you either.

[22]Consider therefore the kindness and sternness of God: sternness to those who fell, but kindness to you, provided that you continue in his kindness. Otherwise, you also will be cut off. [23]And if they do not persist in unbelief, they will be grafted in, for God is able to graft them in again. [24]After all, if you were cut out of an olive tree that is wild by nature, and contrary to nature were grafted into a cultivated olive tree, how much more readily will these, the natural branches, be grafted into their own olive tree!

Some of the difficulty in expounding this section arises from one of Paul's peculiarities, seen most clearly in verses 11-12. Paul often began to discuss a subject without completing it. Drawn away by some related idea, he digressed from the subject he just introduced. Here Paul, after beginning to discuss the future hope Israel, has turned to discuss the effect their rejection has had on the world at large. Because they fell from these privileges, salvation has come to the Gentiles to **arouse my own people to envy and save some of them.** One of God's purposes in giving the gospel to the Gentile world was to thrust upon Israel a craving for their privileges they had lost through their unbelief. Paul wanted us to see that the wonderful privileges the world knows today because Israel fell pale in comparison to the riches that will come through their fullness (v. 12; see also verses 15-16).

But in verse 13 Paul digressed. He has mentioned the Gentiles and the hope they presently enjoy. So here he addressed the Gentiles directly, hoping to stir Israel up to jealousy. His purpose is to warn them against spiritual boasting against Israel. Though His people are in a hardened state, God has not forgotten them. Before the end of this chapter, Paul reminded all of his Gentile readers that although Israel is hostile to the gospel, God loves them for the sake of their fathers (the patriarchs). Paul confidently expected Israel's salvation because he knew God's ways. The hope he has for their salvation rests on their relationship to the patriarchs, the **firstfruits** and the **root.**[4] If Abraham, Isaac, and Jacob are holy in God's eyes, then those descended from them remain holy, despite their present condition of hardening.

Verses 17–24 contain several difficulties. Paul used some key expressions that commentators have had difficulty defining. Problems arise especially in three areas: the **nourishing sap,** the cutting out and re-grafting of the branches, and the identity of **you** addressed in the paragraph. Since I have purposed not to write a technical commentary on Romans, it is sufficient to sketch the possibilities briefly.

The last problem is the most significant, for whatever one says about it determines the meaning of the other two problems. The word **you** throughout verses 17–24 is singular. Cranfield interpreted this as an individualizing singular, directing attention to each individual Gentile.[5] Similarly, Stifler said that it is an address to the Gentile believer.[6] These interpretations create terrible difficulties, even contradicting the rest of the letter since whoever Paul addressed as **you** has been grafted into the olive tree and may be cut out again (vv. 17,21,24). Such a reading suggests that branches God cuts out can again come into condemnation (contra Rom. 8:1).

These observations lead me to propose another way of understanding the addressee of this passage.[7] The singular pronoun **you** addresses no particular individual person, but the Gentile world as a single whole. I believe this interpretation makes sense for the following reasons. First, the Jews whom God cut out of **the olive tree** were not saved Jews who became lost again. He cut them out because of their unbelief (v. 19). Therefore, having a place in the tree means to share in the hope of seeing the fulfillment of the promises. Those promises are the **nourishing sap,** for the sap[8] is the life of **the olive tree.**

To summarize, the **root** refers to the patriarchs and the **nourishing sap** refers to the benefits that flow from the patriarchs. All Jews formerly participated in those benefits, whether they were justified or not. God has now removed the nation of Israel from uniquely sharing the benefits and replaced them with the Gentiles. Jewish people who never practiced faith were in the tree and then cut out. That means that the passage is not a reference to loss of election or loss of salvation, but loss of participation in the benefits flowing from the patriarchs. The singular pronoun addresses the Gentile world. It is the Gentiles as a group who are now in **the olive tree.** They share the **nourishing sap** of the **root**—the benefits flowing from the patriarchs. The Gentiles now may lay hold of the benefits, grasping them by faith. If, however, the Gentiles, like the Jews in Paul's day, refuse faith, God will cut them out of the tree and re-graft Israel. This paragraph (vv. 17-24) is a warning that the Gentiles should not grow proud against Israel. Though Israel is in hardening now, it is not permanent (see v. 25), so the gospel might go to the Gentiles. God grafted them in Israel's place, so they now have hope to share Abraham's blessing. But they stand by faith and Israel fell due to unbelief.[9] God will one day re-graft Israel into their own **olive tree.**

Paul began this chapter by saying that God has not rejected Israel. And as we have already seen, Israel's present condition in rejection and hardening is part of God's plan. But Israel's hardening is no more a part of God's plan than Israel's salvation. Their hardening is only partial, their fall only temporary. As Paul pointed out, if their fall has brought the offer of salvation to the Gentiles, what will their deliverance mean when God accomplishes it?

Paul opened this chapter on a note of hope. So where has all the hope gone? Hope remains in the grace of God, who has even in this present day preserved a remnant of Israel chosen by grace. Similarly, in the future God intends in His grace to restore His people to the place of blessing, a truth Paul addressed next (11:25-32).

5. God will stir Israel to jealousy, bringing them to salvation through faith (11:25-32).

[25]I do not want you to be ignorant of this mystery, brothers and sisters, so that you may not be conceited: Israel has experienced a hardening in part until the full number of the Gentiles has come in, [26]and in this way all Israel will be saved. As it is written:

> **"The deliverer will come from Zion;**
> **he will turn godlessness away from Jacob.**
> **[27]And this is my covenant with them**
> **when I take away their sins."**

[28]As far as the gospel is concerned, they are enemies for your sake; but as far as election is concerned, they are loved on account of the patriarchs, [29]for God's gifts and his call are irrevocable. [30]Just as you who were at one time disobedient to God have now received mercy as a result of their disobedience, [31]so they too have now become disobedient in order that they too may now receive mercy as a result of God's mercy to you. [32]For God has bound everyone over to disobedience so that he may have mercy on them all.

Israel's hardening is only partial and temporary (a hardening in part). In God's covenant (the new covenant) He promised to take away all of Israel's sins through the promised deliverer who will come from Zion. Paul quoted from two passages in Isaiah (59:20-21; 27:9) to make his point. Remarkably, after Israel rejected the Messiah at Pilate's palace, after their mocking at the cross, during Jewish persecution of Christians, Paul quoted predictions of Israel's conversion. Can it be true? Is it possible? The answer must be yes. God remains as faithful to His Old Testament promises as He is to His promises in the New Testament. What God requires of His people, He provides. Therefore, their hardening is only partial and only until the full number of the Gentiles has come in. God has purposed to save a specific group of Gentiles, and when He has accomplished their salvation, He will turn again to Israel. Then all Israel will be saved.[10] As if to emphasize that the salvation is for Israel, Paul quoted Isaiah's promise about the deliverer coming from Zion. That deliverer, Jesus the Messiah, will come from Zion to turn godlessness away from Jacob.[11] What a triumph of grace that will be!

For the present they are in rejection so God might save Gentiles. But God will save them since God's gifts and his call are irrevocable, meaning His promises and calling can never be canceled. He called Israel three and a half millennia ago to be His people. His calling is permanent and cannot go off course permanently through His people's disobedience. Even in their disobedience God loves them for the sake of their fathers. For the present they are disobedient. That means that we Gentiles have obtained a privileged place in receiving God's mercy. But days will come in which they too will receive mercy.

6. Conclusion: God's Unfathomable Wisdom and Knowledge (11:33-36).

[33]Oh, the depth of the riches of the wisdom and
knowledge of God!
How unsearchable his judgments,
and his paths beyond tracing out!
[34]"Who has known the mind of the Lord?
Or who has been his counselor?"
[35]"Who has ever given to God,
that God should repay them?"
[36]For from him and through him and for him are all
things.
To him be the glory forever! Amen.

Consider the wealth **of the wisdom and knowledge of God.** In chapter 9–11 Paul explained the incredible plan God has set up to bring His salvation to the ends of the earth. But it is a strange missionary strategy. If we wanted to bring the gospel to Albania, for example, what would we do? We would probably buy a radio station to beam the gospel into the country. We would recruit people of great faith to smuggle Bibles and other Christian literature into that land. We would evangelize expatriate Albanians to send them back to their country to bear the good news of Jesus. But what has God done? To win Israel, He has taken the hope of the gospel away from them and given it to the Gentiles. Why did He do this? He gave it to the Gentiles to stir Israel to jealousy so they would return to God seeking His blessings.

Here is **wisdom** indeed. Here is inscrutable **knowledge** and **unsearchable judgments.** Here is a plan that can only originate with God Himself. No one else would devise such a plan. No one **has known the mind of the Lord,** and no one **has been his counselor**. Therefore, He owes nothing to anyone in all that He does (see Job 35:7; 41:11; Isa. 40:13-14). What glory this is! What wisdom this is! What grace this is for sinful humanity, Gentiles and Jews! Therefore, God has acted, in all His saving work, by grace and by grace alone. All that He does, He does for His own glory, as Paul explained in verse 36: **For from him and through him and for him are all things. To him be the glory forever! Amen.**

This may be the most difficult lesson any human can learn. God acts for His own sake. His glory, His reputation, is the single most significant motivation for God's activity. If it is the most significant motivation for God's activity, then it must be the crowning motivation of all human activity. Since God acts graciously for the sake of His own reputation, so should those whom He has redeemed by His grace. Paul has sought to teach the Roman Christians about grace. He has explained in chapters 1–11 that Christ has accepted them, and us, by grace. We as Christians today must learn to accept one another by grace. To teach us that part of his lesson, Paul has included chapters 12–15.

At this point in Romans we have covered only a part—a major part, but still only a part—of what Paul wanted to teach. Do not stop reading this book or the epistle to the Romans until you have studied the final chapters of Romans. That is where the point of the book is. In 1 Timothy 3:16-17, Paul teaches us about the profit we may derive from "all Scripture." We may certainly gain "teaching" from Scripture, but there is so much more. God is not so much interested in our intellect as He is in our godliness. Paul wrote chapters 12–15 especially to give us the rest of the profit of Scripture, the "rebuking, correcting and training in righteousness, so that the servant of God may be thoroughly equipped for every good work." Therefore, in these final chapters Paul explained how—in light of God's redeeming grace—we are to "accept one another, just as Christ also accepted us to the glory of God" (Rom. 15:7, NASB).

Notes for Romans 11

[1]There are also echoes of these ideas in Isaiah 6:9-10; 21:3; 44:18; Jeremiah 5:21; Ezekiel 12:2.

[2]This difficult group of psalms includes Psalm 7, 35, 55, 58, 59, 79, 109, 137, and possibly 139.

[3]A. A. Anderson, *Psalms (1-72)*, 1:506.

[4]Another view which is worthy of attention comes from C. K. Barrett, *A Commentary on the Epistle to the Romans,* p. 216. He suggested

that the images of the firstfruit and root refer to the remnant of justified Jews who are "the pledge of the eventual salvation of all Israel." This interpretation is consistent with the immediate context, but in the broader context of the section, Paul began by stressing the role of the patriarchs and participation with them in the promises. Further, Paul called all believers children of Abraham in chapter 4. So in light of the following context (vv. 17-24), it seems more likely that these figures refer to the patriarchs.

[5]2:566-67.

[6]James M. Stifler, *The Epistle to the Romans: A Commentary Logical and Historical*, p. 191.

[7]The solution of this problem requires us to consider the other two.

[8]In Judges 9:9, the olive tree in Abimelech's allegory of the trees says, "Should I give up my oil [lit. "fatness"], by which both gods and humans are honored, to hold sway over the trees?" The fatness here is likely the olive oil itself (as the NIV indicates). Paul's use of the figure demands that the branches share in the fatness.

[9]Cranfield (2:567-68) agreed with this interpretation: "Paul is aware that there is a danger that Gentile Christians will be tempted to despise Jews.... It seems likely that he is reckoning with the possibility (or the actual existence?) of an anti-Semitic feeling within the Roman church reflecting the dislike of, and contempt for, the Jews which were common in the contemporary Roman world."

[10]The statement **all Israel will be saved** means that all the living nation will come to salvation in the kingdom. That nation (and any nation) only exists as it exists on earth. The words **all Israel** occur several times in the LXX with that very meaning. The phrase appears 153 times in the LXX, and the following is a selection of relevant occurrences: Numbers 16:34; Deuteronomy 1:1; 5:1; 11:6; 13:11; 21:21; 1 Chronicles 9:1; 11:1,4,10; 12:38; 13:5-6; Ezra 2:70; 6:17; 8:25,35; 10:5; Nehemiah 7:73; 12:47; 13:26. Therefore, God here promised the salvation of a whole living generation of Israelites.

[11]It is this quotation that demonstrates that in referring to Israel, Paul meant the people descended physically from Jacob, not the church.

ROMANS 12

Romans 12:1 begins the second major section of the book. In chapters 1–11, Paul thoroughly explained his doctrine of grace-righteousness, a right relationship with God through His grace. In 12:1, Paul turned his attention to teaching us how to accept one another by grace. This concern to teach Christians to accept one another dominates Paul's thought in 12:1–15:13.

II. Believers, through their self-sacrifice, must receive each other by grace (12:1–15:13).

This section consists of four subdivisions. (1) Paul used 12:1-2 as a bridge between the chapters 1–11 and chapters 12–15. These verses also serve as an introduction to the exhortations of chapters 12–15. In these two verses Paul called his readers to a life of self-sacrifice based on the mercies of God and to a transformed mind that shows the excellence of God's will. The apostle called his readers to self-sacrifice and a transformed mind, but these are not some marvelous mystical experiences. They occur in decidedly concrete ways. The three subsections that remain contain three particular ways of living out self-sacrifice and the transformed mind. (2) In 12:3-8 Paul called his readers to serve one another by their spiritual gifting. (3) Verse 9 introduces the third subsection and summarizes it, calling for sincere love, and this section extends through 13:10. (4) In 14:1–15:13 Paul explained the issues of Christian liberty based on God's grace.

A. The righteous by faith must practice living sacrifice as they are transformed in their minds (12:1-2).

¹Therefore, I urge you, brothers and sisters, in view of God's mercy, to offer your bodies as a living sacrifice, holy and pleasing to God—this is your true and proper worship. ²Do not

conform to the pattern of this world, but be transformed by the renewing of your mind. Then you will be able to test and approve what God's will is—his good, pleasing and perfect will.

In 12:1-2, Paul called his readers to self-sacrifice, which he described as **your true and proper worship** (KJV, "reasonable service"). He based the legitimacy of his call on **God's mercy** (lit. "mercies" as in KJV). We do not usually make the word **mercy** plural. Yet the plural of such abstract words is fairly common in the biblical languages. In them the plural of mercy refers to all the different merciful acts God has done. It is in this word "mercies" that Paul summarized chapters 1–11, indicating that these chapters form the basis of his appeal in 12:1–15:13. Since God has dealt with us so mercifully, it is only reasonable for us to make our lives living, holy, and acceptable sacrifices for one another.

Paul might have commanded his readers to sacrifice themselves for one another. That, however, would have been out of place in this letter. He has, after all, just spent chapters 1–11 teaching about God's grace. So he exhorted his readers by God's merciful work for us. Paul urged us but he did so without commanding. This is similar to Philemon 8-9 where the word **urge** occurs as well: "Therefore, although in Christ I could be bold and order you to do what you ought to do, yet I prefer to appeal [urge] to you on the basis of love."

Two distinctives appear in the Philemon passage that contrast urging with commanding. First, the act of commanding rests on authority; the act of beseeching rests in relationship. Paul had enormous authority as an apostle. But in his letter to Philemon, he was dealing with a beloved brother in Christ, not with a subject. Therefore, he urged Philemon as a brother in the faith. Second, a commander may dislike those whom he commands, and he may care little whether they like him or not. But urging depends on love. Read what Paul said to Philemon again and observe the distinctions he made. Commanding comes from boldness, but urging comes from a loving relationship.

Since God had shown deep mercy and grace to Paul, he needed to show the same grace to his brothers. The justified by faith now live free from law and condemnation. Even though Christ's apostles could impose law on God's people, Paul, with an apostle's full authority, refused to command. The Roman Christians were God's children, Paul's brothers and sisters in Christ. They were not his to command. Rather, in love, Paul exhorted his readers to do what fits their identity because of God's mercies to them. The imperatives that follow, while undergirded by apostolic authority, were nonetheless his appeal to them (as in Phlm. 8-9).

The mercies of God, by their very nature, define the proper lifestyle for the justified. Verses 1-2 define that lifestyle in two steps, the first in verse 1 and the second in verse 2. The first element of that life style is a **sacrifice** of our **bodies.** To keep us from thinking that this is a call to martyrdom, Paul described it with three adjectives. The sacrifice must be **living, holy, and pleasing to God.**

The sacrifice of martyrdom is a costly sacrifice. Imagine being in a room somewhere with other believers worshiping the Lord. During worship a heavily armed soldier enters the room. In horror our songs cease, our very breath catches in our throats. The soldier says, "Your government has fallen and the new government has condemned all Christians to death. But I will let the rest go if one of you agrees to die." In such a situation many of us would gladly volunteer to die under those circumstances. We have learned the value of laying down our lives for our friends. Some of us might have less pure motives. We realize that a quick death is much more desirable than remaining under persecution. But such a sacrifice, as costly as it certainly is, is far less costly than the one Paul called for. Martyrdom is a dead sacrifice. God's mercies call for **a living sacrifice.** The sacrifice of martyrdom is a once for all sacrifice, but a living sacrifice requires dedication every moment of every day of our lives. Paul excluded all thought of a once-for-all sacrifice when he called it **a living sacrifice.**

Calling this **a living sacrifice** implies something else. Paul explained earlier that we have died and risen with Christ, that we now walk in newness of life, and this life means that we live to God (Rom. 6:1-11). As we grow in our understanding of Christ's work, we grow in our ability to live by faith. As we live by faith, we grow in Christlikeness. Jesus Christ is the preeminent Servant who gave His life a ransom for many. Those who have risen with Him will have the same life.

237

Paul spent all of chapters 12–15 explaining this living sacrifice. It includes serving one another through our spiritual gifting (12:3-8), loving one another sincerely (12:9–13:10), and accepting one another as Christ accepted us (14:1–15:13). This sacrifice is eminently practical and down to earth. It is as practical as meeting other people's needs. The apostle John addressed what laying down our lives for one another means: "we ought to lay down our lives for our brothers and sisters." Then he asked, "If anyone has material possessions and sees his brother or sister in need but has no pity on them, how can the love of God be in that person?" (1 John 3:16-17). Living sacrifice is practical. Living sacrifice is our reasonable service.

The sacrifice he calls for is also a **holy** sacrifice. Holiness is a difficult idea for most modern Christians to understand. We associate holiness primarily with purity of life. But moral purity is not inherent in the meaning of the word. A passage where this is easily seen occurs in the law of Moses: "None of the daughters of Israel shall be a cult prostitute [Hb. "holy woman"], nor shall any of the sons of Israel be a cult prostitute [Hb. "holy man"]" (Deut. 23:17, NASB). Such striking uses of this term demands explanation. It is correct to say that holiness is the condition of being set apart. In the creature this "set-apartness" relates to setting oneself apart to the worship and service of deity. In this sense holiness is not primarily moral purity but a condition of separation. Scripture tells us that we become like the deity we serve (see Pss. 115:4-8; 135:15-18). In Canaanite religion the priests and priestesses became just like the gods they served. They were holy because they were set apart for the worship and service of Baal or other Canaanite gods. Moral purity played no part in their holiness. The character of the deity determines the nature of holiness.

The Bible says that the ground on which Moses stood was holy (Ex. 3:5). We certainly cannot think of ground as characterized by moral purity. It was holy ground because it was where God revealed Himself to Moses. Aaron's garments were holy (Ex. 28:2,4). These garments were holy because they were for use in the sanctuary ministry only. The priests wore ordinary clothing until they went each day to minister in the holy place. Then they had to wear the holy garments. The high priest wore a holy crown (Ex. 29:6). The sacrifices made to ordain the priesthood were holy (Ex. 29:34). Moses used holy oil to anoint the tent of meeting and the ark of the testimony (Ex. 30:25-26). The Sabbath is holy (Ex. 20:8; 31:14-15). The Nazirite was holy for the duration of his vow (Num. 6:8). Moral purity for the Nazirite was irrelevant. He was holy during the days of his separation only. He had to keep himself from any product of the vine, and he could not cut his hair. This is his holiness. The grain offering was most holy to the Lord (Lev. 2:3), so only the priests could eat it. The sin offerings, the burnt offerings, and the guilt offerings were also holy (Lev. 6:25; 7:1). This is why the animals that Israel offered had to be perfect. The requirement that the Lord gave for the burnt offering was that it could have no defect (Lev. 1:3). The animal for the holy offering had to be as much as possible like the Deity to whom it was offered. For an ox or a sheep, that meant that it had to be free of imperfections. It must share the character of God.

But what is holiness in God? The holiness of our God is His separation from all that He is not. One theologian defined God's holiness this way: "His holiness is the collective and consummate glory of His nature as an infinite, morally pure, active, and intelligent spirit."[1] Simplified this means that all that God is sets Him apart from all else that exists. One of the main passages supporting this definition is Psalm 99. The psalmist connects God's holiness with the following; His reign (v. 1); His greatness and exaltation (v. 2); His strength, justice, and righteousness (v. 4); His grace and mercy (vv. 6-8); His willingness to forgive (v. 8); and His work of avenging sin (v. 8). Other passages of Scripture add to our understanding. In Leviticus 10 God's holiness includes His separation from Israel and His wrath. Psalm 98:1 indicates that through His holiness God redeems people in keeping with His covenant (see also Ps. 111:9). Isaiah 57:15 associates His holiness with His condescending grace and eternality. Psalm 89:35 links God's holiness with His faithfulness. Psalm 103 connects holiness with His love and immutability (vv. 1,11-17). Psalm 145 links holiness with His incomprehensibility (vv. 1-3,21). Moral purity is only a very small part of the holiness of God.

So what does it mean that we should offer our bodies as holy sacrifices? We have seen that Old Testament sacrifices had to share as much as possible in the character of God. Paul knew this truth. In fact, he would have expected his readers to know it also too since they had studied the Old Testament. He would have assumed that they understood that they should share the character of God. In the Book of Romans, Paul has emphasized the truth that God is a God of grace. Therefore, grace must be in his mind as he calls the readers to offer themselves as holy sacrifices. As we serve one another in our spiritual gifting (12:3-8), love one another sincerely (12:9–13:10), and accept one another, we will be people of grace, that is how we become holy sacrifices to God.

Paul has spent eleven chapters explaining God's grace so we would know how to treat each other by grace. God has showered His grace on us in the person and work of Jesus. He did it "not because of righteous things we have done" (Titus 3:5), for "no one will be declared righteous in God's sight by the works of the law" (Rom. 3:20). He has taken hostile, sinful people (Rom. 5:6-10) and has made them His sons (Rom. 8:14-17). That is God's grace. He has even planned to save that rebellious and contradictory nation, His people Israel. For He will send "The deliverer. . . from Zion; he will turn godlessness away from Jacob… and take away their sins" (Rom. 11:26-27). Here is grace! God Himself is the model for our living sacrifice. Those who have received God's marvelous grace will live as holy sacrifices by offering themselves to one another in grace.

Finally, Paul urged us to make ourselves sacrifices that are **pleasing to God.** Three passages help us understand what it means to be pleasing to God. Hebrews 13:20-21 is a prayer that includes asking God to equip His people "with everything for doing his will" and "to work in us what is pleasing to him." This teaches us a first truth about a pleasing sacrifice: it is God's work in us. It is not something by which we earn merit with God. This life of self-sacrifice that is pleasing to God is a life lived by grace. The grace of God flows in the sacrificial life.

Two other passages teach us something about what sort of life is pleasing to God. In Philippians 4:18 Paul thanked the Philippian church for the gifts they had sent him to support his ministry through the years. These offerings of their love to him, he said, were "a fragrant offering, an acceptable sacrifice, pleasing to God." The sacrificial language of the verse links it closely with Romans 12:1 and in fact links it with the all of Romans 12–13. To give money to those who are carrying the gospel beyond the boundaries of the established church pleases God. To support those who are suffering persecution for the name of Christ gives delight to the heart of God.

The other passage is Romans 14:18, where Paul reminded us that limiting our freedom in Christ for our brothers is pleasing to God. Serving one another, loving one another sincerely, and receiving one another by grace are sacrifices with pleasing aromas. God receives them and they are pleasing to Him.

Our lives must bear the fruit of grace. We have married Him who rose from the dead (Rom. 7:4) so we can bear fruit to God. The necessity of grace in the justified life is not the necessity produced by law. It is the same necessity that lies in a peach tree. A peach tree must necessarily bear peaches. By necessity it cannot bear bananas. It is the necessity of its own nature, and such is the necessity of grace in the believer's life. This is a holy sacrifice. It is not perfection. It is not morality. It is a life that reflects God's character. Only with such a sacrifice is God well-pleased. Such a life overflowing with grace, such a living sacrifice, is our reasonable service!

The second element of the lifestyle that fits the mercies of God appears in verse 2. **Do not conform to the pattern of this world, but be transformed by the renewing of your mind.** This command has something to do and something to avoid. Negatively, we must avoid the world's efforts to mold us into its values. Positively, we must put ourselves into God's hands to mold us to His will.[2] The Greek verbs translated **conform** and **be transformed** are present tense imperatives, which usually indicate ongoing obligation. The Romans were already subject to this transforming work. Paul used the present tense here to indicate that fact, and that he wants them to keep it up.

This transformation occurs **by the renewing of your minds.** It surprises some Christians to realize that we still need our minds renewed. When we enter the Christian life, we bring with us much from the world. Although we have died to sin, we carry with us our grave clothes, that is, this old body (see Rom. 8:23). Our immaturity makes us think in worldly ways, and so we still act in worldly ways. We need a renewed mind so that we will come to think as God thinks. We need a godly mindset, which takes time. It comes with growth in grace and faith. It comes through the work of God but also through our cooperation. We must recognize our need for a renewed mind and foster the process.

In the context of this letter, the Romans needed a renewed mind. They still evaluated themselves and each other as if they had never experienced God's grace. They condemned one another. They despised one another. They lived as if they had never experienced justifying grace. Here is the core of the problem with the Roman Christians. They needed their minds renewed so they would under-stand the grace God had shown them. They needed their minds re-newed so they would understand the grace God showed to others[3] and so that they would offer God's grace to each other. In this way, they would prove that the will of God is **good, pleasing and per-fect.** Beginning with verse 3, Paul explained the self-sacrifice he urged upon them and the transformation he called them to.

> B. **Those who are righteous by faith and called to living sac-rifice must express God's grace in ministry through their spiritual gifting (12:3-8).**

[3]For by the grace given me I say to every one of you: Do not think of yourself more highly than you ought, but rather think of yourself with sober judgment, in accordance with the faith God has distributed to each of you. [4]For just as each of us has one body with many members, and these members do not all have the same function, [5]so in Christ we, though many, form one body, and each member belongs to all the others. [6]We have different gifts, according to the grace given to each of us. If your gift is prophesying, then prophesy in accordance with your faith; [7]if it is serving, then serve; if it is teaching, then teach; [8]if it is to encourage, then give encouragement; if it is giving, then give generously; if it is to lead, do it diligently; if it is to show mercy, do it cheerfully.

This section appears to be a passage calling God's people to humili-ty, since Paul warned **do not think of yourself more highly than**

you ought. In one sense, this passage *is* dealing with humility. The problem is that modern ideas about humility are not biblical. Many think humility means we are aware of our shortcomings and think less of ourselves because of them. Such humility can be a mask for pride, for it ignores what God has done in us and through us. It does not allow us to recognize the genuine place God has given us in the body of Christ. Biblical humility is much different. It is not thinking lowly of ourselves. Genuine biblical humility is the freedom not to have to worry about ourselves. Genuine biblical humility drives us to find our hope in God and focus our thought on other people. This kind of humility is what this passage is about.

Paul told the Roman Christians to think. . . **in accordance with the faith God has distributed to each of you,** and this faith expresses itself in the role believers play in the body of Christ. The human body has **many members** that differ widely in **function.** So it is with the body of Christ. God has placed us in the body according to His plan, and each of us fills an essential role within that plan. In a very real sense, each of us is God's gift to the church. Therefore, we who have received grace from God must have a proper, though not inflated, evaluation of our worth in the body. We are members of one another as we are members of Christ, **and each member belongs to all the others.** We are essential to each other for spiritual growth. Therefore, each gifted person ought to function according to the role he plays in the body (vv. 3–8). This is the beginning of the life of self-sacrifice, the life appropriate to the mercies of God.

In verses 6-8 Paul lists six gifts that God might give to believers in the church. The major New Testament teaching on gifts appears in 1 Corinthians 12–14. Here we have only a brief passage on the subject, so my comments are brief. No list of the spiritual gifts is the same as any other (see also Eph. 4:11). From that I conclude that the New Testament nowhere gives a complete list of the gifts. Certain representative gifts appear according to the author's purpose when he wrote. The list in this passage appears as part of Paul's call to living sacrifice. We make our bodies a living sacrifice when we serve one another. Yet how can we serve someone we condemn or despise? Only by learning the lesson of grace can we serve others. We might **prophesy** or **serve** or **teach** or **give encouragement** or **give gen-**

erously or help[4] or **show mercy.** But we must do it according to the grace that God has given us.

Romans 12:1-2 contain in essence a call to covenant loyalty. Paul explained the covenant in Romans 1–11. In chapters 12–15 he called the readers to face their covenant responsibility. In the old covenant the great commandment was to love God wholeheartedly (Deut. 6:5). In John 13:34-35 Jesus gave the "new command." It is new only in that it replaces the great commandment God gave in Deuteronomy. The great commandment of the new covenant is "Love one another. As I have loved you, so you must love one another."

In John 15:13 Jesus described His own love for His disciples, the model for their mutual love: "Greater love has no one than this: to lay down one's life for one's friends." Romans 12:1–15:13 is an explanation of that truth. He has called us to living self-sacrifice for one another. We will best prove our share in the new covenant as we love one another sacrificially. We will best offer that living sacrifice by serving one another as God has given us grace in our spiritual gifting. We will best show our covenant loyalty by serving one another. "Love one another," Jesus said. He said that the greatest love is to lay down our lives for our friends.

C. Those who are righteous by faith must offer their living sacrifice through sincere love (12:9–13:14).
    1. Those who have received grace from God should love one another sincerely (12:9-16).

[9]**Love must be sincere. Hate what is evil; cling to what is good. [10]Be devoted to one another in love. Honor one another above yourselves. [11]Never be lacking in zeal, but keep your spiritual fervor, serving the Lord. [12]Be joyful in hope, patient in affliction, faithful in prayer. [13]Share with the Lord's people who are in need. Practice hospitality.**

[14]**Bless those who persecute you; bless and do not curse. [15]Rejoice with those who rejoice; mourn with those who mourn. [16]Live in harmony with one another. Do not be proud, but be willing to associate with people of low position. Do not be conceited.**

The list of commands that begins in verse 9 builds on the opening sentence: **Love must be sincere.** In classical Greek, the root of the word translated **sincere** (literally "unhypocritical") referred to an actor.[5] Since actors are pretenders, the word group came to have the meaning of pretending or pretense. Therefore, the love for which Paul calls is genuine with no "play acting." This love ought to be the basis for overcoming the division within the church. Such genuine love will have no affection for **evil,** but will **cling to what is good.** Those who love genuinely arouse in themselves and for each other brotherly affection, honoring others over themselves (v. 10). They are zealous in spirit and never fail in their concern for one another, thus **serving the Lord.** They show the genuineness of their love for one another by giving to the needs of **the Lord's people,** in this way pursuing **hospitality.**[6] They ought not simply to wait for opportunities to show hospitality, but like Abraham they should pursue them. Sincere love means we bless even our persecutors (v. 14). It means we **rejoice with those who rejoice** and **mourn with those who mourn.** This is what it means to be of the same mind. Anyone who practices this type of sincere love indeed condescends to help **people of low position.** They avoid being **proud** or **conceited** and seek to **live in harmony with one another.**

> 2. Those who love one another with sincere love must avoid avenging themselves on their enemies, leaving vengeance to God and the ministers to whom He has given the execution of justice (12:17–13:7).

[17]Do not repay anyone evil for evil. Be careful to do what is right in the eyes of everyone. [18]If it is possible, as far as it depends on you, live at peace with everyone. [19]Do not take revenge, my dear friends, but leave room for God's wrath, for it is written: "It is mine to avenge; I will repay," says the Lord. [20]On the contrary:

> "If your enemy is hungry, feed him;
> if he is thirsty, give him something to drink.
> In doing this, you will heap burning coals on his head."

[21]Do not be overcome by evil, but overcome evil with good.

When God's people love sincerely, they have no room for vengeance. The grace Paul has taught in Romans should produce in the recipients love that excludes vengeance. Paul ruled out vengeance against anyone. He does not limit this love to the body of Christ. Indeed, in the verses of this section, he extends his call for love to all who come into our relationship, even those who harm us. The grace of God acting in our lives demands that we **Do not repay anyone evil for evil.** It demands that we **live at peace with everyone.** It demands that we treat everyone well, in ways which all will recognize as good. Grace in our lives means that we must **not take revenge** in our relationships. Vengeance belongs to God, as He has said (Deut. 32:35). Therefore, when we receive ill treatment, it is never right for us to respond with hatred and bitterness. Our responsibility is to do whatever we can to make our tormentor's life more pleasant and comfortable. This is the point of Paul's quotation about heaping **burning coals on his head** (see Pro. 2:21-22).[7] Feeding an enemy is the "only vengeance you are to inflict, the coals of red-hot love."[8]

This is the power of grace in a life. In our sufferings grace teaches us that "our struggle is not against flesh and blood" (Eph. 6:12). Grace teaches us that the tormentor is not the real cause of our troubles. Grace teaches us that we are no different from our enemies apart from Christ. Grace teaches us to see the terror behind the persecutor, but to love the persecutor. Grace teaches us to recognize the bondage of sin in the tormentor's life, to grieve over him, longing for him to know Christ's grace. This is how we **overcome evil with good.** Therefore, grace and vengeance are mutually exclusive since one rules out the other.

Notes for Romans 12

[1]Dabney, *Lectures in Systematic Theology*, pp. 172-73.

[2]Paul used the passive imperative here, a difficult form to interpret. Cranfield was probably correct when he suggested that the passive imperative implies that the subject has a responsibility to allow the action of the verb: "The passive imperative [*metamorphousthe*] is consonant with the truth that, while this transformation is not the Christians' own doing but the work of the Holy Spirit, they nevertheless have a real responsibility in

the matter—to let themselves be transformed, to respond to the leading and pressure of God's Spirit" (2:607).

³Cranfield expounded these verses as if the main appeal were for morality, an interpretation that misses the point of the whole book.

⁴The Greek term I have translated "help" (*proistemi*, NIV "lead") needs some discussion. The KJV translates it "rules." The problem with that translation is twofold. First, it does not fit the context, for ruling may involve no service at all since those ruled serve the ruler. While the NT clearly includes service in ruling, the translator must look for equivalents that do not feed improper target language assumptions. Second, the word in Greek does not mean" rule." Cranfield suggested that it refers to "the person, who by virtue of his social status was in a position to be, on behalf of the church, a friend and protector of those members of the community who were not in a position to defend themselves (e.g., the widows, orphans, slaves, strangers)" (2:626-27). The noun form of (*prostatis*) appears in Romans 16:2, where few commentators would translate it "ruler" since it refers to Phoebe, the "helper of many" (NASB). If it means "helper" in the one place (as it surely does), it might have a similar meaning elsewhere. The context here indicates that the verb does indeed mean something like "help." It occurs with teaching, encouraging, sharing, and showing compassion—helping gifts. Therefore, I have rejected "rule" as an appropriate translation of the verb.

⁵Liddell and Scott, *A Greek-English Lexicon*, s.v., "ὑποκρίτης," p. 1886.

⁶The modern American primarily thinks of hospitality as a character quality in the person who has friends and family in his home regularly and makes them feel at home. Hospitality in the first century was very different. One showed hospitality primarily to traveling strangers who would need shelter, provisions, and perhaps even legal protection (see Gen. 18–19, Abraham's provision for, and Lot's protection of, the angels). In the first century, there were no hotels or motels, as we think of them. The only places available for travelers had a bad reputation. Therefore, the Christian traveler urgently needed someone to provide for his needs. The Greek word for hospitality consists of two parts, which mean "love of strangers." This passage does not command Christians to show hospitality to his friends and

family; it teaches us to show hospitality to brothers and sisters in Christ whom we do not even know.

[7]Such is the interpretation given by McKane: "To show kindness and magnanimity to an enemy by satisfying his hunger and thirst is to deal with him in a salutary way… Kindness shown to an enemy, because it is undeserved, awakens feelings of remorse. When the enemy has steeled himself to meet hate with hate and is impervious to threats of revenge, he is vulnerable to a generosity which overlooks and forgives, and capitulates to kindness" (*Proverbs: A New Approach*, pp. 591-92). Other commentators on Romans (such as Cranfield, Murray, Bruce, and Greathouse) hold the same opinion.

[8]James M. Stifler, *The Epistle to the Romans: A Commentary Logical and Historical*, p. 213.

¹Let everyone be subject to the governing authorities, for there is no authority except that which God has established. The authorities that exist have been established by God. ²Consequently, whoever rebels against the authority is rebelling against what God has instituted, and those who do so will bring judgment on themselves. ³For rulers hold no terror for those who do right, but for those who do wrong. Do you want to be free from fear of the one in authority? Then do what is right and you will be commended. ⁴For the one in authority is God's servant for your good. But if you do wrong, be afraid, for rulers do not bear the sword for no reason. They are God's servants, agents of wrath to bring punishment on the wrongdoer. ⁵Therefore, it is necessary to submit to the authorities, not only because of possible punishment but also as a matter of conscience.

⁶This is also why you pay taxes, for the authorities are God's servants, who give their full time to governing. ⁷Give to everyone what you owe them: If you owe taxes, pay taxes; if revenue, then revenue; if respect, then respect; if honor, then honor.

In 13:1-7 Paul continued the emphasis he began in 12:17-21 of loving one another sincerely. This means we must avoid all vengeance. When wronged we must learn to respond with practical acts of love (12:20-21). We must leave vengeance to God because He has reserved it for Himself (12:19). Yet He has also delegated responsibility for avenging wrong to His ministers, the officials of government (13:4). God has not left all justice to the future. Therefore, we may simply do as much as we can to foster peace in all our relationships (12:18). These opening verses, then, explain the role of government in avenging evil. They also explain how Christians should relate to the officials. This relationship is all the more difficult because government officials are often unbelievers. For Paul this was no obstacle. If God has appointed them, they are His ministers. He makes all things work together for good to those who love Him (8:28).

Verses 1-2 lay out the basic principles Paul wanted to address. Christians must submit to the government because God has ordained them to their office. Verses 3-4 primarily focus on the role of God's officials in avenging evil. Finally, 5-7 focus on Christians' responsibilities to God and His officials.

Paul made the command in verse 1 individual with the term **everyone** (Greek, "every soul"). No one in the Christian family is exempt from Paul's teachings on this subject. He called every individual to submit to the government.

Even among Christians, submission is largely misunderstood. Submission is as central to the Christian life as it is misunderstood. In our Christian culture submission has become the inferiority role we assume as wives, children, or employees (see Eph. 5:22–6:9). But this point of view has not understood a key fact about submission. Submission is not for the inferior. Submission is for everyone. Writing to the Ephesian church, Paul called every believer to be filled with the Spirit (5:18), and he explained what he meant in the verses that follow. In this passage, being filled with the Spirit means worshipful, joyful singing (v. 19), constant and consistent thankfulness (v. 20), and submitting to one another in the fear of the Lord (v. 21). This submission is for the wife (vv. 22-24), but it is also for the husband (vv. 25-33). Submission is for children (6:1-3), but it is also for the parents (6:4). Submission is for the slave (6:4-8), but it is also for the master (6:9). Submission, then, is not for the inferior. It is for everyone.

Ephesians contributes one other fact about submission. Submission is what the elite do. The command to submit to one another appears in the second main section of the epistle, beginning with chapter 4. In 4:1 Paul called them to "live a life worthy of the calling you have received." He defined that calling in the first three chapters. God has blessed Christians with every spiritual blessing in the heavenlies in Christ (1:3); predestined them to adoption (1:5) so they would contribute to the praise of the glory of His grace (1:6); redeemed them, forgiving their sins (1:7); sealed them with the promised Holy Spirit who is the guarantee of the promised inheritance

(1:13-14); and gave them life together with Christ (2:5), raising them from the dead (1:6). But most importantly He has enthroned them in heavenly spheres together with Christ to show the surpassing wealth of God's grace in the ages to come (2:7). Christians are the elite of the universe, and these elite are those whom Paul commanded to submit to one another. Submission is the role that even Jesus will assume: "the Son himself will be made subject to him who put everything under him" (1 Cor. 15:28). Submission is for the elite. One commentator on Ephesians suggested that submission is the attitude of princes who yield to one another to accomplish a common goal.[1]

When Paul called his readers to submit to the government, he did not place them in a role inferior to the government. He gave them the position purchased for them by Jesus Christ. They are the elite of the world. This means that it is appropriate for the world's elite to submit to God's officials whom He ordained to bring vengeance on evil.

After calling his readers to **be subject to the governing authorities,** Paul explained why: **there is no authority except that which God has established.** No official of government ever achieves any position without God's specific decree. Therefore, to resist those officials is to resist the decree of God and bring judgment upon oneself. These statements become all the more amazing when we consider the nature of the government under which Paul lived. The men who ruled the Roman empire in the middle of the first century were profoundly immoral men. Nero was the Roman Emperor when Paul wrote Romans. He indulged "in low pleasures and excesses" and surrounded "himself with dissolute companions—habits that the emperor never abandoned."[2] The same source recounts that he exhausted the state treasury and began a program of confiscating the estates of unfortunate nobles. So extravagant was Nero that he left the Roman Empire bankrupt.[3] This is the background of the passage we are reading. This is the background for Paul commands for his Christian readers in Rome to submit to the government. God ordained even Nero himself to be emperor. His was the special duty before God to avenge evil within the Roman Empire.

Therefore, Christians should do what is good under government officials, since it is the prerogative of the state to **bear the sword** and they do not do so **for no reason.** The statement requires little thought or exposition. Swords are not for spanking. The government, which has been **established by God,** has the responsibility to carry out capital punishment. This responsibility includes the assessment of all lesser penalties. The government is the proper administrator of justice, not the church. In fact, Paul here referred to government officials as **God's servants, agents of wrath to bring punishment on the wrongdoer.**

The actual outworking of what Paul said here is clear in general. But in certain specifics it is not so clear. In our day civil disobedience has become a major tool for social change. The civil rights movement used it successfully to accomplish its goals. The pro-life movement has used it to agitate for the abolition of abortion in America. A passage such as Romans 13 might seem to prohibit all civil disobedience. On the other hand, the Lord's apostles were never squeamish about disobeying man's laws when they contradicted God's commands. How do we find our way between what we read here and what we see of the apostles' practice?

First, we must say that whether in obedience to man's laws or in civil disobedience, we must always live in submission to the government. A way exists to break government laws and remain in submission, surprising as it may seem. When we find that we must break government laws to obey God, we must submit to the government in at least two ways. First, we submit to the government in our attitude. It is out of harmony with Christian living to ridicule the government or speak disrespectfully of government officers. Jude warned about those who reject and slander authority (v. 8). Always a Christian ought to respond this way to the government, offering the respect and dignity due to God ordained officials.

Second, we ought to obey the government whenever we can. But when we cannot, we can submissively bear the penalty, unjust as it may be, that the government assesses for our transgressions. We must not engage in accusations or berating. This is not what the Lord did when He found Himself falsely accused. Peter spoke about Jesus' response to false condemnation. Peter held the same view that Paul did about the value of unjust suffering for the Christian: "But if you suffer for doing good and you endure it, this is commendable before God. To this you were called, because Christ suffered for you, leaving you an example, that you should follow in his steps. He committed no sin, and no deceit was found in his mouth. When they hurled their insults at him, he did not retaliate; when he suffered, he made no threats. Instead, he entrusted himself to him who judges justly" (1 Pet. 2:20-23). This is the pattern for all Christian suffering. This means that if the government should decide that we need to suffer, we must bear it in submission. We know that God will produce Christlikeness in us through it (8:28-29). Even this unjust suffering works to our eternal advantage.

One other idea demands a hearing. In the Bible civil disobedience occurs only when the government requires of a believer something that is directly contrary to what the Bible teaches. Consider the cases of Shadrach, Meshach, and Abednego. When Nebuchadnezzar, the Babylonian king and head of the government, demanded that they worship an idol to a false god, all three disobeyed. The government has no God-given right to dictate the object of our worship. But they did not ridicule or berate even those who made such godless decrees. Here is their response to the king:

> King Nebuchadnezzar, we do not need to defend ourselves before you in this matter. If we are thrown into the blazing furnace, the God we serve is able to deliver us from it, and he will deliver us from Your Majesty's hand. But even if he does not, we want you to know, Your Majesty, that we will not serve your gods or worship the image of gold you have set up (Dan. 3:16-18).

They did not find fault or scold. They accepted the king's right to punish them for their refusal. They remained respectfully forthright in their approach to the king. But they refused to strike a compromise between their responsibility to God and their duty to the king.

It is a little more difficult to make application when the issues set by the government do not demand that we violate Scripture. The government, being a pagan entity, may take positions that are ungodly. This is what we should expect. As the song "Am I a Soldier of the Cross" says, this world intends to be no friend to grace. Since this is the case, when should we take issue with the government? In what situations should we engage in civil disobedience? Sometimes we face no government demand to violate Scripture. Sometimes we only face pagan practices in the government or in a society aided by the government. In fact, in these matters we always face the danger of opposing the government because we are rebellious people. The government may not be wrong at all. Peter also addressed this issue. He said, "Live as free men, but do not use your freedom as a cover-up for evil; live as servants of God" (1 Pet. 2:16). When the issues are not clear, we must before God follow our convictions. Some of us will be certain that we should disobey the government. Others will be certain that we should not violate the government's laws.

A good example of this is the abortion controversy. The group Operation Rescue consists of Christians who are certain of their responsibility before God to violate laws to save the lives of the unborn. Other Christians, equally mature spiritually, firmly believe that they should not violate such laws. Each group may practice submission to the government by treating the police and the courts with the respect and dignity due them as ministers of God. The people in the first group, those who practice civil disobedience, must willingly bear whatever penalty the government imposes. The other group obeys the lesser laws, while opposing the sin of abortion. They must minister to those in the first group who suffer under the government's punishment. This is the time to "look after orphans and widows in their distress" (Jms. 1:27) to show to the world pure and undefiled religion.

Submission to the government in America has at least one other meaning. We are, in theory, a government of and by the people. This places on Christian citizens the obligation to be involved in the governmental processes to live out the righteousness that we are in Christ. We ought to practice our citizenship and governmental role so our Christian commitments are obvious. When we sway public opinion, the government will become less pagan. This is a role that comes upon us in America because of our government system. On the other hand, God has not in Scripture given us the responsibility to make the government Christian.[4]

Paul added a final note about our submission to the government. Submission to the government means that we **pay taxes** to support **God's servants** for vengeance. Christians ought to have certain

254

debts. We owe **taxes, revenue, respect,** and **honor.** These we pay because God has ordained them for the support of His servants. We will owe these debts as long as God puts off the final day of judgment. Then these debts we must pay. But the "debt" of vengeance we can leave to God Himself, and to His appointed servants. We must seek to pay no other debt than to do good to all, even to those who harm us.

3. Believers must have no unpaid debts except love, for love satisfies all the law could impose (13:8-10).

8Let no debt remain outstanding, except the continuing debt to love one another, for whoever loves others has fulfilled the law. 9The commandments, "You shall not commit adultery," "You shall not murder," "You shall not steal," "You shall not covet," and whatever other command there may be, are summed up in this one command: "Love your neighbor as yourself." 10Love does no harm to a neighbor. Therefore love is the fulfillment of the law.

With this Paul returned to the subject he started in 12:9, the subject of love for one another. Indeed, the only unpayable debt which we ought to have is **to love one another.** Many have used verse 8 to prove that it is ungodly to incur financial **debt.** While the Bible no where encourages indebtedness, it does not universally condemn it. Both the Old Testament and the New Testament assume debt as a fact of life. The Mosaic law makes provisions for debt. It contains basic laws respecting the imposition of interest on loans (Deut. 23:19-20), places limitations on loan collateral (24:6), and restricts how a creditor may collect the collateral for a debt (24:10-13). Paul himself understood that every person has legitimate debts. Some are mentioned in verses 6-7.

Additionally, the language of the command in verse 8 does not support the absolute prohibition of debt. The Weymouth translation accurately represents the force of the Greek text: "Leave no debt unpaid except the standing debt of mutual love."[5] The point is that Christians should labor to pay off all of their debts. But we need to recognize that the debt of love is finally unpayable. This debt is a constant obligation we have to others. Yet it is a debt that we must pay, even though we will never pay it off.

This call to love is so important to Paul because of the role love plays in the Scriptures. Love is what God sought in the Israelites through the Mosaic law. Most readers are familiar with Deuteronomy 6:5, "Love the LORD your God with all your heart and with all your soul and with all your strength." But this is not the only time Moses challenged his people to love. Moses also said, "And now, Israel, what does the LORD your God ask of you but to fear the LORD your God, to walk in obedience to him, to love him " (10:12). Also, "If you carefully observe all these commands I am giving you to follow—to love the LORD your God, to walk in obedience to him and to hold fast to him…" (11:22). God is so committed to develop love in His people that he promised to provide Israel with a heart to love him (Deut. 30:6). Therefore, Moses concluded his charge to the people in verses 16-20 with two beautiful calls to love God: "For I command you today to love the LORD your God… Now choose life, so that you and your children may live and that you may love the LORD your God."

Love for God leads to love for other people. If we love God, we will love what God loves. We mentioned above the command to love God in Deuteronomy 10:12. In verses 18-19 Moses addressed this issue: "He defends the cause of the fatherless and the widow, and loves the foreigner residing among you, giving them food and clothing. And you are to love those who are foreigners, for you yourselves were foreigners in Egypt." Love is so important that it can replace the law. Paul explained that faith does not annul the law, but that it establishes it (Rom. 3:31). To prove that statement has required all of the intervening discussion. Here he made his point. Love can replace the law for this reason: **Love does no harm to a neighbor. Therefore love is the fulfillment of the law.** This is why no law is necessary for those whom God has declared righteous. Law is not needed in those in whom God is producing love for Himself. That very love will—or at least ought to—lead them to love one another. His love for them will—or at least ought to—be the pattern for their mutual love. Once more, therefore, Paul has called us to "accept one another, as Christ accepted you" (Rom. 15:7). Before he turned to develop that idea more specifically in chapters 14–15, he gave extra motivation for fulfilling his instructions—the near return of the Lord.

> **4. Parenthesis: Since you know that the time of the Lord's coming and the culmination of your salvation is near, give no opportunity to the flesh but live like Jesus Christ in the world (13:11-14).**

[11]**And do this, understanding the present time: The hour has already come for you to wake up from your slumber, because our salvation is nearer now than when we first believed.** [12]**The night is nearly over; the day is almost here. So let us put aside the deeds of darkness and put on the armor of light.** [13]**Let us behave decently, as in the daytime, not in carousing and drunkenness, not in sexual immorality and debauchery, not in dissension and jealousy.** [14]**Rather, clothe yourselves with the Lord Jesus Christ, and do not think about how to gratify the desires of the flesh.**

The second coming of Jesus is among the most powerful motivations for Christian living in the New Testament. Wherever the future hope of the kingdom appears throughout the Bible, the writers associate it with calls to changed lives. Jesus warned His disciples to watchfulness because of His coming (Matt. 25:42). Peter asked, "Since everything will be destroyed in this way, what kind of people ought you to be? You ought to live holy and godly lives as you look forward to the day of God and speed its coming.... So then, dear friends, since you are looking forward to this, make every effort to be found spotless, blameless and at peace with him" (2 Pet. 3:11-12,14). John told his readers, "But we know that when Christ appears, we shall be like him, for we shall see him as he is. All who have this hope in him purify themselves, just as he is pure" (1 John 3:2-3).[6]

The Romans knew the significance of **the present time** since future **salvation** was drawing even closer. Therefore, they must recognize equally the need to live out their identity in Christ (vv. 13-14).

If Christ's coming was **nearer now than when we first believed** for Paul and the Roman Christians in the first century, how much closer now is His coming for us in the twenty-first century?

Paul contrasted **slumber** and **night** and **darkness** with **day** and **light** in this passage. Since the daytime must be the kingdom, the sleep must be the normal life pattern typical of the present age. Paul called us to live already in the light of the coming dawn. We have not yet reached the fullness of the dawn. We have not yet come to the fullness of the kingdom. But we can live the life of the kingdom of God. Paul's command in 12:2 is to avoid conformity to this age. Here he provided the pattern of our transformation. This is the transforming life of God's kingdom lived in the darkness of the present world. In verse 14 he made his point clearer: **clothe yourselves with the Lord Jesus Christ.** The life of the kingdom is the life of Christ. Now we are privileged to put on the Lord Jesus. This is the inner meaning of the exhortation **to put on the armor of light.** Putting on the weapons of light, walking in an orderly fashion, must mean to live by faith in the Son of God. We live now by the power of resurrection life, and we expect His return momentarily. This is the life we must live. If we live it, we will not practice unrestrained sin. Paul lists sins in verse 13 that are completely inconsistent with the life of Christ.

Because of what we have read already in Romans, I conclude that these sins especially characterize the legalist (see chap. 2). Legalism, the curse of the church and of the world, keeps people in darkness. Established in unbelief, legalism denies the value of what Christ has done. It exalts what man can do, making God a liar. Here is the night of this present age. Christ Himself is the light that comes with the dawning of the new day. As we live by faith in Him, serving in our spiritual gifting and loving one another without sham, we will in fact be clothed with the Lord Jesus Christ. We will leave no room for the flesh to fulfill its desires. Here is the life of living sacrifice, a sacrifice holy and acceptable to God. Here is the life transformed, proving that the will of God is good, acceptable, and perfect. But that life has one other key characteristic that Paul addressed in chapters 14–15. It is a life of liberty that is lived in mutual acceptance within the body of Christ.

Notes for Romans 13

[1]Marcus Barth, *The Epistle to the Ephesians*, Anchor Bible, 2:710-14.

[2]*International Standard Bible Encyclopedia*, s.v., "Nero," by S. Angus and A. M. Renwick, 3 (1986): 521.

[3]Ibid., 522.

[4]Compare the statement in J. H. Merle D'Aubigne's *History of the Reformation* (1:72). He described the papacy's temporal power just before the Reformation. "It was in truth the spiritual order which the Church had at first undertaken to defend. But to protect it against the resistance and attacks of the people, she had recourse to earthly means, to vulgar arms, which a false policy had induced her to take up. When once the Church had begun to handle such weapons, her spirituality was at an end. Her arm could not become temporal and her heart not become temporal also. . . After resolving to employ earth to defend heaven, she made use of heaven to defend the earth. Theocratic forms became in her hands the means of accomplishing worldly enterprises. . . The charm ceased, and the power of the Church was lost, so soon as the men of those days could say, She is become as one of us."

[5]Zerwick explained the grammar behind this translation: "Especially in prohibitions it commonly happens that [*me*] with the present imperative [the construction in Romans 13:8] is used to forbid the continuation of an act, and. . .with the aorist subjunctive to forbid a future one (with an absolute prohibition, as distinct from the prohibition 'in principle' conveyed by the present; but the aorist may be used simply because it is more vivid and absolute, or regarding a general case as a particular one: [Matthew 5:42; 6:2f,7; John 5:9] etc.)" (*Biblical Greek,* §246). Only prohibition in the aorist would unquestionably have prohibited all possible debt.

[6]See also Philippians 4:4-7; 1 Thessalonians 5:1-11,23; Hebrews 10:24-25; James 5:7-11; 1 Peter 4:7-11.

ROMANS 14

Since the beginning of his letter, Paul has been preparing his readers for the passage before us. He laid the foundation of the sinfulness of humanity in 1:18–3:20. That foundation takes away all claims to righteousness that anyone can make, including the claims of those who "keep the commandments." In 3:21–8:39 he showed that life with the living God begins and continues only by grace. No works, merit, or obedience can ever begin or sustain life with God. On the contrary, works, merit, and obedience (as requirements of life) only weaken and hinder. They cannot foster life. In 9:1–11:36 Paul showed both Jews and Gentiles their proper place before the grace of God. Israel cannot boast in its national privileges. Their unbelief and God's judicial wrath have (temporarily) set them aside. Gentiles have no reason for boasting either. God's sheer mercy has extended to them the position they now share in salvation. Therefore, as Paul said in 11:32, "God has bound everyone over to disobedience so that he may have mercy on them all." Finally, in 12:1–13:14 Paul called all of his readers, Jews and Gentiles alike, to practice covenant loyalty with one another. This mutual loyalty is a life of sacrificial service to one another. Believers serve each other in their spiritual gifting, in their sincere love for one another, and through submission to authorities.

All of this was necessary because of the factions present in the church at Rome. The evidence of the letter sets a scene of competing factions in the church. One group, the Jewish believers, held that it was necessary for Christians to keep dietary and calendar laws such as the Sabbath. The other group "considered such observances to be a symptom of a weakness in one's Christian faith."[1] Each group had its distinctive way of relating to the other. The first group judged (i.e., condemned) the second for its failure to practice the law. The second group despised the first precisely because it did practice the law. It is key to Paul's purpose in Romans that he wrote to reconcile these two groups. Paul did not actually call these groups "the Jews" and "the

Gentiles." He called them the "weak" and the "strong," respectively. It is likely that he avoided calling them Jews and Gentiles because there were Jews and Gentiles in each group. I have called the groups Jews and Gentiles for simplicity. The Jews likely dominated among the "weak," and the Gentiles likely dominated among the "strong." Significantly, in giving the groups the titles of weak and strong, Paul classified himself with the strong.

Thus, Romans 14:1–15:13 is the culmination of the letter. Here Paul directly addressed the Roman church. He called the church to express the unity produced by the Holy Spirit, to shun the divisiveness of human merit and achievement, and to extend to one another the same grace God has extended to each.

D. Paul called those who are righteous by faith to living sacrifice through accepting one another (14:1–15:13).

This section has five parts: verses 1-3 introduce the specific problem and call on all to avoid judging and despising one another; verses 4-12 address the "weak," charging them to quit passing judgment on God's servants; 14:13–15:4 addresses the "strong," who must in love refuse to flaunt their liberty before their weak brothers since doing so might lead them to violate their consciences. The strong, above all, must walk in love before their brothers. The last two parts are a closing prayer in 15:5-6 and a conclusion to this section in 15:7-13, where Paul called on all believers to accept one another.

We must define four terms before we begin the exposition of the chapter: "strong" and "weak"; "disputable matters"; and "distress" and "stumble." According to the Centenary Translation of the New Testament, in verse 1 Paul warned his readers not to allow the weak into discussions "for the purpose of deciding doubtful points." This is a good translation that points the way in identifying the "disputable matters" referred to in verse 1. The Bible is full of commandments and prohibitions, and God has an abiding interest in preserving our welfare through keeping those precepts. Yet the Bible is silent about large areas of human life. The Bible does not tell us whether to live in Detroit or Des Moines. The Bible does not tell us what kind of car to buy, or whether to buy one. It is silent on movies, ties, and computers. As painful as it may be to many Christians, the Bible is even silent about smoking![2] Shouldn't we make more of the sins that the Bible condemns and less of the practices that we simply don't like?

The "disputable matters" of verse 1 are precisely of this class. They relate to practices that the Bible neither condemns nor approves. One of the central problems in the passage before us is the problem of food. Some of the Romans ate any kind of food. Others, whom are called "weak," ate only vegetables. The New Testament clearly has done away with the food laws of the old covenant (see Mark 7:14-23; Acts 10:13-16). What believers eat today has no bearing on our relationship with God. Yet some Christians in the first century felt an obligation to abide by the dietary law. Diet is one of the "disputable matters."

Is God pleased if we eat beef and not pork? Is God pleased if we eat pork? Paul gave the answer in verse 17: "The kingdom of God is not a matter of eating and drinking, but of righteousness, peace and joy in the Holy Spirit." He answered it again in verse 23: "But whoever has doubts is condemned if they eat, because their eating is not from faith; and everything that does not come from faith is sin."

Then is God pleased or displeased when we eat pork? The answer is that eating pork is not important. God is pleased when we act in faith. If we are convinced that we are right in God's eyes while eating pork, God is pleased. But faith pleases Him. Pork is irrelevant. Faith is what matters.

The new covenant leaves whole areas of life open to our own decisions. God deals with us as with adult sons. In Galatians 4 Paul drew a distinction between being under the law and being under grace. He said that God dealt with Israel under the law as with children, but with those under grace as adult sons. Verse 3 says, "So also, when we were underage, we were in slavery."[3] But when grace came, we received a new position: "So you are no longer a slave, but God's child." (v. 7). To be under law is to be a child. To be under grace is to be an adult.[4] And this is what is meant by "walking in the Spirit" and being "led by the Spirit."

In the old covenant God gave His people commandments covering nearly every aspect of their lives. He told them what to eat (Lev.

11). He told them when not to eat (Lev. 16:29). He told them who their friends and enemies were (Gen. 10; Deut. 20). He told them what to wear and what not to wear (Deut. 22:5,11-12; Lev. 19:19). Furthermore, He told them where to go to the bathroom (Deut. 23:9-14)! Now we don't tell adults what to eat, who to have as friends, what clothing to wear, or where to go to the bathroom. These are things we do for children.

One major difference between the Mosaic covenant and the new covenant is just at this point. God treated the people under the Mosaic covenant as children. He treats us under the new covenant as adults. This is essential to grace. Grace allows the believer to make his own decisions. That is risky, but such risks are inherent in adulthood. Mothers rarely call their adult sons to tell them what to eat, what to wear, or where to go to the bathroom. When they do, we know that something is seriously wrong.

In the new covenant God has given us the indwelling Holy Spirit. This internal guide has come to change our hearts, to produce obedience in us (see Ezk. 36:27). This new internal motivation is God's grace at work in us. This is risky, but the level of risk depends on how much we can trust the Holy Spirit in each other. His trustworthiness means that no real risk involved.

To sum up, the disputable matters of 14:1 are things neither commanded nor prohibited by Scripture. Since God deals with us as adults, the list of disputable matters is much longer in the new covenant than in the old covenant. In Romans 14 the list of doubtful things includes food and Sabbath keeping. We can grant each other freedom in these areas because all of us who are justified have the Holy Spirit who guides us. We must either trust Him or not.

We must now define the "weak" (14:1) and the "strong" (15:1). Paul addressed the weak first (14:4-12). The weak are those who are weak in conscience. They have more restrictions on their consciences than the Scriptures place on us. Verse 14 makes this point clear: "I am convinced, being fully persuaded in the Lord Jesus, that nothing is unclean in itself. But if anyone regards something as unclean, then for that person it is unclean." Paul repeated the same point in verse 23: "But the man who has doubts is condemned if he eats, because his eating is not from faith; and everything that does not come from faith is sin." Conversely, the strong is one whose conscience approximates what Scripture teaches. In one sense the strong is free to do or avoid whatever is neither commanded nor prohibited in Scripture. We should note that Paul classed himself among the strong ("We who are strong" in 15:1).

What we have been describing is the idea of Christian liberty. Christian liberty does *not* mean that it is our right to do whatever Scripture does not condemn. Christian liberty is our freedom to limit ourselves as much as is necessary to help others grow. Paul presented this idea clearly in chapters 14–15. For example, in 14:15 he called the strong to act "in love." This means refusing to lead a weaker brother astray. The kingdom of God is neither food nor drink (14:17). Therefore, it is wrong for the strong to cause a weaker brother to violate his conscience. For this reason Paul said, "It is better not to eat meat or drink wine or to do anything else that will cause your brother to fall" (14:21). In 1 Corinthians 8–10 Paul wrote the longest passage in Scripture on Christian liberty. He wrote, "Therefore, if what I eat causes my brother or sister to fall into sin, I will never eat meat again, so that I will not cause them to fall" (8:13). Later he wrote:

> Though I am free and belong to no one, I have made myself
> a slave to everyone, to win as many as possible. To the Jews
> I became like a Jew, to win the Jews. To those under the law
> I became like one under the law (though I myself am not
> under the law), so as to win those under the law. To those
> not having the law I became like one not having the law
> (though I am not free from God's law but am under Christ's
> law), so as to win those not having the law. To the weak I
> became weak, to win the weak. I have become all things to
> all people so that by all possible means I might save some. I
> do all this for the sake of the gospel, that I may share in its
> blessings (9:19-23).

This is the life style of Christian liberty, and 9:23 especially expresses the motivation of that liberty. Those set free under grace are free to do all things "for the sake of the gospel." The liberty that grace gives supports our ministry of the gospel. No practice can be so dear, no possession so precious, no activity so valuable, that we cannot sacrifice it for the sake of those we wish to serve spiritually.

Then what does it mean to "distress" and "stumble"? To distress means to lead a brother to violate his conscience. This conclusion is clear from 1 Corinthians, where Paul explained "distress" and "stumbling" at the same time.

> Be careful, however, that the exercise of your rights does
> not become a stumbling block to the weak. For if someone
> with a weak conscience sees you, with all your knowledge,
> eating in an idol's temple, won't that person be emboldened
> to eat what is sacrificed to idols? So this weak brother or sister, for whom Christ died, is destroyed by your knowledge.
> When you sin against them in this way and wound their
> weak conscience, you sin against Christ (1 Cor. 8:9-12).

Thus, distressing (or offending) a brother occurs only when the brother stumbles. Stumbling only occurs when he violates his conscience under the influence of my liberty.

Long ago I heard a man relate an experience he had many years earlier. In a faculty meeting at a Christian college, a colleague stood up and rebuked the man relating the story. The colleague said, "I think we ought to censure Dr. Smith, because I saw him playing tennis on Sunday. I was offended that he would do such a thing. Since the Bible teaches that we should not offend one another, I think we should censure him."

Dr. Smith responded, "Brother, I have two questions for you. First, when you saw me playing tennis, did you go and play tennis?"

The man answered, "No. Of course not!"

Dr. Smith then asked, "Are you my weaker brother?"

His antagonist answered, "Of course I am not your weaker brother! I would never play tennis on Sunday."

Dr. Smith said, "Then I cannot offend you. For one can only offend a weaker brother, and only when the weaker brother violates his conscience, led by someone else's liberty."

This brief story illustrates well the issues involved in offending and stumbling. It is the call of grace in Christian liberty to live so that we build up all around us. This is the life of living sacrifice Paul has called us to by God's mercies. This is our reasonable service. This is the life transformed, proving that the will of God is good, acceptable, and perfect. This is how we best serve one another in our spiritual gifting. Here is sincere love. Here is the call to life in Christ. Now that we have defined these terms, we turn to the exposition.

1. Those who are righteous by faith must avoid judging and despising each other in matters of personal preference and simply accept each other (14:1-3).

¹**Accept the one whose faith is weak, without quarreling over disputable matters. ²One person's faith allows them to eat anything, but another, whose faith is weak, eats only vegetables. ³The one who eats everything must not treat with contempt the one who does not, and the one who does not eat everything must not judge the one who does, for God has accepted them.**

In verses 1-3 Paul introduced the specific problem at the Roman church and called on both parties to accept one another. The verb **accept** is basic to the whole segment, but Paul needed the whole passage to explain its meaning. The preceding 13 chapters assure us that acceptance exhibits grace, self-sacrificial service, and love.

Paul addressed his command to accept others specifically to the strong (see 15:1), since they are the ones who are to **accept the one whose faith is weak.** The major responsibility in expressing acceptance falls upon the strong. They are those who have most understood grace. Grace has changed their lives. Grace has set them free. In the church, they are uniquely those who can accept others.

But when those who are strong begin to discuss the **disputable matters,** they must take care not to include the weak. The weak have standards that exceed the requirements of Scripture. They are not wicked or heretical in their commitments. Paul did not rebuke those who eat **only vegetables.** The weak are simply convinced in their consciences that their standards are consistent with their faith in Christ. Therefore, the strong must not attack the conscience of the weak. A professor used to say, "Your conscience isn't always right, but it's never right to violate your conscience." The weak do need to grow, but attacking their standards and leading them to violate their consciences does not help them. They need acceptance, not attack.

By God's grace the body of Christ has room for differences over diet and other areas of disagreement. Unfortunately, people in the church feel that their standards are more important than their brothers. At the church in Rome the weak **judged** (i.e., condemned[5]) the strong, and the strong had **contempt** for the weak.

Observe this distinction: the weak condemn the free, and the free show contempt for the weak. This is a test to help us know where we are spiritually. Do you often find yourself asking, "How can anyone who does that claim to be a Christian?" If you do, you may be among the weak. On the other hand, you may find yourself having contempt for those in the church who are bound by convictions not in Scripture. You may be strong, but you need to learn to **accept** those who differ from you, since **God has accepted them.**

The closing remark of verse 3 is important not only for the strong. The weak need this instruction. Because eating meat was such a problem for the weak at Rome, they would be liable to believe that eating meat was a problem before God. Then, when they saw stronger Christians eating meat, they would likely condemn them. Yet the strong, as well as the weak, are those whom God has received. How quickly we forget the lessons of grace. We conclude, in our faithless arrogance, that God cannot accept anyone who differs from ourselves. But Paul declared that God has already accepted the strong, by grace, as He has the weak. Then the circle of those whom we accept must be as large as the circle of Christ's acceptance. Having set out these basic principles, Paul addressed his concerns first to the weak.

> **2. The weak must receive their strong brothers whom the Lord has accepted, even if they do not follow their diet or worship restrictions, since both will give account of their actions to God (14:4-12).**

[4]Who are you to judge someone else's servant? To their own master, servants stand or fall. And they will stand, for the Lord is able to make them stand.

⁵One person considers one day more sacred than another; another considers every day alike. Each of them should be fully convinced in their own mind. ⁶Whoever regards one day as special does so to the Lord. Whoever eats meat does so to the Lord, for they give thanks to God; and whoever abstains does so to the Lord and gives thanks to God. ⁷For none of us lives for ourselves alone, and none of us dies for ourselves alone. ⁸If we live, we live for the Lord; and if we die, we die for the Lord. So, whether we live or die, we belong to the Lord. ⁹For this very reason, Christ died and returned to life so that he might be the Lord of both the dead and the living.

¹⁰You, then, why do you judge your brother or sister? Or why do you treat them with contempt? For we will all stand before God's judgment seat. ¹¹It is written:

"'As surely as I live,' says the Lord,
'every knee will bow before me;
every tongue will acknowledge God.'"

¹²So then, each of us will give an account of ourselves to God.

The very first Greek word in verse 4 is the singular pronoun **you,** the subject of the sentence. Greek does not need a separately expressed pronoun since the verb form includes the pronoun subject. This means that the pronoun is emphatic. In fact, by placing the pronoun first, in the sentence, it is doubly emphatic. Grammatically, Paul pointed his long, bony finger at the weak brothers in Rome, calling them to account for their actions. "Who are you, of all people," he asked, "to judge another man's servant?"

The rhetorical question **Who are you to judge someone else's servant?** demands that the weak take their proper position in relation to their brothers. Paul showed the Roman Christians that they were fellow servants of the same **master.** Therefore, since the strong obediently serve their master, they owe no account of their actions to their brothers. The strong **will give an account...to God.** They will certainly pass that examination, but not because of their obedience. We have already seen that what God requires, God provides. He has set as His eternal purpose that everyone whom He has justified will become like the Lord Jesus Christ. Since it is His purpose, He will surely accomplish it. None of those whom He foreknew will be missing when it is time to finish our salvation. None of those whom He foreknew will be unlike Jesus. This includes the strong as well as the weak in the church. **The Lord is able to make them stand,** even without the help of self-appointed judges in the church.

In verse 5 Paul provided another principle on Christian liberty and "disputable matters." Personal conviction is the basis for deciding what to do regarding things neither commanded nor prohibited in Scripture. If we are personally convinced that it is inconsistent with our faith to eat meat, then we should avoid meat. But it is equally true that if we are personally convinced that our faith permits us to eat meat, we may indulge freely. God has left it to our personal choice.

The same holds true for the day of worship: **One person considers one day more sacred than another; another considers every day alike.** In the first century, the church experienced the powerful influence of Jewish practices. Believers who came from the synagogue would have favored worshiping on the Sabbath, that is, on Saturday. Believers who did not enter the church through the synagogue would have had little commitment to a particular day of worship.

Nowhere in Scripture has God moved the Sabbath from Saturday to Sunday. No evidence exists before the time of Moses that God had imposed the Sabbath on anyone. In the Mosaic law itself, the Sabbath plays a key role, being the sign of the Sinai covenant (Ex. 31:13). But it is a mistake to think that the Sabbath was only a day. Those who profess to keep the Sabbath keep only one day a week, normally Sunday. The biblical teaching on the Sabbath is much fuller. God commanded Israel to keep the Sabbath day, but that is only one part of the Sabbath law. The rest of the Sabbath law appears in Leviticus 25, where God instructed Israel to allow the ground to lie fallow one year out of seven, the Sabbatical Year (vv. 1-7). During that year they were not to sow their fields or prune their vineyards. Additionally, God did not permit harvesting what grew in the fields or vineyards. As in the days of the wilderness wandering, the food in the fields was for anyone to gather. They might not harvest, but they could gather daily what they needed. The other element of the Sabbath law required that after seven sabbatical years, they should rest another year, the Year of Jubilee (vv. 8-17). So in any 50-year cycle,

Israel should not have plowed, planted, or harvested in the forty-ninth or the fiftieth years.

The reasons for these laws are twofold. First, as God says in Leviticus 25:23, the land of Canaan never really belonged to Israel: God said that the land could not be sold permanently since the land was His—the Israelites were just aliens and tenants. The Sabbath law required that Israel recognize God's ownership of the land, and their role as tenants on it. As tenants, they did not have absolute right to use the land. The Owner stipulated how they might use it.

Second, the Sabbath law, as the sign of the covenant, gave Israel a key test of loyalty to the covenant. It would be fairly easy not to work one day out of seven. But the Sabbath law required no work during the seventh year and during the fiftieth year. The test becomes clear at this point. Would Israel trust God to provide all that they needed to eat during those years of no food production? God pointed out this very issue in Leviticus 25:20-22: "You may ask, 'What will we eat in the seventh year if we do not plant or harvest our crops?' I will send you such a blessing in the sixth year that the land will yield enough for three years. While you plant during the eighth year, you will eat from the old crop and will continue to eat from it until the harvest of the ninth year comes in." It would take enormous faith to refuse to sow and harvest for one year. In the Jubilee it would take even greater faith to go two years in a row without sowing and harvesting.

What God was asking His people to do was to take time simply to enjoy His provision, the salvation He promised in the Mosaic covenant. In the covenant, God promised obedient Israel prosperity in the land. Thus, the issue for Israel was the faithfulness of God. Could they trust Him to fulfill His own promises?

For the weak to claim to keep the Sabbath, but to keep only part of it, is a mark of unbelief in God's people. However, the strong acknowledge that the Sabbath as taught in Scripture is not a requirement for the people of God in the church. The New Testament clearly teaches that the Sabbath is not a requirement for the church. Paul cautioned the Christians in Colossae about allowing anyone to "judge you by what you eat or drink, or with regard to a religious festival, a New Moon celebration or a Sabbath day" (Col. 2:16). He explained that these are "a shadow of the things that were to come; the

reality, however, is found in Christ" (v. 17). In open exasperation at
the Galatian Christians, Paul said, "You are observing special days
and months and seasons and years! I fear for you, that somehow I
have wasted my efforts on you" (Gal. 4:10-11). Here in Romans 14:5
the apostle made it clear that he did not consider keeping the Sabbath
a requirement for Christians since he said, **Each of them should be
fully convinced in their own mind.** To keep any day sacred is a
matter of personal choice, and it is something we do **to the Lord.**[6]

In the church in Rome some kept one day a week as special to
the Lord; others held every day equally holy. We surely cannot think
that those who believed that every day was holy, that all of life was
sacred, were wrong. So Paul permitted both approaches to life before
God. What is necessary is that we live out our faith. We need not keep
Sabbath, but we must follow our consciences. It is the same with food
and with all other "disputable matters." What is important is faith, not
diet or calendars. Faith always pleases God. Faith may lead us to avoid
meat, but it is not the diet that pleases God.[7] Faith may lead us to
keep the Sabbath, but it is not keeping the Sabbath that pleases God.
What pleases God is faith and faith alone (Rom. 14:23; Heb. 11:6).

In verses 7-9 Paul gave the reasons for what he has just said, and
the most foundational statement is in verse 9: **Christ died and returned to life so that he might be the Lord of both the dead and
the living.** This means that no Christian lives disconnected from all
other associations. We live and die **for the Lord** because **we belong
to the Lord.** The Christian does not live "with no other object in
view than his own gratification, for in fact, all Christians live 'to the
Lord', that is, they live with the object of pleasing Christ, they seek to
use their lives in His service, and, when it comes to dying, they glorify
Him by committing themselves to His keeping."[8]

Further, since **each of us will give an account of ourselves to
God,** it is wrong to **judge** or treat other believers **with contempt.**
The fault did not lie exclusively with the weak or with the strong.
Each group was wrong to respond to the other in its own peculiar
way. Since we all live for God's sake, no Christian can judge or show
contempt to other believers.

Distressingly, the modern church preaches far more about practices that are problems in our culture but have no biblical mandate.

Why should we emphasize what the Bible is silent on? Why should we ignore divisiveness (1 Cor. 1–4, and especially 1:10-17 and 3:1-4; Phil. 2:1) or gluttony (Deut. 21:20; Prov. 23:21; Titus 1:12), or gossip (Prov. 20:19; Rom. 1:29; 2 Cor. 12:20; 1 Tim. 5:13), when the Bible does condemn these practices? Why do we ignore Paul's teaching against silly talk and coarse jesting (Eph. 5:4)? These are not "disputable matters." God Himself condemns them. But we act as if we are more righteous than God. We should do what Paul says in verse 11: we should bow before the Lord and confess that He is right. One day we will do just that. Then we all **will give an account of ourselves to God.** Then we will know that His commands were right, and we will see that He was right to justify the weak as well as the strong. Then we will see the nobility of the weak. Then we will know that we should never treat them with contempt. Then we will see the righteousness and strength of faith in the strong. Then we will see that we should never judge them. We will see that God was right all along.

> **3. The strong who are righteous by faith must not flaunt their freedom, so that by their example they can lead the weak to violate their consciences, but they should limit their own freedom for the weak (14:13–15:4).**

[13]Therefore let us stop passing judgment on one another. Instead, make up your mind not to put any stumbling block or obstacle in the way of a brother or sister. [14]I am convinced, being fully persuaded in the Lord Jesus, that nothing is unclean in itself. But if anyone regards something as unclean, then for that person it is unclean. [15]If your brother or sister is distressed because of what you eat, you are no longer acting in love. Do not by your eating destroy someone for whom Christ died. [16]Therefore do not let what you know is good be spoken of as evil. [17]For the kingdom of God is not a matter of eating and drinking, but of righteousness, peace and joy in the Holy Spirit, [18]because anyone who serves Christ in this way is pleasing to God and receives human approval. [19]Let us therefore make every effort to do what leads to peace and to mutual edification. [20]Do not destroy the work of

God for the sake of food. All food is clean, but it is wrong for a person to eat anything that causes someone else to stumble. [21]It is better not to eat meat or drink wine or to do anything else that will cause your brother or sister to fall.

[22]So whatever you believe about these things keep between yourself and God. Blessed is the one who does not condemn himself by what he approves. [23]But whoever has doubts is condemned if they eat, because their eating is not from faith; and everything that does not come from faith is sin.

The first part of verse 13 sums up by exhorting the weak no longer to judge others: **let us stop passing judgment on one another.** Paul then turned to the strong, who bear the greater responsibility in the discord at Rome. While the weak must stop judging their brothers, it is more important for the strong not to flaunt their liberty before their brothers: they must **not to put any stumbling block or obstacle** in front of other believers. It is always a temptation for those who are free to parade their freedom before people who do not understand that freedom. The attitude that displays freedom before the weak is one of scornful disdain for those who do not perceive the value of liberty. It is this very scorn that leads the weaker brother to stumble. He may recognize the grace and freedom living in his brother's life, and recognizing it, he may come to resent his own faith commitments. In his resentment this weaker brother may stumble by violating his own conscience.

Teaching this passage to young people usually arouses a particular response. Did Paul not flaunt his liberty at Antioch when he rebuked Peter for withdrawing fellowship from Gentile brothers (Gal. 2:11-14)? Did he not flaunt his liberty when he took Titus to Jerusalem and refused to allow him to be circumcised (Gal. 2:1-3)? Did Jesus not flaunt His liberty when He ate with publicans and sinners at Levi's house (Mark 2:13-17), or when He refused to fast as the Pharisees did (vv. 18-22), or when He permitted His disciples to pluck grain from the fields on the Sabbath (vv. 23-28)? The students ask, "Isn't it sometimes necessary to flaunt our liberty?" The answer is simple. These examples we have just cited are not what Paul meant in Romans 14–15.

The examples we have given are events in which someone was violating (or was liable to violate) the truth of the Scriptures. Paul said that Peter's actions were not consistent "with the truth of the gospel" (Gal. 2:14). Paul's indignation occurred because Peter violated the gospel itself. In Jerusalem, Paul stood for the truth of grace for the Gentiles in opposing Titus's circumcision. The cases that we cited from Mark's Gospel about Jesus are similar. He was violating cultural standards, not the Mosaic law, to force people, especially Pharisees, to make a decision about Jesus' identity.

The flaunting of liberty in Romans 14 is quite different. The weak are not people who have violated the truth of the gospel or God's grace. They simply have faith commitments that are different from the strong. The very strength of the strong may lead the weaker brothers to violate their own consciences. Therefore, Paul called on the strong not to place **a stumbling block** in the way of a brother. The strong must not encourage the weak to violate their consciences.

This is clear from the following verses in Romans 14. The discussion continues about food. The weak brother considers some food **unclean.** But Paul knew, as do you and I, that **nothing is unclean in itself. But if anyone regards something as unclean, then for that person it is unclean.**[9] He added the basic principle in verse 17: **The kingdom of God is not a matter of eating and drinking, but of righteousness, peace and joy in the Holy Spirit.** He further exhorted the believers to **make every effort to do what leads to peace and to mutual edification. Do not destroy the work of God for the sake of food. All food is clean, but it is wrong for a man to eat anything that causes someone else to stumble.** Finally, he gave his conclusion about eating in verse 21: **It is better not to eat meat or drink wine or to do anything else that will cause your brother or sister to fall.** It is not the food that is the problem. It is the weak faith of certain believers that is the problem. Any flaunting of liberty before these people may weaken their faith and hinder their spiritual growth.

It is for this reason that Paul told his readers, **Do not allow what you know is good be spoken of as evil.** When the weak brother violates his conscience, encouraged by the freedom of his stronger brother, he has sinned. His conscience is not necessarily right, but it is never right for anyone to violate his conscience. So Paul made the point in verse 23: **everything that does not come from faith is sin.** If the weak brother is not capable of seeing the freedom he has in Christ, it is not helpful to him to lead him to practices that violate his own standards. This is why Paul called his readers to **love** in their treatment of weak Christians, since **Christ died** for them too.

You may ask, as others have before, why the strong should limit the exercise of their freedom for the weak. The answer is that the strong always limit themselves for the weak. In mountain climbing the stronger members of the team always move at the pace of the weaker members. If they do not, then the whole team risks disaster. In a family it is the same. When a family brings a new baby home, it is not the baby who changes for the sake of the family. The family changes for the sake of the baby. And oh, how it changes! The parents, who are the mature and strong ones in the home, tiptoe around the house when the baby sleeps. Silence reigns. But when the baby awakens, screaming its hunger to the whole household, what a flurry of activity it arouses! Everybody rushes to meet the needs of the baby. Although the parents begin a program of helping the baby grow up, it is not until the child is much older that the younger starts to change for the older. It is always the role of the strong to change, to limit the exercise of legitimate freedoms, for the sake of the weak.

When the strong do not limit themselves for the weak, disaster follows. Some parents refuse to curtail their socializing with friends and neighbors for a newborn child. In those circumstances the child may suffer physical or emotional neglect or even abuse. That would be disastrous for the child's health. The same is true in the spiritual family. When the strong do not curtail their liberties for the weak in the family, they neglect or abuse the weak spiritually. This is the reason for Paul's warnings: **Do not by your eating destroy someone for whom Christ died,** and **Do not destroy the work of God for the sake of food.** We do not help each other to gracious liberty, to spiritual maturity, by leading the weak to violate their consciences and faith commitments. The weak brother is grieved when he transgresses his own standards "and is afflicted with the vexation of conscience which the consequent sense of guilt involves. It is this tragic result for the weak believer that the strong believer must take into account."[10] Paul described the tragic result in these verses by the extremely strong verb **destroy.** Violating love for the weaker brother can lead to lasting, serious damage to his spiritual life. Paul referred to that damage in verses 22-23. If a weaker brother eats meat, he brings upon himself the guilt of sin, since he "as yet does not possess the inward liberty"[11] to do it. This is sin, since his **eating is not from faith,** and whatever **does not come from faith is sin.**

Therefore, it is in this context that Paul's principle in verse 17 takes on greater significance. The kingdom of God surely is not food or drink. Therefore, the weak must not make food and drink the standards by which to judge their brothers. But even more, the strong must not use food and drink to bring serious damage to the spiritual life of his weak brother. The only significant issues of the kingdom are **righteousness, peace and joy in the Holy Spirit.**

The weak and the strong can unite in their enjoyment and expression of righteousness. Righteousness in Romans is primarily a relational term, not a judicial term. It refers to right relationship. Therefore, they can unite in expressing their right relationship with God and with each other by accepting one another, refusing condemnation and ridicule. They can defer to one another, recognizing that God's acceptance ennobles and justifies them all together, without reference to their disputable matters.

The weak and the strong can unite in their enjoyment and expression of peace. They can live out the reconciliation accomplished by Christ and brought into their experience as God has brought salvation to the Jew first and also to the Greek. This peace will dominate their fellowship as they live in harmony, as Paul prays in chapter 15:5-6: "May the God who gives endurance and encouragement give you the same attitude of mind toward each other that Christ Jesus had, so that with one mind and one voice you may glorify the God and Father of our Lord Jesus Christ." What is more of a demonstration of God's peace than for people with differing standards and commitments to live in harmony with one another, accepting one another, as Christ accepted them? This righteousness and peace will produce joy in the Holy Spirit, since the very life of the community will express the fruit of the Spirit. Hardly anything is more needed in human relationships

277

than a warm, welcoming, forgiving, and accepting community. This is the life of living sacrifice. It is a holy sacrifice acceptable, not only to God, but to man (12:1; 14:18). This is how the strong should help the weak to bear the burden of their consciences and not to please themselves. To these issues Paul turned in chapter 15.

Notes for Romans 14

[1]A. J. M. Wedderburn, *The Reasons for Romans,* p. 60.

[2]Some will object that since the Bible teaches us that our bodies are the temple of the Holy Spirit, we should not smoke. While it is true that smoking is dangerous physically, the Christian church seldom makes such a point about gluttony! I wonder why, since the Bible does condemn gluttony but not smoking. Why should we make more of an issue over things that the Bible is silent on than things that the Bible condemns? Perhaps it because gluttony is more of a problem for modern-day preachers than smoking is. A legalist usually condemns sins that cause very little problems for him. Few preachers have problems with makeup or smoking, yet they are the first to condemn them! Is this legalism or spirituality?

[3]F. F. Bruce, *The Epistle to the Galatians: A Commentary on the Greek Text,* NIGTC, p. 193, shares the same view.

[4]Bruce, p. 200, agrees with this interpretation. Commenting on Galatians 4:7, he said, "Instead of being imprisoned under law…, instead of being under the control of a slave-attendant or in care of guardians and stewards, believers are now full-grown sons and daughters of God; they have been given their freedom and the power to use it responsibly."

[5]Barrett (*Romans,* p. 258) said, "The peculiar danger of the weak is censoriousness; for the weak Christian is apt to suppose that his fellow-Christian, who does something he (the weak man) regards as sinful, must be sinning against his conscience, although in fact his conscience is more enlightened, and does not condemn the course of action in question." Murray (*Romans,* 2:174), discussing the two ways of treating each other, said, "In actual practice these vices appear respectively in the smile of disdainful contempt and in the frown of condemnatory judgment."

[6]Sabbath can teach us very important lessons. One lesson it should teach us is our need to stop laboring for our salvation. God has brought salvation to pass. He will fulfill His own promises without our aid. We will not increase the blessing of God's promise by our obedience. He gives His blessings by grace.

Another lesson we should learn from the Sabbath law is that Sabbath is the time when God finished His work (Gen. 2:1-3). We now await the completion of God's saving work. There is a sense in which we now enjoy God's rest, but there is also a sense in which we have not yet entered into rest. Hebrews 4:11 calls us to "be diligent to enter that rest." The ultimate time of rest awaits the kingdom of God when He will complete our salvation. Then Sabbath will have reached its culmination.

[7]According to v. 6, each one expresses his faith in his thankful response to God.

[8]Cranfield, 2:707.

[9]The New Testament specifically annuls the Mosaic covenant's dietary laws. Jesus said, "'Are you so dull? Don't you see that enters a man from the outside can make him 'unclean.' For it doesn't go into his heart but into his stomach, and then out of his body.' (In saying this, Jesus declared all foods 'clean.')" (Mark 7:18-29; see vv. 14-23 for whole context). In Acts 10 Peter's vision in Joppa had the same effect. God pronounced all foods clean, and the result of this cleansing was the destruction of the barrier between Jews and Gentiles. This is clear since the vision immediately led Peter to minister at Cornelius' house. In Colossians 2:20-23 Paul warned against false teachers who imposed unbiblical commandments. "Since you died with Christ to the basic principles of this world, why, as though you still belonged to it, do you submit to its rules: 'Do not handle! Do not taste! Do not touch!'? These are all destined to perish with use, because they are based on human commands and teachings. Such regulations indeed have an appearance of wisdom, with their self-imposed worship, their false humility and their harsh treatment of the body, but they lack any value in restraining sensual indulgence." Paul gave a similar warning in 1 Timothy 4:2-5, "Such teachings come through hypocritical liars, whose consciences have been seared as with a hot iron. They forbid people to marry and order them to abstain from

certain foods, which God created to be received with thanksgiving by those who believe and who know the truth. For everything God created is good, and nothing is to be rejected if it is received with thanksgiving, because it is consecrated by the word of God and prayer." Finally, Hebrews 13:9 warns, "Do not be carried away by all kinds of strange teachings. It is good for our hearts to be strengthened by grace, not by ceremonial foods, which are of no value to those who eat them." The dietary laws of the Old Testament have no place in Christian living.

[10]Murray, 2:191.

[11]Cranfield, 2:714.

¹**We who are strong ought to bear with the failings of the weak and not to please ourselves. ²Each of us should please our neighbors for their good, to build them up. ³For even Christ did not please himself but, as it is written: "The insults of those who insult you have fallen on me." ⁴For everything that was written in the past was written to teach us, so that through the endurance taught in the Scriptures and the encouragement they provide we might have hope.**

Paul classed himself among the **strong** when he discussed Christian liberty. He commanded the strong to help **the weak** and not merely to seek what pleases themselves. Among young Christians, Paul's teaching about Christian liberty is hard to understand precisely here. They cannot understand that we still might avoid some practice even if the Bible does not prohibit it. Younger Christians have not learned that self-pleasing is not consistent with the Christian life. Christian liberty gives no license. It is self-denying. As we saw especially in chapter 8, the justified live lives like the Messiah, and the Messiah's life was a life of suffering (see Rom. 8:17-27). Jesus Himself suffered and calls us to suffer also so that He might bring us to glory with Him. He did not seek self-gratification in His life. Therefore, the life of the strong must be a life that avoids self-pleasing.[1] It must be a life that seeks to **please our neighbors for their good, to build them up.** Because of our identification with Christ and our justification— that is, by the very nature of our relationships in grace—we must seek to build up one another.

What practice is there that we cherish so much that it is more valuable than the spiritual welfare of other believers? What practice do we cherish so much that it is more worthwhile than the ministry we can have to God's people? This was one of Paul's basic principles of ministry: "I do all this for the sake of the gospel, that I may share in its blessings" (1 Cor. 9:23). Paul gave up his liberty in Christ, living under law, to reach those who were under law. He lived like a Gentile to reach the Gentiles (vv. 19-22). All of this he did to enhance his ministry. Christian liberty is my freedom to bind myself as much as is necessary to help others grow spiritually.

Paul was not the only example of this self-denying liberty, or even the most important example: **For even Christ did not please himself but, as it is written: "The insults of those who insult you have fallen on me."** Cranfield remarked that Paul's statement "sums up with eloquent reticence both the meaning of the Incarnation and the character of Christ's earthly life."[2] Christ lived preeminently to please His Father.[3] Therefore, Paul quoted Psalm 69:9, where the righteous sufferer bears the reproach that God's enemies hurl at Him. Jesus bore men's hostility against God. "The purpose of the reference is to indicate the lengths to which Christ went in His not pleasing Himself."[4] He went to the cross to please someone else. How can we make less a sacrifice for His redeemed people when He made such a sacrifice for us? Therefore, this principle of self-denying liberty is common to the life of Paul, to the life of the King Himself, and to the Old Testament that has given us instruction in order that **we might have hope.** This hope will come as we practice and endure even self-denial for our brothers. Then in the midst of self-denial we will know genuine comfort from the growing love within the church's fellowship. Self-denying liberty is the only true liberty for the Christian.

Now note this point: The suffering that Jesus bore was caused by the enemies of God. This passage imposes no limitation on the source of our suffering, and though it mainly describes relations within the church, it doesn't exclude suffering caused by those outside the faith. Then no wrong that I can suffer, whether from a brother in Christ, or from an enemy of the cross, must require vengeance. Christ's acceptance must extend to all graciously. Even within the church self-denial is the proper method of relating to one another. Since the Son of God Himself denied Himself to receive His enemies (Rom. 5:6-10), self-denial within His fellowship must be free and unconditional. Scripture calls us, as a living sacrifice, to accept one another, as Christ accepted us.

This is the crowning expression of living sacrifice in Romans (see 12:1-2), and being a living sacrifice is possible only for those who have a proper view of themselves and their spiritual ministry in the body of Christ (see 12:3-8). Being a living sacrifice is a true expression of genuine love that foregoes vengeance but does good, even to those who oppose us (see 12:9–13:10).

4. Closing Prayer (15:5-6)

⁵May the God who gives endurance and encouragement give you the same attitude of mind toward each other that Christ Jesus had, ⁶so that with one mind and one voice you may glorify the God and Father of our Lord Jesus Christ.

In a closing prayer Paul asked that God may produce **the same attitude of mind toward each other** in the church at Rome. Unity had failed there because of the spiritual pride of the two groups, the weak and the strong. Paul had to prove their sinfulness to the weak, and God's gracious salvation, so they would learn not to judge their brothers in Christ. His discussion in chapters 3–8 was also essential since those passages would teach the weak brothers at Rome that the strong were righteous in God's eyes. They are righteous even without keeping the law. In short, Paul had to prove to them that the gospel was the law free.⁵

The characteristics mentioned in verse 4, **endurance** and **encouragement,** are gifts from God. He gives them both to us through the Scriptures and through our experiences with each other. He is such a God who would produce unity in the church at Rome, and will do so in any other church. The church experiences these gifts in a much more powerful and consistent way when we learn the self-denying liberty of accepting one another. We experience them when we learn to practice unity.

Paul's (and therefore the Holy Spirit's) deep interest in unity within the church appears in the repeated terms he used for unity in these two verses. He prays that God may grant you **the same attitude of mind toward each other,** praising God **with one mind and one voice.** Paul had already called his readers to be of one mind

(12:16), where he coupled it with a warning against haughtiness and an exhortation to associate with lowly people. In 2 Corinthians 13:11 he connected unity with being at peace and enjoying the blessing of the love and peace of God. Being of one mind also appears in Philippians 2:2-5, where Paul pleaded for the Philippians to make his joy complete. What would complete his joy over them was for them to maintain the same love, to be united in spirit, to have the same purpose. They would do nothing out of selfish motives, but would act with humility of mind, regarding each other as more important than self. Here, in verses 5-8, he showed that this is precisely what Christ did.

Such a same-mindedness results in united praise to God: **with one mind and one voice you may glorify the God and Father of our Lord Jesus Christ.** That praise, according to verse six, has two characteristics. First, it will be "with one mouth" (NIV, **one voice**). The prophets of the Old Testament spoke with one mouth (1 Kings. 22:13; 2 Chr. 18:12). The three Hebrews in Nebuchadnezzar's fiery furnace praised God with one mouth in the furnace (Dan. 3:51). The very unity of the praise is proof that God is at work in the midst of His people. The unity of the prophets is one of the proofs of the inspiration of the Scriptures. Further, the unity of naturally diverse elements in the church shows that God is at work in the church. Christians differ widely in their practices. When unity reigns among them in spite of those different practices, God must be at work in their midst.

Indeed, the very possibility of being **with one mind** is a result of having a spirit of unity. God Himself grants that spirit. Observe further, that this unity is part of glorifying God, which is most acceptable when all who share in Christ's atoning work join, not in organization, but in heart and soul to offer Him the sacrifice of praise. In this way, united as God's children, the Roman Christians would have been able to glorify God most acceptably, as is proper because of Christ.

5. Conclusion: Believers must accept each other as Christ accepted them since He is the minister for both Jews and Gentiles, as the Scripture says (15:7-13).

[7]**Accept one another, then, just as Christ accepted you, in order to bring praise to God. [8]For I tell you that Christ has be-**

come a servant of the Jews on behalf of God's truth, so that the promises made to the patriarchs might be confirmed [9]and, moreover, that the Gentiles might glorify God for his mercy. As it is written:

"Therefore I will praise you among the Gentiles;
I will sing the praises of your name."

[10]Again, it says,

"Rejoice, you Gentiles, with his people."

[11]And again,

"Praise the Lord, all you Gentiles;
let all the peoples extol him."

[12]And again, Isaiah says,

"The Root of Jesse will spring up,
one who will arise to rule over the nations;
in him the Gentiles will hope."

[13]May the God of hope fill you with all joy and peace as you trust in him, so that you may overflow with hope by the power of the Holy Spirit.

The concluding section of this segment consists of four parts. (1) In verse 7 Paul stated the basic application of all that he has been saying since chapter 1. (2) In verses 8-9a he showed that this mutual acceptance is appropriate since Christ is the minister of both the circumcision and the uncircumcision. (3) In verses 9b-12 he cited Scriptures that prove God intended the Gentiles to join Israel in worshiping Him. (4) Paul concluded in verse 13 with another prayer.

Here is Paul's basic application: **Accept one another, then, just as Christ accepted you, in order to bring praise to God.** We can now see what it means to **accept one another.** From the context above, it means weak Christians refuse to judge other Christians whom Christ has justified. We may have overly strict consciences or biblically balanced consciences. But accepting one another means we treat one another with respect and dignity. We recognize in each other the saving work of God. We learn to extend to one another the grace we have received from God. It means that we walk in love toward one another. It means we deny our own desires when they collide with the needs even of a weaker brother. His needs must always be uppermost.

We seek to help him grow, not to attack his standards or lead him to violate them. As Paul said elsewhere, "Therefore, if what I eat causes my brother or sister to fall into sin, I will never eat meat again, so that I will not cause them to fall" (1 Cor. 8:13).

There is more to say about the meaning of **accept.** The Greek word Paul used (*proslambano*) appears in two places that can aid us. First, the Septuagint uses the same Greek word in Psalm 27:10 that appears in Romans 14:1,3; 15:7. David said, "Though my father and my mother forsake me, the Lord will receive me." We do not know the specific historical context for this psalm, but we can conceive of a situation. David never was among his father's favorite children. When Samuel came to Bethlehem to anoint the next king of Israel, he asked Jesse to gather all of his sons. After Jesse assembled the family, Samuel began to search for God's chosen man. God let him know that none of the sons he saw was right (1 Sam. 16:1-13). Why didn't Jesse bring David before the prophet? He left him out tending the sheep. Could it be that Jesse really had no deep regard for David? During David's flight from King Saul, his family had to leave Israel and flee to Moab (1 Sam. 22:3). Based on what we have already seen of Jesse, it is possible that David's parents were on the verge of rejecting him. Yet even in the face of such rejection, David finds hope in God. God, he said, would take him up and "receive" (LXX, *proslambano*) him. What does *proslambano* mean here? In this context it must mean that God would be to David what a mother and father should be. God would give him the welcome, the affection, the warmth, the acceptance we receive when we go home.

Second, Philemon 17 can also help us understand what Paul wants us to do in accepting one another. The situation in this letter is that Onesimus had run away from Philemon his master, a Christian man who lived near Colossae. By sheer coincidence Onesimus had fled about five hundred miles to the most populous city of the Roman empire, Rome. Some have estimated that during Augustus' reign the city had a population of one million. At that time the slave population was about thirty percent of the total.[6] That means there may have been 300,000 slaves in the city. Then, by sheer coincidence, Onesimus met Philemon's friend Paul, who led him to Christ (remember Rom. 8:29-30?). As a new believer, he needed to return to his master, who also was a believer, for it would be important for him to be able to fellowship with Philemon. Paul wrote the letter to urge Philemon to forgive Onesimus. The apostle said in verse 17, "So if you consider me a partner, welcome [*proslambano*] him as you would welcome me." Here is Paul's point in the letter: Accept this runaway slave!

By Roman law Philemon had the right to execute Onesimus for any reason, since the power of the master over the slave was unlimited.[7] Onesimus may even have robbed him (see v. 18). But Paul asked the master to accept the slave, and not merely as a slave: "Perhaps the reason he was separated from you for a little while was that you might have him back forever—no longer as a slave, but better than a slave, as a dear brother. He is very dear to me but even dearer to you, both as a fellow man and as a brother in the Lord" (vv. 15-16). But the acceptance that Paul requested for Onesimus was not merely the kind offered to a new brother in Christ. Paul asked Philemon to accept Onesimus as if he were Paul.

When anyone comes to your home, you welcome them in different ways. We may welcome them tactfully. Someone has defined tact as the ability to make people feel at home when you wish they were. Such people may come into the living room, but we really do not want them anywhere else in the house. On the other hand, we admit our friends to the living room, the kitchen, or the dining room. But we do not really want some of our friends beyond the dining room. Finally, we welcome our most beloved guests anywhere in the house. That is the welcome Paul would expect for himself at Philemon's, and it is the welcome he asked for Onesimus, who was now "a dear brother.".

Here then is acceptance. Paul asked the Roman Christians, both weak and strong, to treat each other as beloved family. He asked them to offer each other the warmth and acceptance of a loving home. It makes no difference that we differ with one another in some of our practices. We are brothers and sisters in Christ. After all, Christ accepted us when we were helpless, ungodly, hostile sinners. Now He has made us His friends, reconciling us through His own death (Rom. 5:6-10). So how can I reject one for whom Christ died? How can I reject one whom Christ has accepted? In the church, we must learn to make a home for one another. It is the grace of God to us. It now must become the grace of God through us to each other.

This accepting attitude glorifies God. To glorify God means to enhance His reputation in the eyes of others. The Old Testament teaches us that the heavens declare God's glory (Ps. 19:1). They show the greatness of God. Scientists say that the universe has millions of galaxies and each one with millions of stars. Our own galaxy alone is supposedly ten thousand light years thick and one hundred thousand light years across.[8] Yet Scripture describes God as measuring the heavens with the span of His hand (Isa. 40:12). When we measure something, we use the largest meaningful available measurement. We measure this page in inches. We measure a room with feet. We measure the earth with miles. The most appropriate measurement for the heavens is God's hand! This must be figurative, of course, but it teaches us something about God's greatness.

Psalm 29 teaches that God glorifies Himself by the majestic thunderstorm. The sound of the storm is the voice of God (Ps. 29:3). The storm reveals the sheer power of God, for with His voice He breaks the cedars of Lebanon. His voice causes the mountains to quake, to skip about like lambs. His voice kindles the lightning. Here is a terrifying revelation of God's power, which can un-create the earth as easily as He created it. Here are two elements of our creation that glorify God. The heavens reveal the greatness of God and the storm reveals His power. But Paul says that people who receive one another glorify God. We often believe that God's glory in the heavens or the thunderstorm is the greater revelation. What could be more moving than to meditate on God's greatness as we behold the stars?

Yet God's self-revelation in the heavens has led no one to faith and life. The thunderstorm has never led anyone to repentance. Perhaps these are not such great revelations of God's glory. Christians who accept one another are a far greater revelation of God's glory than either the heavens or the thunderstorm. When the lost see the heavens or the storm, all they see are atoms in motion. When they see people who really love one another, people who differ but really accept one another, they see something of the greatness and power of God. This is missing from the sky and the storm. No one can explain away genuine love, genuine gracious acceptance. No one can rationalize them. Genuine loving acceptance unmistakably reveals the greatness and power of God. Genuine loving acceptance is not totally explainable. The lost might consider that this could be the revelation of God's glory. It isn't as striking as the thunderstorm, and it isn't as grand as the heavens. But it is powerful beyond comprehension, since it is God's power in the gospel that produces it. This genuine loving acceptance proves that God's grace is real, that we have indeed experienced it. It proves the truth of the gospel.

Paul explained that mutual acceptance is appropriate since Christ is **a servant of the Jews** and **the Gentiles.** He came to confirm **the promises made to the patriarchs** (see chap. 11), but He also came **that the Gentiles might glorify God for his mercy.** Christ makes no distinction between the weak and the strong in His ministry.

This Gentile participation in the worship of God is no new element in the plan of God. This Paul showed in verses 9b-12 by citing four Old Testament passages (2 Sam. 22:50; Deut. 32:43; Ps. 117:1; Isa. 11:10) which prophesy that Gentiles would join Israel in worshiping God. The quotation of 2 Samuel 22:50 (which also occurs in Ps. 18:49) is in a royal psalm in which David celebrated God's saving work on His behalf. Indeed, in David's day God caused the Gentiles to worship Himself by subjecting them to David, His anointed king: **I will praise you among the Gentiles.** But the greater David will subject, not the petty kingdoms of the near east, but all the earth. This He has already begun in the church as He brings people from every tribe, tongue, and nation into His body, the church.

Paul then quoted Deuteronomy 32:43, which is part of the conclusion of the Song of Moses: **Rejoice, you Gentiles, with his people.** Beginning in verse 34 Moses sang about God's vengeance that will vindicate His people when He brings compassion on Israel (v. 36). In that day of vengeance, God will call all the nations to rejoice with God's people. Then He will "make atonement for his land and people" (v. 43). The song specifically refers to the day when Messiah Jesus will set up the kingdom of God on the earth. Then God will judge all the nations. But Messiah Jesus has already atoned for His people. Already the time has come for the nations to rejoice with Israel. We do rejoice with Israel, for among our brothers and sisters in Christ are the redeemed remnant of Israel.

The third quotation (Rom. 15:11) comes from Psalm 117:1, where the psalmist calls the nations to rejoice with Israel because of

God's loyal love to them: **Praise the Lord, all you Gentiles; let all the peoples extol him.** God's love towers over them, and His faithfulness is everlasting. This psalm is part of the Egyptian Hallel (Pss. 113–118) sung during Passover. They all celebrate God as Israel's Savior. We have learned from Romans that God is not the God of the Jews only (see Rom. 3:29-30). Therefore, if God brings salvation to Israel, it must mean salvation for the world. This is what God said in Isaiah to His Servant: "It is too small a thing for you to be my servant to restore the tribes of Jacob and bring back those of Israel I have kept. I will also make you a light for the Gentiles, that my salvation may reach to the ends of the earth" (Isa. 49:6). It is what Paul said in Romans 11:11-12: "Again I ask, Did they stumble so as to fall beyond recovery? Not at all! Rather, because of their transgression, salvation has come to the Gentiles to make Israel envious. But if their transgression means riches for the world, and their loss means riches for the Gentiles, how much greater riches will their full inclusion bring!"

The final quotation that proves the appropriateness of mutual acceptance is from Isaiah 11:10: **The root of Jesse will spring up, one who will arise to rule of the nations; in him the Gentiles will hope.** This verse occurs in the section of Isaiah that many have called the "Book of Immanuel" (Isa. 7–12). This section foretells the coming of one who will be "God with us." Chapter 11 promises that the nations will come to the root (11:10) and branch (11:1) of Jesse. This will happen in the time when the Spirit-anointed Ruler will rule the world with wisdom, strength, and the fear of the Lord. He will be the final ruler who will judge the nations with righteousness and equity. Then the nations will put their trust in Him. Already the firstfruits of the nations are fulfilling this prophecy. Therefore, God has always planned for Israel and the Gentiles to stand shoulder to shoulder praising Himself through the ministry of His Messiah. In the body of Christ the Gentiles and Jews must learn to accept one another. We may still differ with each other, but we must offer each other the very grace that we have equally received from God.

Verse 13 is another prayer for the Romans Christians to experience God's **joy** and **peace** and to **overflow with hope by the power of the Holy Spirit.** The prayer, in some ways, is a summary of the whole book. Paul emphasized the joy and peace that we have in

Christ, thus building their faith (chaps. 1–8). Here he prayed that God would fill them with joy and peace in believing. The result of such joy and peace in believing is the hope they have in Christ (especially chaps. 8 and 11). They would then experience the joy and peace of receiving one another by grace, and they would grow in hope through the Holy Spirit. Paul prayed for these things on their behalf, knowing this was the will of God.

Conclusion (15:14-33)

Paul has now completed the main portion of his message. This section has the character of personal notes more than pastoral exhortation. The segment consists of five parts. (1) Verse 14 states Paul's confidence that the Romans will be able to carry on with what he has taught them. (2) In verses 15-21 Paul explained he has written as the apostle to the Gentiles, and as such he hoped to offer all the Gentiles, the ones in Rome included, as a pleasing sacrifice to God. (3) Verses 22-29 describe Paul's ministry plans, which include a trip to Jerusalem and a trip to Spain by way of Rome. (4) Verses 30-32 contain a prayer request for Paul's ministry in Jerusalem. (5) Verse 33 pronounces a blessing on the Roman Christians.

A. Paul's confidence in the Roman believers (15:14).

¹⁴I myself am convinced, my brothers and sisters, that you yourselves are full of goodness, filled with knowledge and competent to instruct one another.

After such a lengthy letter about the problems at Rome, we might suppose that Paul had no confidence in the Romans' compliance, but verse 14 shows that he did. They had two qualities that nurtured this confidence in him. The Romans were **full of goodness** and **filled with knowledge** ("perfectly well instructed" in the Jerusalem Bible has the right idea). Denney explained this goodness as kindness, "the charity on which such stress is laid in chapter xiv as the only rule of Christian conduct."⁹ Further, they surely understood well what Paul had been saying.

Paul's certainty of their disposition to kindness and of their understanding encouraged him further. He was sure that they were **competent to instruct one another.** They needed no further instruction from Paul about unity. Because of their kindness and understanding, they would have been able to guide each other in carrying out Paul's teaching. The verb translated **instruct** in this verse refers to verbal appeal to a hostile will or disposition. That appeal seeks to improve the attitude that brings about repentance so that no punishment is needed.[10] Although opposition would arise in the church, Paul confidently expected to see them carry out all he had taught them. Here again is the grace of Paul's attitude. He accepted even these divisive Roman Christians the same way Christ accepted him.

B. Paul wrote boldly as a minister by God's gracious power so the Gentiles would be his offering sanctified by the Holy Spirit (15:15-21).

[15]**Yet I have written you quite boldly on some points to remind you of them again, because of the grace God gave me** [16]**to be a minister of Christ Jesus to the Gentiles. He gave me the priestly duty of proclaiming the gospel of God, so that the Gentiles might become an offering acceptable to God, sanctified by the Holy Spirit.**

[17]**Therefore I glory in Christ Jesus in my service to God.** [18]**I will not venture to speak of anything except what Christ has accomplished through me in leading the Gentiles to obey God by what I have said and done—** [19]**by the power of signs and wonders, through the power of the Spirit of God. So from Jerusalem all the way around to Illyricum, I have fully proclaimed the gospel of Christ.** [20]**It has always been my ambition to preach the gospel where Christ was not known, so that I would not be building on someone else's foundation.** [21]**Rather, as it is written:**

"**Those who were not told about him will see,
and those who have not heard will understand.**"

This section has three subdivisions. The first subdivision (vv. 15-26) explains Paul's boldness in writing to the church in Rome. The second one (vv. 17-19) takes up the theme of Paul's boldness in all of his ministry. The third one (vv. 20-21) gives one of Paul's basic ministry objectives.

Paul has written **quite boldly** to the Romans, not to instruct them in some new revelation, but to remind them of what they already know. But he is bold because of the grace that God has extended to him by making him **a minister of Christ Jesus to the Gentiles.** God, in grace, has given him a ministry to discharge and performa. He offers the Gentiles as a **an offering acceptable to God.** Cranfield, after studying the Old Testament usage of Paul's language, concluded that Paul views himself as filling the role of a Levite assisting Christ's priestly ministry.[11] This was no mere job for Paul. He was the Messiah's assistant who labored in His sacrificial work, a sacred work before God that called him to be bold and was **sanctified by the Holy Spirit.**

This has given him boldness when dealing with the things of God (15:17). Paul had no other reason for boldness. Nothing that he did by himself had any significance worth mentioning. But he knew that **what Christ has accomplished through me in leading the Gentiles** had spiritual significance. All of his teaching and work, including the **power of signs and wonders,** had occurred **through the power of the Spirit of God.** It was due to the Spirit's work that Paul had been able to **fully proclaimed the gospel of Christ,** and he did so **from Jerusalem all the way around to Illyricum,** that is, throughout the regions of Syria, Asia, and Greece—roughly what we would call the Balkans.

All of this Paul did based on a fundamental principle: he labored only in places **where Christ was not known,** that is, where no gospel witness had already been established. Rather, Paul always sought new unplowed fields to plow and sow. This principle is congruent with Isaiah's statement in Isaiah 52:15. Those who had not been **told** or **heard** the message of Messiah would hear it from the mouth of the apostle.

C. Paul planned to visit the believers in Rome on his way to Spain after completing the ministry of the Greek saints for the poor in Jerusalem (15:22-29).

²²**This is why I have often been hindered from coming to you.**

²³**But now that there is no more place for me to work in these regions, and since I have been longing for many years to visit you,** ²⁴**I plan to do so when I go to Spain. I hope to see you while passing through and to have you assist me on my journey there, after I have enjoyed your company for a while.** ²⁵**Now, however, I am on my way to Jerusalem in the service of the Lord's people there.** ²⁶**For Macedonia and Achaia were pleased to make a contribution for the poor among the Lord's people in Jerusalem.** ²⁷**They were pleased to do it, and indeed they owe it to them. For if the Gentiles have shared in the Jews' spiritual blessings, they owe it to the Jews to share with them their material blessings.** ²⁸**So after I have completed this task and have made sure that they have received this contribution, I will go to Spain and visit you on the way.** ²⁹**I know that when I come to you, I will come in the full measure of the blessing of Christ.**

There were reasons Paul had not yet made it to Rome. **This is why I have often been hindered from coming to you** refers back to verse 20. The Romans already had the foundation of the gospel, and Paul was busy laying it elsewhere. But he had an opportunity to come to Rome on his way to Spain which was more unplowed territory. He had longed deeply to come to Rome, and it was finally possible. One of the secondary purposes of this letter becomes clear now (v. 24). Paul asked for aid from the Roman Christians for his Spanish mission when he passed through Rome.

In the meantime, between the writing of the letter and his trip west, Paul was going **to Jerusalem in the service of the Lord's people there.** (The text literally says "serving the saints," and the most immediate reference would be to serving the saints in Jerusalem.) Through persecution the Christians in Jerusalem had fallen into poverty. But the believers from **Macedonia and Achaea** had planned to send some **contribution for the poor among the Lord's people in Jerusalem.** The verb form of **contribution** appears elsewhere in the New Testament in the sense "share" or "contribute" (see Gal. 6:6; Phil. 4:15). The word group is based on the word translated "common." It thus emphasizes commonness or joint participation that occurs in a community. The saints in Jerusalem were poor. The saints in Greece felt a commonness between themselves and the saints in Judea. Thus, the Greek believers wished to share with their fellow believers in Judea the resources that God had given them.

Verses 26-27 provide an important contribution to the New Testament's teaching on giving. The major New Testament passage on giving is 2 Corinthians 8–9, where Paul gave the basic principle that helps us better understand his meaning here. In 2 Corinthians 8:13–14 he spelled out the principle of equality: families practice equality in the distribution of family resources, and so it is in the church. But this equality in distribution doesn't mean we say to our families on payday, "There are five of us and each of us gets twenty percent of the family's resources. When you use up your twenty percent, though, you'll have to wait till next payday. If you get sick, you may just have to make do if you've used up your twenty percent." The equal distribution of resources means that all the family's resources are available to all the family members to meet anyone's need. Family catastrophes lead the whole family to rally its resources to meet the need. Families do this even if only one member of the family is hurting. It should be this way in the family of God. Paul challenged the Corinthians to help with the offering for the Judean saints: "Our desire is not that others might be relieved while you are hard pressed, but that there might be equality. At the present time your plenty will supply what they need, so that in turn their plenty will supply what you need. The goal is equality" (2 Cor. 8:13–14).

Paul provided us here with a basic insight on giving. The New Testament teaches three specific objects to which we should give our money. Romans 15 gives two of them, and the first appears in verses 25–26: we give to those in Christ's family who are in need. A second one is that others outside the family may receive our giving, as Paul instructed the Galatians, "Therefore, as we have opportunity, let us do good to all people, especially to those who belong to the family of believers" (Gal. 6:10). But this is like the distribution of funds within the human family. We have primary responsibility for the members of our own families. When funds are available, it is right to give to worthy causes outside the family. But the family comes first.

Paul provided a third area (the second in Romans 15) to which we can give our money: **They were pleased to do it, and indeed they owe it to them.** The New Testament teaches us to give to those who have ministered to us spiritually. Paul instructed Timothy that elders who work hard are worthy of financial support (1 Tim. 5:17). The same point occurs in Galatians 6:6, where Paul stated that the one who receives instruction should share all good things with the one who teaches. Jesus Himself taught that "the worker is worth his keep" (Matt. 10:10).[12] Therefore, the Gentile Christians in Rome had an obligation to share with their Judean brothers and sisters since the latter have ministered in spiritual things to them. Paul was completing his ministry, not only to the Judean saints, but also to the Gentile saints. They would receive reward for their service. He then planned to travel to Spain by God's blessing.

D. **Paul desired earnest prayer for his deliverance from unbelievers in Judea, for the reception of his ministry among the saints, and for a joyous trip to be with the believers in Rome (15:30-32).**

[30]**I urge you, brothers and sisters, by our Lord Jesus Christ and by the love of the Spirit, to join me in my struggle by praying to God for me.** [31]**Pray that I may be kept safe from the unbelievers in Judea and that the contribution I take to Jerusalem may be favorably received by the Lord's people there,** [32]**so that I may come to you with joy, by God's will, and in your company be refreshed.**

Wedderburn believed it's possible that Paul expected hostility from the Judean saints toward the offering from the Gentiles.[13] The whole letter calls for Jews and Gentiles in the church to learn to accept one another. Many of the strong brothers in the church at Rome might find it difficult to support such a ministry to Jewish brothers as Paul has undertaken. Only the growing power of grace will lead them to support it. The minority of weak brothers at Rome might resent help from Gentiles going to the Jerusalem church. Thus, Paul has first taught them about God's grace. Then he taught them grace for one another. Here at the end of the letter he asked them to **pray** for grace in the Jewish Christians of Jerusalem **that the contribution I take to Jerusalem may be favorably received by the Lord's people there.** This prayer will not be a mere recitation of requests. Paul asks them, **by our Lord Jesus Christ and by the love of the Spirit,** to struggle together with him in prayer. He also asked them to pray that he would **be kept safe from the unbelievers in Judea,** a prayer that God answered after a fashion. Then, delivered of his ministry and from the unbelieving, he could come to Rome joyfully and **in your company be refreshed.**

E. Paul's Signature Closing (15:33).

[33]The God of peace be with you all. Amen.

This verse contains Paul's signature closing, one very similar to the benediction in his other twelve letters in the New Testament (see 2 Th. 3:17-18); he included another one in 16:21b. This benediction should normally be the end of the epistle. Indeed, a whole century of scholarship has held that the epistle originally ended here, and that someone else added chapter 16 for some particular reason. While I reject these conclusions as unwarranted, I can speculate about what happened. It may be that Paul originally intended to end the letter here, but then learned of Phoebe's trip to Rome (see 16:1). He then may have added chapter 16 as a sort of introductory letter for her to the church there, with a list of greetings to provide her with relevant introductions to key people in the city who could help her. Since this is thoroughly speculative, based on the most limited evidence, we may profitably leave it.

Notes for Romans 15

[1]Cranfield gave this caution about self-denial: "That it would be perverse to read into Paul's [decision not to please himself] any notion that everything which is delightful to one ought to be avoided simply because it is delightful (a notion which the ill-informed not infrequently ascribe to the Puritans and their heirs) should be obvious.

What is meant here by not pleasing oneself is not pleasing oneself regardless of the effects which one's pleasing oneself would have on others. What Paul is forbidding in particular is that strong Christians should please themselves by insisting on exercising outwardly and to the full that inner freedom which they have been given, when to do so would be to hurt a weak brother's faith" (2:731).

[2]Cranfield, 2:732.

[3]But there is no question about whether Jesus would please the Father. Jesus was always pleasing to God. Rather, Jesus' whole ministry simply gave new opportunities for His Father to enjoy His pleasure in the Son.

[4]Cranfield, 2:733.

[5]Wedderburn, p. 65.

[6]Peter Garnsey and Richard Saller, *The Roman Empire: Economy, Society and Culture* (Berkeley: University of California Press, 1987), p. 83.

[7]Alan Watson (*Roman Slave Law* [Baltimore: Johns Hopkins University Press, 1987], p. 120) quoted Justinian's *Institutes* 1.8.1 to this effect. He also cited (p. 119) Seneca (*On Anger*, 3.40.1-3): "To chide a person who is angry is only to incite his rage. You should approach him with various gentle appeals, unless you are such an important person that you can reduce his anger just as the Deified Augustus did when he was dining with Vedius Pollio. One of his slaves had broken a crystal cup. Vedius ordered him to be seized and to be put to death in an unusual way. He ordered him to be thrown to the huge lampreys which he had in his fish pond. Who would not think he did this for display? Yet it was out of cruelty. The boy slipped from the captors' hands and fled to Caesar's feet asking nothing else other than a different way to die: he did not want to be eaten. Caesar was moved by the novelty of the cruelty and ordered him to be released, all the crystal cups to be broken before his eyes, and the fish pond to be filled in." Watson explained that "Augustus's response was extralegal but was permitted by his position of power" (p. 120).

[8]A light year is approximately six trillion miles, the distance light travels in a year. This means that the galaxy is sixty quadrillion miles thick and six hundred quadrillion miles across!

[9]James Denney, "St. Paul's Epistle to the Romans," in *The Expositor's Greek Testament*, 2:711. He cited Galatians 5:22; Ephesians 5:9;

and 2 Thessalonians 1:11 as supporting his contention. Note that *mestoi* and *pepleromenoi* appear in Romans 1:29!

[10]*TDNT,* s.v., "[*noutheteo*]," by Johannes Behm, 4 (1967): 1019-20.

[11]Cranfield, 2:755.

[12]The fourth area to which we ought to direct our funds appears in a passage like Philippians 4:14-18, where Paul indicated that the church's financial support of his ministry was an acceptable sacrifice to God. It would bring them great reward, both temporally and eternally. Thus, the fourth area to which we can direct some of our funds, according to the New Testament, is to missions.

[13]*Reasons,* pp. 37-41.

ROMANS 16

Commendation and Greetings (16:1-27)

If my conjecture at the end of the previous chapter is correct, then Paul learned just before sending his letter to Rome that Phoebe was going to Rome on some sort of business. So he added this sixteenth chapter to introduce her to the people at Rome and to ask them to help her in her business.

Chapter 16 has five parts. (1) Paul introduced Phoebe to the church in Rome and asked for their help (vv. 1-2). (2) Paul sent greetings to some of the saints in Rome, partly as an expression of his regard for them and partly as an introduction of them for Phoebe (vv. 3-16). (3) Paul warned the Romans against those who violated Paul's teaching on grace, promising their quick end (vv. 17-20). (4) Paul sent greetings to the church from several of the men who were with Paul in Corinth (vv. 21-23). (5) Paul closed the whole book with an expanded doxology (vv. 25-27).

A. Paul's commendation of Phoebe (16:1-2).

¹I commend to you our sister Phoebe, a deacon of the church in Cenchreae. ²I ask you to receive her in the Lord in a way worthy of his people and to give her any help she may need from you, for she has been the benefactor of many people, including me.

Paul introduced Phoebe to the church in Rome. This woman is no idle member of the church in Cenchreae,¹ for Paul identified her as **a deacon** or servant of the church and **the benefactor of many people** including Paul himself. These verses have caused much discussion in the history of the doctrine of the church. The Greek word *diakonos* in verse 1 is translated **deacon** elsewhere only three times (Phil. 1:1; 1

Tim. 3:8,12 with the related verb occurring in v. 10), but it is normally translated "servant" or "minister" (see Matt. 20:26; John 2:5; Rom. 13:4; 15:8; 2 Cor. 3:6; Eph. 3:7). The issue arises about whether a woman can be a deacon. Was Phoebe a deacon of the church in Cenchreae? The problem becomes more acute since deacons have tended to become a sort of governing board for the church.

A review of the uses of *diakonos* in the New Testament allows one to draw the following conclusions. Both secular and New Testament uses of *diakonos* indicate that the term refers to the type of servant who does for others what they cannot or should not do for themselves. Further, this kind of servant serves others under the authority of someone else. For example, in secular Greek *diakonos* referred to a servant in the home who served under the master's authority for the benefit of the members of the master's household; Christ was a servant for us in redemption under the authority of the Father (Rom. 15:8); Paul was a servant under God's authority to various churches (Eph. 3:7; Col. 1:23,25); and the government is a servant under God's authority for the good of society (Rom. 13:4). The handful of technical uses of the term *diakonos* (rendered "deacon"; see list above) for specific servants in the church refer to those who serve the church under the authority of Christ and the elders of the church.

One fact is clear from a survey of *diakonos* in the New Testament. Those who serve as "deacons" never sit as a deliberative or governing body. Therefore, since Paul called Phoebe **a deacon** (or "servant") of the church, the apostle did not mean that she was part of the governing board. Rather, she was one who took a lowly position of service to help others in the church.

One can easily think of areas of service that would be improper or even impossible for a man to carry out in a church with widows and orphans. It is likely that Phoebe played such a role. But she was not only a servant of the church, she was a helper of many—and particularly of Paul. Phoebe was a woman who had learned God's grace. She served others. Thus, Paul asked the Roman church to help her in her business in Rome in a way that was **worthy of his people.** Perhaps to help her get acquainted with other believers in Rome, Paul added the list in verses 3-16.[2] In this way, the Roman church was able to enjoy the blessing of servant believers too.

B. Paul greets various brothers and sisters in the church in a way that befits the saints (16:3-16).

³Greet Priscilla and Aquila, my co-workers in Christ Jesus. ⁴They risked their lives for me. Not only I but all the churches of the Gentiles are grateful to them.

⁵Greet also the church that meets at their house.

Greet my dear friend Epainetus, who was the first convert to Christ in the province of Asia.

⁶Greet Mary, who worked very hard for you.

⁷Greet Andronicus and Junia, my fellow Jews who have been in prison with me. They are outstanding among the apostles, and they were in Christ before I was.

⁸Greet Ampliatus, my dear friend in the Lord.

⁹Greet Urbanus, our co-worker in Christ, and my dear friend Stachys.

¹⁰Greet Apelles, whose fidelity to Christ has stood the test.

Greet those who belong to the household of Aristobulus.

¹¹Greet Herodion, my fellow Jew.

Greet those in the household of Narcissus who are in the Lord.

¹²Grect Tryphena and Tryphosa, those women who work hard in the Lord.

Greet my dear friend Persis, another woman who has worked very hard in the Lord.

¹³Greet Rufus, chosen in the Lord, and his mother, who has been a mother to me, too.

¹⁴Greet Asyncritus, Phlegon, Hermes, Patrobas, Hermas and the other brothers and sisters with them.

¹⁵Greet Philologus, Julia, Nereus and his sister, and Olympas and all the Lord's people who are with them.

¹⁶Greet one another with a holy kiss.

All the churches of Christ send greetings.

What an honor it would be for the apostle to the Gentiles to single one's name out of a whole city for mention and commendation in Scripture! The commendations he gave are enviable. He called these people his **co-workers in Christ** (v. 3; see v. 9), his **dear friend** (vv. 5, 9, 12), his fellow prisoners who were **outstanding among the apostles** (v. 7). He referred to some who maintained **fidelity to Christ** (v. 10), as people who **worked hard in the Lord** (v. 12), **chosen in the Lord** (v. 13). Paul said of Priscilla and Aquila, **They risked their lives for me.** Therefore, all the churches of the Gentiles were thankful to them. This is high praise. It would be interesting to know whether these were all strong, or all weak, or if the list includes a mixture. It is certainly possible that the list is a mixture of the weak and strong. Once again, Paul received all whom Christ received.

The names that appear here make an interesting study. A few names we recognize from other passages of Scripture, such as Priscilla and Aquila, and Rufus. Priscilla and Aquila joined Paul in tent-making (Acts 18:2). Rufus may be the same man mentioned in Mark 15:21, the son of Simon of Cyrene. From that point, few of the names are familiar. However, those who study names have made some important discoveries about this list. Ampliatus, Urbanus, Stachys, Herodion, Asyncritos, Phlegon, Hermes, Patrobas, Hermas, Philologus, and Julia were all common slave names. Of the 23 individuals mentioned, 11 in the list are slave names.

Paul had never been to Rome. Therefore, it is likely that he did not know many of the average people in the pew. It is likely that this list represents the leaders of the church in Rome. About this we should notice at least verses 4, 10, 11, 14, and 15. In these verses Paul referred to **the church that meets at their house** and those who were **with them.** Here are probably at least three, and possibly five small congregations that met in Rome, making up the larger church at Rome. But it seems that the leaders of the church are slaves. Could something similar to this happen in the American church? The leaders of American churches tend to be the bankers, lawyers, and physicians, and (woe on our heads) the seminary trained. It seems that graduate education or professional employment (the more money the better) is the infallible sign of spiritual leadership. The mindset of today is that sanitation workers are never spiritual! This attitude did not exist in the first century church. The church accepted all who were spiritual because of their spiritual qualifications. Anyone who was mature in the faith could become a leader. Thus, what Paul said in 15:14 is true. He said, "I myself am convinced, my brothers and sisters, that you yourselves are full of goodness, filled with knowledge and competent to instruct one another." They were already practicing what they would teach, to some degree. Oh that we might learn that worldly attainment is not a sign of spirituality. Oh that we might learn to accept one another, as Christ accepted us, and thus bring glory to God.

C. Believers must avoid false doctrine and must trust in God (16:17-20).

[17]I urge you, brothers and sisters, to watch out for those who cause divisions and put obstacles in your way that are contrary to the teaching you have learned. Keep away from them. [18]For such people are not serving our Lord Christ, but their own appetites. By smooth talk and flattery they deceive the minds of naive people. [19]Everyone has heard about your obedience, so I rejoice because of you; but I want you to be wise about what is good, and innocent about what is evil.
[20]The God of peace will soon crush Satan under your feet. The grace of our Lord Jesus be with you.

Before closing his epistle, Paul gave his readers a final warning about **those who cause divisions and put obstacles in your way that are contrary to the teaching you have learned**. After reading this letter, we must conclude that this includes those who continue to condemn or despise their brothers for whom Christ died. They cause division and offenses contrary to Paul's teaching in this letter. The Roman believers must **watch out** for such people and **keep away from them.**

Such divisive, offensive people **are not serving our Lord Christ.** Instead they serve **their own appetites** (literally, "their bellies"). This is such an appropriate figure of speech, especially when we remember what caused division in the church in the first place. They flatter people to win them to their own clique. They use **smooth talk** to hide the actual intent of their hearts. They capture the unwary with their deceit, fracturing the gracious and precious unity of the Lord's church.

Paul spoke with such boldness and confidence to the Roman believers because of their known **obedience.** Throughout the world they were known as people of faith. In Romans 1:5 Paul described his ministry as aimed at leading the Gentiles to "the obedience of faith," which the New International translated "the obedience that comes from faith." This expression is difficult to understand, but we must discuss it to understand 16:19 (and 16:26). At least seven different possible interpretations exist for this expression.[3] Several translations handle the phrase as does the NIV. While this translation adequately represents a truth about obedience and faith, it does not fit the context of the book well. A better interpretation would be "to call people from among all the Gentiles to the obedience which faith is?"[4]

Paul has not extended two calls to the Gentiles, to obedience and to faith. He has called them to only one thing—faith, and faith is obeying the gospel. Remember that Paul praised the Romans in 1:8 because their faith was being reported all over the world. Here in 16:19 he praised them because their obedience has reached all. These are, for Paul, the same thing. I am not saying that obedience and faith are equivalent ideas. But there is an obedience to the gospel that can only be faith. Paul's letter to the Romans rejects works as the means of righteousness; it rejects rule keeping as a way of properly relating to God. Paul did not here take back what he has said up to this point. The only obedience that pleases God is faith. Consequently, Paul greatly rejoiced over the Roman believers. He longed for them to be **wise** (well-skilled) in doing **good,** but **innocent** (novices) in doing **evil.**

They could take heart in this condition. They would suffer Satan's opposition. But **the God of peace** would soon **crush Satan** under their feet. All who learn to live by grace can share this hope. By God's grace, no one opposes us (see 8:31), not even Satan himself. So Paul added a prayer, **The grace of our Lord Jesus be with you.**

D. Paul and others send greetings to the church in Rome (16:21-24).

[21]**Timothy, my co-worker, sends his greetings to you, as do Lucius, Jason and Sosipater, my fellow Jews.**

²²I, Tertius, who wrote down this letter, greet you in the Lord.

²³Gaius, whose hospitality I and the whole church here enjoy, sends you his greetings.

²⁴Erastus, who is the city's director of public works, and our brother Quartus send you their greetings.

Verses 21-24 contain a series of greetings from those who were with Paul in Corinth when he wrote his letter. Just as he did in the list in verses 3-16, Paul here placed both the high and the lowly on equal footing. He accepted others as Christ accepted him. Paul's list begins with the most well-known of his associates, **Timothy,** whom he called **my co-worker.** Acts shows that Timothy was Paul's companion on some of his travels, and the apostle mentioned him in several letters and even wrote two of them to his son in the faith (see 1 Tim. 1:2; 2 Tim. 1:2). Erastus was **the city's director of public works.**[5] On the other end of the social spectrum is **Tertius.** His name in Latin means "third." Similarly, **Quartus** in Latin means "fourth." From the meaning of these names, it is possible that these two were slaves. Paul practiced in his own associations what he commended to others. The probability is that Tertius was the amanuensis (a secretary or scribe) whom Paul used in writing the book.[6]

E. Benediction (16:25-27)

²⁵Now to him who is able to establish you in accordance with my gospel, the message I proclaim about Jesus Christ, in keeping with the revelation of the mystery hidden for long ages past, ²⁶but now revealed and made known through the prophetic writings by the command of the eternal God, so that all the Gentiles might come to the obedience that comes from faith— ²⁷to the only wise God be glory forever through Jesus Christ! Amen.

Paul closed his letter with a benediction. Consistent with all that he has said to this point in the letter, he addressed the benediction to God—**him who is able to establish you.** The faith of the Roman believers would not establish them. Their works would certainly not establish them. It was God alone who would establish them, as Paul's gospel proclamation about Jesus Christ showed. Paul received that message by revelation, which was **hidden for long ages past** but **now revealed** to him. God had commanded its revelation **through the prophetic writings** to lead the Gentiles to "the obedience which faith is" (**the obedience that comes from faith,** NIV; see above on v. 19). The gospel is the profound wisdom of God, shown **through Jesus Christ.** We say with Paul: **to the only wise God be glory forever through Jesus Christ! Amen.**

Notes for Romans 16

[1]Cenchreae was the port city of Corinth on the Aegean Sea (Harold G. May, *Oxford Bible Atlas*, pp. 89-90). This is one of the indications that Paul wrote Romans from Corinth.

[2]So Cranfield, 2:783: ". . . so long a list of greetings, though without a parallel elsewhere in the NT, makes quite good sense in connexion with v. 1f, since it would have served to give Phoebe an immediate introduction to a large number of individuals in the Christian community in Rome."

[3]Cranfield (1:66) gave these: "(i) 'obedience to the faith (i.e., to faith in the sense of *fides quae creditur*, the body of doctrine accepted); (ii) 'obedience to faith' (i.e., to the authority of faith); (iii) 'obedience to God's faithfulness attested in the gospel'; (iv) 'the obedience which faith works'; (v) 'the obedience required by faith'; (vi) 'believing obedience'; (vii) 'the obedience which consists in faith'." Cranfield's view is the same as my interpretation above.

[4]This is the genitive of apposition.

[5]The Greek term Paul used here (*oikonomos*) was the proper title for the city treasurer in Corinth in his day (*ISBE*, s.v., "Erastus," 2[1982]:126, by Gary A. Lee).

[6]Douglas J. Moo, *The Epistle to the Romans*, The New International Commentary on the New Testament (Grand Rapids, MI: Wm. B. Eerdmans Publishing Co., 1996), 1.

APPENDIX

1 JOHN 1:9
CONFESSION AS A TEST, BUT OF WHAT?

Note: This article was originally published in *Bibliotheca Sacra* 172 (April–June 2015): 162–77. Reprinted by permission.

No biblical book demonstrates more obviously the impact of context on meaning than 1 John. Choice of a hypothesis for its purpose determines the options for its interpretation in a more obvious way than for some other books of the Bible. This study suggests a refinement on other proposals of purpose for the book, a refinement that redirects the interpretation. The special aim is to suggest a significantly different reading of 1:5–10 and particularly of verse 9. The thesis is that verse 9 in John's argument gave evidence to use to identify reliable teachers in view of the recent secession of false teachers from the community. The importance of 1 John 1:9 in Christian life teaching must surely make the study crucial. But if the thesis of this study is correct, it bears profoundly upon one's conception of Scripture and ecclesiastical practice.

The Purpose of 1 John

Students of 1 John cite 5:13 as stating the book's purpose: "These things I have written to you who believe in the name of the Son of God, in order that you may know that you have eternal life." Some add other statements of purpose, such as 1:3, "that you may have fellowship with us," or 2:1 "that you may not sin."[1] From these and other similar references, the implication is that John's book aims at one of two goals, to give either tests of fellowship or tests of life. The test of fellowship view[2] addresses the question of intimate relationship with God, or how one may live in close fellowship with

309

God. The test of life view addresses assurance of salvation, or what is a genuine Christian.[3]

Rarely do commentators include 1 John 2:26 as a purpose statement, "These things I have written to you concerning those who are trying to deceive you."[4] Is this a statement of purpose? In form, it is not, but in function it is, and the immediate context supports this. Chapter 2:18–25 prepares the reader for verse 26. And 4:1–3 adds to this emphasis. The readers must guard against false prophets and test "to see whether they are from God; because many false prophets have gone out into the world" (v. 1).[5] Akin acknowledges this, but he sees the major issue differently: "Whereas the Gospel of John is written with an evangelistic purpose, 1 John is penned to provide avenues of assurance whereby a believer can know he has eternal life through the Son."[6]

But why was this assurance necessary for the readers? What role does 2:26 play in explaining the purpose of John in writing the letter? The material from 1 John chapters 2 and 4 suggests that questions had arisen in the minds of the original audience about their own relationship with God in view of the departure of the false teachers. Those who left seem to have been trusted members of the community, even leaders (4:1–3). Their departure resulted from charges of being false prophets, even antichrists: "Even now many antichrists have arisen; from this we know that it is the last hour. They went out from us, but they were not really of us" (2:18–19). This departure left the audience without a clear understanding of two decisive issues. First, if these formerly trusted teachers were so wrong, how is right relationship with God to be determined? Second, who now can be trusted? These are the questions that John must address and bring to resolution.

What contextual data impel such a reading? Several points need to be addressed. First, to whom does "we" refer in the opening chapter? Second, what does verse 3 mean? Why is it necessary for the reader to have "fellowship with us"? Does this express cause-effect or something else? Third, what is the relationship between the subordinate clauses and main clauses of verses 6–10? Fourth, what is the meaning of the terms "confess," "forgive," and "cleanse"? A series of implications grow from answering these questions.

Addressing the Difficulties of 1 John 1:9
The Referent "We"

The referent of the pronoun "we," common in this passage, may seem so rudimentary as to be needless to address. Some commentators simply ignore it in favor of more theological concerns. It becomes important in verses 5 to 10, where differing views arise about the identity of the pronominal reference. In verses 1 to 5 it is much clearer. Thus Strecker says, "One could more correctly judge that the author uses 'we' in order to assert membership in the 'circle. . . of "apostolic" witnesses.'".[7]

Expositors of 1 John consistently assume a change in the referent, as in the first chapter.[8] They argue for a broadening of the referent of the pronoun "we." Hiebert is representative: "The claims indicated in verses 6, 8, and 10 seem clearly to represent views advanced by the false teachers. John's 'we' is inclusive, embracing himself and his readers, as well as the false teachers."[9] Only rarely do the authors explain why they make this shift. Christie offers five reasons, one of which is most cogent for this study: an exclusive view of the referent "'we' has difficulty explaining how the apostles could ever be characterized as not having *the* truth or *the* Word *in* them, as well as the fact that it does not harmonize with the other tests, or with John's purpose."[10]

But the problem Christie raised remains. How could the apostles be included? Two comments will suffice here. First, the syntax assists in understanding how the apostles are involved. Verses 6-10 are, after all, examples of a third-class condition. Debate goes on whether one should analyze the conditions as present general or future more probable. Given the discussion to follow, here the condition is present general. It relates to all time (to all who present themselves as "tradition bearers"), and this conclusion leads to the second comment. Apostles are not less subject to confirmation of their divine appointment than are other tradition bearers. No further evidence for the truth of this idea is necessary than Paul's second Corinthian epistle. People do make claims to apostolic authority, even today. Their claims must be open to testing.

How should this material be evaluated? In response to Christie's argument, it is not at all necessary that the testimony be solely apostolic. Paul mentioned over five hundred brothers (1 Cor. 15:6) who saw the risen Jesus. More narrowly, in seeking a replacement for Judas, the apostles identified two men from the number of those who "accompanied us all the time that the Lord Jesus went in and out among us" (Acts 1:21). Any number of people who had witnessed the incarnation and resurrection appearances of Jesus may have been present in Ephesus as John was writing. These would be authoritative witnesses, but they would not be people for whom apostasy was impossible. In short, John addressed a situation that involved a group of tradition bearers or authoritative teachers of the church, which might include even second generation believers who had heard the consistent testimony of the apostles. Wider issues, though, also need to be surfaced.

In this passage determining the referent of "we" affects the interpretation of the whole passage. If it is an inclusive "we," then the choice is between the "tests of fellowship" and "tests of life" approaches. Yet neither of these tests resolves the difficulty of addressing 2:26 and 5:13 in the construction of the message and purpose of the book.

In the book's opening verses, it seems best to identify the referent of the pronoun as original apostolic witnesses of the resurrection.[11] Kruse rightly states, "When he [John] writes about having heard the message from the lips of Christ, or having seen him and touched him, or about bearing witness to the message of eternal life, he always uses the first person plural form."[12] At least for verses 1–5 there is wide consensus in identifying "we" as apostolic witnesses. Meanwhile, the referent of this pronoun does not change throughout chapter 1.

It is certainly possible that John could have had a different referent in mind. However, if there is a change, one would expect a contextual marker. Just such a marker comes in 2:1–2. In those verses the author gives three key indications that he is moving on from the concepts he developed in chapter 1. First, is the personal address that begins verse 1, *teknia mou*. While the audience is surfaced in the first chapter (with references to "you" in verses 3 and 5), 2:1 contains the first direct identification of the audience and address to them. Second, the chain of first-person plurals is broken with *tauta grapho humin*, establishing a new development in the discourse. Third, the text moves away from the simple opposition of "we—you" with the new conditional clause, *kai ean tis hamartei*, the indefinite pronoun generalizing the reference beyond the twofold pattern established in the first chapter. Without obvious contextual markers to the contrary earlier in the text, it is best understood if one allows the first-person plural to remain consistent through verse 10. The authoritative teachers of the church are in view. It is their credibility that is at stake with the bona fides that mark them out.

The importance of these observations cannot be overstressed. As 1:7 states, it is the consistent testimony of these authoritative witnesses of the Word of Life that causes the scales to turn in favor of John's teaching against the views of the secessionists. Without the consistent testimony of the eyewitnesses, the debate between John and his opponents becomes merely a balance of probabilities between two options. The consistent testimony and life pattern of the apostolic witnesses confirm the truth of John's position. This study proposes that the following reading best accounts for the data reviewed to this point. False teachers have left the congregation, but they seem at one time to have been trusted leaders. Their departure has now left those who remain confused about whom to trust. Thus John—after a statement of one of his basic theses—offers tests for leadership. How could believing readers know whom to trust among their leaders? John uses "we," not because he was in danger of going astray himself, but because some with whom he had been allied had gone astray in practice and doctrine, and he feared others would do so as well in the future. "We" then refers to authoritative teachers of the church. The conditional sentences in 1:6–10 are third class, not warning that John himself would go astray, but that there may be others in the future who would.

This approach does not rule out relevance or application to those who are not leaders or in authority, but it does allow the reader to see three things. First, it explains why John included himself. Second, it explains what impact the false teachers had on the message of the book. And third, it explains why John wrote "so that you may know that you have eternal life" (5:13)

What Does John Mean By "Fellowship"?

"The word *fellowship* is difficult to define. Various suggestions for English translations have been 'fellowship,' 'partnership,' 'communion,' or 'community.'"[13] Harris rightly suggests that the word implies some shared reality, in particular, "the apostolic (eyewitness) testimony about who Jesus is."[14] The word is relatively rare in the New Testament, occurring only seventeen times, and only four times in John's writings, all of them in 1 John 1:3, 6, 7. This makes determining John's meaning all the more difficult.

This *koinonia* is something that John wants the readers to maintain (note the present subjunctive *echete*), but by implication, the false teachers did not have it. To fellowship with John and the other authoritative teachers of the church (all of whom bear the testimony about the incarnate Son of God) is in fact to fellowship with God and His Son (1:3). One may infer from this, then, that *koinonia* is relationship with God, beginning with salvation. Akin insightfully addresses this very issue with three points. First, the apostolic preaching of the incarnation was the means of bringing about fellowship with God for John's readers (v. 3). Second, fellowship expressed itself as they walked in the light as God is in the light (v. 6). This implies loving the brothers, since God is himself is love (4:7–8, 16). Akin concludes, "Fellowship with the Father and his Son, then, is essentially the same thing as having eternal life."[15] The implication is that one who claims "fellowship" with God but has none with the authoritative teachers actually has no relationship with God. This interpretation fits well with 1:5, which introduces what is likely John's opposition to basic positions of the false teachers. So, to shun fellowship with the authoritative messengers is to reject fellowship with God.

Verses 6 and 7 draw out this conclusion. If apparently authoritative teachers claim fellowship with God, but they "walk in darkness" (in the context, they reject the interpretation of the message of God that other apostolic teachers have given),[16] it is obvious that they have rejected fellowship with God. There can be no fellowship with God without the apostolic testimony.[17]

If this is the correct reading, then 1:3 offers no support for the idea of "losing fellowship"[18] with God that is advocated by such commentators as Duffy, who states, "Unconfessed sin results in a barrier between God and the Christian as far as fellowship is concerned. It has eternal consequences only in that being out of fellowship with God reduces one's opportunities for reward."[19]

The Protases and Apodoses in 1 John 1:6-10

Verses 1:6-10 share a common syntactical arrangement. Each begins with a conditional clause (a protasis with *ean* and the subjunctive) followed by the apodosis at the end of each verse. In English readers tend to think of them as expressing cause and effect. On the condition that "A" happens, the result, "B" will follow. It is difficult to break free of this framework. It results in statements like the following: "This forgiveness and cleansing, issuing from the faithfulness and justice of God, are conditional upon confession."[20] Akin comments, "There are basically three kinds of relationships between the 'if' part (protasis) and the 'then' part (apodosis) of all conditional sentences. The relationship can be cause and effect, evidence and inference, or equivalence. . . In 1 John 1:6 the effects of 'lying' and 'not doing the truth' are caused by the claim of fellowship with God and yet living in death."[21] Even those who propose one of the other of Wallace's categories have difficulty removing from their discussion of this passage the cause-effect relationship. What follows examines these verses to see if cause-effect will work.

After the statement of his first thesis in verse 5, "that God is light, and in Him there is no darkness at all," John proceeds to apply it to the circumstances he addresses in the book. In verses 6, 8, and 10 he takes up claims made by his opponents and shows them to be false.[22] He intersperses two verses that give his own point of view.

In verse 6 John offers the (negative) claim: "If we say that we have fellowship with Him and *yet* walk in the darkness." For modern English readers this clause can be slightly confusing, but it is offering two claims. The first part of the conditional clause claims fellowship with God. The second claim of the clause is that the person making the claim walks in darkness. From John's point of view, walking in darkness includes at least three things. That darkness is the sphere of sin, false teaching about Christ, and hating the brothers. These are the charges that John will continue to bring against the false teachers. His readers would likely agree with him as to his definitions.[23] What is essential is to compare the statement with verse 5: "there is no darkness in God at all." One who has fellowship with God should be in the light, yet the claimant is in the darkness.

The apodosis of the sentence follows in verse 6: "we lie and do not practice the truth." Here it becomes important to test Akin's view that the protases and apodoses of the passage should be read as cause and effect.[24] Did the claimants suddenly become liars by claiming to have fellowship with God, all the while walking in darkness? Or, were they already liars? Is that the reason they claimed fellowship though walking in darkness? It seems reasonable to conclude that they were already liars. What, then, does it mean that they were lying and not doing the truth?

John's writings are rich in use of the *aleth*-word group, Accordance lists 93 instances in John's works (55 in John; 16 in 1 John; 10 in Revelation; and the rest in the remaining two letters). But John's use of its antonym, *pseud*- and its related terms, has only 14 recorded instances (once in John; four times in 1 John; and nine times in Revelation). What is remarkable, is that its use is to classify anyone described by it with Satan (John 8:44; Rev. 3:9; 16:13) or with false prophets or false apostles (1 John 4:1; Rev. 2:2). Is this a result of an accomplished condition?

Rather than cause and effect, the relationship between the protasis and apodosis must be "evidence-inference," what Cotterell and Turner call a "Grounds-CONCLUSION relationship." They state, "In the case of *grounds-CONCLUSION* relations, one kernel offers the evidence on the basis of which the second is to be accepted."[25] It turns out that there are quite a few of these in the New Testament. One example will illustrate the point: "For if we believe that Jesus died and rose again, even so God will bring with Him those who have fallen asleep in Jesus" (1 Thess. 4:13). Faith in the resurrection of Jesus is evidence that one should believe in the resurrection of those who have already fallen asleep in him. It is the contention here that all of the conditional statements in 1 John 1:6–10 should be read this way. Thus, in verse 8, the claim that one "has no sin"[26] is the evidence that the claimants were self-deceived and had no truth in themselves (on this compare John 8:44, again, and Satan, again!). In the same way one could read 1 John 1:7 and 9 with the pattern of evidence-conclusion. These verses have a structure parallel to the other verses in the context, so the reader would naturally assume a parallel relationship.

Verse 7 becomes much more important because of this approach. The protasis gives information, not about the Christian life in general, but about the reliability of leaders in the Christian community. How do Christians who are troubled about their own relationship with God, troubled especially because of false teaching, know whom to trust? How do they know what message to embrace? The seventh verse provides an answer: "but if we walk in the light as He Himself is in the light, we have fellowship with one another, and the blood of Jesus His Son cleanses us from all sin." Again, the pronoun "we" retains its referent from verses 1–6: the authoritative teachers. Those who may be trusted are people who walk in the light because God is light, and they meet the three tests of 1 John: they practice righteousness (e.g., 2:1–6);[27] they teach truth about Jesus (e.g., 2:18–25); and they love the children of God (e.g., 3:10–12). A reliable teacher is one whose way of life coheres with the way of life that the apostles pursued. Accordingly, they fellowship with John and the apostolic band and, more importantly, with the God the apostles represent. Furthermore, their doctrine also coheres. These two evidences make it clear that "they walk in the light," and more, "that the blood of Jesus God's Son cleanses them from all sin." Walking in the light is the evidence that they are cleansed through the continuing work of Jesus in their lives. Von Wahlde's comment is apt: "The most extensive means of refuting the opponents is by providing tests and ways to know if the claims are true and actual. Specifically the author insists that every prerogative claimed by the opponents. . . has to be tested in terms of both correct belief and ethics."[28]

The Meaning of Confession, Forgiveness, and Cleansing

The most important issues of this study revolve around the key terms in verses 7 and 10—"confession," "forgiveness," and "cleansing," though few commentaries on 1 John spend much time explaining the concept of forgiveness and cleansing. This leaves several options open for interpretation.[29] More frequently in devotional literature confession is counted as a means of restoring or maintaining fellowship with God.[30]

The view of this study is that 1 John 1 aims to identify those who in reality have relationship with God so that the people of the community will know whom to follow. The evidence so far seems to support such a position. What then would forgiveness and cleansing mean in such a setting?

As to cleansing, John uses the verb *katharizo* and related words only a few times.[31] Perhaps the most important uses are in John's Gospel. In John 15:2–3 Jesus uses the image of "cleansing" or "purifying" to convey the idea of preparation for fruitfulness. The vine-dresser "purges" (*kathairei*) the branch so that it will be *katharos*. The effect is that the branch will bear more fruit. The branch was not fruitless before; its purging is not punitive but enhancing. A leader who walks in the darkness is not fit for the life of the community and will not be fruitful in it.

Forgiveness, by contrast, would seem to be a simple issue. It is the cancellation of the penalty due to sin. Yet the Bible uses the word in a variety of contexts. Two are immediately important. One relates to the cancellation of the eternal penalty for sin (because it has been paid by the work of Christ). Key references on this are found throughout the New Testament, but especially in Matthew 26:28 and Colossians 2:13. The other category of forgiveness is temporal, the cancellation of the temporal consequences of sin. The evidence for this is more limited in the New Testament, but a case can be made from passages such as James 5:15[32] and John 5:14. To the man healed at the pool of Bethesda Jesus said, "Behold, you have become well; do not sin anymore," so that nothing worse happens to you." The implication of Jesus' statement appears to be that the malady from which the healed man suffered was initiated by his sin. Now that he is healed, the temporal consequence of his sin is removed. But there remains the possibility that further sin would bring worse suffering into his life. In the Old Testament there is abundant evidence for the category of temporal forgiveness, especially in Leviticus 4 and 5, since the penalties remitted to the worshiper who brings either the sin (or purification) offering or the guilt (or restitution) offering would be temporal.

These two senses seem fairly likely. One other category is possible, derived from the difficult passage in Matthew 6:12–15. There Jesus grounds forgiveness on the sinner's prior forgiving of others (see the parallel in Luke 6:17; see also Mark 11:25). If God's forgiveness in Matthew 6:12–15 is eternal forgiveness, a problem arises. Faith alone is no longer enough for salvation. If the forgiveness is temporal, it is not clear what the temporal consequence would be. The Sermon on the Mount appears to be talking, not about specific Christian life issues but about the conditions for entry into the kingdom (see Matt. 5:17–20 and 7:13–27).[33] If this is the context, forgiveness could be eschatological, amounting to permission to enter the kingdom. Only those who forgive have the righteousness that goes beyond that of the Pharisees and so are allowed to enter the kingdom. This category may help solve the problem posed in Matthew 18:35.

One of the results of this study is that there is not a clear passage that defines forgiveness as restoration to intimacy in the family. The question is, which of these categories best fits the context of 1 John 1:9? It appears that the first is best—the eternal cancellation of sin's penalty. If fellowship is a synonym in John's works for salvation; if the issue is the distinction to be made between light and darkness, categories that exclude one another, especially in John; if the problem is false teachers who are the spirit of antichrist—then the proper way to read forgiveness is as eternal, the cancellation of the eternal penalty for sin because Jesus has paid the penalty by his work. This forgiveness cannot, then, be conditioned upon confession.

Confession. The Greek word *homologeo* is often treated etymologically. The *log-* part of the word means "to say," and the *homo-* part means "same." Thus Hiebert can say, "To 'confess' means literally 'to say the same thing, to agree with.'"[34] To be sure Hiebert does not hold that simple agreement is all that is necessary. Anyone who follows this view has sensed that more is needed than agreeing with God. Thus, Hiebert explains,

"More is involved than a general acknowledgment of one's sinfulness; it is the confession of sinful deeds to God. . . . A believer must frankly be willing to say the same thing about his sins (the sins he is conscious of having committed) that God says about them. Christians must acknowledge their sins for what they are, rather than using some flowery designation that conceals their true character. The present tense calls for such confession as their standing practice. The confession should be as wide as the actual guilt."[35]

For those who see 1 John 1:9 as a key to gaining forgiveness from God, simple confession is never enough; what is required is true confession.[36] It is an act of prayer in which one acknowledges sin to God. After all, the verse continues that he is faithful and righteous in forgiving sins and cleansing from all unrighteousness. Consequently, true confession brings about cleansing and forgiveness of sin.

Is this, though, a sound way of approaching the meaning of a word? It is clear that *homologeo* can mean to agree, as in *exomologeo* in Luke 22:6, where Judas "agreed" to the plan to hand Jesus over to his enemies for pay. The standard lexicon for New Testament Greek, though, records only one example of such a meaning in the New Testament, Acts 23:8 (where it may not mean agree at all; it appears to fit with the lexicon's third category better than with the second[37]). The various forms of *homologeo* and *exomologeo* occur thirty-six times in the New Testament. The lexicon lists most of the uses of the uncompounded verb (19 out of 26), not as meaning confess in prayer but "to acknowledge someth[ing], ordinarily in public, *acknowledge, claim, profess, praise.*"[38] The compounded verb occurs ten times, none of which occurs in prayer in the New Testament. All are used, one way or another, to refer to a public acknowledgement. The word group does appear in the context of confession of sin, but in the New Testament (1 John 1:9 aside) never in prayer. In the Septuagint confession in prayer using this word group does occur, but rarely, as in 1 Kings 8:31–35; 2 Chronicles 6:24; Daniel 9:4 and 20. But out of 135 occurrences of the various forms of the word group, these are the only places where such usage occurs. Most of the time the reference is to some sort of public proclamation with special reference to public praise of God (and this includes virtually all of the references in Psalms, where *exomologeo* translates the Hebrew verb *yadah*). In the New Testament the rarity continues:

Confession of sin is not a theme that is found often in the NT. It is found in only four other places. It occurs in the Synoptic accounts of the ministry of John the Baptist when people came confessing their sins to be baptised by him (Matt 3:6; Mark 1:15). It is also found in James 5:16, where, in the context of praying for the sick, people are urged to confess their sins and pray for each other that they may be healed. People in Ephesus confessed their 'evil deeds' and burned their magical books during the ministry of Paul in that city (Acts 19:18). In each of these cases confession of sin was public, not private (i.e., not just between the individual and God). It may then be the case that here in 1:9 the author also has in mind public confession of sin.[39]

To make matters even more pointed, John never elsewhere uses the word group for prayer. He uses it most often in one of two ways. For example, John 1:20 says, "And he confessed, and did not deny, and he confessed, 'I am not the Christ.'"[40] Here the expression seems to mean something like "he went on record" or "made a public statement for the record." The other major usage is common in 1 John, of making public statements, as in 1 John 4:2–3, where a prophet may be tested by his statements about Jesus. One last use may be mentioned that appears in both testaments and also in John's writings, of publicly identifying with someone (e.g., John 9:22; Rev. 3:5; compare also Matt. 10:32 and the opposite 7:23). The Septuagint's language of prayer may be preserved in Matthew 11:25 where the New American Standard reads, "I praise Thee, O Father," translating *exomologeo* as "praise."

This discussion prompts doubt that 1 John 1:9 is even about prayer. John never uses the "confess" word group that way, and the Bible broadly only rarely does.[41] This means that reading the word "confess" should not lead to a default assumption that prayer is in view.[42] Additionally it should be clear that 1 John 1:9 does not say that confession is made to God.[43] What else could it be, then? This review of usage suggests one option: the public acknowledgement of one's sins. Can it be that God expects of everyone, as a condition of being forgiven, public acknowledgement of sins?

The course of the argument in this study leads in another direction altogether. "We" in 1 John 1 refers to authoritative teachers, and the relationship between the clauses in verses 6–10 is evidence-inference or *grounds-CONCLUSION*, to use the terms introduced earlier. The implication is that confession is a public act of leaders that alerts the hearers that they are reliable teachers.[44] Kruse supports at least this part of the argument: "The author projects a situation in which people acknowledge their sins in an ongoing way. He portrays authentic Christian living as involving honest and ongoing acknowledgement of one's sins."[45]

Then what must Christian leaders do? Must reliable leaders publicly announce all their sins? Of course not. However, it is a mark of authenticity, as when Christian leaders allow the people to enter their lives, know some of their weaknesses, identify with them in their struggles.

In this area, discernment is necessary. "Need to know" must be the standard. People do not need to know every possible failing and struggle, but they need to know some. When in public ministry, whether pulpit, lectern, or counseling room, a personal acknowledgement of weakness, an anecdote of failure will actually serve the purpose of communication, illustrating the very point at issue.

Summary and Implications

John wrote to a community that had seen schism. False teachers who were the spirit of antichrist (4:3) had left the church, but they had gained a hearing before they left and apparently were trusted among the people. Their departure left the people troubled, not knowing whom to trust or what to believe about themselves and their relationship with God. Thus John had two goals in writing, to show readers how to identify reliable teachers, and to confirm believers in their faith (5:13; cf. the poetic passage in 1 John 2:12– 14).

The tests for reliable teachers begin, but do not end, in chapter 1 and they include walking in the light and confession (that is, public acknowledgement) of sins. It now seems clear that walking in the light includes verse 9. Those who live by faith make it plain that they do not deserve the status they have. They make it plain that they live depending entirely upon Jesus by their freedom to even discuss their sins. It is that freedom that makes it clear that they are forgiven and cleansed from all sin. Additionally, though, walking in the light includes fellowshipping with the apostles and other authoritative teachers of the church in the doctrine of Christ. So, as verse 7 says, by walking in the light they prove, not only that they are cleansed, but also that they share fellowship with the apostles, whose fellowship is with the Father and with his Son Jesus Christ (v. 3). Therefore both their doctrine and their behavior cohere with the apostolic doctrine and life.

No church and no ministry group can claim to be genuinely Christian that does not meet these criteria. Christians are indeed called to service, and that service must be rooted in a commitment to the apostolic message and the apostolic life pattern. These are tests of reliable ministry.

Notes for Appendix

[1] See Robert W. Yarbrough, *1–3 John*, Baker Exegetical Commentary on the New Testament (Grand Rapids, MI: Baker Academic, 2008), 46.

[2] For a brief survey of the tests of life and tests of fellowship views, with a listing of their proponents, see Gary W. Derickson, "What is the Message of 1 John?" *Bibliotheca Sacra* 150 (January–March 1993): 89–105. A variant of the tests of fellowship approach comes from Yarbrough, who says that John "writes in order to stabilize and enhance the existence of 'church' in the locale he addresses: 'The term "church" is not used, but *koinonia* meaningfully interprets the reality of the believing community' (Painter 2002: 128)" (*1–3 John*, 41).

[3] A fuller treatment of these views will follow in the discussion of verses 6–10.

[4] Daniel Akin, *1, 2, 3 John*, New American Commentary, ed. Ray Clendenen (Nashville: Broadman & Holman, 2001), 31–32, is an exception. Akin holds the tests of life view. Brown also identifies 1 John 2:26 as a major issue in the book: "Above (Introduction IV) the thesis was proposed that 1 John is a response to a struggle with Johannine adversaries" (Raymond E. Brown, *The Epistles of John: Trans-*

lated, with Introduction, Notes, and Commentary, Anchor Yale Bible [New Haven: Yale University Press, 2008], 180). Implicitly Stephen S. Smalley accepts this as an important theme for the book, though on page 17 he indicates his view of the book's purpose as "concerned essentially with the conditions for true Christian discipleship. The two main divisions of the letter set out these conditions and exhort the readers to live in the light (1:5–2:29) as children of God (3:1– 5:13)" (*1, 2, 3 John,* Word Biblical Commentary. Accordance/Thomas Nelson electronic ed. [Waco: Word Books, 2007], 15).

[5]Urban C. von Wahlde, *The Gospel and Letters of John: Commentary on the Three Johannine Letters,* vol. 3, Eerdmans Critical Commentary (Grand Rapids: Eerdmans, 2010), 17. He says, "At the time 1 John was written, there was an internal theological crisis dividing the Johannine community. This crisis was caused by two divergent interpretations of the community's traditions. The crisis had gotten to the point that some in the community had left, evidently to form their own community guided by their own beliefs.

"It is clear that 1 John was written to deal with this crisis. However, the Letter is not aimed primarily at the opponents but at the author's own followers. The author speaks to those who have remained faithful to him and faithful to the tradition as he understood it. The author is not in direct dialogue with his opponents. Consequently, the majority of his Letter explains how his views differ from those of the opponents and why the opponents have no right to make their claims."

For similar views see also Colin G. Kruse, *The Letters of John,* Pillar New Testament Commentary. Accordance electronic ed. (Grand Rapids: Eerdmans, 2000), 51; I. Howard Marshall, *The Epistles of John,* New International Commentary on the New Testament. Accordance electronic ed. (Grand Rapids: Eerdmans, 1978), 14– 15; Georg Strecker and Harold W. Attridge, *The Johannine Letters: A Commentary on 1, 2, and 3 John,* Hermeneia (Minneapolis: Fortress, 1996), 19–20.

[6]Akin, 1, 2, 3 John, 31–32.

[7]Strecker and Attridge, *The Johannine Letters,* 12. This interpretation for verses 1–5 is all but a consensus. Brown calls the group "the tradition-bearers and interpreters" (*Epistles of John,* 95). See also Yarbrough, *1–3 John,* 40–41. W. Hall Harris III, *1, 2, 3 John—Comfort and*

Counsel for a Church in Crisis (Galaxie Software, 2003), 59. However, Harris sees a change with verse 5: "The author goes on to explain the ethical implications of this description in the following verses, both for the claims of the opponents and for the author's readers" (ibid., 60).

[8]Yarbrough titles this section "C. Implications of God's Character for the Christian Life (1:6–10)" (*1–3 John*, 52). See also for similar approaches Gary M. Burge, *The Letters of John*, ed. Terry C. Muck, NIV Application Commentary. Accordance electronic ed. (Grand Rapids: Zondervan, 1996), 64; W. Hall Harris III, *1, 2, 3 John*, 60–61; Marshall, *The Epistles of John*, 109–110; Strecker, *The Johannine Letters*, 28-29; and Brooke Foss Westcott, ed., *The Epistles of St. John: The Greek Text with Notes and Essays*, 4th ed., Classic Commentaries on the Greek New Testament (New York: Macmillan, 1902), 18; D. Edmond Hiebert, An Expositional Study of 1 John: Part 2: An Exposition of 1 John 1:5–2:6,"*Bibliotheca Sacra* 145 (July– September 1988): 332. References could be further multiplied. Marshall says concerning verses 6–10, "In each case, the writer's reply is to compare the statement with the actual way of life of the persons who made it and hence to show that the claims were false. Then he goes on to indicate in each case how people who wished to have fellowship with God could really have it."

[9]Hiebert, "An Expositional Study of 1 John," 332. For other representatives see also Westcott, *The Epistles of St. John*, 18–19; Marshall, *The Epistles of John*, 109– 110; Strecker, *The Johannine Letters*, 28–29; Brown, *The Epistles of John*, 197; Smalley, *1, 2, 3 John*, 20-21.

[10]George Bryan Christie, "An Interpretive Study of 1 John 1:9," 33–34.

[11]For a good discussion of the alternatives for 1:1–4, see Brown, *The Epistles of John*, 158–61.

[12]Kruse, *The Letters of John*, 61. He further argues (p. 52) that the editorial "we" is ruled out by the sense perception verbs that fill the opening three verses. Strecker likewise writes, "One could more correctly judge that the author uses 'we' in order to assert membership in the 'circle. . . of "apostolic" witnesses.' In any case, the emphatic backward reference to the past time of salvation and the stress on the eyeand ear-witness have a 'historically' accentuating function" (*The*

Johannine Letters, 12). He continues, "It is not really possible to understand the terminology used in vv. 1–4 as nothing more than a transferred, spiritualistic manner of speaking" (ibid., 14). This he holds in spite of rejecting an eyewitness author for the book!

[13]Harris, 1, 2, 3 John—Comfort and Counsel for a Church in Crisis, 55.

[14]Ibid.

[15]Ibid. Compare a similar view in Brown, *The Epistles of John*, 170, who commented on 1 John 1:3: "The 'you' are the 'Those who have not seen and yet have believed' of John 20:29." See also Akin, *1, 2, 3 John*, 56; Harris, *1, 2, 3 John*, 55–56; and Kruse, *The Letters of John*, 60–61.

[16]See Charles P. Baylis, "The Meaning of Walking 'In the Darkness' " (1 John 1:6)," *Bibliotheca Sacra* 149 (April–June 1992): 221. Yarbrough comes to a similar conclusion: "This is the means whereby sinners become children of God; otherwise they are children of the devil, a state of affairs that Christ has come to undo" (*1–3 John*, 41).

[17]See on this Kruse, *The Letters of John*, 57–58; and Strecker, *The Johannine Letters*, 19–20. Von Wahlde (*The Gospel and Letters of John*, 34) extends the discussion. In commenting on verse 3 he says, "Within the context of the community dispute it has a specific polemical intent, for the author will explicitly argue later (2:22–24) that unless one believes properly in the Son one cannot be said to believe properly in the Father."

[18]Contra Hiebert, "An Expositional Study of 1 John," 336; and Thomas S. Baurain, "The Development of the Johannine Concept of Fellowship" (ThM thesis, Dallas Theological Seminary, 1980), 39.

[19]R. Michael Duffy, Review of "The Judgment Seat of Christ in Theological Perspective, Part 1: The Judgment Seat of Christ and Unconfessed Sins," by Samuel L. Hoyt, *Bibliotheca Sacra*, January–March 1980, 32–39, in *Journal of the Grace Evangelical Society* 5 (1992): 92.

[20]John R. W. Stott, *The Letters of John: An Introduction and Commentary*, Tyndale New Testament Commentaries. IVP/Accordance electronic ed. (Downers Grove, IL: InterVarsity, 1988), 83.

[21]Akin, *1, 2, 3 John*, 71, note 122; see also Marshall, *The Epistles of John*, 108. In addition to the reference to Wallace, see an extended discussion of the possible relationships between "kernels" in Peter

Cotterell and Max Turner, *Linguistics and Biblical Interpretation* (Downers Grove, IL: InterVarsity, 1989), 188–229. Akin is not entirely consistent in dealing with the relationship between the clauses. On page 56 he observes: "The reality of this fellowship is shown in the readers' walking in the light as God is in the light (cf. 1 John 1:6–7). Loving one's brothers and sisters in Christ is, in turn, evidence of being in the light (cf. 1 John 2:–911; it is the equivalent of knowing God [cf. 1 John 4:8; also 4:16])." This is the view that the present study takes (what he calls evidence and inference), but it is not the same as the cause and effect interpretation he offers. It is not uncommon among the commentaries to analyze the relationships between the clauses ambiguously, leaving the concept undefined. As an example, von Wahlde, *The Gospel and Letters of John*, 46, simply calls the apodosis the "consequence" of the protasis.

[22]See Marshall, *The Epistles of John*, 109–110.

[23]Baylis makes a good case that faith in the gospel is at the heart of the idea: "Those who do not receive eternal life through Jesus Christ reject that revelation from God (light). They walk 'in the darkness'; they do not believe His word." See his article, "The Meaning of Walking 'In the Darkness' (1 John 1:6)," 221. If the main object of vv. 6–10 were to teach about Christian life, his view would suffice. However, given the context of 1 John, there must be some moral element to walking in the light. Baylis's view is sound but needs tweaking, which we will suggest below. Akin, 1, 2, 3 John, 72–73, escapes the problem of his cause effect reading of these verses by defining obedience out of "walking in the light," a move that the very next section of the book makes impossible. For the "morality view" see for example Smalley, 1, 2, 3 John, 23: "'Living in the light' thus implies a 'conscious and sustained endeavour to live a life in conformity with the revelation of God' (Brooke, 15). In Pauline language this means living in complete openness to him who 'searches our hearts' (Rom 8:27), and meeting the challenge to behave morally while living 'a new life' (Rom 6:4; cf Matt 5:14‑16; Luke 16:8b; Eph 5:8–14; Col 1:12–14; Phil 2:15; 1 Thess 5:5). It is in God's light that "we see light" (Ps 36:9)." See also D. Edmond Hiebert, "An Expositional Study of 1 John: Part 2: An Exposition of 1 John 1:5–2:6," *Bibliotheca Sacra* 145, no. 579 (Jul 88): 332; Marshall, *The Epistles of John*, 110.

[24]This study is not in debate with Akin. Most of the major commentaries treat the conditional sentences in this passage the same way. Akin, in a well-argued commentary, has simply given a very clear and concise discussion of the issues.

[25]Cotterell and Turner, *Linguistics and Biblical Interpretation*, 211.

[26]Though older commentators hold that the claim made in verse 8 is a claim to sinlessness (see David Smith, "The Epistles of John," *The Expositor's Greek Testament: Commentary* [New York: George H. Doran, n.d.], 172), it is far less common in more recent studies, since John's usage is against it. Brown, for example, proposes the translation "We are free from the guilt of sin" (*The Epistles of John*, 205). His discussion properly refers the reader to the same phrase (*hamartian echein*) in John 9:41; 15:22, 24; 19:11 (ibid., 205–06). The implication of the phrase is that those who have committed sin are liable to punishment for it. The clearest of these references is 15:22. The penalty of those who have seen Jesus' work without a response of faith is greater than if they had seen none of his works. The distinction made here between *reatus culpae* and *reatus poenae* goes at least as far back as Anselm, *Summa Theologica* (Rome: Forzani, 1894), Question 80, Article 8, Objection 4, and elsewhere; see also Richard Baxter and William Orme, *The Practical Works of the Rev. Richard Baxter*, vol. 12, *The Life of Faith* (London: James Duncan, 1830), 302.

[27]Marshall holds that one must live "a life that is compatible with being in the light, a life that is free from sin" (*The Epistles of John*, 109–110). To his credit he attributes this to the cleansing work of Christ, not to the moral strength of the believer.

[28]Von Wahlde, *The Gospel and Letters of John: Commentary on the Three Johannine Letters*, 21. See also Marshall's summary of 1:6–10, *The Epistles of John*, 109–110.

[29]A former student of mine believed that she was not saved unless she had confessed all her sins. More to the point, Brown says, "Perhaps the best explanation (Hoskyns, Schneider, B. Weiss, Wilder) is to stress that the author of I John is not worried about *initial* justification but about the forgiveness of sins committed as a Christian. When people first believe and come to the light, their sins are forgiven. They may sin again; yet if they try to walk in the light, the blood of Jesus, which cleanses from all sin, cleanses from these sins as well"

(*The Epistles of John*, 202). There are two sorts of forgiveness here, but it is not entirely clear what Brown, a Roman Catholic, might mean by the distinction. Harris uses the same language as Brown but surely means something different: "The author is not worried about the initial justification (salvation) of the people to whom he is writing. Rather he is reassuring them about forgiveness of sins committed *after* having become Christians" (*1, 2, 3 John*, 63–64). See also Smalley, *1, 2, 3 John*, 26. Yet these contrasting ends of the theological spectrum do not clearly spell out what is meant by forgiveness.

[30]This appears to be Harris's point, *1, 2, 3 John*, 63–64. "From a human standpoint, our fellowship can be marred by sin. The promise of confession is forgiveness and cleansing" (Eric E. Kress, *Notes for the Study and Exposition of 1st John* [The Woodlands, TX: Kress Christian Publications, 2002], 35).

[31]John 2:9; 3:25 for ritual purification; 13:10-11 and 15:3, with a pun on *kathairo* in 15:2; in the epistles, only in 1 John 1:7 and 9; Revelation has six more occurrences, but with substantially different senses.

[32]See Daniel R. Hayden, "Calling the Elders to Pray," *Bibliotheca Sacra* 138 (July–September 1981): 258–66, who argues for this position.

[33]Entering the kingdom is not synonymous with entering salvation. Jesus said in the Beatitudes: "Blessed are the poor in spirit, for theirs is the kingdom of heaven. . . Blessed are the meek, for they shall inherit the earth. . . Blessed are the pure in heart, for they shall see God" (Matt. 5:3, 5, and 8). Jesus' sermon is about entering into the final experience of salvation, future salvation, what Paul called in Romans 8:30, glorification. The only way to enter the kingdom, according to the sermon, is to have an "exceeding righteousness." A full exposition of this concept would require more space than is available here, entailing reviewing the meaning of the introduction and conclusion of the sermon and a discussion of what "father" and "brother" mean in the sermon.

[34]Hiebert, "An Expositional Study of 1 John," 335. Against this view see Yarbrough, *1–3 John*, 63, note 13: "The oft-heard claim that it means 'to say the same thing as' (Hiebert 1991: 66), while technically true in some Classical Greek passages (LSJ 1226), lacks lexical

backing in NT usage. The claim owes its existence to a semantic root fallacy (cf. Carson 1996a: 28–33). In few if any NT passages where *homologeo* appears can one make sense of a text by using the translation 'to say the same thing as.'" The etymology of a word may be useful on the condition that the context makes it clear that the author is playing on the etymological background of the word. Otherwise contextual usage must guide analysis of the meaning of any word.

[35]Ibid.

[36]See also Marshall, *The Epistles of John*, 113; Yarbrough, *1–3 John*, 64.

[37]BDAG, 708.

[38]William Arndt et al., *A Greek-English Lexicon of the New Testament and Other Early Christian Literature* (Chicago: University of Chicago Press, 2000), 708.

[39]Kruse, *The Letters of John*, 68. The comment applies only to the use of the verb *homologeo*, not to the concept that is clearly implied in the so-called Lord's prayer in both its appearances. It should be added that the noun, *homologia* occurs only five times, 2 Cor 9:13; 1 Tim 6:12–13; Heb 3:1; 4:14; 10:23, and never relates to prayer or the confession of sin. It relates to the confession of the faith or of Jesus.

[40]Brown gives the same evidence: "The idea of public confession also receives support from the four uses of *homologein* in GJohn (1:20; 9:22; 12:42) which involve public professions in relation to Jesus" (*The Epistles of John*, 208).

[41]"Confession of sin is not a theme that is found often in the NT. It is found in only four other places (Matt 3:6; Mark 1:15; Jms. 5:16; and Acts 19:18). In each of these cases confession of sin was public, not private (i.e., not just between the individual and God). It may then be the case that here in 1:9 the author also has in mind public confession of sin" (Kruse, *The Letters of John*, 68). Even in the Apocrypha, the one use associated with confession of sin (Sir. 4:26) is about public confession, not prayer.

[42]"All the parallels and background given thus far suggest that the Johannine expression refers to a public confession rather than a private confession by the individual to God (although the latter view was held by Augustine, Oecumenius, Bede, and Theophylact)" (Brown, *The Epistles of John*, 207–208).

[43]"The fact that in the rest of 1 John 1:9 God alone is the agent of forgiveness does not prove that the confession is to God rather than to the Community (*pace* Schnackenburg, *Johannesbriefe* 86), for both 1:7 (the previous 'But if' condition) and 1:3 show that relations to God are in a Community context" (Brown, *The Epistles of John*, 208; contra Akin, *1, 2, 3 John*, 75, note 132, and Strecker, *The Johannine Letters*, 32).

[44]Dike takes a similar view: "After investigation the verdict was made that the individual walking in light is the one confessing his sins—the believer, while the individual walking in darkness is the person denying his sins—the non-believer. The conclusion was amplified further with the resolution that the believer could not be described as ever walking in darkness (denying his sins), but that he is always characterized as walking in light (confessing his sins)" (Darryl G. Dike, "The Confession Question" (Th.M. Thesis, Dallas Theological Seminary, 1986), 48. See also von Wahlde, *The Gospel and Letters of John*, 52–53: "In this sense, 'confess' does not refer to a ritual act. It is a public acknowledgment of one's overall attitude and conviction regarding the possibility/reality of sin."

[45]Kruse, *The Letters of John*, 68.

BIBLIOGRAPHY

Anderson, A. A. *Psalms* (1–72). New Century Bible Commentary. Grand Rapids: William B. Eerdmans Publishing Co., 1972.

Baker's Dictionary of Theology, 1960. Everett F. Harrison, Geoffrey W. Bromiley, Carl F. H. Henry, eds. Grand Rapids: Baker, 1960. See "Depravity, Total," by Charles C. Ryrie.

Barrett, C. K. *A Commentary on the Epistle to the Romans.* Harper's New Testament Commentaries. New York: Harper & Row, Publishers, 1957.

Barth, Markus. *Ephesians.* Anchor Bible. 2 vols. Garden City, NY: Doubleday & Co., Inc., 1974.

Berkhof, Louis. *Systematic Theology.* 4th edition. Grand Rapids: William B. Eerdmans Publishing Co., 1941.

Bird, Michael. *Romans*, The Story of God Bible Commentary, ed. Tremper Longman III and Scott McKnight. Grand Rapids: Zondervan, 2016.

Blackman, Philip. *Mishnayoth : Pointed Hebrew Text, English Translation, Introductions, Notes, Supplement, Appendix, Indexes, Addenda, Corrigenda.* 2nd ed., rev., corrected, enl. Gateshead Eng.?: Judaica Press, 1977.

Blackman, Philip, ed. *Mishnayoth.* 2nd ed. 7 vols. Gateshead, UK: Judaica Press, Ltd., 1977.

Bradley, K. R. *Slaves and Masters in the Roman Empire: A Study in Social Control.* New York: Oxford University Press, 1984.

Bridges, Jerry. *Trusting God Even When Life Hurts.* Colorado Springs: Navpress, 1988.

Bruce, F. F. *The Epistle to the Galatians: A Commentary on the Greek Text.* New International Greek Testament Commentary. Grand Rapids: William B. Eerdmans Publishing Co., 1982.

---. *The Epistle of Paul to the Romans: An Introduction and Commentary.* Tyndale New Testament Commentaries. Grand Rapids: William B. Eerdmans Publishing Co., 1963.

Campolo, Tony. *The Kingdom of God is a Party*. Dallas: Word Publishing Co., 1990.

Chafer, Louis Sperry. *Systematic Theology*. 8 vols. Dallas: Dallas Theological Seminary, 1947–1948.

Childs, Brevard S. *Memory and Tradition in Israel*. Studies in Biblical Theology. Naperville, OH: Alec R. Allenson, Inc., 1962.

Cotterell, Peter, and Turner, Max. *Linguistics and Biblical Interpretation*. Downers Grove, IL: InterVarsity Press, 1989.

Cranfield, C. E. B. *A Critical and Exegetical Commentary on the Epistle to the Romans*. International Critical Commentary. 2 vols. Edinburgh: T&T Clark, 1975, 1979.

D'Aubigné, J. H. Merle. *History of the Reformation of the Sixteenth Century*. Translated by H. White. 5 vols. New York: American Tract Society, n.d.

Dabney, Robert L. *Lectures in Systematic Theology*. Reprint ed. Grand Rapids: Zondervan Publishing House, 1972.

De Vaux, Roland. *Ancient Israel: Social Institutions*. 2 Vols. New York: McGraw-Hill Co., 1965.

Dentan, R. C. *The Knowledge of God in Ancient Israel*. New York: Seabury Press, 1968.

Edersheim, Alfred. *The Life and Times of Jesus the Messiah*. 2 vols. New York: Longmans Green and Co., 1950.

Ellingworth, Paul, and Nida, Eugene A. *A Translator's Handbook on Paul's Letters to the Thessalonians*. New York: American Bible Society, 1976.

Expositor's Greek Testament. 5 vols. "St. Paul's Epistle to the Romans," by James Denney. Grand Rapids: William B. Eerdmans Publishing Co., 1967.

Greathouse, William M. *Romans*. Beacon Bible Expositions. Kansas City, MO: Beacon Hill Press of Kansas City, 1975.

Grogan, Geoffrey W. *What the Bible Teaches About Jesus*. The Layman's Series. Wheaton, IL: Tyndale House, 1979.

International Standard Bible Encyclopedia, 1979–1988. See "God, Names of," by R. J. Way.

Interpreter's Dictionary of the Bible, 1962. See "Sojourner," by T. M. Mauch.

Jeremias, Joachim. *The Parables of Jesus*. 2nd rev. ed. Translated by S. H. Hooke. New York: Charles Scribner's Sons, 1972.

Ladd, G. E. *A Theology of the New Testament*. ed. Donald A. Hagner, Rev. ed. Grand Rapids: William B. Eerdmans Publishing Co., 1993.

Law, Robert. *The Tests of Life: A Study of the First Epistle of St. John*. 3rd ed. Grand Rapids: Baker Book House, 1968; reprint ed., Edinburgh: T&T Clark, 1909.

Liddell, Henry G., and Robert Scott. *A Greek-English Lexicon*, 1886. 9th ed. See "uJpokrivthV."

Lloyd-Jones, D. M. *Romans: An Exposition of Chapter 6 — The New Man*. Grand Rapids: Zondervan Publishing House, 1972.

---. *Romans: Chapters 7:1–8:4: The Law: Its Functions and Limits*. Grand Rapids: Zondervan Publishing House, 1973.

Louw, Johannes P., and Eugene A. Nida. *Greek-English Lexicon of the New Testament Based on Semantic Domains*. 2 vols. New York: United Bible Societies, 1988.

Lull, Timothy F., ed. *Martin Luther's Basic Theological Writings*. Foreword by Jaroslav Pelikan. Minneapolis: Fortress Press, 1989.

Lyall, Francis. *Slaves, Citizens, Sons: Legal Metaphors in the Epistles*. Grand Rapids: Zondervan Publishing House, 1984.

MacArthur, John F. *The Gospel According to Jesus*. Grand Rapids: Zondervan Publishing House, 1988.

May, Herbert G. *Oxford Bible Atlas*. 3rd edition. New York: Oxford University Press, 1984.

McKane, William. *Proverbs: A New Approach*. Old Testament Library. Philadelphia: Westminster Press, 1970.

Moo, Douglas J. *The Epistle to the Romans*. The New International Commentary on the New Testament. Grand Rapids, MI: Wm. B. Eerdmans Publishing Co., 1996.

---. *Romans 1–8*. Wycliffe Exegetical Commentary. Chicago: Moody Press, 1991.

Moulton, James H., and George Milligan. *The Vocabulary of the Greek Testament Illustrated from the Papyri and Other Non-literary Sources*. See "kovlasiV."

Murray, John. *The Epistle to the Romans: The English Text with Introduction, Exposition and Notes*. New International Commentary on the New Testament. 2 vols. Grand Rapids: William B. Eerdmans Publishing Co., 1959, 1965.

Noth, Martin. "The 'Representation' of the Old Testament Proclamation." In *Essays in Old Testament Hermeneutics*, pp. 76–88. Edited by Claus Westermann. Translated by James L. Mays. Richmond, VA: John Knox Press, 1963.

Nygren, Anders. *Commentary on Romans*. Philadelphia: Muhlenberg Press, 1949.

Orlie, Olaf M. *The New Testament: A New Translation*, 1961.

Passover Haggadah. No publication data.

Perowne, J. J. S. *The Book of Psalms*. 2 vols. Grand Rapids: Zondervan Publishing Co., 1976.

Pink, A. W. *The Sovereignty of God*. Grand Rapids: Baker Book House, 1930.

Ringgren, Helmer. *The Faith of the Psalmists*. Philadelphia: Fortress Press, 1963.

Ringness, Thomas A. *The Affective Domain in Education*. Boston: Little, Brown & Co., 1975.

Robertson, A.T. *Word Pictures in the New Testament*. Nashville, TN: Broadman Press, 1933.

Ryrie, Charles C. *Balancing the Christian Life*. Chicago: Moody Press, 1969.

Stifler, James M. *The Epistle to the Romans: A Commentary Logical and Historical*. Chicago: Moody Press, 1960.

Stott, John R. W. *The Epistles of John: An Introduction and Commentary*. Tyndale New Testament Commentary. Grand Rapids: William B. Eerdmans Publishing Co., 1978.

Strack, Hermann L., and Billerbeck, Paul. *Kommentar zum Neuen Testament aus Talmud und Midrasch*. 6 vols. Munich, Germany: C. H. Beck'sche Verlagsbuchhandlung, 1982.

Theological Dictionary of the New Testament. See "ἀββά," 1:5–6, by Gerhard Kittel; "νουθετέω," by Johannes Behm, 4:1019–22; "υἱός, υἱοθεσία" 8: 334–99, by Peter Wülfling von Martitz, Georg Fohrer, Eduard Schweizer, Eduard Lohse, and Wilhelm Schneemelcher.

Theological Dictionary of the Old Testament, 1977. See "['anaph]," 1:348-60, by Jan Bergman and E. Johnson.

Ernst Jenni and Claus Westermann, *Theological Lexicon of the Old Testament* (Peabody, MA: Hendrickson Publishers, 1997), s.v., "צדק, ṣdq to be communally faithful, beneficial," by K. Koch.

Theologisches Handwörterbuch zum Alten Testament, 1994. See "[ṣdq] gemeinschaftstreu/heilvoll sein," by K. Koch, 2:507-30.

Von Rad, Gerhard. *Genesis: A Commentary.* Old Testament Library. Philadelphia: Westminster Press, 1972.

Walvoord, John F. *Jesus Christ Our Lord.* Chicago: Moody Press, 1969.

Webster's Encyclopedic Unabridged Dictionary of the English Language, 1989. See "freedom."

Wedderburn, A. J. M. *The Reasons for Romans.* Minneapolis: Fortress Press, 1991.

Weiser, Artur. *The Psalms: A Commentary.* Old Testament Library. Translated by Herbert Hartwell. Philadelphia: Westminster Press, 1962.

Westcott, B. F. *The Epistles of John: The Greek Text with Notes.* Grand Rapids: William B. Eerdmans Publishing Co., 1966.

Zerwick, Maximilian. *Biblical Greek Illustrated by Examples.* Rome: Pontifical Biblical Institute, 1963.

ALSO FROM
SEVEN INTERACTIVE

❖ ❖ ❖ ❖ ❖ ❖ ❖ ❖ ❖ ❖

Called To Reign: The Bride of Christ and the
Unfolding Story of God's Kingdom People
by Rick Edwards

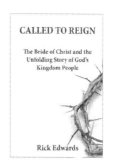

Called to Reign is a study of who we are as the people of God, what He has in store for us, and how we are to live in this age. It is a call for Christians to live as the Bride of Christ, but it's also a call for the local church to teach the story of God's kingdom deliberately and strategically. For many, the Bible is little more than an ancient collection of random stories that are disconnected and largely irrelevant. Church educators and Christian publishers often foster this misconception (inadvertently) by developing curriculum plans that study isolated biblical texts but never consider the broader narrative of the Bible. Rick Edwards, a pastor, publisher, and Christian educator, argues that the ancient Hebrew wedding, as understood by Jesus and the biblical writers, provides a model for understanding the biblical story and, consequently, all of human history. *Called to Reign* can be found on Amazon.com.

Seven Interactive provides publishing resources for the local church and those who lead it. If you're interested in publishing through Seven Interactive, please visit SevenInteractive.com or email us at Admin@SevenInteractive.com.

ABOUT THE AUTHOR

Jim Allman is Professor of Old Testament Studies at Dallas Theological Seminary where he has been teaching for more than 17 years. Prior to that Jim taught for 18 years in Memphis, Tennessee at Mid-South Bible College (later Crichton College).

Jim earned a Th.M in Old Testament in 1977 and a Th.D in Old Testament in 1984. He has led Bible conferences in India, Canada, Poland, Australia, and Siberia. Jim also has taught at colleges in Australia, Ukraine, and at a seminary in South India. He continues to stay busy preaching and teaching on a regular basis.

Jim and his wife of 47 years (and counting) have three children and 10 grandchildren.

If you wish to contact Jim, you may do so by emailing Admin@SevenInteractive.com.

Made in the USA
Columbia, SC
25 November 2017